T0330987

THE WAR ON
WEALTH

Fact and Fiction in British Finance Since 1800

Frontiers of Accounting and Financial History

Print ISSN: 2737-5706
Online ISSN: 2737-5714

Accounting and financial history underlies the history of all organisations, civilisations, politics, institutions and societies. Its ambit is, therefore, very wide in scope and chronology. However, the study of accounting and financial history is mainly centred within the realm of social science faculties in universities where the institutional norm is for researchers, including accounting and financial historians, to produce journal articles for specialists in the same field. Many serious scholars see this journal fetishism as a limitation, and there is an appetite for producing more substantial works that enable the accounting and financial historian to engage with their subject matter in greater depth. Furthermore, while the subject's remit is very wide, a relatively small and specialised audience reads most of what accounting and financial historians produce in journals. This series, therefore, a) gives scholars the opportunity to explore their subject matter in greater depth; and b) reach a wider audience, given the fundamental nature of the subject. The focus will, therefore, be on single-authored works rather than edited volumes, and the subject matter will be eclectic in its composition. Proposals are encouraged from accounting and financial historians and all those interested in exploring the frontiers of this broad, changing and exciting subject.

Published

Frontiers of Accounting and Financial History – Vol. 3

THE WAR ON WEALTH

Fact and Fiction in British Finance Since 1800

Ranald Michie

Durham University, UK

World Scientific

NEW JERSEY · LONDON · SINGAPORE · BEIJING · SHANGHAI · HONG KONG · TAIPEI · CHENNAI · TOKYO

Published by

World Scientific Publishing Co. Pte. Ltd.
5 Toh Tuck Link, Singapore 596224
USA office: 27 Warren Street, Suite 401-402, Hackensack, NJ 07601
UK office: 57 Shelton Street, Covent Garden, London WC2H 9HE

Library of Congress Cataloging-in-Publication Data
Names: Michie, R. C., 1949–   author.
Title: The war on wealth : fact and fiction in British finance Since 1800 /
    Ranald Michie, Durham University, UK.
Description: New Jersey : World Scientific, [2023] | Series: Frontiers of accounting and
    financial history, 2737-5706 ; vol. 3 | Includes bibliographical references and index.
Identifiers: LCCN 2022056897 | ISBN 9789811270727 (hardcover) |
    ISBN 9789811270734 (ebook) | ISBN 9789811270741 (ebook other)
Subjects: LCSH: Finance--Great Britain--History. | Capitalists and financiers--Great Britain--
    History. | Finance--Fiction. | Capitalists and financiers--Fiction.
Classification: LCC HG186.G7 M52 2023 | DDC 332.0941--dc23/eng/20230130
LC record available at https://lccn.loc.gov/2022056897

British Library Cataloguing-in-Publication Data
A catalogue record for this book is available from the British Library.

For any available supplementary material, please visit
https://www.worldscientific.com/worldscibooks/10.1142/13261#t=suppl

Desk Editors: Nambirajan Karuppiah/Kura Sunaina

Typeset by Stallion Press
Email: enquiries@stallionpress.com

Printed in Singapore

I dedicate this book to my two children:

Alexander Uisdean Michie, born in Durham on 8 December 1989, and Jonathan Iain Michie, born in Durham on 5 April 1992.

With them, life goes on.

Preface

I shall welcome any adverse criticism on the conclusions reached, provided the criticisers read the work entirely through before attacking the conclusions, and also provided any contrary views are facts substantiated by statistical evidence, and are not simply generalities brought forward for the express purpose of attack.

> Alfred Herbert Gibson, *The Fall in Consols and Other Investments since 1897*, p. iii (London: 1908).

This book is the culmination of over 50 years of reading and research in financial history. It began when I went to Aberdeen University in 1967, where I completed an MA and a PhD, continued through a career spent at Durham University (1974–2014), and then concluded with a post-retirement phase at Newcastle University (2014–present). Over these years, I have never lost my enthusiasm for financial history, and this is the ninth book I have written on the subject. Though it is my last, it is merely a stage on a journey that I will never complete. Accompanying me on various stages of that journey were my parents, James Michie (1922–1973) and Mary Macleod (1922–1991), my brother, Uisdean Michie (1945–2015), my wife, Dinah Brooks (1956, married 1981), and my two children, Alexander (1989) and Jonathan (1992). I owe them everything but gave little in return. My obsession with financial history left little for others. Finally, without the invitation of David Oldroyd, to publish in a series he was editing, this book would never have been written, and without the help of my friend, Francis Pritchard, it would never have been made ready for publication.

This book rests heavily on my published work, which I list below.

'North-East Scotland and the Northern Whale Fishing, 1752–1893', *Northern Scotland*, 3 (1977/1978).

'The Transfer of Shares in Scotland, 1700–1820', *Business History*, 20 (1978).

'The Social Web of Investment in the 19th Century', *Revue Internationale d'Histoire de la Banque*, 18 (1979).

'Aberdeen and Ceylon: Economic Links in the 19th Century', *Northern Scotland*, 4 (1979/1980).

'Options, Concessions, Syndicates, and the Provision of Venture Capital, 1880–1913', *Business History*, 23 (1981).

'The Formation of the Greenock Stock Exchange, 1888–1900', *Scottish Industrial History*, 4 (1981).

Money, Mania and Markets: Investment, Company Formation and the Stock Exchange in 19th Century Scotland (Edinburgh: John Donald, 1981).

'Investment and Railways in 19th Century Scotland', *Scottish Industrial History*, 5 (1982).

'Trade and Transport in the Economic Development of North-East Scotland in the 19th Century', *Scottish Economic and Social History*, 3 (1983).

'Crisis and Opportunity: The Formation and Operation of the British Assets Trust, 1897–1914', *Business History*, 15 (1983).

'Income, Expenditure and Investment of a Victorian Millionaire: Lord Overstone, 1823–1883', *Historical Research*, 58 (1985).

'The London Stock Exchange and the British Securities Market, 1850–1914', *Economic History Review*, 38 (1985).

'The London Stock Exchange and the International Securities Market, 1850–1914', in R.V. Turrell and J.J. Van Helten (eds.), *The City and the Empire* (Collected Seminar Papers) Vol. 1 (London: Institute of Commonwealth Studies, 1985).

'The London and New York Stock Exchanges, 1850–1914', *Journal of Economic History*, 46 (1986).

'The Myth of the Gold Standard: An Historian's Approach', *Revue Internationale d'Histoire de la Banque*, 32–33 (1986).

'The Performance of the 19th-Century International Gold Standard', in W. Fischer, R. Marvin McInnis and J. Schneider (eds.), *The Emergence of a World Economy 1500–1914 — Papers of the IX International Congress of Economic History* (Stuttgart: 1986) (with J. Foreman-Peck).

The London and New York Stock Exchanges 1850–1914 (London: Allen & Unwin, 1987).

'Different in Name Only? The London Stock Exchange and Foreign Bourses c. 1850–1914', *Business History*, 30 (1988).

'Dunn Fisher & Co. in the City of London 1906–1914', *Business History*, 30 (1988).

'The Finance of Innovation in Late Victorian and Edwardian Britain: Possibilities and Constraints', *Journal of European Economic History*, 17 (1988).

'The Canadian Securities Market, 1850–1914', *Business History Review*, 62 (1988).

'The London Stock Exchange and the British Economy, 1870–1930', in J.J. van Helten and Y. Cassis (eds.) *Capitalism in a Mature Economy* (London: 1989).

'London als Wirtschaftszentrum, 1871–1939', in G. Brunn and J. Reulecke (eds.), *Metropolis Berlin: Berlin als deutsche Hauptstadt im Vergleich Europäischer Hauptstädte 1871–1939* (Bonn/Berlin: 1992).

The City of London: Continuity and Change 1850–1990 (London: Macmillan, 1992).

'The City of London and International Trade, 1850–1914', in D.C.M. Platt with A.J.H. Lathan and Ranald Michie (eds.), *Decline and Recovery in Britain's Overseas Trade, 1873–1914* (London: Macmillan, 1993) (also Postscript).

R.C. Michie (ed.), *The Industrial Revolution: Financial and Commercial Services* (Oxford: Blackwell, 1994) (Introduction).

'The London and Provincial Stock Exchanges, 1799–1973: Separation, Integration, Rivalry, Unity', in D.H. Aldcroft and A. Slaven (eds.) *Enterprise and Management* (Aldershot: Scholar Press, 1995).

'The City of London: Functional and Spatial Unity in the 19th Century', in H.A. Diedericks and D. Reeder (eds.) *Cities of Finance* (Amsterdam: North-Holland, 1996).

'The International Trade in Food and the City of London since 1850', *Journal of European Economic History*, 25 (1996).

'London and the Process of Economic Growth since 1750', *The London Journal*, 22, 1 (1997).

'Friend or Foe: Information Technology and the London Stock Exchange since 1700', *Journal of Historical Geography*, 23, 3 (1997).

'Anglo-American Financial Systems, 1800–1939', in P. Cottrell and J. Reis (eds.) *Finance and the Making of the Modern Capitalist World, 1750–1932* (Madrid: 1998).

'Insiders, Outsiders and the Dynamics of Change in the City of London Since 1900', *Journal of Contemporary History*, 33, 4 (1998).

'The Invisible Stabiliser: Asset Arbitrage and the International Monetary System since 1700', *Financial History Review*, 15 (1998).

'Stock Exchanges and Economic Growth, 1830–1931', in P. Cottrell, G. Feldman and J. Reiss (eds.), *Finance and the Making of Modern Capitalism* (Aldershot: Ashgate Press, 1999).

The London Stock Exchange: A History (Oxford: Oxford University Press, 1999).

'Economic History: A Doomed Love Affair', in P. Hudson (ed.), *Living Economic and Social History* (Glasgow: Economic History Society, 2001).

'One World or Many Worlds? Markets, Banks, and Communications, 1850s–1990s', in T. de Graaf, J. Jonker and J.J. Mabron (eds.), *European Banking Overseas, 19th–20th Centuries* (Amsterdam: 2002).

'Banks and Securities Markets, 1870–1914', in D.J. Forsyth and D. Verdier (eds.), *The Origins of National Financial Systems: Gerschenkron Revisited* (London: 2003).

'The City of London and British Banking, 1900–1939', in C. Wrigley (ed.), *A Companion to Early 20th-Century Britain* (Oxford: 2003).

'The City of London and the British Government: The Changing Relationship', in R.C. Michie and P.A. Williamson (eds.), *The British Government and the City of London in the 20th Century* (Cambridge: 2004).

'A Financial Phoenix: The City of London in the 20th Century', in Y. Cassis and E. Bussière (eds.), *London and Paris as International Financial Centres* (Oxford: 2005).

'Der Aufstieg der City of London als Finanzplatz: Vom Inlandsgeschäft zum Offshore-Centrum?' in C.M. Merki (ed.), *Europas Finanzzentren: Geschichte und Bedeutung im 20. Jahrhundert* (Frankfurt 2005).

'The City of London as a European Financial Centre in the 20th Century', in *Europäische Finanzplätze im Wettbewerb* (Stuttgart: Bankhistorisches Archiv-Beiheft 45, Franz Steiner Verlag, 2006).

The Global Securities Market: A History (Oxford: Oxford University Press, 2006).

'The City of London as a Global Financial Centre, 1880–1939: Finance, Foreign Exchange and the First World War', in P.L. Cottrell, E. Lange and U. Olsson (eds.), *Centres and Peripheries in Banking: The Historical Development of Financial Markets* (Aldershot: Ashgate Publishing Company, 2007).

'The City of London and the British Regions: From Medieval to Modern', in W. Lancaster, D. Newton and N. Vall (eds.), *An Agenda for Regional History* (Newcastle upon Tyne: Northumbria University Press, 2007).

'Reversal or Change? The Global Securities Market in the 20th Century', *New Global Studies* 2 (2008).

Guilty Money: The City of London in Victorian and Edwardian Culture, 1815–1914 (London: Pickering and Chatto, 2009).

'The London Stock Exchange and the British Government in the 20th Century', in S. Battilossi and J. Reis (eds.), *State and Financial Systems in Europe and the USA: Historical Perspectives on Regulation and Supervision in the 19th and 20th Centuries* (Aldershot: Ashgate Publishing Company, 2010).

'The Emergence and Survival of a Financial Cluster in Britain', in *Learning from Some of Britain's Successful Sectors: An Historical Analysis of the Role of Government* (BIS Economics Paper No. 6, Department of Business Innovation and Skills, 2010).

'Securities, Markets, Exchanges and the Finance of Economic Growth: A Global and Historical Perspective', in J. Morilla, J. Hernández Andreu, J.L. García Ruiz y and J.M. Ortiz-Villajos (eds.), *Homenaje A Gabriel Tortella: Las Claves del Desarrollo Económico y Social* (Madrid: LID Editorial Empresarial, 2010).

'Exchanges in Historical and Global Context', in L. Harris (ed.), *Regulated Exchanges: Dynamic Agents of Economic Growth* (Oxford: Oxford University Press, 2010).

'Gamblers, Fools, Victims or Wizards? The British Investor in the Public Mind, 1850–1930', in D.R. Green, A. Owens, J. Maltby and J. Rutterford (eds.), *Men, Women and Money: Perspectives on Gender, Wealth, and Investment 1850–1930* (Oxford: Oxford University Press, 2011).

'The Battle of the Bourses? Competition between Stock Exchanges in the 20th Century', in L. Quennouëlle-Corre and Y. Cassis (eds.), *Financial Centres and International Capital Flows in the 19th and 20th Centuries* (Oxford: Oxford University Press, 2011).

'British and American Banking in Historical Perspective: Beware of False Precedents', *History and Policy,* December 2011 (with S. Mollan).

'The Stock Market and the Corporate Economy: An Historical Perspective', in G. Poitras (ed.), *Handbook of Research on Stock Market Globalization* (Cheltenham: Edward Elgar, 2012).

'The City of London and International Banking in the 19th and 20th Centuries: The Asian Dimension', in S. Nishimura, T. Suzuki and R.C. Michie (eds.), *The Origins of International Banking in Asia: The 19th and 20th Centuries* (Oxford: Oxford University Press, 2012).

'The City of London as an International Commercial and Financial Centre in the 20th Century', *Enterprise and Society*, 13(2) (2012) (with S. Mollan).

'Too Big To Fail': UK Financial Services Reform in History and Policy', *Economic Affairs*, 32(3) (2012).

The City of London in Literature: Place, People and Pursuits [published online by Gresham College] (London: 2013).

'Financial Capitalism', in L. Neal and J.G. Williamson (eds.), *The Cambridge History of Capitalism. Vol. 2. The Spread of Capitalism: From 1848 to the Present* (Cambridge: Cambridge University Press, 2014).

'Big Bang in the City: An Intentional Revolution or an Accident', *Financial History Review*, 21 (2014) (with Chris Bellinger).

'Bursting the Bubble: The 2007 Northern Rock Crisis in Historical Perspective', in A.T. Brown, A. Burn and A. Doherty (eds.), *Crises in Economic and Social History: A Comparative Perspective* (Woodbridge: The Boydell Press, 2015) (with Matthew Hollow).

'Nature or Nurture: The British Financial System since 1688', in M. Hollow, F. Akinbami and R. Michie (eds.), *Complexity and Crisis: Critical Perspectives* on the Evolution of American and British Banking (Cheltenham: Edward Elgar, 2016).

'Securities Markets', in Y. Cassis, R. Grossman and C. Schenk (eds.), *The Oxford Handbook of Banking and Financial History* (Oxford: Oxford University Press, 2016).

British Banking: Continuity and Change from 1694 to the Present (Oxford: Oxford University Press, 2016).

'Jewish Financiers in the City of London: Reality versus Rhetoric, 1830–1914', in C. Hofmann and M.L. Müller (eds.), *History of Financial Institutions: Essays on the History of European Finance, 1800–1950* (London: Routledge, 2016).

Banks, Exchanges and Regulators: Global Financial Markets from the 1970s (Oxford: Oxford University Press, 2021).

'Conan Doyle and the City of London: Critic, Apologist, Realist or a Man of His Time?' (Unpublished Paper).

Contents

Chapter 1

Introduction: Making Judgements

This book marries a factual study of the British financial system since 1800 to its fictional portrayal, with the aim of integrating reality and perception. Regardless of the stability that the British banking system delivered between 1867 and 2007, or the success of the City of London as an international financial centre throughout the entire period, there was always a cloud of suspicion over the financial sector. This mattered because perception influenced the decisions made both within the financial system and by those with power over it, such as successive governments. Democratically elected governments respond to public pressure, and that is driven by perception rather than reality. In 2000, the Nobel Prize economist, Robert Shiller, complained that judgements about the US financial system were based on "superficial opinions" rather than "in-depth analysis."[1] This is particularly the case in a modern economy as the complexity of the financial system made it difficult for the public to understand the rationale behind what was happening. Finance was very exposed to criticism because it operated in an intermediary capacity, and so those who saved, invested, borrowed, bought, sold or were simply advised always had grounds for complaint. Added to that was the latent hostility found in British society towards foreigners and Jews, as both played a prominent role in finance. Finally, as finance had the power to create plutocrats or paupers, it drew antagonism, simultaneously, from those who wanted to overthrow and those who wanted to maintain the established order.

---

[1] R.J. Shiller, *Irrational Exuberance* (New York: 2000), p. 75.

Further fuelling the divide between reality and perception when judging Britain's financial system was the fact that it increasingly performed a global role. This meant that much of what it did was not directly related to Britain and so was neither understood nor appreciated by the British people. Britain became the hub of a dense international network that linked national financial systems across the world, with the City of London being one of the foremost financial centres from the eighteenth to the twenty-first centuries.[2] It was in the years after 1850 that financial services emerged as an important sector within the economy, valued for itself and not simply for what it did. By the First World War, Britain's financial sector was servicing the needs of the world economy, not just Britain and its Empire, and that remained the case a century later. The changes made to maintain Britain's position as a supplier of financial services to the world were often resented at the time by those who continued to view UK banks and markets as operating exclusively in the interests of the domestic economy. One consequence, for example, was the increasing domination of Britain's financial system by banks and markets located in London, which acted not only as the interface between the UK and the world but also as the hub for international financial transactions.[3]

Writing in 1914, no less an economist than J.M. Keynes was so impressed by what the British financial system had achieved that he wrote, "I believe our banking system, and indeed the whole intricate organism of the City, to be one of the best and most characteristic creations of that part of the genius and virtue of our nation which has found its outlet in 'business.'"[4] This was praise indeed from an expert on the working of the monetary and financial system. That he later became a leading critic of this financial system, both in terms of the way it operated and of failing the needs of the British economy, provides conclusive evidence that facts alone, even when interpreted by an expert as qualified as Keynes, could never be left to speak for themselves. It was never possible to possess a complete understanding of complex financial systems, especially when that involved making predictions about future outcomes

---

[2]UK International Financial Services, *The Future: A Report from the UK Based Financial Services Leaders to the Government* (H.M. Treasury, May 2009), p. 19.

[3]The Corporation of London, The Competitive Position of London's Financial Services: Final Report (London: 1995); UK International Financial Services, *The Future*.

[4]J.M. Keynes, 'The Prospects of Money', *Economic Journal*, 24, 633 (1914).

based on current projections. Even when connecting the past to the present, the conclusions reached were influenced by the conditions prevailing when the judgements were made. Before the impact made by the First World War, Keynes was extrapolating from Britain's place in an open and dynamic world economy. By the 1930s, that world had been transformed, as had Britain's place within it, requiring a radical re-evaluation of previous judgements.[5] There are no self-evident truths when re-examined in the light of new evidence and the use of new analytical tools. Nevertheless, decisions were made based on what was believed to be true at the time, whether they had been arrived at, in the words of Shiller, by "in-depth analysis" or "superficial opinions." If the aim is to understand past behaviour, it is a necessary to understand perception as well as reality as both influenced outcomes.

Though the factual evidence is open to interpretation, at least the material exists from which to assemble a coherent narrative, using institutional and business records, government reports, census and other data, as well as contemporary observations and descriptions. In contrast, there is nothing that can be used to indicate what people believed to be true. In this book, I have turned to novels, though the result is often disappointing. One example is Charles Dickens's novel, *Dealings with the Firm of Dombey and Son, Wholesale, Retail, and for Exportation*. This was published in 1848 and is a book of 1,006 pages. Its title implies that it is about the activities of a firm of City of London merchants. However, there is virtually no detail and little comment on what business it did. Dombey and Son appear to own ships and trade with the West Indies, but, beyond that, nothing more is revealed. The owner of the firm, Paul Dombey, left the running of the business to his office manager, Carker, spending long periods absent from the office. Without Carker, the business collapsed, but Carker died a wealthy man as a result of the money he had made. As a source for the public perception of the City of London as a commercial and financial centre, this novel is of little value.[6] In contrast, other novelists such as Charlotte Riddell did provide both detail and comment on the contemporary world of trade and finance, but their work has long been

---

[5] J.M. Keynes, *The General Theory of Employment, Interest and Money* (London: Macmillan, 1935), ch. 12 The State of Long-Term Expectation.
[6] C. Dickens, *Dealings with the Firm of Dombey and Son, Wholesale, Retail, and for Exportation* (London: 1848).

ignored though it was popular at the time it was written.[7] It was common for novelists to incorporate contemporary concerns into their work no matter how tangential it was. An example is the 1910 novel by Rider Haggard, *Queen Sheba's Ring*. Though set almost entirely in Africa, the story incorporates contemporary concerns about Britain's preparedness for war, and this is made clear. "People who refuse to be ready to fight must fall and become the servants of those who are ready."[8] Many novels capture the contemporary perception of bankers and the status of stock exchanges, and who was blamed for speculative outbursts, bank failures, investor losses and financial crises, especially when the search is extended beyond a few literary giants recognised by posterity to those whose work commanded mass appeal at the time. From these, the London Stock Exchange emerges not as an institution of global importance but one where investors were cheated out of their money. Similarly, the City of London did not generate public pride because of its success as an international financial centre but as a place populated by Jews and foreigners, whose only interest was to amass power and money regardless of the cost to others. Novels also allow the changing perception of bankers to be traced. They were viewed with suspicion in the first half of the nineteenth century, becoming respected and trusted in the first half of the twentieth century, and then resuming a position of suspicious characters by the beginning of the twenty-first century.

Lying at the heart of the perception of the financial system was the question of trust, because of the intangible nature of much that took place in banks and markets. Lord Byron captured this in his poem, *Don Juan*, which appeared around 1820. "O Gold! I still prefer thee unto paper, which makes bank credit like a bank of vapour."[9] Whether it involved the promises made in bank notes, stock and bond certificates, and derivative contracts or the counterparties to any deposit, loan, sale or purchase,

---

[7]For a novel that features the work of a City accountant, see C. Riddell, *George Geith of Fen Court* (London: 1864).

[8]H. Rider Haggard, *Queen Sheba's Ring* (London: The Thames Publishing Company, 1910), pp. 151, 214. He was picking up on the work of other popular authors, such as William Le Queux, who wrote two novels that provided detailed accounts of Britain being invaded by the French and Russians in the 1890s and then the Germans before the First World War. W. Le Queux, *The Great War in England in 1897* (London: 1894) and *The Invasion of 1910* (London: 1906).

[9]L. Byron, *Don Juan* (1818/23).

a financial transaction involved a high degree of trust that payments would be made and assets transferred. Without trust, it was impossible for a bank to operate, as they could be brought down by the spread of a rumour, whether true or false. When the Bank of England was formed in 1694, its bank notes contained the words that "I promise to pay on demand" an equivalent sum in gold. The same was true for financial markets. The motto of the London Stock Exchange, dating from its foundation in 1801, was *Dictum Meum Pactum*, or "My Word is my Bond." Without trust, there was a reluctance to use the services of a broker. When capturing the importance of trust in all financial transactions, novelists picked up on the depth and diversity of contemporary views regarding finance. In turn, novels helped shape perception among those who read them, magnifying the importance of individual financiers rather than anonymous companies and the everyday routine of their numerous employees. Similarly, novels ignored the constant ebb and flow of the market, focussing instead on speculative booms and bank failures. All this contributed to the perception of finance that was at variance with reality, but exerted an enormous influence nevertheless.

Though not above suspicion, accountants, like lawyers, were regarded as trusted professionals and were rarely subjected to criticism. Few novels featured accountants, and when they did appear, it was as characters who were honest and lacked the imagination to commit financial fraud. In Peter Milwain's 2006 novel, *The Honest Accountant*, Keith Platt was described as efficient, careful and conscientious. "He liked the perfect symmetry of the balance sheet where everything had to have its place."[10] In contrast, in the 2010 novel focusing on tax evasion, *Crossfire*, by Dick Francis and Felix Francis, the scheme was devised by Roderick Ward, a self-employed "dodgy young accountant." He was later murdered by his associates.[11] It was only rogue accountants that committed crimes and they were not considered representative of their profession. Accountants largely escaped public condemnation as they were not directly involved in money-making, while there was a lack of understanding of the work that they did because of its highly technical nature. The result was that one large and expanding part of the financial community, with a reputation for probity, was largely omitted from the public's perception of finance in

---

[10]P. Milwain, *The Honest Accountant* (Lochmaben: Solway Publishing Company, 2006), p. 1.

[11]D. Francis and F. Francis, *Crossfire* (London: Michael Joseph, 2010), pp. 73–75.

general, and that extended to many other groups.[12] The problem with the public's perception of those in finance is that it was coloured by the negative reputation of particular groups, and that was the product of the actions of a few individuals who generated widespread publicity. Furthermore, in making its judgements, the public had difficulty distinguishing between genuine criminal acts and the inevitable losses resulting from the normal course of business, especially when it involved unrealistic expectations among investors. Financial crime was continually evolving, blurring distinctions between moral and legal judgements, as with insider trading or tax evasion.[13] Crimes, supposed or otherwise, were committed by and against those in finance. The real crimes included thefts of property, and their loss did generate a degree of sympathy, but there was always the underlying feeling that those in finance could afford it because they were wealthy. In contrast, the wealth possessed by those in finance made them powerful, and moral judgements were passed on how this money had been

---

[12] See D. Budden, *No Accounting for Murder* (London: 1986); D. Francis, *Risk*, Michael Joseph, London 1977; D. Francis and F. Francis, *Crossfire*, pp. 73–75; L.P. Hartley, *A Perfect Woman* (London: 1955); J. Malcolm, *A Back Room in Somers Town* (Glasgow: William Collins, Sons and Co., 1984); J. Malcolm, *The Godwin Sideboard* (Glasgow: William Collins and Sons, 1984); J. Malcolm, *The Gwen John Sculpture* (London: Collins, 1985); J. Malcolm, *Whistler in the Dark* (London: Collins, 1986); J. Malcolm, *Gothic Pursuit* (London: Harper Collins, 1987); J. Malcolm, *Mortal Ruin* (London: Harper Collins, 1988); J. Malcolm, *The Wrong Impression* (London: Collins, 1990); J. Malcolm, *Sheep, Goats and Soap* (London: Harper Collins, 1991); J. Malcolm, *A Deceptive Appearance* (London: Macmillan, 1992); J. Malcolm, *The Burning Ground* (London: 1993); J. Malcolm, *Hung Over* (London: 1994); J. Malcolm, *Into the Vortex* (London: 1996); J. Malcolm, *Simpson's Homer* (London: 2001); J. Malcolm, *Circles and Squares* (London: 2003); J. Malcolm, *Rogues' Gallery* (London: 2005); B. Marshall, *The Bank Audit* (London: 1958), published in the USA as *The Accounting* (Boston: Houghton Mifflin, 1958); F.H. Mel, *The Accountant* (London: Remington & Co., 1894); Milwain, *The Honest Accountant*; P.H. Newby, *The Barbary Light* (London: Faber and Faber, 1962); Riddell, *George Geith of Fen Court*; P. Robinson, *Dry Bones that Dream* (London: Constable and Company, 1995); C. Smith, *The Speaking Eye* (London: Hammond and Hammond, 1955); C. Smith, *The Deadly Reaper* (London: Hammond and Hammond, 1956); C. Smith, *The Case of Torches* (London: Hammond and Hammond, 1957); F. Weldon, *The Life and Loves of a She-Devil* (London: Hodder and Stoughton, 1983).

[13] See S. Wilson, *The Origins of Modern Financial Crime: Historical Foundations and Current Problems in Britain* (London: Routledge, 2014); S. Toms, 'Financial Scandals: A Historical Review', *Accounting and Business Research*, 49 (2019).

gained and what it was used for. Judging from the repeated casual references in numerous novels over the course of the nineteenth and twentieth centuries, and into the twenty-first, in the eyes of many, there was something tainted about money, and that influenced the public's attitude towards those in finance because of their close connection to the whole process of money-making. The impression generated from so many novels was that banks failed, leaving depositors penniless, investors lost money on the stock exchange, while fraudulent financiers pedalled a host of get-rich-quick schemes through which the undeserving were made rich and the deserving were impoverished. Justice only came when financiers were beaten at their own game and either forced to disgorge their accumulated wealth or committed suicide because they could not face the losses they routinely inflicted on others. This justice was even sweeter when it reached those financiers considered alien, such as foreigners and Jews.[14]

---

[14]For a selection of stories that give a flavour of the public's attitude towards the world of finance, see the following list. This aspect of fact, fiction and finance will be explored in later chapters.

Mrs Alexander, *What Gold Cannot Buy: A Novel* (London: F.V. White, 1895); G. Allen, 'The Great Ruby Robbery' (1892), in M. Cox (ed.), *Victorian Tales of Mystery and Detection* (Oxford: 1992); W. Besant, *All Sorts and Condition of Men* (London: 1882); W. Besant, *The Fourth Generation* (London: Chatto and Windus, 1900); H. Blyth, 'The Accusing Shadow', in M. Cox (ed.), *Victorian Tales of Mystery and Detection* (Oxford: 1992); G. Boothby, The Duchess of Wiltshire's Diamonds (1897), in H. Greene (ed.), *The Complete Rivals of Sherlock Holmes* (Harmondsworth: 1983); M.E. Braddon, *Birds of Prey: A Novel* (London: Ward, Lock and Tyler, 1867); M.E. Braddon, Levison's Victim (1870), in M. Cox (ed.), *Victorian Tales of Mystery and Detection* (Oxford: 1992); J. Buchan, *The Gap in the Curtain* (London: 1932); L. Charteris, *Boodle: Stories of the Saint* (London: Hodder and Stoughton, 1934); G.K. Chesterton, *The Innocence of Father Brown* (1910/11), in *The Complete Father Brown* (London: 1981); A. Christie, *Parker Pyne Investigates* (London: 1932); W. Collins, *A Rogue's Life* (London: 1856); W. Collins, *The Dead Secret* (London: 1857); W. Collins, *Who Killed Zebedee?* (London: 1881); J. Conrad, *Heart of Darkness* (London: 1902); J. Creasey, *The Case of the Murdered Financier* (London: 1937); G. Elliot, *Middlemarch* (London: 1871/2); J.S. Fletcher, *The Charing Cross Mystery* (London: 1923); J. Galt, *A Rich Man; or, He Has Great Merit, Being the Autobiography of Archibald Pack, esq. Late Lord Mayor of London* (1836), reprinted in W. Roughead, *A Rich Man and Other Stories by John Galt* (London & Edinburgh: T.N. Foulis, 1925); E. Gaskell, *North and South* (London: 1855); G. Gissing, *The Nether World* (London: 1889); G. Gissing, *Eve's Ransom* (London: 1895); G. Gissing, *The Crown of Life* (London: 1899); J. Hatton, *In the Lap of Fortune; A Story Stranger than*

A flavour of these casual references comes in William Le Queux's 1899 novel, *The Bond of Black*, "The rich stockbroker is merely a lucky gambler; and the company promoter is but a liar whose ingenuity is such that by exaggeration he obtains money out of the public's pockets to float his bubble concerns."[15]

Fiction (London: Frederick Warne and Co., 1873); J. Hatton, *John Needham's Double* (London: 1885); W. Heseltine, A Family Scene during the Panic at the Stock Exchange in May 1835, *The Lady's Magazine* (London) 9 July 1836; H. Hill, *Millions of Mischief: The Story of a Great Secret* (London: 1905); A. Hope, *Tristram of Blent: An Episode in the Story of an Ancient House* (London: 1901); E.W. Hornung, *Raffles: The Amateur Cracksman* (London: 1899); F. Hume, *Lady Jim of Curzon Street* (London: 1905); F. Hume, The Greenstone God and the Stockbroker (1893), in M. Cox (ed.), *Victorian Tales of Mystery and Detection* (Oxford: 1992); D. Jerrold, *A Man Made of Money* (London: 1849); A.E.W. Mason, *The House in Lordship Lane* (London: Hodder and Stoughton, 1946); Mrs M. Oliphant, *The Fugitives* (London: 1879); Mrs M. Oliphant, The Lady's Walk (1883), in M. Cox (ed.), *Victorian Ghost Stories* (Oxford: Oxford University Press, 1997); Mrs M. Oliphant, The Stockbroker at Dinglewood (1868), in *Neighbours on the Green* (London: Macmillan and Company, 1889); Mrs M. Oliphant, An Elderly Romance (1879), in *Neighbours on the Green* (London: Macmillan and Company, 1889); Mrs M. Oliphant, My Faithful Johnny (1880), in *Neighbours on the Green* (London: Macmillan and Company, 1889); Mrs M. Oliphant, The Wonderful History of Mr Robert Dalyell (1892), in *The Ways of Life and Other Stories* (London: Smith, Elder & Co., 1897); Mrs M. Oliphant, Queen Eleanor and Fair Rosamund (1886), in *A Widow's Tale and Other Stories* (London: 1898); Mrs M. Oliphant, Mademoiselle (1889), in *A Widow's Tale and Other Stories* (London: 1898); B. Pain, *Eliza's Husband* (London: 1903); B. Pain, *Exit Eliza* (London: 1912); B. Pain, *Eliza's Son* (London: 1913); E. Phillips Oppenheim, *The Mysterious Mr Sabin* (London: 1905); H. Rider Haggard, *Colonel Quaritch V.C.* (London: 1888); F.E. Smedley, *Frank Fairleigh, or Scenes from the Life of a Private Pupil* (London: 1850); G. Sutherland, *East of the City* (London: 1998); J. Tey, *The Man in the Queue* (London: Peter Davies, 1953); W.M. Thackeray, *The Book of Snobs: Sketches of Life and Character* (London: 1846); A. Trollope, *Can You Forgive Her?* (London: Chapman & Hall, 1864/6); E. Wallace, *A Debt Discharged* (London: 1916); E. Wallace, *The Joker* (London: Hodder and Stoughton, 1926); F. Warden, *City and Suburban: A Novel* (London: F.V. White and Company, 1890); F. Warden, *Something in the City* (London: John Long, 1890); H.G. Wells, *Ann Veronica* (London: 1909); O. Wilde, *The Model Millionaire* (1891), in *The Complete Works of Oscar Wilde* (London: 1948/66); F. Wills Crofts, *Inspector French's Greatest Case* (London: Wm. Collins Sons & Co., 1924); Mrs H. Wood, *East Lynne* (London: 1861); V. Woolf, *The Voyage Out* (London: 1915).

[15] W. Le Queux, *The Bond of Black* (London: 1899) ch. 13.

Economic Performance in Fact and Fiction

Novels are a dangerous source to use for perception as their misuse can easily lead to misconceptions. Building on a mixture of contemporary views and later research, which suggested that the British economy was in decline from the 1870s onwards, in 1981, Martin Weiner published an influential book, *English Culture and the Decline of the Industrial Spirit.* This book argued that the cause of economic decline was that by the late nineteenth century the British people had become antagonistic towards manufacturing, taking as evidence the views expressed in a small number of contemporary novels.[16] This argument resonated with those, both at the time and later, who believed that capitalism contained the seeds of its own decay and that was what was taking place in Britain. One of these was the influential socialist George Bernard Shaw, who mixed fact and fiction when expressing this view in his 1887 novel, *An Unsocial Socialist.* "When my father made his fortune we had the start of all other nations in the organization of our industry and in our access to iron and coal.... But now our customers have set up in their own countries improved copies of our industrial organization.... Our profits are vanishing, our machinery is standing idle." To Shaw, the cause was obvious with "capitalists living on the interest of foreign investments."[17]

What contemporaries, who were critical of Britain's economic performance, latched onto was the unequal distribution of income and wealth, which was converting it into a nation of rentiers and so depriving it of the entrepreneurs required to respond to new challenges and opportunities.[18]

---

[16]M.J. Weiner, *English Culture and the Decline of the Industrial Spirit, 1850–1980* (Cambridge: 1981), pp. 128, 145. See B. Collins and K. Robbins (eds), *British Culture and Economic Decline* (London: 1990): Robbins, pp. 5, 21; Rubinstein, p. 6; W.D. Rubinstein, *Capitalism, Culture and Decline in Britain, 1750–1990* (London: 1993).

[17]G.B. Shaw, *An Unsocial Socialist* (London: Constable and Company, 1887, reprint 1914), pp. 20–21, 63, 91–94, 98–99, 198–199, 209, 212, 264–267.

[18]L.G. Chiozza Money, *The Nation's Wealth: Will It Endure?* (London: 1914), p. 104; Sir G. Paish, The Export of Capital and the Cost of Living, *The Statist,* 14th February 1914, p. 8. See W.D. Rubinstein, *Wealth and Inequality in Britain* (London: 1986); W.D. Rubinstein, The Wealth Structure of Britain in 1809, 1860–1861, and 1906, in D.R. Green, A.J. Owens, J. Maltby and F. Rutterford (eds), *Men, Women and Money: Perspectives on Gender, Wealth, and Investment, 1850–1930* (Oxford: 2011); W.D. Rubinstein, *Men of Property: The Very Wealthy in Britain since the Industrial Revolution,* 2nd ed. (London: 2006).

Mulhall claimed in 1896 that "Nearly 80 per cent of the total wealth is held by 1.5 per cent of the adult population." He added that "Fortunes over £5,000 are multiplying much faster than those under £5,000, which is the reverse of what is desirable, and this congestion seems to increase in intensity the higher we go."[19] According to Chiozza Money, whose book, *Riches and Poverty*, was very popular from its publication in 1905, "A group of about 120,000 people, who with their families form about one-seventieth part of the population owns about two-thirds of the entire accumulated wealth of the United Kingdom."[20] Faced with this weight of accumulated wealth, enjoyed by a privileged elite, it was only to be expected that the economy would lack the dynamic drive exhibited by earlier generations. One example was the retired banker Lord Overstone, who lived on a large fortune inherited from his father and uncles. When he died in 1883, his estate was valued at £5.3 million, split between land (£3.1m) and securities (£2.2m). He was unable to spend more than half his income, even when financing the building of a country house or the wedding of his only daughter.[21] To quote Chiozza Money again, "The congestion of so much of the entire income and accumulated wealth of the United Kingdom in a few hands has a most profound influence upon the national development. It means that the great mass of the people — the nation itself — can progress only in such fashion as is dictated by the enterprise or caprice of a fraction of the population." To him, "The possessors of wealth exercise the real government of the country."[22]

What those who took a negative view of Britain's economic performance before 1914 missed, especially those using it to call for radical social and political change, was that the British economy was being forced to undergo structural change due to a combination of rising

---

[19]M.G. Mulhall, *Industries and Wealth of Nations* (London: 1896), p. 100. See W.H. Mallock, *The Nation as a Business Firm: An Attempt to Cut a Path through Jungle* (London: 1910), pp. 173, 234–235, 243, 250; A.D. Webb, *The New Dictionary of Statistics* (London: 1911), p. 629; A.M. Carr Saunders and D.C. Jones, *A Survey of Social Structure of England and Wales* (Oxford: 1927), pp. 115–116.

[20]L.G. Chiozza Money, *Riches and Poverty*, 11th ed. (London: 1914), pp. 79, 339. See J. Camplin, *The Rise of the Plutocrats: Wealth and Power in Edwardian England* (London: 1978), p. 37.

[21]D.P. O'Brien (ed.), *The Correspondence of Lord Overstone* (Cambridge: 1971), pp. 14–47, 1273–1275: Memorandum by Lord Overstone on his Wealth, 1875.

[22]L.G. Chiozza Money, *Riches and Poverty*, p. 141.

per capita income at home and growing competition from abroad. As the first industrial nation and the first urban consumer society, Britain developed and then supplied the goods and services required by an industrialising and urbanising world. These included not only mass-produced textiles, machinery, ships, locomotives and armaments but also all the varied products required to equip homes, offices, shops, schools, hospitals, dockyards and military establishments. What poured out of Britain were carpets, tiles, paint, pens, ink, paper, envelopes, ledgers, manuals, textbooks, medicine, surgical equipment and uniforms; and lifestyle and leisure items like ornaments, books, magazines, clothes, drinks, cigarettes, biscuits, golf clubs, cricket bats, footballs, sheet music, toys and fashion items. In addition, Britain was the leading provider of the services that allowed the international economy to function such as shipping, communications, insurance and credit; the merchants, brokers, agents and markets linking buyers and sellers around the world; the supplier of professional services such as law and accountancy; and the producer and distributor of the coal that kept the world's steam shipping moving. Finally, Britain was the dominant international investor, supplying indebted governments with funds and financing the building of railway systems round the world, as well as the finance required to open up the earth's mineral and agricultural resources.[23] This made Britain prosperous and wealthy and there was no sign that this was waning before the First World War, though other countries were catching up and even surpassing

---

[23] I began studying modern British economic history at Aberdeen University in 1967 and then taught the subject at Durham and Newcastle universities between 1974 and 2020. For many years, the work of Sydney Pollard provided the standard account and he was a leading exponent of the view that the British economy was in long-term decline before the First World War: S. Pollard, *The Development of the British Economy, 1914–1990*, 4th ed. (London: Edward Arnold, 1992). Pollard himself began to revise his negative view of the pre-1914 British economy even before the 4th edition came out in 1992. See S. Pollard, *Britain's Prime and Britain's Decline: British Economy, 1870–1914* (London: Edward Arnold, 1989). Since then, there has been a gradual rehabilitation of Britain's economic performance from 1870 to 1914, led especially by Nicholas Crafts. See N. Crafts, *British Relative Economic Decline Revisited*, CEPR Discussion Paper (2011). Though the view that the British economy performed poorly before 1914 remains popular, it is increasingly disputed in the specialist literature and can no longer be taken as uncontested. See R. Floud, J. Humphries and P. Johnson (eds), *The Cambridge Economic History of Modern Britain: Vol. 2, Growth and Decline, 1870 to the Present* (Cambridge: Cambridge University Press, 2014).

it, as was the case with the USA. One measure of Britain's success was that it was running a balance of payments surplus of £200 million (c £10bn in 2021) on the eve of the First World War and had accumulated a portfolio of foreign assets valued at £4 billion (£200bn in 2021), or 40 per cent of the international total.[24]

When a more positive view of Britain's economic performance before 1914 is taken, alternative evidence from contemporaries is available to support it. The slow progress of motor car and electrical manufacturing before 1914, for example, which had been blamed on either entrepreneurs or investors, and used as evidence of decline, was mainly caused by restrictive legislation, according to contemporary experts, and once relaxed these industries prospered.[25] Similarly, Weiner's claim that late Victorian Britain had developed an anti-industrial culture was found to be highly exaggerated. He had based it on the views of very few novelists, selecting those who took a negative view of business while ignoring those who wrote in praise of manufacturers.[26] When the search is widened, there were many writers who took a positive view of industry from the 1850s to the First World War, including Charles Kingsley, Mrs Craik, Joseph Hatton, Isabella Banks, John Oxenham, Cutcliffe Hyne, R.H. Bretherton and E.F. Benson.[27] What the use of novels by Weiner reveals is the danger of taking a very narrow approach and selecting only those that support the thesis being put forward. Instead, it is necessary to achieve as much

---

[24] See R.C.O. Matthews, C. Feinstein and J. Odling-Smee, *British Economic Growth 1856–1973: The Post-War Period in Historical Perspective* (Oxford: Oxford University Press, 1982), ch. 5. For overseas investment see M. Edelstein, *Overseas Investment in the Age of High Imperialism: The United Kingdom, 1850–1914* (London: 1982).

[25] See R.C. Michie, The Finance of Innovation in Late Victorian and Edwardian Britain: Possibilities and Constraints, *Journal of European Economic History*, 17 (1988).

[26] See M.J. Weiner, *English Culture and the Decline of the Industrial Spirit, 1850–1980*. This thesis was examined from a number of perspectives in B. Collins and K. Robbins, *British Culture and Economic Decline*. See also F.M.L. Thompson, *Gentrification and the Enterprise Culture: Britain 1780–1980* (Oxford: 2001) and W.D. Rubinstein, *Capitalism, Culture and Decline*.

[27] C. Kingsley, *Yeast: A Problem* (London: 1851); D.M. Mullock (Mrs Craik), *John Halifax, Gentleman* (London: 1856); J. Hatton, *The Tallants of Barton* (London: Frederick Warne & Co., 1867); Mrs G. Linnaeus Banks, *The Manchester Man* (London: 1876); J. Oxenham, *Rising Fortunes: The Story of a Man's Beginnings* (London: 1899); C.J. Cutcliffe Hyne, *Thompson's Progress* (London: 1903); R.H. Bretherton, *An Honest Man* (London: 1909); E.F. Benson, *The Osbornes* (London: 1910).

breadth as possible, in terms of both novels and novelists, extending from the literary giants to the pedestrian toilers.

Agenda

The intention of this book is to combine fact and fiction to provide a full evaluation of not only what took place in Britain's financial sector over the course of the last 200 years but also what people perceived was happening and so made their judgements accordingly. Over the course of the nineteenth and especially twentieth centuries, British governments became both more willing to intervene and were expected by the public to do so. In turn, the nature of that intervention was governed by public perception rather than a careful evaluation of what was required to improve the efficiency of the financial system so that it served its customers better, whether they were savers and investors, lenders and borrowers, or simply those who made and received payments. Acting as a driver to government intervention was the direct involvement of the British public in investment. This began with purchases of the National Debt, which rose to huge proportions during the wars with France between 1793 and 1815. It then took a new turn in the 1840s when investors were attracted by the prospects of the stocks and bonds issued by railway companies. There then followed successive speculative booms during which British investors bought into railways and mining companies operating all round the world as well as a growing number of domestic industrial and commercial enterprises. Though always a minority, these investors grew in number helping to make the London Stock Exchange the largest in the world by the First World War. In addition, all major British cities possessed their own stock exchanges, providing a market for the shares issued by local companies. Meanwhile, British investors faced with falling domestic returns turned to foreign investment, with the securities issued by governments and companies from the Empire and Latin America being especially popular, though the United States was, by far, the most popular.

Despite the increasing diversification of investment before the First World War, there was a prevailing view that most investors were both ignorant and naïve, easily seduced by current fads, and so lost out when pursuing investment objectives other than UK government debt of British property. The effect was to generate calls for greater protection for investors after each bout of speculation, but these came to little before the First World War, other than more stringent requirements on the information presented in prospectuses and improved accounting procedures. The majority view was that investors were a tiny elite who did not warrant intervention to preserve them from their follies. It was not until after the First World War that serious attempts were made to provide greater investor protection, as the number involved had expanded enormously due to public participation in response to patriotic appeals by the government to purchase war bonds. That then spilled over into mass participation in domestic stock issues in both the 1920s and 1930s when the returns on alternative investments were low. Losses made on these, and the continued exposure of the dubious practices used to persuade investors to buy new issues, led to a growing demand for greater protection. These demands were ultimately met after the Second World War through both legislation and pressure of the London Stock Exchange to ban particular practices. As it was, the high levels of taxation and the greater complexity of financial products led to investment being placed in the hands of the professional fund managers. They employed expert staff to research and undertake the process of selecting which stocks to purchase. In turn, they were displaced by models that simply replicated a particular index, leaving little scope for individual choice and speculative booms. The result was that investment moved into and out of the public arena while the composition of investors was transformed from the individual to the institutional. This had inevitable consequences for the perception of investment and investors.

Another area of finance that experienced great swings in perception was that of bankers. Over the course of the nineteenth century, the structure of British domestic banking was transformed. At the beginning of the nineteenth century, there were numerous individual banks with a high failure rate, whereas by the end there were a few large and stable banks managed from London but with numerous branches spread across the entire country. Until the financial crisis of 2007/2008, these large banks commanded universal trust making British banking the most respected in the world. The managers of these banks were regarded as highly conservative individuals, pillars of the community, who could be trusted to look after their customers' money. However, they were disliked because of their refusal to provide borrowers with the funds they wanted on the terms they desired. That perception then changed as a result of the financial crisis of 2007/2008, which they were blamed for causing because of their reckless behaviour. In terms of perception, this returned bankers to the position they had held until the late nineteenth century. A similar transformation and reversal took place with international bankers. Initially they were regarded as possessing undue influence over government, able to dictate the fate of nations. That changed over the course of the nineteenth century while never wholly disappearing. Referred to as merchant bankers, they were seen as providing British merchants and manufacturers with the credit that was essential for the conduct of an international business, and British investors with access to profitable and safe investment opportunities around the world. The result was that they became increasingly respected. It was only after the Big Bang in 1986, with an influx of American investment banks, that the way they were regarded changed as they were, once again, seen as possessed of enormous power which they exercised recklessly for their own ends, culminating in the financial crisis of 2007/2008.

Bankers were not the only financial intermediaries who attracted public attention. Over the course of the nineteenth century, there was a growing change in the way that business was organised, and this created a new type of financier, initially labelled a company promoter. The era of individual and family enterprise, combining ownership and control, gave way to that of the public company, involving a separation between those who managed an enterprise and those who provided the capital, received the profits or bore the losses. This process began with the railways which were simply too big and complex to be financed by a small group of individuals and required the expertise of a large and experienced staff to be run successfully. Other businesses of this kind were then added over the course of the nineteenth century, providing essential services such as electricity and telecommunications. It was also applied to highly risky enterprises such as mining ventures around the world where the possibility of total loss was combined with the chance of incalculable gain. However, the most marked feature was the conversion of existing privately owned businesses into public companies and involving the participation of investors not only as holders of bonds but also shares, which gave them ownership rights. This separation between ownership and control opened up opportunities for those without any direct connection to business to participate directly in the potential profits whether it was a speculative mining venture in a distant land or a well-established British business supplying familiar products such as beer, soap or tobacco. However, it also created opportunities for those bringing mining opportunities to the public's attention or converting existing private enterprises into public companies to present misleading information regarding future prospects, or hide the possibility of total loss. Despite the returns generated by these investments, the prevailing view was that those handling the flow of funds, the company promoters, thrived by selling investors the stocks of worthless companies. Shares issued by foreign mining companies and domestic industrial enterprises were considered especially dubious though they were favourites among risk-taking investors and generated a huge speculative interest. Though relatively little money was invested in these mining and industrial companies, the spectacular gains and, frequently, losses that they left investors with coloured the perception of investment both before the First World War and subsequently.

The huge issue of government debt during the First World War enticed ever more investors to dabble in stocks between the wars, especially the shares of British manufacturing companies. The effect was to perpetuate the belief that investors were being cheated by company promoters. Though never wholly disappearing, those beliefs were present after the Second World War, despite the absence of speculative booms and bursts, apart from individual stocks, in the much more regulated environment of the 1950s, 1960s and 1970s. During the 1980s and 1990s, controls over markets and safeguards for investors were lessened, because of the suppression of risk taking that they caused. The result was to encourage investors to buy the shares of less established companies, lured by the prospect of large gains rather than steady returns, as well as explore more esoteric financial products. As a consequence, there was some reappearance of the negative views attached to those who issued and traded such securities, especially if the outcome was losses not gains. However, investment became, increasingly, the preserve of the professional fund managers acting on behalf of huge financial institutions, handling the collective savings of the many. That element involving individuals, and with a high exposure to risk, were relatively few, though investors were quick to accuse those who advised them of providing misleading information if the returns did not turn out as promised, regardless of the risks involved. By then, company promoters had successfully relabelled themselves as investment bankers, which was the term long in use in the USA.

Developing from the prominence given to the Rothschilds as financiers in the nineteenth century, Jews were believed to occupy a prominent, and even dominant, place within the British financial system. Certainly, Jews were important in merchant banking, international finance, commodity broking and bullion dealing, but were almost nonexistent in retail banking or accountancy. Nevertheless, the entire financial sector was strongly associated with Jews in the eyes of the public. From biblical times Jews were seen as money lenders who charged exorbitant rates of interest and imposed impossible terms on those who borrowed from them. This view was then transferred to Jewish financiers in Britain. In the fiction of pre-1914 Britain, it was Jewish financiers, especially from Germany, who were depicted as those engaged in floating worthless companies and manipulating shares prices. This was despite the likes of the Rothschilds becoming establishment figures, trusted by governments and investors, while the major frauds were committed by non-Jewish English financiers. Though the anti-Jewish rhetoric faded after the First World War, it remained in the background, before largely dying away after the Second World War.

Both the structure and functioning of the City of London and its perception changed over the course of the last 200 years. The City was transformed from a largely commercial centre serving the needs of the British economy, the British population and the British government to a financial one meeting the demands of an integrated global economy. Despite this transformation, throughout those years, the perception of the City remained negative though the reasons why that was so changed over time. Initially, the City was used as a term for a particular part of London, whose inhabitants made their money in a somewhat mysterious fashion, through buying and selling, borrowing and lending, rather than activities whose value was tangible and easy to understand. As the City became increasingly a business district, with the residential population in decline, perception was based on the fabulous wealth accumulated by the merchants and, especially bankers, who did business from offices located there. This wealth allowed them to occupy fine houses in the West End of London and rise in society through marriage and the acquisition of titles and landed estates. The wealth possessed by those in the City fostered both envy and even hatred, which was transferred, collectively, to the City of London as that was where such fortunes were made and such people flourished. Finally, as the City became more impersonal, as its activities were undertaken by companies not individuals, and was increasingly obscure and global, it became identified as the physical manifestation of capitalism and so associated with inequalities, exploitation, instability and imperialism in the eyes of those opposed to the operation of financial markets and the power exercised by banks and companies. Especially in the twentieth century, the City of London became the personification of the British financial system, attracting blame whenever the economy was in difficulty, business was performing poorly and crises took place.

Attitudes towards finance were heavily influenced by perception as much as reality. What the financial system did went either undetected or was taken for granted, such as the provision of a means of payment, safe and secure investments, and credit and finance for individuals and business. In the place of a full appreciation of what the financial sector did, judgements were made based on what was both unusual and dramatic, such as speculative booms and slumps, spectacular frauds committed by high-profile financiers and the collapse of a bank after a rush by depositors to withdraw their savings. None of these was commonplace, especially between 1866 and 2007, but each left a lasting impression. Combined with an underlying ignorance of what was required to deliver a functioning financial system that was simultaneously resilient and responsive to demands, the result of this impression was a perspective that greatly undervalued the importance of finance. Added to that was the association made between Jews and finance, which built on a latent anti-Semitism, and the identification of banks and financial markets with the excesses of capitalism, then a powerful portfolio of perceptions existed that could quickly drive a hostile interventionist agenda from the government of the day.

Chapter 2

Investment: From Private to Public to Private

Introduction

Investment takes many different forms, ranging from the personal and private to the public and transparent. The personal and private included the use of savings by individuals and partners, the direction of reinvested profits by the management of large businesses and control of funds by politicians and administrators within government. All this was undertaken internally, with little opportunity for the public to monitor what was taking place or pass judgements on the outcomes. At all times, these personal and private financial flows outweighed the public and transparent. The construction and ownership of property, ranging from homes through offices to factories, shops and warehouses, was one of the single most important investments and it took place largely in a private business. Even when funds were channelled through a financial intermediary such as a bank, this was usually done through private negotiation between lender and borrower. What this meant was that most investment that took place at any one time was done in secret, passing unnoticed by the public regardless of the amount involved or its results. Rather than the word "investment," the term "capital formation" is used by those attempting to capture the process through which an economy constantly renews and replaces infrastructure and equipment and adds to what already exists. In contrast, there is another use of the word "investment," which involves the acquisition of financial assets including deposits in banks, the ownership of land, buildings and enterprises, and loans made to governments and businesses.[1] Though much of this was conducted in private, it also involved a significant public element, when ownership took the form of stocks issued by joint-stock companies and loans that had been converted into bonds. Once these stocks and bonds were quoted on the market provided by stock exchanges, rather than being closely held, they entered the realm of the public and transparent. The sale of these stocks and bonds, and their subsequent trading, was conducted in the full glare of publicity, with current prices being circulated, encouraging speculative interest driven by market-sensitive information. This was in complete contrast to "capital formation" but both could be labelled investment.[2]

The difference between investment as capital formation and investment as the acquisition of financial assets had implications in terms of perception. What contemporaries had available to them was what was visible and measurable, not unseen and unknown. That favoured a focus on investment not as "capital formation" but as the acquisition of financial assets. Even within investment as the acquisition of financial assets, it was that involving stocks and bonds that attracted the most attention, receiving the greatest publicity. This was already the case in the eighteenth century when, in order to finance its expenditure in successive wars, the government borrowed extensively. This had led to the founding of the Bank of England in 1694 and the organisation of the South Sea Company, contributing to the speculative bubble of 1720. It also led to the creation of a permanent government debt in 1751 through the issue of fixed-interest securities, which were transferable. As the amount in circulation grew, and these were actively traded, the London Stock Exchange was founded in 1801 to provide the National Debt with a permanent market. Beginning in the 1820s, the London Stock Exchange provided a market for the government debt of other countries as well as corporate stocks and bonds, and this trading expanded rapidly after the Railway Mania of the 1840s. The result was that the public increasingly identified investment with the quoting and then trading of stocks and bonds on the London Stock Exchange. To later commentators, Britain's financial revolution became associated

---

[1] Contrast the approach of Matthews, Feinstein and Odling-Smee, *British Economic Growth, 1856–1973*, with that of R.W. Goldsmith, *Comparative National Balance Sheets: A Study of Twenty Countries, 1688–1978* (Chicago: 1978).

[2] See R.C. Michie, 'Financial Capitalism', in L. Neal and J.G. Williamson (eds), *The Cambridge History of Capitalism. Vol. 2. The Spread of Capitalism: From 1848 to the Present* (Cambridge: Cambridge University Press, 2014).

with the founding of the Bank of England and the creation of the National Debt rather than the development of the banking system and process through which the Industrial Revolution was financed.[3] The confusion this led to was that many judgements about the pace, nature and composition of investment were based on what was happening on the London Stock Exchange rather than the actual process of capital formation or even a complete picture of holdings of financial assets. The securities quoted on the London Stock Exchange do not capture the underlying process of capital formation, as only selected areas of the economy obtained finance through the issue of stocks and bonds. They also provide a distorted reflection of British holdings of financial assets as the London Stock Exchange increasingly emerged as the hub of the international securities market.[4] As early as 1889, the eminent statistician and economist, Robert Giffen, cautioned against using the paid-up value of securities when making judgements about capital formation. "It is only a certain part of the whole savings which goes to the Stock Exchange, and seeks new securities of the kind dealt with there."[5]

The weakness of such judgements about British investment based on the securities quoted on the London Stock Exchange can be seen by looking at the period from 1853 to 1913. At first, the impression is generated that the London Stock Exchange is becoming central to the process of investment taking place in Britain. The value of the securities quoted rose from £1.2 billion in 1853 to £9.6 billion in 1913, and they were an increasingly diverse collection as corporate stocks and bonds became more important, at the expense of the National Debt. In 1853, the National Debt accounted for 70 per cent of the value of all securities quoted on the London Stock Exchange. A further 8 per cent was taken up with the debt of foreign governments and the stocks and bonds of foreign railways, with another 16 per cent comprising the stocks and bonds of British railways that left only six per cent to represent the rest of the economy. Considering the importance of urban property and rural land as assets at this time, the

---

[3] See R.C. Michie, 'Nature or Nurture: The British Financial System Since 1688', in M. Hollow, F. Akinbami & R. Michie (eds), *Complexity and Crisis: Critical Perspectives on the Evolution of American and British Banking* (Cheltenham: Edward Elgar, 2016).

[4] See R.C. Michie, 'Securities Markets', in Y. Cassis, R. Grossman and C. Schenk (eds), *The Oxford Handbook of Banking and Financial History* (Oxford: Oxford University Press, 2016).

[5] R. Giffen, *The Growth of Capital* (London: 1889), pp. 153–154.

securities quoted on the London Stock Exchange did not even reflect investment as a financial activity. By 1913, the National Debt had shrunk to only 11 per cent of the value of securities quoted on the London Stock Exchange, but it remained a poor mirror for the holding of financial assets let alone capital accumulation in the economy. Foreign government debt was 21 per cent of the total, but much of this was held abroad, especially that from other European governments. The value of UK railway stocks and bonds had dropped to 13 per cent of the total while that of foreign railways comprised 31 per cent. Again, much of the foreign railway stocks and bonds were held abroad, especially that of the US railroads. That left 22 per cent of the securities quoted at the London Stock Exchange being those issued by companies, most of which were British. These did include ones operating across manufacturing, mining and services such as banking, insurance, shipping and retailing. Nevertheless, sectors such as agriculture, property and the professions remained completely unrepresented while much of manufacturing obtained its finance through informal channels and reinvested profits, especially newly emerging components.[6] One example of the divergence between visible and invisible was the relative proportion of foreign assets quoted on the London Stock Exchange compared to overall holdings. In 1913, an estimated 18 per cent of UK assets were foreign, including government debts and the stocks and bonds belonging to railway companies operating throughout the globe. However, the proportion of securities quoted on the London Stock Exchange that were foreign was, at least, 52 per cent. Any contemporary basing their judgement on what they saw quoted on the London Stock Exchange would, inevitably, overestimate the importance of foreign investment. One was J.A. Hobson, leading him to suggest that there was a strong connection between investment and imperialism, which then became widely believed. His book *Imperialism: A Study*, published in 1902, was highly influential. In it, he claimed that "By far the most important economic factor in Imperialism is the influence relating to investments." He defined imperialism as the "depraved choice of national life, imposed by self-seeking interests which appeal to the lusts of quantitative acquisitiveness and of forceful domination," adding that "It is not too much to say that the modern foreign policy of Great Britain has been primarily a struggle for profitable markets for investment." The result was

---

[6]For an example of this view see W.P. Kennedy, *Industrial Structure, Capital Markets and the Origins of British Economic Decline* (Cambridge: Cambridge University Press, 1987).

that "Great Britain has been becoming a nation living upon tribute from abroad, and the classes who enjoy this tribute have had an ever-increasing incentive to employ the public policy, the public purse, and the public force to extend the field of their private investments, and to safeguard and improve their existing investments."[7]

The Process of Investment, 1815–1914

Whether investment was personal and private or public and transparent, it was all drawn from the collective savings of the nation. As each investment decision had consequences for the whole, it is necessary to capture all that was taking place. With the government playing a very limited role in the economy, either nationally or locally, directly or indirectly, between 1815 and 1914, investment decisions were largely driven by individual preferences and market forces. Housing, for example, which was the single most important investment, whether viewed as capital formation or asset acquisition, was undertaken as a market transaction. Until the First World War, virtually all UK housing was privately rented rather than being provided by the state or owner occupied. As rented houses required careful monitoring and constant management, investment in them was usually arranged through a lawyer, who was at the centre of a local network linking investors, builders and property developers.[8] Those investing in property were attracted by the high yield and the ownership of a tangible asset, and accepted the lack of liquidity, the need for supervision and maintenance, and the absence of income when it was unlet or tenants defaulted on payments.[9] These risks meant that property investment was left to those with the required knowledge, experience and time.[10] A few of

---

[7]J.A. Hobson, *Imperialism: A Study* (London: 1902) pp. 51–53, 368.

[8]A. Offer, *Property and Politics 1870–1914: Landownership, Law, Ideology and Urban Development in England* (Oxford: Oxford University Press, 1981) pp. 57–60, 76, 80–87, 89, 205–207.

[9]*Scottish Railway Gazette*, 2nd February 1850; *The Edinburgh Property Review*, 24th May 1879.

[10]Heritable Securities Investment Association (BT2/124), East of Scotland Financial Company (BT2/176), Scottish Heritable Security Company (BT2/274), North British Property Investment Company (BT2/395), Caledonian Heritable Security Company (BT2/407), Glasgow Heritable Securities Company (BT2/485), National Property Investment Company (BT2/560), Kilmarnock Property Investment Company (BT2/565),

these networks of individuals were organised as companies, providing an insight into the risks involved in property investment. The Heritable Property Trust Company, for example, raised £10,000 from 40 investors in 1876, but collapsed within five years as it was unable to generate sufficient income to service its debts.[11] One of the risks that was frequently underestimated by property investors was that of liquidity, especially when developments were financed through short-term borrowing from banks, accepting deposits from savers or issuing redeemable bonds to the public. The money obtained in that way could be withdrawn on demand or the property repossessed if interest payments were not maintained.[12] At times, when money was plentiful, interest rates low and economic conditions promising, investors were lured into all manner of property-related ventures, borrowing additional funds to finance their projects. They then faced a liquidity crisis when credit tightened, interest rates rose and property values fell. The complete scenario can be seen from the experience of the lawyer, Sir Alexander Anderson. In the 1860s, he had invested heavily in developing a housing estate in the suburbs of Aberdeen, using money borrowed from banks. After the Overend Gurney financial crisis of 1866, he was unable to sell the building plots, but the banks demanded repayment. He escaped bankruptcy by selling his entire property portfolio to the newly formed City of Aberdeen Land Association. This company then sold shares to investors and attracted deposits directly from savers, allow-

---

Land Feuing Company (BT2/575), Heritable Property Trust Company (BT2/586), Edinburgh and Glasgow Heritable Company (BT2/589), Heritable Estates Company (BT2/604), Trinity Land Company (BT2/605), Property Investment Company of Scotland (BT2/606), Scottish Equitable Property Improvement and Investment Company (BT2/609), Company of Heritable Proprietors (BT2/630), Provincial Heritable Trust Association (BT2/633), Mercantile Heritage Company (BT2/645), Prudential Heritable Property Trust (BT2/649), General Property Investment Company (BT2/652), Alliance Heritable Security Company (BT2/667), United Kingdom Heritable Securities Company (BT2/695), Real Estate Security Company (BT2/714), Heritable Syndicate (BT2/716), Victoria Estates Company (BT2/735), North Albion Property Investment Company (BT2/736), Western Heritable Property Company (BT2/741), Aberdeen and Northern Heritable Property Company (BT2/840).

[11] Heritable Property Trust Company (BT2/586): Letter from Walter Paton, manager, to the Registrar, 21st May 1886. For a similar example see the North British Property Investment Company (BT2/395): Petition to Lords of Council and Session, 12th April 1905.

[12] Craigmore Pier Company (BT2/631): Letter from Mitchell, Johnston & Co. to the Registrar 14th July 1889.

ing it to repay the money owed to banks. Such was the success of this strategy that the Association began investing in property in Glasgow but was then caught up in the collapse of the market there after the failure of the City of Glasgow Bank in 1878. On that occasion, only a personal loan from the wealthy Baird family of Glasgow saved the Association from collapse.[13]

The housing market was subject to extreme volatility and illiquidity as demand rose and fell, with periods of shortage being followed by over-building, leading to a surplus. Whereas in the early 1880s, it was felt that "House property seems to be a drug in the market,"[14] it was back in vogue during the 1890s, when interest rates were again very low. The result was a nationwide house building boom which lasted until the early twentieth century. That left a glut of houses which pushed down prices and rents for most of the ten years prior to the First World War. *The Estates Gazette*, for example, contained regular reports from estate agents complaining about the stagnation in the housing market, and the difficulty they experienced in both selling property on behalf of owners and obtaining rents sufficient to cover expenses. What recovery there was came to an end with the financial crisis of 1907, after which banks and building societies were reluctant to lend to those providing property as collateral. The housing

---

[13] J. Craik, J. Eadie, and J. Galbraith, *Memoirs and Portraits of One Hundred Glasgow Men* (Glasgow: 1886) p. 411; Western Heritable Property Company (BT2/741): Petition by the City of Aberdeen Land Association, 10th July 1882; Edmonds & Macqueen, lawyers, to Alexander Anderson, 11th June 1880; Alexander Anderson to Alexander Jopp, 8th April 1865, Minutes of Meetings of the Trustees and Commissioners on the Sequestrated Estate of Sir Alexander Anderson, Aberdeen, 26th October 1874, 9th November 1874; Alexander Anderson to Robert Fleming, London 13th January 1875, 9th February 1875, 18th February 1875, 18th March 1875; Alexander Anderson, Circular Letter, December 1874; City of Aberdeen Land Association, Memorandum and Articles of Association, 1875, Minutes of Meetings of Directors 4th January 1876, 4th July 1876, 1st January 1877, 6th November 1877, 5th June 1883, 18th July 1883, 2nd June 1884, 1st July 1884, 2nd March 1886, 7th December 1886, 5th April 1887, 5th April 1892; Annual report 1876–1887; Report by the Committee of Directors relative to loans on house property in Glasgow, 10th January 1877; Report by Alexander Anderson on Glasgow Loans, 10th June 1880; Edmonds & Macqueen to Alexander Anderson, 11th June 1880; Alexander Anderson to Edmonds and Macqueen 16th June 1880; Memorandum by Alexander Anderson, 16th July 1880; The Scottish Equitable Property Improvement Company: Prospectus, 1875; The Real Property Trust: Prospectus, 1876.

[14] *Aberdeen Free Press*, 28th January 1882, 26th October 1886.

market was then further depressed by the 1909/1910 budget as this introduced taxes on land values.[15] The depressed state of the property market became the subject of a national investigation in 1914. The conclusion it reached was that since 1905 the combination of the overhang of property from the last boom, rising building costs, increased property taxes and stationary rents had made building and owning houses an unattractive investment. The result was that investors deserted the property market and turned to stocks and bonds before the First World War. As investment in housing was private and personal, while the purchase of stocks and bonds was public and transparent, the reason for the shift escaped those whose focus was the latter, even though the cause was found in the former.[16]

Another area of investment that largely escaped public notice was that of agricultural land. The fortunes of this market were inextricably linked to the state of British agriculture, and this faced growing foreign competition from 1870, leading to a collapse in the prices paid for its products. This affected the rents that farmers could pay, pushing down the income that land could generate and thus its attractions for investors.[17] Sustaining what demand there was for rural land was the status that the ownership of an estate conferred. In 1881, Brodrick observed that "The man who buys land buys not only what may pay him so much per cent, but what may give him social position, and power over his tenants and neighbours."[18] Even that appeal faded as land values continued to fall. By 1892, the *Estates Gazette* reported that "Men who have made money in business … seem now but little disposed to take on themselves the ownership of

---

[15] *Aberdeen Free Press*, 22nd April 1896, 1st May 1896; *The Estates Gazette*, 2nd January 1904, 24th December 1904, 30th December 1905, 29th December 1906, 5th January 1907, 21st December 1907, 28th December 1907, 4th January 1908, 11th January 1908, 26th December 1908, 9th January 1909, 18th December 1909, 1st January 1910, 24th December 1910, 31st December 1910, 23rd December 1911, 28th December 1912, 3rd January 1914, 10th January 1914, 26th December 1914, 2nd January 1915.

[16] The Land: The Report of the Land Enquiry Committee (London: 1914) Vol. 2: Urban, pp. 87–90; Scottish Land: The Report of the Scottish Land Enquiry Committee (London: 1914) pp. 382, 388–390, 407; J.H. Lenfant, *British Capital Export, 1900–1913*, University of London Ph.D. 1949, pp. 136, 150.

[17] Norton, Trist & Gilbert, 'A Century of Land Values: England and Wales', *The Times*, 20th April 1889.

[18] G.C. Brodrick, *English Land and English Landlords* (London: 1881) pp. 112, 261.

land."[19] There was little recovery in the land market before the First World War.[20] Existing landowners stopped adding to their holdings and instead were forced to make disposals in order to maintain their lifestyle, unless their heirs could make a fortunate marriage. Those willing to purchase rural land were the farmers, making them owner-occupiers rather than tenants.[21]

Business in general had long been conducted by owner-managers because of the need for close supervision due to the high level of risk, with finance coming from informal networks of closely connected individuals.[22] This continued to be the case for most businesses right up to the First World War.[23] In the shipping industry, for example, the ownership of individual vessels was largely restricted to investors who knew the risks involved. Throughout the port communities of UK, there were clusters of

---

[19] *Estates Gazette*, 2nd June 1892.

[20] J.F.L. Rolleston, 'Commercial and Financial Aspects of "Back to the Land"', *Financial Review of Reviews*, September 1907, p. 27; J.F.L. Rolleston, 'The Taxation of Land Values', *Financial Review of Reviews*, April 1909, p. 5.

[21] S.W. Martins, *A Great Estate at Work: The Holkham Estate and Its Inhabitants in the Nineteenth Century* (Cambridge: 1980) pp. 65, 267–269; F.M.L. Thompson, *English Landed Society in the Nineteenth Century* (London: 1963) pp. 306–307; D. Sutherland, *The Landowners* (London: 1968) p. 45; D. Cannadine, 'Aristocratic Indebtedness in the Nineteenth Century: The Case Re-opened', *Economic History Review*, 30, 1977, 647; D. Cannadine, 'The Landowner as Millionaire: The Finances of the Dukes of Devonshire, c.1800 c.1926', *Agricultural History Review*, 25 and 26, 1977/1978, 90; J. Franklin, *The Gentleman's Country House and Its Plan, 1835–1914* (London: 1981) pp. 36–39; H.A. Clemenson, *English Country Houses and Landed Estates* (London: 1982) p. 97.

[22] R. Giffen, *Stock Exchange Securities* (London: 1877) p. 153.

[23] A.K. Cairncross, *Home and Foreign Investment, 1870–1913* (Cambridge: 1953) pp. 84, 90, 95–96; P.L. Cottrell, *Industrial Finance, 1830–1914: The Finance and Organization of English Manufacturing Industry* (London: 1980) pp. 34–36; M.A. Utton, 'Some Features of the Early Merger Movements in British Manufacturing Industry', *Business History*, xiv, 52 (1972); L. Hannah, 'Mergers in British Manufacturing Industry, 1880–1918', *Oxford Economic Papers*, 26, 14, 18 (1974); Memorandum on Joint Flocks by W.S. Davidson, January 1844; William Leslie junior to William Leslie 3rd May 1844, 25th September 1844, 3rd May 1844, 9th June 1845, 3rd September 1845, 3rd July 1846, 3rd August 1846; James Shand, a merchant in Calcutta (Bruce, Shand, Stewart and Company) to his father, William Shand, an Aberdeenshire landowner; James Shand to William Shand, 9th June 1845, 3rd September 1845, 3rd July 1846, 3rd August 1846.

such investors.[24] These private networks even facilitated foreign investment given the willingness of individuals to emigrate, the wealthy to
travel and the mercantile community to trade, and the greater ease with
which these were undertaken. Once investment opportunities were spot-
ted, often in the Empire but not exclusively so, informal networks were
tapped for funding. Unless or until businesses were converted into joint-
stock companies, whose stocks and bonds were sold to investors and
traded on the London Stock Exchange, this personal and private investment passed unnoticed among the public.[25]

The investment that was already in the public spotlight was the
National Debt. The most important bond issued by the UK government
was that yielding three per cent, referred to as consols, which was short
for consolidated stock. The amount in circulation had risen to huge proportions during the wars with France between 1793 and 1815, attracting

---

[24] J. Mackenzie, 'Ship Owning by Shares and by Single Ship Limited Companies',
Accountants' Magazine, 2, 103–107 (1898); A.M. Dunnett, *The Donaldson Line: A
Century of Shipping, 1854–1954* (Glasgow: 1960) pp. 5, 13–17, 55–56; G.R. Taylor,
Thomas Dunlop and Sons: Ship-owners, 1851–1951 (Glasgow: 1951) p. 33; P.L. Cottrell,
'The Steamship on the Mersey, 1815–1880: Investment and Ownership', in P.L. Cottrell
and D.H. Aldcroft (ed.), *Shipping, Trade and Commerce: Essays in Memory of Ralph
Davis* (Leicester: 1981) pp. 145, 154–155; R. Craig, 'William Gray and Company: A West
Hartlepool Shipbuilding Enterprise, 1864–1913', in Cottrell and Aldcroft (ed.), *Shipping,
Trade and Commerce*, p. 17; The "Klyde" Steamship Company (BT2/1162). See also
London and Edinburgh Shipping Company (BT2/155), Aberdeen and Glasgow Steam
Shipping Company (BT2/1026), Dundee Lochline Steam Shipping Company (BT2/1040),
Dundee Gem Line Steam Shipping Company (BT2/1097), Albany Shipping Company
(BT2/1127).

[25] G.B. Magee and A.S. Thompson, *Empire and Globalisation: Networks of People, Goods
and Capital in the British World, c. 1850–1914* (Cambridge: Cambridge University Press,
2010) pp. 171–179, 212, 219, 229–355; P. Thompson, *The Edwardians: The Remaking of
British Society* (London: 1975) pp. 97, 101, 298; A. Leslie, *Mr Frewen of England: A
Victorian Adventurer* (London: 1966) pp. 53–55, 86, 145; See A.E. Smith, *George Smith's
Money: A Scottish Investor in America* (Madison, Wisconsin: 1966); Counsel for
Emigrants, Aberdeen 1834; Sequel to the Counsel for Emigrants, Aberdeen 1834; J.M.
Gibbon, *The Scot in Canada: A Run through the Dominion* (Aberdeen: 1907); W.A. Baillie
Grohman, 'Cattle Ranches in the Far West', *Fortnightly Review*, xxviii, 1880. See W.A.
Baillie Grohman, *Camps in the Rockies* (London: Sampson Low, Marston, Searle &
Rivington, 1882) pp. 426–431; M.G. Mulhall, *The English in South America* (Buenos
Ayres: 1878) pp. 598–599.

vast numbers of investors as a result.[26] In 1852, Ward recommended the National Debt to investors because "The funds of the English government afford an unquestionably safe investment; and they are a kind of property which is more readily than most others turned into cash."[27] Similarly Playford, in the 1860s considered that "The Public Funds, undoubtedly, will for many years to come, be the favourable medium for employing spare money, particularly in small sums and for uncertain periods."[28] The problem that investors faced was that as the size of the National Debt remained static between 1815 and 1914, while demand increased, the price rose and the yield fell. Such were the attractions of the National Debt to investors prioritising security and liquidity that the government was able to reduce the interest paid from 3 to 2.5 per cent, beginning in 1888, leaving holders with large losses when interest rates began to rise again after 1896.[29] The consequence was that the National Debt became an increasingly unattractive investment from the mid-nineteenth century onwards, valued solely by banks and other financial institutions as a temporary home for idle funds. The effect was to force investors to seek alternatives that involved greater risk than lending to the UK government, especially after the conversion of consols from a 3 per cent to a 2.5 per cent yield in 1888. Among those alternatives were the debts of foreign governments, despite the greater risk of default, as these paid a higher rate of interest, and the bonds issued by the growing number and

---

[26] A.D. Gayer, W.W. Rostow and A.J. Schwartz, *The Growth and Fluctuations of the British Economy, 1790–1850* (Oxford: Clarendon Press, 1953) p. 409; P. Colquhoun, *A Treatise on the Wealth, Power, and Resources of the British Empire* (London: 1815) p. 276.

[27] R.A. Ward, *A Treatise on Investments* (London: 1852) p. 195.

[28] F. Playford, *Practical Hints for Investing Money: With an Explanation of the Mode of Transacting Business on the Stock Exchange* (London: 1856 and 1865) p. vii.

[29] *The Financier: A Daily Record of the Money Market, Investments and Trade*, 1st March 1879; W.W. Wall, *How to Invest in Railways* (London: 1903) p. 50; Bell, Begg and Cowan, Stockbrokers, Edinburgh, Monthly Circular, January 1883, July 1885, May 1893, October 1895, December 1895, January 1896; D.R. Green and A. Owens, 'Gentlewomanly Capitalism? Spinsters, Widows, and Wealth Holding in England and Wales, c. 1800–1860', *Economic History Review*, lvi, 510–511, 520–521 (2003); D. Walker and Watson, *Investor's and Shareholder's Guide* (Edinburgh: 1894) pp. 23–26; *The Scottish Banking and Insurance Magazine*, June 1883; *Aberdeen Free Press*, 22nd April 1896, 1st May 1896; W. Graham, *The One Pound Note in the History of Banking in Great Britain* (Edinburgh: 1911) p. 226.

variety of companies, especially foreign railways, as these were being constructed all over the world.[30]

The most obvious domestic investment was directly in business as that promised a higher rate of return but with an accompanying higher level of risk.[31] Either by starting an enterprise as a joint-stock company or through the conversion of an existing one into a joint-stock company, investment in business could be opened to the wider public. The ownership of a joint-stock company was divided into stocks. Stocks could be bought by investors as an investment as it gave them the right to a share of the profits by way of dividends and a capital gain if they rose in price and were then sold. A joint-stock company could also borrow through the sale of bonds to investors. Bonds promised a fixed rate of return and, unlike a loan, could be bought and sold. Holding back investor participation in business was the liability attached to the ownership that went with it, and that extended to corporate stocks. Whereas a bond was a debt with any loss capped at the amount invested, that was not the case with corporate stocks. They incurred the same liability as the partners in a business, which meant covering all losses, and that could extend far beyond the amount invested. This exposure to such risks had a material effect on the ability of a business to attract outside investors.[32] It was reported in 1826 that "The prospect of unlimited liability for obligations constructed by others is enough to discourage a cautious man from adventuring in a joint enterprise."[33] Until this barrier was removed, it stopped most investors from participating in businesses other than those they were engaged in

---

[30] G.A. Jamieson, 'On Some of the Causes and Effects of the Fall in the Rate of Interest', *Accountants' Magazine*, 1, 12 (1897); C. Deuchar, 'Investments', *Journal of the Federation of Insurance Institutes of Great Britain and Ireland*, 1, 307–325 (1898); *The Investor's Monthly Manual*, February 1908, August 1910; *Financial Review of Reviews*, January 1906; A.H. Gibson, *The Fall in Consols and Other Investments since 1897* (London: 1908) p. 69; F.A.H. Woolf, *The Stock Exchange: Past and Present* (London: 1913) pp. 1, 101; F.W. Paish, *Long-Term and Short-Term Interest Rates in the United Kingdom* (Manchester: 1966) pp. 53, 56; J. Johnson and G.W. Murphy, 'The Growth of Life Assurance in UK since 1880', *Economic and Social Studies*, 25, 155 (1957).

[31] *Inverness Journal and Northern Advertiser*, 17th December 1824.

[32] J. Scott and M. Hughes, *The Anatomy of Scottish Capital* (London: 1980) pp. 20, 34–37; B.L. Anderson and P.L. Cottrell, 'Another Victorian Capital Market: A Study of Banking and Bank Investors on Merseyside', *Economic History Review*, 28, 599 (1975).

[33] *Parliamentary History and Review* — Reports of the proceedings of the two houses of Parliament during the session of 1825 (London: 1826) p. 711.

themselves or were run by friends, relatives and trusted associates.[34] Throughout these years, there were constant reminders to investors of the risks involved in business with well-publicised bankruptcies, leaving debts which had to be covered by the shareholders.[35] This led to growing calls for investors in corporate stocks to be granted limited liability, which would limit their losses to the amount they had invested. Writing in 1870, after that privilege had been granted, Leone Levi stated that, "It is just and reasonable that shareholders, who take no part in the management, who cannot exercise any influence on the amount of confidence awarded to the firm beyond what results from the amount of capital invested, should have a liability limited to the amount of their shares."[36] In 1886, Thomson reflected that "There are many enterprises of a more or less hazardous nature, which no private capitalist would care to undertake on his own responsibility but which there would be plenty of individuals willing to take a share in provided that their risk was limited to a certain known amount." In his opinion, "Most people are willing to risk a small portion of their money in an investment, if they know that there is a fair chance of profit being made and a limit to the amount they can be called upon to pay should the affair prove a failure."[37] Prosser in 1898 commented on

---

[34]P. Johnson, *Making the Market: Victorian Origins of Corporate Capitalism* (Cambridge: 2010) pp. 110, 126–127, 146, 163, 230; L. Newton and P. Cottrell, 'Female Investors in the First English and Welsh Commercial Joint-Stock Banks', *Accounting, Business and Financial History*, 16, 316 (2006); R. Brown, 'The Genesis of Company Law in England and Scotland', *Juridical Review*, 13, 198 (1901); J.R. Christie, 'Joint-Stock Enterprise in Scotland before the Companies Acts', *Juridical Review*, 21, 129–132 (1909); J.B. Jefferys, *Trends in Business Organisation in Great Britain since 1856, with Special Reference to the Financial Structure of Companies, the Mechanism of Investment and the Relations between the Shareholder and the Company*, University of London Ph.D., 1938, p. 169; H.A. Shannon, 'The Coming of General Limited Liability', *Economic History Review*, 2, 373 (1931); T. Hadden, *Company Law and Capitalism* (London: 1972) p. 16; J. Anderson, *To the Shareholders of the North British Australasian Loan and Investment Company* (privately printed: 1848) p. 18.

[35]'Scottish Banking Institutions', in W. Chambers, *The Book of Scotland* (Edinburgh: 1830), p. 349; W. Mitchell, *Our Scotch Banks* (Edinburgh: 1879) pp. 26, 75; Clydesdale Banking Company BT2/123: Number of shareholders; *The Scottish Banking and Insurance Magazine*, December 1880.

[36]L. Levi, 'Joint-stock Companies', *Journal of the Royal Statistical Society*, xxxiii, 16 (1870).

[37]T. Thomson, 'The Effect on Commerce of the Law of Limited Liability', *Journal of the Institute of Bankers*, lvii, 502, 506 (1886).

"The outstanding benefit which may be derived from incorporation is limitation of liability."[38] Napier in 1901 had a similar view. "Joint-stock companies have rendered an enormous number of undertakings possible which from the amount of capital required could not have been carried out by a capitalist or a group of capitalists."[39]

Before the introduction of general limited liability from the 1850s, the exposure of investors to the losses of a business was addressed by individual acts of Parliament. These conferred limited liability on investors and had been used as a way of attracting investors to such high-risk enterprises as overseas trading companies, like the East India Company, and banks, including the Bank of England, or those with large capital requirements as with canals in the late-eighteenth century and water and gas companies in the early nineteenth century. However, the real breakthrough, leading to mass investor participation, came with the railways because of the scale of their financial requirements. These railway companies were formed through private acts of Parliament that limited the liability of investors to the paid-up value of the shares for which they had subscribed. Though the railway companies did raise funds through borrowing from banks and the issue of bonds, they were reliant upon investors buying shares. Without the funds that shareholders provided, a railway company lacked the collateral required to raise a loan from a bank or tap bondholders for funds. All businesses needed access to venture capital which was normally largely obtained from private sources through informal networks. These were inadequate in the case of a railway. A railway had to be completed in its entirety, connecting one population centre to another, before it could expect to become profitable, but construction costs, operating expenses and likely revenue to be generated were little more than guesses. It was those who bought shares that took the risk that the railway would prove a success as they ranked behind creditors, including bondholders, when a bankrupt business was being wound up and its assets disposed of. Once the early railway lines proved successful, and began paying dividends to their stockholders, investors were attracted to their stocks, knowing their liability was capped.[40]

---

[38] J. Prosser, 'The Incorporation of Trading Companies', *Accountants' Magazine*, 2, 226 (1898).

[39] T.B. Napier, 'The History of Joint-Stock and Limited Liability Companies', in *A Century of Law Reform* (London: 1901) p. 400.

[40] *The Bankers' Circular*, 31st January 1831; T.R. McCullough, *Dictionary of Commerce* (London: 1832) pp. 898–899; F. Mewburn, *The Larchfield Diary: Extracts from the Diary*

However, it was not the transformation of corporate stocks into safe investments that was the focus of public attention from the 1820s until the 1850s but the speculation in them that took place, in the belief that prices would rise and investors would make large gains. Fuelled by rumour and press comments, the Railway Mania of the mid 1840s featured a frenzy of buying and selling.[41] Contemporaries compared the Railway Mania to the South Sea Bubble of 1720.[42] Perpetuating the legacy of the Mania as a speculative bubble was the continuing references to it in later years, none more so than those by the journalist D. Morier Evans. In 1852, he reflected that the whole of society had been "entangled in the mania" and as the

of the Late Mr Mewburn, First Railway Solicitor (London: 1876) pp. 7–8; C. Fenn, *A Compendium of the English and Foreign Funds and Principal Joint-stock Companies* (London: 1838) pp. 140, 145; *The Economist*, 17th August 1844, 27th September 1845, 4th October 1845, 18th November 1848; *Railway Record*, 12th November 1845; *The Scottish Railway Shareholder's Manual* (Edinburgh: 1849) p. 12; W. Vamplew, 'Sources of Scottish Railway Share Capital before 1860', *Scottish Journal of Political Economy*, 17, 437 (1970); T.R. Gourvish and M.C. Reed, 'The Financing of Scottish Railways before 1860: A Comment', *Scottish Journal of Political Economy*, 28, 21 (1971).

[41] T. Tooke, *A History of Prices* 6 vols (London: 1838–1857) Vol. 1, p. 278, Vol. 2, pp. 149–258, 274, Vol. 4, pp. 66–67, Vol. 5, pp. 234, 242; *The Bankers' Circular*, 29th May 1829, 24th July 1829, 20th August 1830, 31st December 1830, 31st January 1831, 13th December 1833; *The Bankers' Magazine and Journal of the Money Market*, May 1844, June 1845; *Railway Record*, 1st February 1845, 19th November 1845, 1st February 1845, 19th November 1845; *Illustrated London News*, 4th November 1843, 3rd February 1844, 24th February 1844, 23rd August 1845, 13th December 1845, 28th February 1846, 10th February 1849, 15th November 1851; *Economist*, 13th April 1844, 25th October 1845, 28th March 1846, 8th May 1847, 20th November 1847; *The Times*, 2nd July 1845, 28th July 1845, 7th August 1845, 30th August 1845, 14th October 1845, 25th October 1845; *Dundee, Perth and Cupar Advertiser*, 17th February 1825, 9th September 1836, 28th October 1845; *Edinburgh Weekly Journal*, 1st December 1824, 29th December 1824, 3rd May 1826, 16th July 1826, 30th October 1844; *Aberdeen Herald*, 23rd January 1836, 15th November 1845, 22nd September 1849, 6th July 1850; *Scottish Railway Gazette*, 25th September 1847, 26th May 1849, 14th December 1850.

[42] John Gray, London, to John Buddle, Newcastle, 7th February 1825; A. Romney, *Three Letters on the Speculative Schemes of the Present Times and the Projected Banks* (Edinburgh: 1825) p. 3; Sir A. Alison, *England in 1815 and 1845* (London: 1845) p. 82; Mewburn, *The Larchfield Diary*, pp. 68, 70, 82; H. Cockburn, *Memorials of His Time* (Edinburgh: 1856) p. 432; *Journal of Henry Cockburn, 1831–1854* (Edinburgh: 1874), 23rd April 1836, 28th November 1845; J. Mitchell, *Reminiscences of My Life in the Highlands* (London: 1883) pp. 31, 59, 166; A. Moffat, *Scottish Railways: Their Present and Future Value Considered as an Investment for Capital* (Edinburgh: 1849) p. 3.

contagion spread "the passion of the public was stimulated by the most daring species of stock gambling that ever darkened the page of history."[43] In his 1859 work on *Facts, Failures and Frauds*, he considered that "It is with the railway mania of 1845 that the modern form of speculation may be said to begin, and the world has not yet recovered from the excitement caused by the spectacle of sudden fortunes made without trouble, and obscure individuals converted, as if by magic, into millionaires."[44] To many casual observers, the experience of the Railway Mania and other speculative outbursts condemned the whole process of investment as irrational exuberance when left to market forces. In contrast, when examined from the perspective of the investor, faced with frequent twists and turns in the price of railway stocks, their actions were perfectly rational. This can be seen from the comments in the monthly circular of Robert Allan, an Edinburgh stockbroker, between 1842 and 1860. During 1844, he reported on "a multiplicity of new railway schemes — some good, many bad." By the end of that year, he considered that "The mania for new railway schemes has now cured itself." That turned out not to be the case. In April 1845, he wrote that "Railways are still commanding the larger portion of public attention." It was not until November that he pronounced the end of the speculative boom. A sustained recovery did not take place until the early 1850s, but there were numerous rises and falls in the intervening years. Even that recovery was interrupted by the Crimean War between 1854 and 1856, and it was not until the end of that decade that railway stocks finally became a favoured holding for those investors looking for security and a regular income.[45]

The Railway Mania left three legacies. One was a transport system that met the needs of a modern, urban, industrial economy by being reliable, regular, fast, accessible and cheap. No other transport system delivered that until the coming of the internal combustion engine. Another was an investment that attracted the savings of a population that was growing in wealth. The paid-up capital of British railways grew from £246 million

[43] D. Morier Evans, *City Men and City Manners: The City, or The Physiology of London Business* (London: Groombridge & Sons, 1852) pp. 72, 77, 81, 97.

[44] D. Morier Evans, *Facts, Failures and Frauds: Revelations Financial, Mercantile, Criminal* (London: 1859) p. 2.

[45] Circular of Robert Allan, Stockbroker, Edinburgh 1842–1860. See J. Taylor, *Boardroom Scandal: The Criminalization of Company Fraud in Nineteenth-Century Britain* (Oxford: Oxford University Press, 2013) p. 241; *Economist*, 22nd January 1887.

in 1850 to £1,335 million by 1912. The final one was to link investment in joint-stock companies with speculative outbursts. Despite that connection, the demand from investors for such an investment grew, outdistancing even the ability of the expanding railway network to satisfy it. The yield on the shares of UK railways, for example, fell from an average of five per cent in 1873 to 3.3 per cent in 1900, as they became the safe investment of choice, replacing the National Debt, rural land and house property.[46]

With the success of railways apparent by the mid-nineteenth century, and a growing appetite among investors for corporate stocks and bonds, the obvious solution was to extend limited liability to all forms of business.[47] In his manual for investors, Withers wrote in 1914 that "The limitation of liability has had a very great effect in quickening the readiness of investors to place their savings in all kinds of joint-stock enterprise."[48] In 1855, an Act of Parliament was passed that allowed all businesses, with a few exceptions and restrictions, to register as joint-stock companies with limited liability. Between 1862 and 1913, a total of 146,097 joint-stock companies were formed under these acts.[49] Nevertheless, investing in corporate stocks and even bonds continued to be regarded as highly risky, being dependent upon the quality of the management, the degree of competition, the state of the market and fluctuations in the wider economy, as the yearly toll of bankruptcies spelled out. This continued to confine most investors in a company to a group closely connected to its management or with a detailed knowledge of the risks involved. The continued vibrancy of provincial stock exchanges right up to the First World War indicates the

---

[46]See G.R. Hawke and M.C. Reed, 'Railway Capital in the United Kingdom in the Nineteenth Century', *Economic History Review*, 22 (1969); R.J. Irving, *The North Eastern Railway Company, 1870–1914: An Economic History* (Leicester: 1976) pp. 154–157.

[47]Napier, 'The History of Joint-Stock and Limited Liability Companies', p. 400; M. Freeman, R. Pearson and J. Taylor, 'A Doe in the City: Women Shareholders and Early nineteenth Century Britain', *Accounting, Business and Financial History*, 16, 271–273 (2006); Newton and Cottrell, 'Female Investors in the First English and Welsh Commercial Joint-Stock Banks', 316, 320–327, 332–335; J. Taylor, *Creating Capitalism: Joint-Stock Enterprise in British Politics and Culture, 1800–1870* (Woodbridge: Boydell and Brewer, 2006) p. 11.

[48]H. Withers, *Stocks and Shares* (London: 1914) p. 30.

[49]*Stock Exchange Official Intelligence* (London: 1914) p. 1706.

existence of localised pools of knowledgeable investors.[50] As *The Economist* observed in October 1914, "Quotations of such securities are affected almost entirely by local knowledge of industrial conditions, and do not respond, as gilt-edged stocks and debentures do, to phases of stringency or ease in the money market, or to influences of politics at home or abroad; nor do they take their tone from London."[51]

Despite the greater risks that came with business investment, there was a major shift, between 1850 and 1914, from the National Debt and landed property towards corporate stocks and bonds issued by companies operating at home and abroad.[52] This was accompanied by a huge broadening in the range of joint-stock securities held by British investors both in terms of geography and composition.[53] Some of these appealed to the risk takers as noted in 1869 by Bartlett and Chapman. "It is the class of persons who will, with the chance of obtaining a prize, venture their money, knowing that they may, instead of the prize, get a blank, that send forth from this mighty and beating heart of commerce and enterprise those currents of wealth which set and keep the industry of the world in motion, and give it, in place of the mere animal enjoyments of barbarism, the

---

[50] S.F. Van Oss and F.C. Mathieson, *Stock Exchange Values: A Decade of Finance, 1885–1895* (London: 1895) p. lix; A.R. Hall, *The London Capital Market and Australia, 1870–1914* (Canberra: 1963) pp. 18, 38, 41, 44–45, 51–52, 55, 58–59, 114–116; G.L. Ayres, *Fluctuations in New Capital Issues on the London Money Market, 1899–1913*, pp. 188–189, 202, 209; W.A. Thomas, *The Provincial Stock Exchanges* (London: 1973) pp. 64–71, 119, 123, 133, 171–180, 187, 246–249, 316–318; W.A. Thomas, *The Stock Exchanges of Ireland* (Liverpool: 1986) pp. 15, 154–157, 221; J. Butt, 'The Scottish Oil Mania of 1864–1866', *Scottish Journal of Political Economy*, 12, 206 (1965); *Aberdeen Free Press*, 19th July 1889.

[51] Business on the Provincial Stock Exchanges, *Economist*, 31st October 1914, 786.

[52] *Stock Exchange Official Intelligence* (London: 1914) p. 1706.

[53] 1884 from *Burdett's Official Intelligence* (London: 1885); 1913 from *The Stock Exchange Official Intelligence* (London: 1914). Foreign bonds payable abroad were excluded under the assumption that these would not be held extensively by UK investors. The division between fixed interest and equities is an approximate figure. Stocks and bonds for US railways are not differentiated in 1884, whereas in 1913 the figure can be split between £805 million in shares and £925 million in bonds. The assumption is made for 1884 and 1913 that other than government debt and UK railway debenture, guaranteed, and preference stocks, all the rest are equities. This overstates equities.

comforts and luxuries of civilised life."[54] Many of these ended in failure.[55] However, most investment in securities was dominated by the safe and secure. Apart from the debts of governments, backed by their ability to tax an entire population, corporate bonds paying a fixed rate of interest and issued by railways and urban utilities were far more popular than stocks despite the introduction of limited liability.[56] Unless attracted by the out-right gamble that were the shares in overseas mining companies, it was investments whose returns appeared predictable that proved the most attractive. In 1907, J&P Coats had a paid-up capital of £11 million owned by 17,000 shareholders and it possessed a virtual monopoly in the supply of cotton thread, an essential household product at the time.[57] Even when investing in companies producing everyday essentials, there was no guarantee of success. Brewery companies appeared to have guaranteed returns and this made them attractive investments in the 1880s, but that changed after 1900 when competition intensified, prices fell and profits

---

[54] W. Bartlett and H. Chapman, *A Handy-Book for Investors* (London: 1869) pp. 340–341.

[55] *The Investors' and Stock Exchange Magazine* (London: January 1863); *The Investment Journal, Money, Land and Share Market Chronicle* (London: February 1863); K. Robinson, *The Mining Market* (London: 1907) pp. v, 12–13, 95–97, 107; L.E. Hopkins (ed.), *The Universal Railway Manual* (London: 1911) p. 1; R.L. Nash, *Money Market Events* (London: Effingham Wilson, 1869) pp. 12, 16; P.L. Cottrell, 'London's First "Big Bang"? Institutional Change in the City, 1855', in Y. Cassis and P.L. Cottrell (eds), *The World of Private Banking* (Farnham: Ashgate, 2009) pp. 83, 90.

[56] Sir G. Paish, 'Great Britain's Capital Investments in Individual Colonial and Foreign Countries', *Journal of the Royal Statistical Society*, lxxiv, 167–168, 185–187 (1911); Paish, 'The Export of Capital and the Cost of Living', pp. 5–8.

[57] 'A Black Year for Investors', *Blackwood's Edinburgh Magazine*, 127, 274–276; Viscount Goschen, *Essays and Addresses on Economic Questions, 1865–1893* (London: 1905) p. 232; J. Turner, 'Holding Shareholders to Account: British Banking Stability and Contingent Capital', in N. Dimsdale and A. Hotson (eds), *British Financial Crises since 1825* (Oxford: Oxford University Press, 2014) p. 143; Cottrell, *Industrial Finance*, pp. 34–35, 92–95, 180–184; T. Nicholas, 'Enterprise and Management', in Floud, Humphries and Johnson (eds), *The Cambridge Economic History of Modern Britain*, Vol. 2, p. 248; B. Lenman and K. Donaldson, 'Partners' Incomes, Investment and Diversification in the Scottish Linen Area, 1880–1921', *Business History*, 13, 9–10 (1971); M. Blair, *The Paisley Thread Industry* (Paisley: 1907) p. 63; R. Smith, 'An Oldham Limited Liability Company, 1875–1896', *Business History*, 4, 37–38, 41 (1961/1962).

disappeared.[58] An investment in bonds also involved risks if the general level of interest rates changed while governments and companies regularly defaulted, as with the Argentinian government and US railroads in the 1890s.[59] No investment was risk free and so investors had to take their chances with what was available. Under the circumstances, investors looked to investments in companies with which they were familiar either because they knew the managers, the business or the location. Some of these turned out well, as with those who invested in Argentine railways because they knew the country. In contrast, those who invested in US cattle ranches, because they trusted the people involved, experienced large losses. Whether organised as a company or not, investment in business brought with it great risks, which were magnified when it took place in a foreign country where conditions were different.[60]

---

[58] K. Watson, *Industrial Finance in the UK: The Brewing Experience, 1880–1913*, Oxford D.Phil, 1990, pp. 91, 105, 184.

[59] C.F. Speare, 'Selling American Bonds in Europe', in W.H. Hull (ed.), 'Bonds as Investment Securities', *Annals of the American Academy of Political and Social Science* (Philadelphia: September 1907) pp. 80–82; C.F. Speare, 'Europe's Interest in American Securities', in T. Gibson (ed.), *Special Market Letters for 1898* (New York: 1909) pp. 104–105. See S.F. Van Oss, *American Railroads and British Investors* (London: 1893) p. 168.

[60] C. Lewis, 'British Railway Companies and the Argentine Government', in D.C.M. Platt (ed.), *Business Imperialism, 1840–1930* (Oxford: 1977) pp. 404, 415, 424; B. Attard, 'From Free-Trade Imperialism to Structural Power: New Zealand and the Capital Market, 1858–1868', *Journal of Imperial and Commonwealth History*, 35, 507, 519 (2007); B. Grohman, 'Cattle Ranches in the Far West', xxviii (1880); 'Outlying Professions', *Blackwood's Edinburgh Magazine*, 136 (1884); J.S. Tait, *The Cattle Field of the Far West* (Edinburgh: 1884) pp. 13–14; W.G. Kerr, 'Scottish Investment and Enterprise in Texas', in P.L. Payne (ed.), *Studies in Scottish Business History* (London: 1967) pp. 367–371; W.T. Jackson, *The Enterprising Scot: Investors in the American West after 1873* (Edinburgh: 1968) pp. 98–100; W.G. Kerr, *Scottish Capital on the American Credit Frontier* (Austin, Texas: Texas State Historical Association, 1976) p. 20; W.C. Holden, *The Espuela Land and Cattle Company* (Austin, Texas: 1970) pp. 44, 53, 246; W.M. Pearce, *The Matador Land and Cattle Company* (Norman, Oklahoma: 1964) pp. 13–14, 34, 72, 124, 150; H.R. Mothershead, *The Swan Land and Cattle Company, Ltd.* (Norman, Oklahoma: 1971) pp. 11, 90, 182–183; W.H. Marwick, 'Scottish Overseas Investment in the 19th Century', *The Scottish Bankers Magazine*, XXVII, 111–112 (1935/1936); The Espuela Land and Cattle Company: Memorandum and Articles of Association, 1884; Prairie Cattle Company (BT2/1003); Texas Land and Cattle Company (BT2/1075); H.H. Bassett (ed.), *Business Men at Home and Abroad* (London: 1912): see entry for William Fry.

As early as the 1860s, it was becoming impossible for investors to keep track of the many securities in existence, let alone possess the detailed knowledge required in order to make an informed decision on which ones to invest in. Writing in 1875, Scrathley considered that it was "very difficult for an investor with this immense variety before him even if he be possessed of a fair knowledge of such matters, to make a wise selection, while, in the case of ordinary persons, almost entirely destitute of any such knowledge, the task is nearly a hopeless one."[61] Echoing this in 1909 was the eminent actuary and chairman of the Prudential Insurance Company, Sir Joseph Burn, who was of the opinion that "Considerable experience and knowledge of a special kind is of course required in order to enable one to decide what is and what is not a suitable investment for a given purpose."[62] In 1914, C.K. Hobson criticised investors for their lack of knowledge of investment opportunities abroad. "There appears to be still a large class of investors which, inadequately informed as to foreign and colonial securities, and unwilling to take the trouble to find out about them, continues to invest in British securities with a low yield but of better standing."[63] Investors were conscious of the risks and rewards that came from investing in corporate stocks and bonds, and how difficult it was to separate those which delivered solid returns in the shape of capital gains and income streams from those which turned out to be complete failures.[64] In 1881, Nash suggested that "The mortality amongst new securities is enormous."[65] A similar verdict was reached by the *Money-Maker Manual* in 1901 when it claimed that "There have been hundreds of companies that have shown signs of decay before the first annual meeting, and gradually rotted to death."[66] Reviewing the survival rate of joint-stock companies in 1906, or fifty years after the passing of the limited liability acts, Henry

---

[61] A. Scrathley, *On Average Investment Trusts* (London: 1875) p. 8.

[62] Sir J. Burn, *Stock Exchange Investments in Theory and Practice* (London: 1909) p. 1.

[63] C.K. Hobson, *The Export of Capital* (London: 1914) pp. 23–25.

[64] J. Wagstaff Blundell, *Telegraph Companies Considered as Investments* (London: Effingham Wilson, 1869) pp. 3–7, 14, 20–21; The Investors' Guardian, *Guide to Investments* (London: 1873) p. 21.

[65] R.L. Nash, *A Short Inquiry into the Profitable Nature of Our Investments*, 3rd ed. (London: 1881) p. 124.

[66] *The Money-Maker Manuals for Investors No 1: How to Commence Investing* (London: 1901) p. 31.

Lowenfeld estimated that only 1 in 5 lasted 10 years.[67] Nevertheless, if investments were to be made, investors had no choice but to take risks as there were no certainties from the mid-nineteenth century onwards.[68]

The environment within which investors operated was changing constantly throughout the 1850–1914 period, with much attention being paid to outbursts of speculation, spectacular corporate failures and sudden government defaults.[69] A flavour of what investors had to cope with between 1890 and 1914, for example, can be gleaned from the *Investor's Monthly Manual*. During 1891 and 1892, investors were still reacting to the crisis of 1890, when one of London's leading investment banks, Barings, almost collapsed and had to be rescued by intervention from the Bank of England. That was followed by a prolonged period when investors shunned any stocks or bonds considered risky. What followed in 1894 was a dramatic reversal, which lasted into 1895 and 1896, when there was a speculative boom in South African gold mines. By 1897, investors were again prioritising safety because of "The frequent defaults of foreign governments and the loss of large sums in various enterprises abroad." Instead, investors favoured "home industrial undertakings," including a revival of interest in electric lighting and manufacturing companies. For the early twentieth century, the war in South Africa had a major influence on investors, and this was still being felt in 1905. "The heavy government borrowings necessitated by the war had the effect of absorbing enormous amounts of capital which, in normal years, would have been employed in industrial enterprise, while the savings, which ordinarily find their way into securities, were largely reduced by increased taxation.... With the completion of the process of digestion in connection with the war issues, and a gradual accumulation of savings, capital has found its way into the

---

[67] H. Lowenfeld, 'Investment Crazes', *The Financial Review of Reviews*, 162, 166, 169 (March 1906).

[68] Giffen, *Stock Exchange Securities*, pp. 153–159.

[69] *Aberdeen Herald*: 29th March 1862, 25th June 1864, 29th December 1866, 11th November 1871, 14th August 1875; *Aberdeen Free Press*: 1st January 1876, 3rd January 1876, 17th January 1876, 23rd March 1876, 1st May 1876, 24th May 1876, 26th May 1876, 20th July 1876, 2nd October 1876, 9th October 1876, 8th January 1877, 10th February 1877, 22nd March 1877, 3rd November 1881, 28th January 1882, 18th May 1882, 10th July 1888, 19th July 1889, 10th August 1889, 26th October 1889, 27th December 1889, 27th February 1892, 5th October 1895, 22nd April 1896, 1st May 1896.

stock markets in a more considerable stream than for years previously." Other influences on the behaviour of the stock market were to be found in the state of the business cycle, fluctuations in interest rates and changes in taxation. By 1908, more speculative conditions had returned with the shares of motorcar manufacturing companies being in demand. "The man who does not mind taking some risk would do well to watch the motor share market closely." In contrast, consols and UK railway stocks were to be avoided because they could no longer be relied upon to maintain their value and deliver a satisfactory yield. Investors were being advised to construct a diversified portfolio which was "not a question of arithmetic, for it depends on judgement, knowledge, experience, courage, and, last of all, good fortune." Within this portfolio, high-risk enterprises were to be avoided. "Looked at coolly, the flotation of an industrial company is really an extraordinary thing, involving a wonderful exercise of faith on the part of the investor ... the value of industrial investments is conditioned by the personality of the managers, and ... as these conditions are unknown to the ordinary investor there should be a higher return on the shares to balance the element of uncertainty." That message was repeated in 1909 and applied to all new companies. "Investment in a new company is carried out by most people with so little information that loss or profit is reduced to a matter of bad or good luck." However, another speculative boom took place in 1910, which centred on oil companies and rubber plantations. "People are out for speculation, and whether in rubber or in mines or in oils or in railways, they mean to have their fling."[70]

What this meant was that in the 25 years before the First World War, investors had to take account of the collapse of one of the leading investment banks, Barings, in 1890, the failure of the largest building society, the Liberator, in 1892, a financial crisis in Australia in 1892 and the USA in 1893, the boom in South African gold mining shares in 1895 and the worldwide financial crisis of 1907. There was also a succession of speculative bubbles involving companies manufacturing bicycles and then motor cars, producing oil and rubber, or running cinemas and ice skating

---

[70] *Investor's Monthly Manual*: June 1891, January 1892, May 1892, December 1892, November 1894, December 1895, September 1896, April 1897, November 1897, February 1901, December 1902, September 1904, December 1904, February 1905, March 1905, July 1906, October 1906, January 1908, February 1908, July 1908, February 1909, May 1909, July 1909, November 1909, February 1910, March 1910, August 1910, August 1911.

rinks. The number of companies providing cinemas, for example, rose from 3 in 1908 to 544 in 1913, with the early ones paying 40 per cent dividends before competition led to a collapse in profits. In addition to these specifically financial influences, investors had to cope with political crises at home, ranging from domestic labour disputes and agitation for Irish independence to conflict in South Africa between 1898 and 1902 and military scares that eventually led to the outbreak of the First World War in 1914. All these influenced the pace and pattern of investment. In addition, there were consequences from the conversion of the National Debt to a lower rate of interest in 1888, which affected all fixed income bonds, and the effects of taxation which undermined the housing market and altered the attractiveness of foreign as opposed to domestic securities in favour of the latter.[71] Throughout these years, a process was taking place in which British investors were learning from their past mistakes and improving their ability to make balanced judgements on the respective merits of the investments available to them, taking all variables into account.[72] At each stage, there were mistakes and setbacks, as well as successes and triumphs.[73] Writing in 1909, the *Canadian Financial Post* considered that "The most wide-awake financier in the world, the Britisher, who looks out from the City on all quarters of the globe, has been quietly absorbing much of our most promising material."[74] However,

---

[71] *Financial Review of Reviews*: 'The Investments of British Capital Abroad', November 1906, pp. 353, 359; G. Jamieson, 'Chinese Investments and Finance', December 1906, p. 452; G. Withers, 'English Investors and American Securities', March 1907, p. 33; H. Lowenfeld, 'The Investor's Mind', November 1907, pp. 16–17, P.F. Martin, 'Local Investments in British India', July 1908, pp. 19–20; E.E. Williams, 'British Capital and Legal Protection in Foreign Countries', July 1909, p. 35; P.F. Martin, 'Mexico as a Field for Investment', August 1909, p. 27; P.F. Martin, 'How Latin Americans Invest their Money', August 1911, p. 24; M.A. Raffalovich, 'Russia as a Field for Investment', August 1912, pp. 10–12.

[72] Lenfant, *British Capital Export*, pp. 30, 47–49, 56, 63–64, 104–105, 116, 130, 136, 150; E.J. Cleary, *The Building Society Movement* (London: 1965) pp. 124, 151–152; A. Essex-Crosby, *Joint-Stock Companies in Great Britain, 1890–1930*, University of London M.Com. 1938, pp. 40, 132; R. Low, *The History of the British Film, 1906–1914* (London: 1949) pp. 15–20.

[73] J.B. Sturrock, *Peter Brough: A Paisley Philanthropist* (Paisley: 1890) pp. 20, 34, 57, 114–118, 117–118, 155, 211; M.B. Rose, 'Diversification of Investment by the Greg Family, 1800–1914', *Business History*, xxi, 91–93 (1979).

[74] *Canadian Financial Post*, 23rd January 1909. See G.P. Marchildon, *Promotion, Finance and Mergers in Canadian Manufacturing Industry, 1885–1918*, London School of

these achievements remained largely hidden in the glare of publicity that followed the daily fluctuations of stock prices and the periodic speculative outbursts. In his 1909 book, *All About Investment*, Lowenfeld pointed out that "Every stock exchange security, no matter what its nature, is a speculation, for it is liable to rise and fall in value, and to a greater or lesser extent may fail to fulfil its promises."[75] These fluctuations captured the public imagination in a way that the steady accumulation of safe assets did not. Like an iceberg, judgements about investment were made based on that portion that was visible, and the even smaller part that attracted public comment, not the greater part that lay beneath the surface.

British Investment After 1914

Before the First World War, there were a number of established trends in British investment. One was the declining importance of rural land and the National Debt as a home for savings and their replacement with the stocks and bonds issued by joint-stock companies, especially railways, irrespective of where they operated. Between 1830 and 1913, holdings of corporate stocks and bonds grew from 1.2 per cent of national assets to 18.3 per cent. Another trend was the acquisition of foreign assets, which grew from 2.7 per cent of national assets in 1830 to 17.8 per cent in 1913, much of which was also in corporate stocks and bonds. By 1914, British investors owned foreign assets worth $18.3 billion at current prices out of a world total of $43.8 billion, or almost half. This position was to be totally transformed again over the next one hundred years beginning with the impact made by the First World War.

The most marked feature of the twentieth century was the greatly enhanced role of the government within the whole process of investment. Not only during both world wars, spanning 1914/1918 and 1939/1945, but

Economics Ph.D. 1990, p. 63; C.K. Morris, *Canada: For British Gold and British Enterprise* (London: 1910) pp. 19, 184; F.W. Field, *Capital Investments in Canada* (Toronto: 1911) pp. 9, 17–19, 41–43, 45, 84–88; *Monetary Times Annual*, January 1914; F.W. Field, 'How Canadian Stocks are Held', *Monetary Times Annual*, January 1915; *Canadian Financial Post*, 23rd January 1909; 'Prospects of Canadian Land Mortgage Companies', *Accountants' Magazine*, 111, 495–498 (1899); D.B. Adler, *British Investment in American Railways, 1834–1898* (Charlottesville, USA: 1970) pp. 71–72, 143, 153, 159; S. Jones (ed.), *Banking and Business in South Africa* (New York: 1988) p. 43.
[75] H. Lowenfeld, *All About Investment* (London: 1909) p. 236.

also after the Second, the state either directly controlled much of the investment that took place or influenced its volume and direction. It was not until after the ending of exchange controls in 1979 that relative freedom was returned to financial markets, enhanced by further measures in the 1980s, such as the privatisation of state assets, the ending of rent controls and the sale of local authority housing. Even then, there was no return to the situation that had prevailed before the First World War. The government continued to dictate the investment agenda across large parts of the economy, as in education, health and transport, while most of the key decisions were taken in the head offices of multinational companies, often foreign owned, or internalised within banks whose operations spanned the globe. The result was to make investment, once again, private and opaque, as it had been before the nineteenth century, though public attention continued to focus on the performance of those corporate stocks quoted on the London Stock Exchange even though they remained a poor representation of the structure of the UK economy, and much came under the control of investors from abroad. As in the years before the First World War, there was a large gulf between the reality of investment and the public perception of what was taking place, but it was the latter rather than the former that often drove the actions of government.[76]

This perception was inherited from the position that had prevailed before the First World War, and then reinforced by the speculative boom that followed it and the harsh economic conditions facing many businesses in the 1920s and 1930s. That boom left a legacy of overcapitalised and poorly performing companies that failed to deliver what had been promised to investors. At the same time, increased taxation and reduced profits deprived many owners of businesses of the funds that they had previously used to finance their investments. The informal financial networks and reinvested profits broke down in many cases, forcing businesses to consider issuing stocks and bonds in order to obtain the finance they required. However, many businesses were no longer as profitable as they had been in the past, especially those operating in the traditional industries, and so their stocks and bonds were unattractive to investors.

---

[76]See Goldsmith, *Comparative National Balance Sheet Capitalism, Culture and Decline*; R.C. Michie, 'The London Stock Exchange and the British Government in the Twentieth Century', in S. Battilossi and J. Reis (eds), *State and Financial Systems in Europe and the USA: Historical Perspectives on Regulation and Supervision in the Nineteenth and Twentieth Centuries* (Aldershot: Ashgate Publishing Company, 2010).

The overall effect was to suggest that the market-based process of investment had failed.[77]

This combination of a speculative boom, followed by a shortage of finance in certain sectors, was picked up by one of the twentieth century's most famous economists, J.M. Keynes. In his *General Theory of Employment, Interest and Money*, which was published in 1936, he launched an attack on finance through the issue of stocks and bonds. "Our knowledge of the factors which govern the yield of an investment some years hence is usually very slight and often negligible.... Certain classes of investment are governed by the average expectation of those who deal on the Stock Exchange as revealed in the price of shares, rather than by the genuine expectations of the professional entrepreneur.... A conventional valuation which is established as the outcome of the mass psychology of a large number of ignorant individuals is liable to change violently as the result of a sudden fluctuation of opinion due to factors which do not really make much difference to the prospective yield; since there will be no strong roots of conviction to hold it steady."[78] Those comments by Keynes, written during the global depression of the 1930s, were sufficient to condemn market-based capitalism for many, and stimulate a search for a radical alternative. This built on earlier critics of capitalism leading to inevitable calls for investment to be placed under the central direction of the government, where it could be managed and controlled. In that way, investment would be made to serve the collective interests of the entire community. At the very least, the guidance of bankers, acting as intermediaries between savers and borrowers, was preferred to the lottery of the marketplace in determining the direction of investment. That then became the direction of travel after the Second World War.[79]

What these critics were ignoring was the completely altered environment within which investment took place as a result of two world wars and a world depression. During the First World War, government debt increased massively. The National Debt rose from £0.7 billion in 1913 to £7 billion in 1918 at current prices. Most of this debt was raised within Britain, but a significant proportion came from the USA. In contrast,

---

[77] C. Swinson, *Regulation of the London Stock Exchange: Share Trading, Fraud and Reform, 1914–1945* (London: Routledge, 2018) pp. 38–40, 45–47, 50–55.

[78] Keynes, *The General Theory of Employment*, ch. 12 'The State of Long-Term-Expectation'.

[79] See R.C. Michie, 'Financial Capitalism'.

foreign assets held by private investors were surrendered to the government and then sold off, especially those denominated in US$s. The same happened during the Second World War when the government's domestic debt ballooned. By 1945, the UK had become a net debtor nation as the government had borrowed $43.5 billion from the USA and the Empire, as well as selling most of the remaining overseas assets, which were worth $6.5 billion. The government then continued to borrow to finance the nationalisation of major industries, such as the entire railway network, and to cover its inability to balance expenditure and revenue in most years. At the same time, the level of taxation increased enormously to finance both the wars and then remained at a high level in the decades that followed. Whether it was the incomes of individuals or the profits of businesses, the government took a large share of the total, greatly diminishing that which was left for discretionary investment. Those with funds to invest also had available to them, as in the early nineteenth century, holdings of the National Debt. In 1926, investors were being advised to invest in the National Debt because, according to Davies, "If you want the nearest approach to absolute safety combined with ready marketability, stick to the 5 per cent War Loan."[80] After the Second World War, the attractions of the National Debt greatly diminished because of the effects of inflation on all fixed-interest securities. This forced investors to look elsewhere if they were to maintain the value of their investment when adjusted for inflation.[81]

As an investment, housing was also badly affected by action taken during the First World War. Rent control was introduced in 1915 and not finally abolished until 1989, destroying the value of rented housing as an investment for much of the twentieth century. What replaced the private investor in housing was a combination of the state and owner occupation. From the 1930s, and especially after the Second World War, local

---

[80] E. Davies, *What to Look for in a Prospectus* (London: 1926) p. 47.

[81] S. Homer, *A History of Interest Rates* (New Brunswick: Rutgers University Press, 1963) pp. 208–209, 409; C.K. Harley, 'Goschen's Conversion of the National Debt and the Yield on Consols', *Economic History Review*, 29, 105–106 (1976); J. Clapham, *The Bank of England* (Cambridge: 1944) p. 428; B. Supple, *The Royal Exchange Assurance: A History of British Insurance, 1720–1970* (Cambridge: 1970) pp. 309–331; Johnston and Murphy, 'The Growth of Life Assurance in UK', p. 155; H.A.L. Cockerell and E. Green, *The British Insurance Business, 1547–1970* (London: 1976) p. 71; E.V. Morgan and W.A. Thomas, *The Stock Exchange: Its History and Functions* (London: 1962) pp. 122, 190.

authorities stepped in to provide housing for rent. That ended in the 1980s when the Conservative government reversed the policy by allowing tenants to buy their homes. A more permanent response to legislation and taxation was the expansion of owner occupation, which was long given favourable tax treatment while home ownership was made increasingly attractive as house prices rose steadily. The driving force behind these changes was legislation and taxation. A similar combination influenced investment in stocks and bonds. Faced with a highly unstable international environment between the wars, and then restrictions on foreign investment after the Second World War, the acquisition of overseas assets was also removed as an option for investors.[82] The result was to direct the attention of investors towards companies operating within Britain. As in the past, investors were mainly attracted to those companies that manufactured products or supplied services that were familiar to them. In response, there was a steady conversion of established businesses into joint-stock companies and mergers to create ever larger units. Large companies were favoured by the increasingly important institutional investors, as their shares were more easily bought and sold. Between the wars, there continued to be a speculative interest in companies that promised high returns from a foreign mineral discovery or new technology.[83]

---

[82]Rubinstein, *Wealth and Inequality in Britain*, p. 87; M. Ball and D. Sunderland, *An Economic History of London, 1800–1914* (London: Routledge, 2001) pp. 185–187, 194.

[83]A.W. Kirkaldy, *British Finance During and After the War, 1914–1921* (London: 1921) p. 137; K. Heinemann, *Popular Investment and Speculation in Britain, 1918–1987*, University of Cambridge Ph.D., 2017, pp. 5–11, 23–30, 42–53; A.S.J. Baster, 'A Note on the Colonial Stock Acts and Dominion Borrowing', *Economic History*, 2, 604 (1930/1933); D.H. MacGregor, 'Joint-Stock Companies and the Risk Factor', *Economic Journal*, xxxix, 4 (1929); F. Lavington, *The English Capital Market* (London: 1921) pp. 202–203, 219–221; R.F. Henderson, *The New Issue Market and the Finance of Industry* (Cambridge: 1951) pp. 55, 83–84, 154; J. Turner, 'Holding Shareholders to Account: British Banking Stability and Contingent Capital', in Dimsdale and Hotson, *British Financial Crises*, pp. 143, 166; D.M. Ross, 'Industrial and Commercial Finance in the Interwar Years', in R. Floud, J. Humphries and P. Johnson (eds), *The Cambridge Economic History of Modern Britain*, Vol. 2, pp. 411, 425–426; W.A. Thomas, *The Finance of British Industry, 1918–1976* (London: 1978) pp. 24, 48–50; S. Haxey, *Tory MP* (London: Victor Gollancz (Left Book Club) 1939), p. 41; Heinemann, *Popular Investment and Speculation in Britain*, pp. 5–11, 23–30, 42–53; H.D. Wynne-Bennett, *Investment and Speculation*, pp. 322–324; C. Maughan, *Markets of London* (London: 1931) p. 9; C. Brooks, *Something in the City: Men and Markets in London* (London: 1931) p. 99; Hannah, *The Rise of the*

After the Second World War, many of the corporate stocks favoured in the past were no longer available with the nationalisation of the railways and utilities. In their place, investors turned even more to the shares of Britain's largest industrial and commercial companies, as well as those of the banks and insurance companies. This encouraged the process of amalgamation that had begun before the First World War and continued during the 1920s and 1930s. The growing scale of these businesses made it easier for them to finance themselves from internal sources rather than tapping outside investors.[84] What increasingly disappeared after the Second World War were the numerous local enterprises beloved of knowledgeable investors, as they were absorbed into national or even international companies. It was in 1973 that the local stock exchanges finally disappeared in a merger with the London Stock Exchange as there was no longer a need for a market for locally held stocks.[85] What also disappeared were the highly risky companies engaged in exploring for minerals or developing a new technology. Instead, these processes took place largely within existing companies, being financed through internal financial flows according to management decisions.[86] Though the abandonment of

---

Corporate Economy, pp. 58–60; K. Heinemann, 'Investment, Speculation and Popular Stock Market Engagement in 20th-Century Britain', *Archiv für Sozialgeschichte*, 56, 254–256 (2016); J. Kinross, *50 Years in the City: Financing Small Business* (London: 1982) p. 73; F.W. Hirst, *Wall Street and Lombard Street: The Stock Exchange Slump of 1929 and the Trade Depression of 1930* (New York: 1931) pp. 80–81; Share Pushing: Report of the Departmental Committee Appointed by the Board of Trade, 1936/7, cmd 5537 (London: 1937) pp. 6, 17; H. Meredith, *The Drama of Money-Making: Tragedy and Comedy on the London Stock Exchange* (London: 1931) pp. 179, 188; H.E. Peters, *The Foreign Debt of the Argentine Republic* (Baltimore: 1934) pp. 1, 33; R.F. Henderson, *The New Issue Market*, pp. 55, 83–84, 154; Wynne-Bennett, *Investment and Speculation*, pp. 322–324; A. Citizen, *The City Today* (London: New Fabian Research Bureau, 1938) pp. 29, 36.

[84] Ross, 'Industrial and Commercial Finance in the Interwar Years', Vol. 2, pp. 411, 425–426; Thomas, *The Finance of British Industry*, pp. 24, 48–50, 90–92; Haxey, *Tory MP*, p. 41.

[85] Hannah, *The Rise of the Corporate Economy*, pp. 3, 105, 216; Thomas, *The Provincial Stock Exchanges*, pp. 64–71, 119, 123, 133, 171–180, 187, 246–249, 316–318; Thomas, *The Stock Exchanges of Ireland*, pp. 15, 154–157, 22.

[86] Heinemann, 'Investment, Speculation and Popular Stock Market Engagement', pp. 264–269; N. Macrae, *The London Capital Market: Its Structure, Strains and Management* (London: 1955) pp. 102–103; Johnson and Murphy, 'The Growth of Life Assurance in the

exchange controls in 1979, and then the reduction in taxation during the 1980s and 1990s, did restore an element of freedom to the stock market, it never returned to the speculative activity witnessed before the First World War and even between the wars. That was now conducted through private and opaque channels, or not at all, being left to venture capitalists in the USA.[87]

Conclusion

With the exception of the National Debt, the process of investment was a private affair before the nineteenth century, when considered the acquisition of financial assets. When viewed as capital formation, it was entirely private. That changed with the Railway Mania of the 1840s as that merged capital formation and the acquisition of financial assets, and brought investment much more into the public spotlight. The spread of joint-stock

---

UK', p. 155; W. Paish, *Business Finance* (London: 1961) p. 96; W.M. Clarke, *The City in the World Economy* (London: 1965) p. 12; G. Clayton and W.T. Osborn, *Insurance Company Investment: Principles and Policy* (London: 1965) pp. 22, 27, 34–35, 49, 67, 68; J. Moyle, *The Pattern of Ordinary Share Ownership, 1957–1970* (Cambridge: 1971) p. 7; A. Jenkins, *The Stock Exchange Story* (London: 1973) p. 178; Thomas, *The Finance of British Industry*, pp. 115–117, 145–147; L. Dennett, *The Charterhouse Group, 1925–1979: A History* (London: 1979) p. 146; W.A. Thomas, *The Big Bang* (Oxford: 1986) p. 17; J.J. Fishman, *The Transformation of Threadneedle Street: The Deregulation and Re-regulation of Britain's Financial Services* (Durham, NC: 1993) pp. 36–37; M. Clarke, *Citizens' Financial Futures: The Regulation of Retail Investment Financial Services in Britain* (Aldershot: 1999) pp. 11–12, 179, 183; A. Gleeson, *People and Their Money: 50 Years of Private Investment* (London: 1981) pp. 1–2, 135; *The Stock Exchange Official Yearbook*, 1985/1986 (London: 1986); Rubinstein, *Men of Property*, pp. 284–298; G.B. Blakey, *The Post-War History of the London Stock Market, 1945–1992* (Didcot: Mercury, 1993) pp. 155–116; J. Rutterford and L. Hannah, 'The Rise of Institutional Investors', in D. Chambers and E. Dimson (eds), *Financial Market History: Reflections of the Past for Investors Today* (CFA Institute Research Foundation: 2016) pp. 242–264.

[87]Cairncross, *Home and Foreign Investment, 1870–1913*, p. 95; A.R. Hall, 'A Note on the English Capital Market as a Source of Funds for Home Investment Before 1914', *Economica*, n.s. XXIV, 63 (1957); Cairncross, 'The English Capital Market Before 1914', pp. 143–146; A.R. Hall, 'The English Capital Market Before 1914: A Reply', *Economica*, n.s. xxv, 340–343 (1958); A.K. Cairncross, *The British Economy since 1945: Economic Policy and Performance, 1945–1990* (Oxford: Blackwell, 1992) p. 24; Pollard, *The Development of the British Economy*, pp. 9, 85, 102.

enterprise in the following years ensured that the distinction between capital formation and the acquisition of financial assets remained blurred, when the subject of investment arose. For many, the process of investment was identified with the issue of stocks and bonds by companies and their quotation on the London Stock Exchange. The securities quoted on the London Stock Exchange became a proxy for the composition of the nation's investment and their performance a measure of its success or failure. The result was a very distorted picture of investment. The relationship between listed securities and capital formation was a very poor one as much consisted of government debt, created to finance military conflict, while huge areas of the economy never resorted to the issue of stocks and bonds for finance. Consequently, the public perception of investment was at great variance to reality. Foreign investment was greatly overrepresented before the First World War, for example, while domestic housing did not feature. After the Second World War, the nationalisation of railways and utilities removed their securities from the list of quoted stocks and bonds only to have them reappear with privatisation from the 1980s.

The distortion even extended to the perception of the nature of investment. Whereas capital formation was a continuous process, as depreciation was made good and improvements financed, activity on the London Stock Exchange involved constant fluctuations in the price of both stocks and bonds. As they paid a fixed return, bonds were very sensitive to variations in interest rates, which led to constant adjustments as funds flowed between them and alternatives. Corporate stocks were even more volatile as they adjusted to supply and demand and responded to company-specific rumours and announcements. Some stocks were very sensitive to the circulation of information, such as those developing a new product or service, using a new technology or exploring for minerals and oil, as success or failure could mean large gains or losses. It was around these stocks that speculative manias developed, as the future was unknown, and could deliver huge profits or spell total disaster. As it was the most extreme price changes that generated the greatest public comment even among financial assets, the process of investment became associated with gambling and the outcome akin to a lottery. For those reasons, there was always a desire among many to subject the whole process of investment to control, either from government or the banks. In that way, the direction of investment could reflect public preferences and be conducted in such a way that eliminated fluctuations and speculative bubbles. This desire was greatly magnified as a result of the experience of government control during two world wars compared to the intervening years of mass unemployment when market forces were allowed full reign. What was lost after the Second World War was the element of risk taking that was a vital element in the investment process despite the mistakes and losses. There was no certainty that collective control over investment would achieve better results, especially when subjected to political and other biases, but much of its outcomes were hidden from view. Similarly, the decisions made by banks and multinational corporations were taken in secret and their results never fully revealed. Instead, the public was left with the evidence generated by trading on the London Stock Exchange upon which to base its judgements, as these were widely reported. In turn, it was that perception that exerted a strong influence on the actions taken by government. This interaction between reality and perception can be seen even more markedly when it was the behaviour of investors that was being observed.

Chapter 3

Investors: From the Few to the Many to the Few

Introduction

Many have a poor opinion of the behaviour of investors when the business was left to individuals following their own judgement rather than bankers, professional fund managers or government employees. Individual investors were considered vulnerable to all forms of scams, were believed to be easily seduced by the latest fad and were seen to indulge in speculation without regard for fundamentals. The result was that they lost all they had staked, and this had damaging consequences for the economy. In the late nineteenth century, investors were accused of favouring foreign rather than home investment; in the inter-war period, they were criticised for neglecting domestic manufacturing; and in the post-war years, they were believed to ignore long-term investment in favour of short-term gains. The founder of the Social Democratic Federation, Henry Hyndman, wrote in 1892 that investors would "rush into new enterprises" and had "a mania for speculation" which was driven by "an eager anxiety to get rich without toil."[1] J. Ramsay MacDonald, the leader of the Labour Party, and then Prime Minister between the wars, considered in 1909 that investors were driven by fads and panics and fell victim to the lure of "an attractive

---

[1]H.M. Hyndman, *Commercial Crises of the Nineteenth Century* (London: 1892) pp. 10, 42.

prospectus," "swindling undertakings" or a "foolish business proposition."[2] Reaching a similar conclusion was the radical economist, J.A. Hobson, whose writings had a huge following. In 1911, he expressed his opinion that "No inconsiderable part of the capital invested every year never materialises in any serviceable shape, but simply passes from the pockets of foolish or unfortunate investors into those of unscrupulous or reckless financiers who float bogus companies, or palm off shares, which have slight value, at exaggerated prices."[3] He argued in his study of modern capitalism, which first appeared in 1894, that leaving investment to investors was a fundamental flaw. He claimed in the 1926 edition that, "The whole system is one of betting."[4] Another who had a very negative view of the behaviour of investors was J.M. Keynes, whose analysis helped determine government policy after the Second World War. In his seminal work, *The General Theory of Employment, Interest and Money*, which was published in 1936, he likened the actions of investors to those of gamblers. "When the capital development of a country becomes a by-product of the activities of a casino, the job is likely to be ill-done."[5] As the behaviour of individual investors could not be changed by legislation, the inevitable recommendation was a much greater role for the state, with individual investors being regulated, marginalised or eliminated.

Encouraging government intervention was the association between investors and gambling. At the very least, investors had to be protected from themselves. Others went further, suggesting that individuals should be entirely removed from the investment process and replaced by either government officials under the direction of elected politicians or trained professionals such as bankers. Only then would it be possible to prevent the self-harm individual investors inflicted on themselves and the damage to the economy resulting from their reckless actions. The problem with such views was that they were often driven by time-specific events and circumstances rather than an examination of the challenges and opportunities investors faced and the long-term consequences of the decisions they took. Instead, they were a product of an anti-capitalism ideology or

---

[2] J. Ramsay MacDonald, 'The Export of Capital', *The Financial Review of Reviews*, 16–19 (April 1909).

[3] J.A. Hobson, *The Economic Interpretation of Investment* (London: 1911) p. 24.

[4] See J.A. Hobson, *The Evolution of Modern Capitalism*, 1926 ed., pp. 243, 256.

[5] Keynes, *The General Theory of Employment*, ch. 12 'The State of Long-term Expectation'.

based on observing the culmination of a speculative bubble, the aftermath of a major corporate failure, the default of a government on its borrowing or the reporting of a well-publicised trial for financial fraud. Both Hyndman and MacDonald were socialists while Hobson had witnessed a speculative bubble in the 1890s involving South African gold mining. Keynes formed his views in the 1920s, in the aftermath of the instability caused by the First World War, and then refined them in the 1930s, in the wake of the Wall Street Crash and during a global economic depression. At the time each wrote, the folly of the investor appeared obvious, as were the wider consequences for the economy. Assessments made, with the benefit of a wider and longer-term perspective, have reached different conclusions but the judgements of contemporaries remained to influence later generations. What needs to be understood was that investors were captives of the environment within which they operated, deprived of the foresight that came with hindsight. Keynes was the one who recognised this, which made him reluctant to recommend the wholesale replacement of the decisions made by individuals with that of the state, but that reservation was lost during the years of government direction that followed the six years of war between 1939 and 1945.[6]

Without an appreciation of the changing nature of investors and the environment within which they operated, judgements about their behaviour become part of the battle between the relative merits of decisions being left to the free will of the individual and those of decisions subjected to collective authority and central direction. There is a constant conflict between the belief that considers individuals as rational decision-makers, delivering the best possible outcome, and that which presses for suppression of choice and its replacement by centralised decision-making as the only way of serving the entire community. In this conflict of ideas, events could tilt the balance in one direction or the other. Wars and crises favoured intervention while peace and stability encouraged a laissez faire attitude. When assessing the behaviour of investors, the environment within which they operated has to be acknowledged. Otherwise, the verdict of contemporaries is accepted even though they made their judgement on the basis of partial evidence. Investor behaviour was influenced by

---

[6]See R.C. Michie, 'Gamblers, Fools, Victims or Wizards? The British Investor in the Public Mind, 1850–1930', in D.R. Green, A. Owens, J. Maltby, J. Rutterford (eds), *Men, Women and Money: Perspectives on Gender, Wealth, and Investment 1850–1930* (Oxford: Oxford University Press, 2011).

such variables as the volatility of prices, changes in interest rates and exchange rates, and the impact of government policies, especially taxation, as well as expectations about the future which might not be fulfilled. This is understood today and the past is no different. In 2021, Maddison Darbyshire, in the *Financial Times*, spelled out the current predicament faced by professional fund managers as a result of the conditions created by central bank intervention since the Global Financial crisis of 2008 and during the Pandemic that broke out in 2019. "Millions of savers face dwindling options for a return on their cash amid ultra-low interest rates. As a result, wealth managers said clients were increasingly moving their money into equity markets.... Advisers noted that savers who were unfamiliar with stock market investment were particularly vulnerable to scams, as they searched for lower-risk options with comparable rates of return."[7] This situation had implications for investors even though the process was now handled by professional fund managers as Anne Richards, the chief executive of the fund managers, Fidelity International, spelled out, also in 2021. "About two-thirds of Britons have a stake in the stock market through their pension, whether they know it or not."[8] In the earlier era, when those decisions were left in the hands of individuals, contemporaries like Hyndman, MacDonald, Hobson and Keynes saw only foolish investors who gambled and lost, not the predicament they faced when taking decisions about a future that was hidden from them.

The Investor Before 1914

In the century before the First World War, the size and composition of the investing public were transformed along with the environment within which they operated. No longer was the investor confined to a tiny minority faced with a choice between holding the National Debt and channelling their savings into loans and property through informal networks. Though the number of investors remained small relative to the total population, it expanded rapidly in breadth and depth as more of the middle class accumulated savings and began to purchase corporate stocks and

---

[7]M. Darbyshire, 'NS&I Rate Cut Drives Savers into Investments', *Financial Times*, 9th January 2021.

[8]A. Richards, 'Transmission Revamp Will Reshape the Financial World', *Financial Times*, 18th August 2021.

bonds. In turn, these investors had available to them a growing variety of securities.[9] As the *Investor's and Shareholder's Guide* observed in 1894, "If there is a wide variety among investments, there is a corresponding variety, in respect both to their requirements and their tastes, among investors themselves — comprising every shade, from the conservative believer in nothing but the funds, to the speculative investor who is content to face the risk of loss for the sake of a 10 or 20 per cent return or a prospective increase in market value."[10] As early as 1873, the London periodical, *Capital and Investment*, claimed that "The class of investors is constantly and rapidly increasing in number."[11] In 1913, the *Investor's Guide*, published by the *Financial Times*, suggested that there has been an "enormous increase in the number of investors" and the "multiplication of securities."[12] An estimate made in 1897 identified around 380,000 investors in joint-stock companies.[13] In 1901, a higher number was put forward in the *Stock Exchange Gazette*. Based on a survey of 6,630 companies, and allowing for double counting, they calculated that there were 455,000 people in the UK who invested in corporate stocks and bonds.[14] Counting only those with a minimum holding of £1,000, the *Financial Review of Reviews* came up with a figure of 190,000 investors in 1904. In 1906, they increased this to 250,000.[15] The number of investors in joint-stock companies, other than railways, does appear to have risen from only 50,000 in 1860 to as many as 500,000 by 1914, with participation growing strongly in the 10 years before the First World War. A recent estimate suggests that the number of investors in total may have grown to as many as 720,000 in this period, helped by such legislation as the Married Women's

---

[9]J. Maltby and J. Rutterford, 'She Possessed Her Own Fortune: Women Investors from the Late 19th Century to the Early 20th Century', *Business History*, 48, 222–224, 230–234 (2006); R.J. Morris, 'The Middle Class and the Property Cycle During the Industrial Revolution', in T.C. Smout (ed.), *The Search for Wealth and Stability* (London: 1979) p. 92, 101–102, 110; Cairncross, *Home and Foreign Investment*, pp. 84–88.

[10]Walker and Watson, *Investor's and Shareholder's Guide*, p. 262.

[11]*Capital and Investment*, 15th February 1873.

[12]'Investor's Guide', *Financial Times* (London: 1913) p. 5.

[13]W. Hickman and S. Aubrey, *Stock Exchange Investments: Their History, Practice, and Results* (London: 1897) p. 172.

[14]*The Stock Exchange Gazette: A Weekly Journal for Investors and Their Advisers*, 28th December 1901.

[15]*The Financial Review of Reviews*, November 1904, February 1906.

Property Act of 1882, which allowed a married woman to own shares in her own right.[16] These investors were located throughout the British Isles. There were dense pools of investors sufficient to support a network of local stock exchanges by 1914, including five in Scotland and three in Ireland, as well as ones in every major English and Welsh city. London was home to the world's largest stock exchange. These stock exchanges catered to distinct investor communities that were large, active and growing. Writing in 1910, Powell reported on "A class of utterly obscure concerns, most of them quite local in scope, of which the small and secretive investor is particularly enamoured.... That which is local and palpable he understands and trusts. That which is distant and invisible he only dimly realises as existing at all." In contrast, the wealthiest investors and especially financial institutions favoured those securities paying a fixed rate of interest and backed by governments and municipalities.[17]

The growing volume and variety of stocks and bonds in circulation made it impossible for a single individual to have sufficient knowledge to make an informed judgement about them all. Hayes Fisher in 1912 stated that "No private investor can hope to watch his own holdings efficiently even if he spent the whole of his time in the work." This did not mean that investors acted blindly as most "have no desire to speculate."[18] Instead, investors directed their funds to those securities where they possessed a degree of inside knowledge or opted for the security of fixed interest. "Between the one investor, who can afford to run no risk at all, and the other, to whom the loss of £1,000 is a mere incident, there is a great gulf fixed."[19] As a replacement for consols, for example, investors chose bonds paying a higher rate of interest but considered equally safe.[20] Confirming that contemporary assessment of the choices made by investors is Stone's comprehensive statistical survey of the distribution of British portfolio foreign investment between 1865 and 1914. He estimated that this collective portfolio amounted to £4.1 billion spread over 150 different countries.

---

[16]D.R. Green, A. Owens, J. Maltby and J. Rutterford, 'Lives in the Balance: Gender, Age and Assets in Late Nineteenth Century England and Wales', *Continuity and Change*, 24, 27–31 (2009).

[17]E.T. Powell, *The Mechanism of the City* (London: 1910) pp. 95–97, 116, 140–142, 165.

[18]W. Hayes Fisher, *Investing at Its Best and Safeguarding Invested Capital* (London: 1912) pp. 13, 18, 23, 37.

[19]Hayes Fisher, *Investing at Its Best*, pp. 13, 18, 23, 37.

[20]Gibson, *The Fall in Consols and Other Investments since 1897*, p. 69.

There was an overwhelming preference for the securities of countries offering an attractive rate of return, and a proven record of servicing their debts, rather than those with a dubious borrowing history regardless of the rate of interest they were offering. The USA was the most popular destination with 21 per cent, followed by Canada, Australia and New Zealand (10 per cent), Argentina (9 per cent), India (8 per cent), South Africa (6 per cent), Brazil (4 per cent) and Russia (3 per cent). Further evidence of the risk-averse preferences of investors was that 68 per cent was invested in bonds, paying a fixed rate of interest, and only 23 per cent in shares, where dividends depended upon current profits. This was ideal at a time of falling prices, as was the case from 1873 to 1896, and very modest inflation subsequently. Finally, Stone revealed that 36 per cent of the total was loans to governments while 32 per cent went to railways and 6 per cent to utilities. The figure for mining and plantations, the riskiest of all types of foreign investment, was only 10 per cent.[21]

Faced with this enormous variety of securities to choose from, individual investors picked different strategies to follow. "Some investors are attracted by the tempting dividends on the shares, and others by the charming combination of simplicity and security supposed to exist in the debentures" was a comment made in 1884.[22] Nash, in 1881, considered that "Throughout the different grades of securities, different investors are found to fancy each." British government debt appealed to the most risk averse, being "the most readily marketable securities in the world" while shares in steamship companies were "risky investments" as they were "subjected to greater variations from prosperity to reverse and back again." Shares in small companies were only for those who could "watch over and control its operations."[23] There were those investors who commanded large fortunes and so could take large risks. In 1910, Harley Withers was of the opinion that there were a number of individuals who possessed the knowledge, expertise and funds to make the buying and selling of stocks and shares a financial success. "With real information of this kind at his disposal, and with plenty of money at his command … this specially endowed kind of speculator can increase his capital with practical certainty, and sometimes very rapidly. But he is not of the general

---

[21] I. Stone, *The Global Export of Capital from Great Britain, 1865–1914: A Statistical Survey* (London: 1999) p. 6.

[22] 'Scottish Capital Abroad', *Blackwood's Edinburgh Magazine*, 136, 470 (1884).

[23] Nash, *A Short Inquiry*, pp. 1, 7, 93, 102, 112.

public."[24] There was, for example, a closely connected group in Glasgow who made money through backing copper mines in Spain, gold mines in India and dynamite manufacturing in the UK between 1866 and 1909.[25]

However, the investing public also placed increasing reliance upon professionals to provide them with advice, with stockbrokers, bankers, accountants and lawyers being regularly consulted. Lawson complained in 1884 that investors had become too dependent upon the advice they provided. "So much of the work of investment is done at second hand through agents and brokers, that the small capitalist has no training to think for himself."[26] Withers reported in 1914 that "A good firm of brokers will have a good set of clients, who will follow their lead and subscribe to the issue."[27] The Glasgow merchant, William Stirling, took advice in the 1880s from his stockbrokers, Kerr, Anderson, Muir and Main. In 1889, another Glasgow investor, W.N. Neilson, an engineer, turned to his stock-brokers, J. & G. Moffat, for recommendations.[28] In January 1914, Max Aitken (Lord Beaverbrook), the Canadian financier who had relocated to London, was assisting the Irish landowner, Edward Alfred Goulding (Lord Wargrave), to remodel a portfolio of stocks and bonds in 50 different companies ranging from railways through industrials to mining and plantations and spread across the USA, Canada, Argentina, Africa and India.[29] Arthur Grenfell, another City financier, maintained a list of "some 2,000 private clients" whom he advised in the years before the First World War.[30] These professionals largely catered to the wealthy investor as they could justify the time and expense involved in keeping them informed because of the dealing fees generated. That left the growing number of

---

[24] Withers, *Stocks and Shares*, p. 354.

[25] N. Crathorne, *Tennants' Stalk: The Story of the Tennants of the Glen* (London: 1973) pp. 138–141; W.J. Reader, *Imperial Chemical Industries: A History, Vol. 1: The Forerunners, 1870–1926* (London: 1970) pp. 24–31; S.G. Checkland, *The Mines of Tharsis: Roman, French and British Enterprise in Spain* (London: 1967) pp. 16–18, 105–106, 111–113, 123–124, 126–127, 132, 138, 186.

[26] W.R. Lawson, *The Scottish Investors' Manual* (Edinburgh: 1884) p. 16.

[27] Withers, *Stocks and Shares*, p. 100.

[28] Kerr, Anderson, Muir and Main to William Stirling, 4th December 1884; J. & G. Moffat to W.N. Neilson 12 February 1889.

[29] Edward Alfred Goulding, Lord Wargrave, Investment Ledger, January 1914 (Beaverbrook collection, House of Lords).

[30] Arthur Grenfell to Earl Grey 29th November 1906; Memorandum by Arthur Grenfell on the Canadian Agency, 1914.

small investors without access to professional advice. Bartlett and Chapman pointed this out in 1869. After noting that "Persons who possess large sums of unemployed money find no difficulty, under ordinary circumstances, in ascertaining the best way of investing it," they posed the question of "What are the uninitiated to do, in the midst of such diversified and powerful attractions as these present, some drawing in one direction, and some in another, but all promising safe and profitable returns? …They must do something with their money, for it is profitless as long as it is hoarded, and brings but little profit if invested in consols or other Government Stock." Some investors could "obtain reliable information" but many could not.[31] One response was found in the growth of fund managers, with one of the first being the Foreign and Colonial Government Trust, founded in London in 1868. Investment trusts were designed to replicate what wealthy investors were already able to do, which was to assemble a diversified portfolio and thus reduce the risks of investing. This is what Robert Fleming had done in Dundee in the 1870s before relocating to London in the 1890s. Another was Alexander Henderson (Lord Faringdon) who had trained as an accountant with Deloitte in the 1860s before becoming a stockbroker in the 1870s. After a career advising family, friends and clients, he set up an investment trust in 1909. When the Scottish American Investment Company was formed in 1873, specialising in US railroad bonds, it immediately attracted 461 investors. It was then followed in 1874 by the Scottish American Mortgage Company which bought up US mortgage loans, and it was equally successful. Many mortgage companies established in the USA and the British colonies already accepted deposits from British investors, acting through a network of agents such as lawyers and stockbrokers. It was but a small step to establish companies in Britain that would provide an institutional channel for these funds. As new investment opportunities appeared, investment companies were quick to be formed in order to take advantage of them, whether it involved investing in emerging economies or new technology.[32]

---

[31] Bartlett and Chapman, *A Handy-Book for Investors*, pp. 1, 169, 187, 339–341.

[32] Scrathley, *On Average Investment Trusts*, p. 8; 'Scottish Capital Abroad', *Blackwood's Edinburgh Magazine*, 136, 471 (1884); C.H. Marshall, 'Dundee as a Centre of Investment', in *British Association, Handbook of the Dundee Meeting*, p. 351 (1912); R.B. Weir, *A History of the Scottish American Investment Company Limited, 1873–1973* (Edinburgh: 1873) pp. 3–8; Jackson, *The Enterprising Scot*, pp. 7, 17–19, 36–39, 45, 268, 276; J.C. Gilbert, *A History of Investment Trusts in Dundee, 1873–1938* (London: 1939) pp. 5–8,

What these investment trusts were doing was also being carried out by insurance companies, as they expanded their investment horizons from the 1870s onwards.[33]

Despite the rise of the institutional investor before the First World War, the field remained dominated by individuals taking their own decisions, with or without professional advice. In its mission to educate investors, the *Financial Review of Reviews* made a study of these investors in the years before the First World War. It was concerned that investors were being led astray by "individual whim and personal fancy" or, as Durran explained in 1913, were acting under the influence of information picked up from "the newspaper, at the dinner table, and in the clubs." What the *Financial Review of Reviews* recommended for individual investors of more limited means was "the careful selection of securities and practising diversification," because "It is not possible for an individual investor to personally analyse the thousands of investments which are dealt in on the Stock Exchange." After asking readers to submit their portfolios for inspection, which over a thousand did, they discovered that the use of a diversified portfolio was already common practice. From a study of this sample of a thousand, it emerged that investors prioritised safety over return and achieved that by holding 15 different stocks in a portfolio with an average value of £8,700. The advantage of this approach was that it recognised that "In investments, as in everything else, the unknown must always contain the possibilities of disaster, and the science of investment consists, so far as is possible, of eliminating all risks." However, these risks had to be taken because, as Martin pointed out in 1908, the "Three

---

40–41, 56–59, 80–85; D. Wainwright, *Henderson: A History of the Life of Alexander Henderson, First Lord Faringdon, and of Henderson Administration* (London: 1985) pp. 14, 15, 18, 23, 59, 65, 72, 92, 95; W.N. Smith, *Robert Fleming, 1845–1933* (Haddington: Whittinghome House, 2000) pp. 67, 116, 139, 144; J.H. Busby, *The London Trust Company Ltd., 1889–1964* (London: 1964) p. 7; Bell, Begg and Cowan, Stockbrokers, Edinburgh, *Monthly Circular*, January 1883, July 1885, May 1893, October 1895, December 1895, January 1896; 'Prospects of Canadian Land Mortgage Companies', *Accountants' Magazine*, 111, 495–498 (1899).

[33] Letter to Bell, Cowan, stockbrokers, Edinburgh, from Alexander Turnbull, manager, Scottish Widows Fund Life Assurance Society, Edinburgh 25th September 1895, 19th October 1895, 9th March 1896, 12th March 1896, 31st March 1896, 13th April 1896, 15th June 1896, 18th January 1897; Johnston and Murphy, 'The Growth of Life Assurance in UK', p. 155.

per Cents, or the most conservative of Home Railway stocks ... have dwindled in capital value, while, in several cases, the low rate of interest paid has become yet lower."[34] By 1913, Rossi concluded that "Since 1897 great progress has been made in the science of investing, the British investor having tasted the fruits of progress is not likely to return to the prejudices and narrow-mindedness of former days.... Nowadays investors do not ask where a stock is situated, they merely ask whether the stock is safe, sound and non-speculative."[35]

It took until 1905 for the *Financial Review of Reviews* to refine its scientific approach to investment. Once it had done so, it bombarded readers with advice about how to achieve the best returns. Their top recommendations included the bonds issued by British industrial and commercial companies and the securities belonging to British railway companies operating abroad, especially in Argentina, because they offered a higher yield for lower risk. In contrast, they warned investors against participating in speculative outbursts, such as that of 1910, which they labelled "The Rubber Madness in the City." In Lawson's judgement, the "Fabulous dividends like those which rubber shareholders have been drawing lately cannot in the nature of things last. They betoken abnormal and exceptional profits which are sure to be levelled down by keen competition." Reid went further suggesting that investors had been persuaded "into buying shares in companies that can be made to pay only by reason of a development bordering on the miraculous."[36] They also warned

---

[34] *The Financial Review of Reviews:* October 1904, December 1904, February 1905, May 1905, June 1905, July 1905, August 1905, November 1905, December 1905, January 1906; 'British and Foreign Railway Dividends Compared', January 1906, p. 36; A.J. Wilson, 'Can Home Railway Common Stocks Solidly Rally?', June 1906, p. 457, H. Lowenfeld, 'Trustee Investments: A Plea for Wider Powers', October 1906, p. 260; 'Is Ancestor-Worship Conducive to Sound Investment?', October 1906, pp. 265–266; 'The Investments of British Capital Abroad', November 1906, pp. 353, 359; H. Lowenfeld, 'The Money Market Article and the Private Investor', February 1907, p. 25; G. Withers, 'Collective and Individual Stability', January 1907, p. 22; H. Lowenfeld, 'How to Select Investments', March 1907, p. 14; Lowenfeld, 'The Investor's Mind', pp. 16–17, P. Rossi, 'A Non-Political Explanation of the Fall in Consols', May 1913, pp. 144–146; W. Durran, 'How the Public Forms an Opinion on Stocks', September 1913, p. 675.

[35] P. Rossi, 'A Non-Political Explanation of the Fall in Consols', *The Financial Review of Reviews*, 144–145 (May 1913).

[36] W.R. Lawson, 'The Rubber Madness in the City: The Gamble in Shares', *The Financial Review of Reviews* (June 1910); T.H. Reid, 'The Rubber Madness in the City: The Risks

investors against investing in those companies manufacturing motor vehicles. "There is but little to be gained by entering the ranks of the pioneer investors in a new industry, whilst there is everything to be lost by so doing.... The finding of capital for motors and motor-bus concerns ought to be left to the trade and to those investors who are practical engineers and are following the entire movement with the closest attention." That article was written by Henry Lowenfeld who strongly advocated the merits of a diversified portfolio. "On the whole my long and very varied experience amongst investors has proved to me that a calm and judicial selection of investments is the only way in which investment success is to be achieved. All crazes or temporary excitements warp the judgement of investors — they are therefore pernicious in their general effect."[37] What Henry Lowenfeld preached above all was geographical distribution to counter the home bias exhibited by investors because they were "not able to estimate the risks attached to lending money in distant lands.... Every capitalist, being afraid of an unknown risk, endeavours to employ his money on a security which he personally knows." To Lowenfeld, geographical diversification was the perfect solution to what investors desired. "All investors have much the same investment aim for they all wish their capital to be quite safe and their income adequate; while they also desire that there should always be an opportunity to sell the investments held without trouble, and at a price higher than that which they originally paid for them." Though "such a state of perfection is practically unattainable," he argued passionately that geographical distribution came closest to achieving it.[38]

The problem with Lowenfeld's attempt to persuade investors to adopt a particular model was that the investing community was so diverse and becoming more so, in this process which J.A. Hobson labelled the democratisation of investment.[39] Mitchell, in 1879, referred to "family trustees, ladies of independent means, our landed gentry, and the highest class of our professional and mercantile men ... who look with suspicion on any

and Dangers of Rubber Cultivation', *The Financial Review of Reviews*, 17, 31 (June 1910).

[37] Lowenfeld, 'Investment Crazes', pp. 162, 166, 169.

[38] Lowenfeld, *All About Investment*, pp. 23–25, 30–56, 69–72, 99–101, 167, 185–186, 196, 236, 254, 258.

[39] J.A. Hobson, 'Do Foreign Investments Benefit the Working Classes?' *The Financial Review of Reviews*, 26 (March 1909).

abnormally high rate of dividend or interest."[40] Lawson, in 1884, split investors into the "Three-fourths ... who ... are bona fide holders" and "The other fourth, who merely gamble."[41] Montagu Williams, in 1892, reported that "Among the women of the beau monde, Stock Exchange gambling is rapidly becoming as dire a disease as baccarat and horse-racing."[42] Conversely, in 1893, Van Oss was of the view that "Investors as a rule are of a cautious temperament, though they do not always act cautiously." What he acknowledged was that "In the human breast the hope of gain proves stronger than the fear of loss," and that "it is the pluck to take risks for the sake of gain which has made this country great and prosperous..., and there is no reason why people should altogether avoid speculative investments; provided they exercise due caution."[43] Powell, in 1910, reached a similar conclusion. "The investor cannot be prevented from taking risks. In a very real sense the progress of the world depends, as human society is at present organised, upon his willingness to take them."[44] Talbot, in 1911, considered that, "In the matter of railway pioneering the British financier is probably the greatest plunger."[45] In the judgement of Hartley Withers in 1914, "The real investor looks most of all to security of income and least to the hope of capital appreciation, while the pure speculator sets no store by income, and looks entirely to the chance of being able to make a big profit by a resale." He added that "It is the safest rule for investors who hold ordinary securities to look upon them as a concession to the gambling spirit, which is strong in nearly all of us, and to regard them as the speculative sauce which seasons the investment salad."[46]

The problem was that it was this "gambling spirit" that was picked on by the growing newspaper press of the nineteenth century and read by an increasingly literate population from the 1820s onwards. Additional coverage then came from reporting the subsequent court cases when investors attempted to recover their losses or crooked financiers were

[40] Mitchell, *Our Scotch Banks*, p. 139.

[41] Lawson, *The Scottish Investors' Manual*, p. 35.

[42] M.S. Williams, *Round London, Down East and Up West* (London: 1892) pp. 221, 224, 258–259.

[43] Van Oss, *American Railroads and British Investors*, pp. 34, 67, 94, 148, 152.

[44] Powell, *The Mechanism of the City*, pp. 95–97, 116, 140–142, 165.

[45] F.A. Talbot, *The Railway Conquest of the World* (London: 1911) p. 104.

[46] Withers, *Stocks and Shares*, pp. 315–317, 327.

prosecuted. Building on the legacy of the South Sea Bubble of 1720, and reinforced by the Railway Mania of the 1840s, the result was to portray the investor as a naïve, foolish or reckless individual whose gambling ruined themselves and wasted the nation's savings. There was no appreciation that investor behaviour changed over time as lessons were learnt and conditions changed. In 1892, the *Investors' Review* reported that "The Public has been so systematically victimised by the abuse of the Limited Liability Acts in the creation of bubble companies that it is now impossible to get them to look at any but the choicest." By 1896, they were reporting on "The Fever of Speculation and its Risks," dating the change to the end of 1894.[47] The impression of being foolish, naïve gamblers was also confirmed in two official inquiries carried out in the 1870s, even though they reflected conditions at a particular moment in time.[48] Also helping to cement the image of investors as naïve fools were the comments made in growing number of self-help investment publications. These publicised the traps that investors had fallen into in the past, with the implication being that without the advice found in these publications, investors would suffer the same fate.[49] The effect of the way investors were reported was to create a lasting impression that they knew little about what they were doing, which was far from the truth in most cases.[50]

---

[47] *The Investors' Review*, Vol. 1 (London: 1892) pp. 2, 90, 264; 5 (1895), p. 41; 8 (1896), 'The Fever of Speculation and Its Risks'.

[48] Select Committee on Loans to Foreign States, Report (London: 1875) p. 66; London Stock Exchange Commission: *Report of the Commissioners and Minutes of Evidence* (London: HMSO, 1878) pp. 14, 284.

[49] G. Omnium, *A Handy Guide to Safe Investments* (London: 1858) p. 88; *The Stock Exchange Observer* (London: 9th February 1875); E.C. Maddison, *On the Stock Exchange* (London: 1877) p. 241; *The Financial Register and Stock Exchange Manual* (London) p. vii (1877), p. v (1878), p. vi (1879); Nash, *Money Market Events*, pp. 12–16; Nash, *A Short Inquiry*, pp. 30, 115, 124–127; *The Scottish Financier* (Glasgow: October 1883) p. 3; *Stock and Share Review* (London: February 1884); H. Phillips, *Phillips' Investors Manual* (London: 1887) pp. 31, 35, 127, 199; A Banker's Daughter, *A Guide to the Unprotected in Every-day Matters Relating to Property and Income* (London: 1891) pp. 1–4, 8; Walker and Watson, *Investor's and Shareholder's Guide*, pp. 23, 53, 109–110, 198, 230–242, 262, 267; A. Baines, *The Popular Handbook of Finance* (London: 1894) p. 147.

[50] M. Lobban, 'Nineteenth Century Frauds in Company Formation: *Derry v. Peek* in Context', *Law Quarterly Review*, 2, 5, 7, 13, 15, 17, 19, 20–21 (1996); M. Lobban, '*Erlanger v. The New Sombrero Phosphate Company* (1878)', in C. Mitchell and

   This impression was then confirmed time and again because of the high mortality among newly promoted companies before the First World War. The available statistics showed that only one in five new companies survived 10 years. Scott, in 1906, considered that "It can only be sheer foolhardiness on the part of the investor which impels him to dabble in newly-born ventures where the average rate of infantile mortality reaches the truly appalling figure of 82 per cent during the first 10 years of infancy." His advice was that that "the investor will find that old-established securities are always capable of supplying every reasonable investment requirement, and … in no case should he allow himself to be tempted by prospectus allurements…. The dangers attending all new companies lie in the fact that it is usually impossible to foresee what adverse circumstances and conditions may unexpectedly appear to blast a promising company's prospects." That did not mean that such companies lacked the support of investors but only that it was best left to those who were familiar with the industry and the people involved.[51] Without doubt, the investment that appealed most to the gambling spirit among investors was the shares of mining companies, especially those operating abroad. Mining was at the forefront of speculative booms from the 1820s to the First World War and helped to perpetuate the image of the foolish and naïve investor who gambled away a fortune.[52] In 1850, an investment in a mine was described as "An adventure beset with so much risk and peril that no man of ordinary prudence would venture much on them."[53] The Edinburgh stockbroker, Robert Allan, warned his clients in 1853 not to consider mining investments because "for one that yields a fair return, 10 will probably go to the wall."[54] In 1901, Napier considered mining

---

P. Mitchell (eds), *Landmark Cases in the Law of Restitution* (London: Hart Publishing, 2006) p. 129; *Aberdeen Free Press*, 14th December 1886.

[51] *The Financial Review of Reviews*: G. Withers, 'Patent Rights and Latent Dangers', April 1906, pp. 290, 294; 'Present Investment Opportunities', June 1906, pp. 433, 469, 471; L.G. Scott, 'The Rich Man Can Speculate: The Poor Man Dare Not', June 1906, pp. 483–486; C. McLaren, 'Prospects for Iron and Steel Investments', October 1906, pp. 248–249; H. Lowenfeld, 'Shares as Investments', February 1911, pp. 5, 17; M.M. Mason, 'Dangers of Colliery Shares', November 1913, p. 903; T. Good, 'Some Shareholding Hazards', October 1913, pp. 791–792.

[52] R. Burt, 'The London Mining Exchange, 1850–1900', *Business History*, xiv, 124 (1972).

[53] *The Curious and Remarkable History of the Royal British Bank* (London: 1850) p. 62.

[54] Circular of Robert Allan, stockbroker (Edinburgh: March 1853).

companies, as "pure gambles."[55] In the same year, the *Money-Maker Manual* was of the opinion that "Of all concerns brought before the notice of the public the mining company is the most risky." Nevertheless, investors continued to buy the shares in mining companies because of the promise of fabulous returns.[56] As Robinson explained in 1907, "It is the uncertainty in mining, the gambling chance, which serves to enlist so much of the world's capital in mining enterprises."[57]

For those reasons, mines continued to attract investors, whether it was those exploring for gold, silver and copper around the world or tin, lead and coal in the UK. The reason was self-evident as Pike pointed out in 1864, "When a mine pays, it pays well."[58] They might be the rare exception, but they did exist. An estimated, 90 per cent of the hundreds of US mining companies backed by British investors, from the 1870s to 1900, paid no dividends, and that was typical of the situation around the world. However, that meant that 10 per cent did pay dividends and these could be enormous. Buying shares in a mining company was akin to purchasing a lottery ticket.[59] With the world being opened up by exploration and

---

[55] Napier, 'The History of Joint-Stock and Limited Liability Companies', p. 413.

[56] *The Money-Maker Manuals for Investors, No. 1: How to Commence Investing* (London: 1901) pp. 30–31, 39; *No. 2: A New Dictionary of Mining Terms*, p. 14. See Earl of Cardigan, 'Can Money be Profitably Invested in Land?', *Financial Review of Reviews*, 83 (August 1906).

[57] Robinson, *The Mining Market*, pp. v, 12–13, 95–97, 107.

[58] J.R. Pike, *Britain's Metal Mines: A Complete Guide to the Laws, Usages, Localities and Statistics* (London: 1864) p. 9. See R.L. Nash, *The Australasian Joint-Stock Companies Year Book* (Sydney: 1900) p. xxix; H.P. Davis, *The Davis Handbook of the Cobalt Silver District* (Toronto: Canadian Mining Journal, 1910) pp. 32–34; Assistant Secretary, Standard Stock and Mining Exchange to Edwin Brady and Company, Boston, 17th November 1913.

[59] C.C. Spence, *British Investments and the American Mining Frontier, 1860–1901* (Ithaca: 1958) pp. 9, 13, 34, 68, 77–79, 82, 91, 113–115, 216–219, 220–223, 227, 261–266; A.W. Currie, 'British Attitudes toward Investment in North American Railroads', *Business History Review*, xxxiv, 194 (1960); J.F. Rippy, *British Investments in Latin America, 1822–1949* (Minneapolis: 1959) pp. 17–18, 25, 32, 46, 57, 68–69; 'Scottish Capital Abroad', *Blackwood's Edinburgh Magazine*, 136, 478–479 (1884); Harveyhill Copper Company BT2/478; Flemington Coal Company BT2/495; Seville Sulphur and Copper Company BT 2/507; Nantile Vale Slate Quarry Company BT2/540; Canadian Copper and Sulphur Company BT2/648; Clyde Coal Company BT2/690; Niddrie and Benhar Coal Company BT2/1146; Achill Plumbago and Talc Company BT 2/1180.

railways, the possibilities of a successful mining operation were bound-less. Africa attracted increasing attention from British investors from the 1880s onwards. Randolph Churchill was one of the many who got involved and lost money as a result. He wrote in 1892 that "No more unwise or unsafe speculation exists than the investment of money in exploratory syndicates."[60] Like many, he was drawn in by the prospects of an unknown land and seduced by the transformation of the mining indus-try through improvements in geological science, the development of drill-ing machinery, the use of chemicals and the construction of railways. Reunert claimed in 1893 that "The proved mineral wealth of South Africa is already one of the wonders of the world, but what is not so generally realised is the vast extent of the still unexplored and undeveloped regions of the vast country."[61] After the discovery of huge gold deposits in the Witwatersrand in the 1890s, there was a widespread belief that all of Africa was mineral rich.[62] For the lucky few, a share in a South African gold mine was the gateway to a fortune in the thirty years before the First World War. By 1914, South Africa was responsible for 38 per cent of world gold production.[63] Nevertheless, despite the huge publicity attached

---

[60]R.S. Churchill, *Men, Mines and Animals in South Africa* (London: 1892) pp. 236, 281, 329.

[61]T. Reunert, *Diamonds and Gold in South Africa* (London: 1893) pp. 117, 120.

[62]C.S. Goldman, *South African Mines: Their Position, Results, and Development, Together with an Account of Diamond, Land, Finance, and Kindred Concerns*, 3 vols. (London: 1895–6) pp. vi, xiv–xv; Reunert, *Diamonds and Gold in South Africa*, pp. viii, 38–48, 117, 120; F.H. Hatch and J.A. Chalmers, *The Gold Mines of the Rand: A Description of the Mining Industry of Witwatersrand, South African Republic* (London: 1895) pp. 2–3, 291.

[63]S.H. Frankel, *Investment and the Return to Equity Capital in the South African Mining Industry, 1887–1965* (Oxford: Blackwell, 1967) Tables 6, 9, pp. 28, 124; C. Newbury, *The Diamond Ring: Business, Politics and Precious Stones in South Africa, 1867–1947* (Oxford: Oxford University Press, 1989) pp. 54, 80, 114, 127, 142; R.V. Kubicek, *Economic Imperialism in Theory and Practice* (Durham, NC: Duke University Press, 1979) pp. 50–54, Table 3.1; G. Blainey, 'Lost Causes of the Jameson Raid', *Economic History Review*, 18, 353 (1965); R.V. Kubicek, 'The Randlords of 1895: A Reassessment', *Journal of British Studies*, 11, 101–102 (1972); P. Richardson and J.J. van Helten, 'The Development of the South African Gold-Mining Industry, 1885–1918', *Economic History Review*, 37, 334 (1984); J.J. van Helten, 'Empire and High Finance: South Africa and the International Gold Standard, 1890–1914', *Journal of African History*, 23, 529–548 (1982); I. Phimister, 'Corners and Company-Mongering: Nigerian Tin and the City of London, 1909–1912', *Journal of Imperial and Commonwealth History*, 28 (2000); S. Chapman,

to the speculative booms in overseas mining companies, collectively they were a very small part of the total foreign investment.[64] George Paish estimated in 1914 that only £0.3 billion or 7.5 per cent of the £4 billion total had been invested in mining.[65] This tallied with the assessment of the *Financial Review of Reviews* in 1905 which arrived at a figure of five per cent for mining investments in the portfolios which had been submitted to it.[66]

Ranking alongside mines as among the riskiest of investments were those of British manufacturing companies developing a new technology. George Withers considered in 1906 that "The remarkable discovery of today is relegated to the scrapheap tomorrow.... Not one patent in a hundred proves to be of any commercial value, and ... of the few patents which are commercially successful scarcely ever does one of them achieve any solid financial results for the investor."[67] In 1914, Henry Withers considered that "It is almost impossible to regard as genuine investments these securities of any company formed to develop a new industry, to work a new patent, or to undertake any new enterprise that has not been actually tested under business conditions. However attractive the estimates and probable the success may seem there must always be an element — or several elements — of uncertainty and a trail of speculation across it."[68] *The Money-Maker Manual* for 1901 had grouped mines and industrials as "the lodestars that usually attract the small investor; the bait

'Rhodes and The City of London: Another View of Imperialism', *Historical Journal*, 28, 647–666 (1985); R.V. Turrell and J.J. van Helten, 'The Rothschilds, The Exploration Company and Mining Finance', *Business History*, 28, 181–205 (1986).

[64] A.L. Mikkelsen, *The Market Practice and Techniques of London Issuing Houses in Connection with Sovereign Bond Issues and Their Role in Facilitating Access to Sovereign Borrowers to the London Capital Market, 1870–1914*, Kings College, London Ph.D., p. 150 (2014); G.W. Paish, *Long-Term and Short-Term Interest Rates in the United Kingdom*, pp. 53, 56; Rippy, *British Investments in Latin America*, pp. 17–18, 25, 32, 46, 57, 68–69; Hopkins, *The Universal Railway Manual*, pp. 37–40.

[65] G. Paish, 'Great Britain's Capital Investments in Other Lands', *Journal of the Royal Statistical Society*, lxxii, 472 (1909); Paish, 'The Export of Capital and the Cost of Living', pp. 5, 8. See Stone, *The Global Export of Capital from Great Britain, 1865–1914*, p. 6.

[66] *The Financial Review of Reviews*, January 1905, June 1905, July 1905, November 1905.

[67] G. Withers, 'Patent Rights and Latent Dangers', *The Financial Review of Reviews*, 290, 294 (April 1906); 'Present Investment Opportunities', *The Financial Review of Reviews*, 433, 469, 471–472 (June 1906).

[68] Withers, *Stocks and Shares*, p. 101.

being either the small nominal value, or otherwise a big dividend."[69] The assessment of the *Financial Review of Reviews* in 1904 was that "Taking industrial Investments as a whole, the British public have lost more money in them than they have ever made out of them."[70] Hopkins in 1911 felt that industrials were best left to the investor who was "an expert in each particular trade."[71] In 1909, Fithian had expressed the same view because they required "to be kept under close observation."[72] The universal view was investors should leave investment in the shares of companies developing a new technology to those with the required knowledge, experience and connections.[73] According to the *Financial Review of Reviews* in 1904, that is what normally happened as the shares "are all allotted to the friends and the business connections of the vendors, to the complete exclusion of the general public."[74] The result, according to the London financier, Leopold Joseph, in 1911, was that "Industrial stocks here in England have more or less a local character, and are locally held."[75] Nevertheless, investors who wanted to gamble on the success of a new technology continued to purchase the shares of newly promoted manufacturing companies, enticed by the prospects of large profits if the venture was successful. In 1904, the *Financial Review of Reviews* had reported that "some of the most successful investors … confine themselves exclusively to this class of security. Many large fortunes have been made out of industrial investments, and innumerable instances could be cited in which capital invested in trading companies has been doubled and trebled in the

---

[69] *The Money-Maker Manuals for Investors: No. 4 Scientific Speculation* (London: 1901), p. 57.

[70] *The Financial Review of Reviews*, October 1904.

[71] L.E. Hopkins (ed.), *The Universal Railway Manual*, p. 1.

[72] A.R. Foster, 'Cotton Spinning Companies as Investments', *The Financial Review of Reviews*, 39–40 (February 1907); E.W. Fithian, 'The Beneficial Effect of International Investment on British Trade', *The Financial Review of Reviews*, 22–23 (February 1909).

[73] H.A. Shannon, 'The Limited Companies of 1866–1883', *Economic History Review*, 4, 382, 387 (1933); MacGregor, 'Joint-Stock Companies and the Risk Factor', p. 4; Lavington, *The English Capital Market*, pp. 202–203, 219–221.

[74] *The Financial Review of Reviews*, November 1904.

[75] L. Joseph, 'Industrial Finance: A Comparison between Home and Foreign Developments', a paper delivered to the National Electric Manufacturers' Association, Institution of Electrical Engineers, London, 25th April 1911, p. 8. See the example of the Monotype Machine Company. Monotype Machine Company BT 2/1147: Peter Fleming, company secretary, to the registrar of companies. 8th December 1886.

short space of two or three years."[76] There were plenty of previous examples where the early backers of a new technology had emerged with huge profits. These included local tramways and a number of London underground lines.[77] It was not a lack of enthusiasm among investors that prevented the success of the electric lighting companies but the restrictive legislation of 1882, which was not amended until 1889.[78] One new technology heavily backed by investors before the First World War was the manufacture of motor vehicles, with speculative booms in 1905–1907 and again in 1911–1914. These followed on from a mania for companies producing bicycles and rubber tyres in the mid-1890s, sparked by the success enjoyed by the early investors in these industries. What made the motor car industry such a hazardous investment was the uncertainty over which mode of propulsion would prove to be the most successful, with steam, battery and petrol all having their early backers.[79]

Investors appeared eager to support whatever looked likely to produce profits in the years before the First World War, whether it was companies producing motor cars in Britain or rubber in Malaya. In response to public enthusiasm for ice skating, by 1910, 200 companies had been formed to provide the rinks required.[80] Whereas the majority of investors avoided risk, favouring the known and the certain, even they could be persuaded to divert a small portion of their savings to the unknown and the uncertain if a spectacular profit beckoned, while there also existed a small minority ready to gamble on whatever took their fancy.[81] As Aubrey noted in 1896,

---

[76] *The Financial Review of Reviews*, October 1904.

[77] T.C. Barker and M. Robbins, *A History of London Transport*, Vol. 1 (London: 1963) p. 268, Vol. 2 (London: 1974) pp. 35, 38, 67, 117–118.

[78] R.H. Benson, 'Episodes of Business and Finance', in *Lady Wantage, Lord Wantage: A Memoir* (London: 1907) pp. 304–305.

[79] A.E. Harrison, *Growth, Entrepreneurship and Capital Formation in the United Kingdom's Cycle and Related Industries, 1870–1914*, University of York Ph.D., pp. 57, 60, 68–69, 354, 358–359, 364–368, 373, 382, 441–442, 439, 459, 467 (1977); A. Du Cross, *Wheels of Fortune: A Salute to Pioneers* (London: 1938) pp. 81–82, 177, 209; J. Lloyd, *Rolls-Royce: The Growth of a Firm* (London: 1978) pp. 15–20, 39.

[80] Powell, *The Mechanism of the City*, pp. 95–97, 116, 140–142, 165.

[81] Ward, *A Treatise on Investments*, pp. 1–4, 35, 93, 101; Maddison, *On the Stock Exchange*, pp. 147, 241; J.C. Lorimer, 'Accountants in Their Relation to Public Companies', *Accountants' Magazine*, 3, 255 (1899); Jefferys, *Trends in Business Organisation in Great Britain Since 1856*, pp. 200–201, 209–210, 215, 228, 233–234, 237–239, 241, 248, 250, 273–275, 279, 281–283, 435; J.B. Jefferys, 'The Denomination and Character of Shares,

"There is always a large speculative fund ready to be embarked in anything likely to yield high profits."[82] An insight into the activities of these risk-taking investors in the Edwardian era can be obtained from the collective biographies put together by H.H. Bassett.[83] What emerges is that their investments were often closely related to their business, occupation or location, indicating that they were operating from a strong foundation of knowledge and experience. Many of these investors also took a cosmopolitan attitude to their investments, benefitting from their international exposure and the insight that provided into particular activities and countries. Some investors took a highly focused approach, concentrating on a specific business or country, while others adopted portfolio diversification, spreading themselves widely across different enterprises and countries. What was evident in each case was the depth of knowledge and experience, and a web of connections, that lay behind every decision made, which was far removed from the popular image of the investor as a naïve and foolish gambler. A few examples suffice to prove this assessment. H.C. Allen trained as an accountant and then joined the Buenos

---

1855–1885', *Economic History Review*, xvi, 50–52 (1946); P.L. Cottrell, *Investment Banking in England, 1856–1882: Case Study of the International Financial Society*, University of Hull Ph.D., pp. 93, 108, 200, 354, 374, 596, 837, 868 (1974); 'Investor's Guide', *Financial Times* (London: 1913), pp. 79, 99.

[82] W.H.S. Aubrey, *Stock Exchange Investments: The Theory, Methods, Practice and Results* (London: 1896) p. 7.

[83] H.H. Bassett (ed.), *Men of Note in Finance and Commerce* (London: 1900/1901): entries for John Brinton, Wilberforce Bryant, Major Peter Chalmers. Cory Brothers, Alexander Fleming, Sir Charles Tennant; Bassett, *Business Men at Home and Abroad*: Entries for H.C. Allen, W.E. Allen, A.E. Anthony, J. Arrowsmith, R. Ashworth, H. Austin, George Balfour, J.R. Bartlett, Sir J.S. Barwick, H.A. Beeching, W.H. Blackie, R.W. Booth, A.B. Bosher, J.S. Bradley, W. Braithwaite, H. Brechin, A. Brodie, J.J. Clark, C. Collard, J.H. Collins, G. Davidson, S.F. Edge, R.C. Fielding, Joseph Fraser, Walter de Frece, William Fry, H.J. Gardiner, W.G. Gordon, G.J.F. Grant [An Edinburgh solicitor with interests in Edinburgh property and overseas oil companies], Robert Grey, P. Griffith, R.T. Harper, F.L. Heyn, H. Hiscott, C.F. Hitchins, J. Hood, J. Inglis, J. Irvine, F.V. Japp, E. Jardine, R.H. Jones, J.Y. Kennedy, C.E. Keyser, D. Lewis, J. Lorrain, W.F. Maclaren, H.R. Mansfield, J.M. Matthews, J. McEwan, J. McFarland, William Mendel, H.H. Montgomery, J.F.E. Mullett, W.S. Pearce, G. Reeves-Smith, G. A Riddell, E. Ruffer, H.K. Rutherford, W. Scott, R.T. Smith, Nathaniel Spens, M. Stevens, J.F.W. Stuart, D.A. Sutherland, J. Torbock, E.H. Turnbull, Sir M.L. Waechter, G.L. Waldron, C.H. Walker, Sir G. White, J. Wickett, Sir John Wilson, St John Winne, C. Young.

Ayres Southern Railway. He became a large investor in that railway along with the Buenos Ayres Western Railway, the Central Uruguay Railway Company and the Great Western of Brazil Railway Company. Sir J. S. Barwick was "A coal owner, quarry owner, interested in shipbuilding, and is a large shareholder in Furness, Withy and Company." S.F. Edge was one of the pioneers of the British motor industry with investments in various cycle, motor and tyre companies. Joseph Fraser had developed tea, coffee and rubber plantations in Ceylon and was a shareholder in a number of these. Walter de Frece was a large shareholder in theatres and music halls and promoted the Variety Theatres Controlling Company. F.L. Heyn was a Belfast merchant and shipowner with investments in a range of local enterprises, British and Foreign railways, and industrial, commercial and shipping companies. H. Hiscott was a London merchant "interested in rubber and produce estates in the East being a large importer of general produce from all parts." C.F. Hitchins was an engineer and one of the pioneers of the British vacuum cleaner industry with investments in the British Vacuum Cleaner Company and the Southern Counties Vacuum Cleaner Company. J. Irvine was a Liverpool-based West Africa merchant who had shares in many West African gold mining companies. F.V. Japp was a London ship manager and broker who was a large shareholder in six steamers as well as the Anglo-Algerian Steamship Company and La Commerciale Steam Navigation Company. E. Jardine, a manufacturer of lace-making machinery in Nottingham, invested in railways and industrial companies. D. Lewis was a Welsh brewer with a diversified portfolio comprising shares in breweries, banks, tin works, coal mines, saw mills, insurance companies and dry docks. W.F. Maclaren, a Glasgow printer and publisher, had interests in numerous rubber plantations with an aggregate value of £3.5 million. H.R. Mansfield was a clay goods manufacturer in Coalville with investments in the National Brick Company, the Coal and Iron Development Syndicate and the Welsh Coal company. J.M. Matthews, a Gloucester furniture manufacturer, had interests in a local insurance company and a brick maker as well as the Cairo City Properties Company. J. McEwan, a London tea merchant, invested in rubber plantations. J. McFarland was a Londonderry engineer with investments in railways, shipping companies and mines. W.S. Pearce was a London businessman who specialised in investing in amusement companies. J.F.W. Stuart was a Manchester banker with large investments in various engineering and rubber companies. J. Torbock was a Middlesbrough iron ore merchant with investments in a local steel company and mining companies in North Africa and India. Sir G. White was a Bristol stockbroker who was a major investor in the Bristol Tramways and Carriage Company, Imperial Tramways and the British and Colonial Aeroplane Company. J. Wickett was a copper smelter and manufacturer in Redruth with investments in 10 tin mining companies operating in either Cornwall or Malaya. C. Young was a Glasgow retailer who invested in the Rangers Football Club and the Scottish Canadian Fruit and Land Company.

What emerges from a review of investors before the First World War was how numerous and diverse they were. The numbers were a product of what was happening to Britain from the 1820s as it was transformed into the world's first urban/industrial economy whose growing population was in receipt of among the highest incomes in the world, while the low level of taxation and lack of welfare provision encouraged the practice of thrift. The diversity reflected the complexity of human nature and the change they experienced over their lives as well as the challenges and opportunities each faced. Some prioritised safety while others gambled on the current novelty, but all faced the dilemma of what to do with their money as it was no longer possible to trust to previous investment favourites. The National Debt, mortgages and property no longer delivered the guaranteed returns and certainty of retaining its value that they had in the past, forcing a search for alternatives, which became more acute as the nineteenth century progressed. At the same time, the revolution in transport and trade, driven by railways and steam shipping, transformed investment horizons delivering a world of new opportunities to the investor. Access to these opportunities at home and abroad was made possible by the coming of joint-stock companies with limited liability, as this made it possible for investors to participate in activities once confined to privileged individuals and private networks. The democratisation of investment exposed investors not only to the lure of speculation and the depredations of criminals but also to participation in profitable businesses that had once been closed to them. Following on from railways and utilities, these included a widening range of industrial and commercial enterprises and extended into services with banking, insurance, retailing and shipping. Joint-stock companies also provided investors with an easy means of investing abroad whether it was the relatively safe stocks and bonds of foreign railways and utilities, moderately risky land and property mortgages, or the outright gambles on mineral discoveries or rubber plantations. Though much was made of the losses experienced on all these investments, investors in general received higher returns than if they had persisted with the old favourites, while a few became fabulously wealthy as a result of the risks they took. However, much of this remained hidden from view while the predictable path of speculative bubbles and the litany of company failures were all too visible. As a result, it was the latter that generated the image of the pre-1914 investor as a foolish and naïve gambler rather than being seen as clever, cautious and connected as so many were.

Investors Since 1914

The world occupied by investors before 1914 was shattered by the events that began with the First World War, continued through the economic, financial and monetary difficulties of the 1920s and 1930s, and were then deepened by the Second World War. It was not only the environment that was fundamentally altered but also the circumstances of the individual investor as high levels of taxation deprived them of much of the income that they had been at liberty to dispose of as they wished. The number of people in receipt of high incomes shrank dramatically once taxation was taken into account. Taxation also exerted a great influence on the way investment was carried out, and the investments that were made. Increasingly, investment was channelled through institutions and tax efficiency became as important as the actual nature of the assets purchased. No longer was investment the preserve of the individual because it became a function of the state, professional fund managers, the board of directors of a company or a bank while that which was personal was directed into the owner occupation of homes, losing its direct connection to calculations of risk and return. The contrast between the pre-1914 and post-1945 world was enormous, with the decades between the wars being ones of transition.

Nevertheless, the perception of the individual investors as naïve and foolish gamblers who had to be protected from themselves and fraudsters remained in terms of taxation and legislation. As investors could not be trusted to act responsibly, legislation was required to control what they could do whether it involved the direct intervention of the state or measures favouring particular types of investment and greater institutional control. The effect was to take the investment process out of the hands of the individual, where it had rested before 1914 and largely remained before 1939. At the same time, the high levels of taxation imposed reduced both the number of individual investors, from the high reached during the First World War, and the amount they had available to them. It was only with the lowering of taxation and the privatisation of state assets in the 1980s that the individual investor regained some importance, but only to a limited degree and one fundamentally different from that of the pre-1914 or even pre-1939 era. Despite speculative booms such as the privatisation issues of the 1980s and the Dot.Com bubble of the late 1990s, the activity of British investors remained subdued. There was to be no return to the speculative manias of the nineteenth and early twentieth centuries. The perception may have remained but the substance was lacking. In the place of the shares issued by joint-stock companies was the purchase of a house for occupation or rent and this attracted much less criticism.[84]

This transformation in the fortunes of the investor and their behaviour was not apparent after the end of the First World War, despite the enormous changes caused by the disposal of US$ securities and the defaults among sovereign borrowers such as Russia. Purchasing the debt issued by the UK government to finance the war had swelled the number of investors enormously and they were eager to purchase stocks and bonds in the heady optimism that followed the end of the conflict. The result was a speculative boom in 1919/1920 with investors sucked into backing companies that briefly flourished and then collapsed. These ranged from domestic industrials to the usual crop of overseas mines.[85] In 1924, one writer, Wynne-Bennett, was already warning that "Gambling in mining shares should not be entertained by anyone who is not prepared to face the loss of all the money embarked in such ventures."[86] There were always investors who were drawn to companies promising high returns and it appeared that the 1920s were no different from the years that had preceded the war. Kinross reflected that in the late 1920s "practically any rubbish could be sold."[87] This was not confined to domestic stocks but

---

[84] Rubinstein, *Wealth and Inequality in Britain*, pp. 73, 76–83, 87, 97, 128–129; Rubinstein, *Men of Property*, pp. 103–105, 218; Heinemann, *Popular Investment and Speculation in Britain*, pp. 5–11, 23–30, 42–53.

[85] Maughan, *Markets of London*, p. 9; Brooks, *Something in the City*, p. 99; Hannah, *The Rise of the Corporate Economy*, pp. 58–60; Heinemann, 'Investment, Speculation and Popular Stock Market Engagement', pp. 254–256.

[86] Wynne-Bennett, *Investment and Speculation*, pp. 322–324.

[87] Kinross, *50 Years in the City*, p. 73.

involved participation in the speculative boom in the USA, which ended with the Wall Street Crash of 1929. In 1931, in the aftermath of "The spectacular crash and panic, which ended the boom in America," Hirst claimed that "a few big London speculators were said to have lost millions through dabbling too long in American stocks and shares." He added that Britain's own speculative mania in the late 1920s had resulted in "The collapse of rubbishy stocks, which had attracted buyers during the boom, accounted for a depreciation of good securities, which necessarily suffered from enforced liquidation."[88] Despite that collapse, there continued to be investors willing to speculate in the 1930s. The 1937 investigation into share pushing reported a "lack of prudence and inexperience" among many investors, concluding that "It is not surprising that frauds in share dealings have become more common."[89] A 1938 publication of the New Fabian Research Bureau referred to a "flood of rotten companies which have made their appearance in recent years — gramophone, artificial silk and the rest, according to the fashion of the moment."[90] These comments were reminiscent of the pre-war era as were the continuing attractions of South African gold mines, supporting the continuing perception of investors as naïve and foolish gamblers.[91] Much less reported were the growing attractions of collective investments such as those managed by insurance companies and investment trusts. A new form of collective investment was added in the 1930s in the form of unit trusts. These allowed investors to hold equities in a diversified portfolio, and so reduce their risks while gaining exposure to capital gains.[92]

Important as the effect the First World War had been, it was with the Second World War that a major change in investors took place. Whereas the top 10 per cent of the population owned 86 per cent of the wealth in 1936, their share had fallen to 64 per cent in 1973. The consequences were quickly apparent to contemporaries like the investment banker, Lionel Fraser. Writing in 1949, he reflected that before the war, "With low taxation and good profits, a section of the population was always seeking opportunities for employing its money to greater advantage, and at times

---

[88] Hirst, *Wall Street and Lombard Street*, pp. 80–81.

[89] Board of Trade, *Share Pushing*, pp. 6, 17.

[90] A. Citizen, *The City Today*, pp. 29, 36.

[91] H.A. Meredith, *The Drama of Money-Making*, pp. 179, 188; H.E. Peters, *The Foreign Debt of the Argentine Republic*, pp. 1, 33.

[92] Henderson, *The New Issue Market*, pp. 55, 83–84, 154.

at considerable risk. Capital could be raised locally, and largely through the personal knowledge and standing of the firm concerned; there was no need for the employment of an intermediary organisation such as an issuing house." In contrast, "at the moment we are going through a phase when too little courage and enterprise are being shown, and too many are looking merely for security. It is to be hoped that phase will soon pass, for no nation can remain great unless it numbers amongst its citizens those who are prepared to be courageous, enterprising, and far sighted."[93] Writing in the same year, Cowen was much less optimistic. "The substantial investors of independent judgement still exist, but in diminishing numbers; as old fortunes are broken up through death they are certainly not being rebuilt by the younger generation."[94] His pessimism was justified. Between the wars, there had continued to exist a substantial cohort of wealthy investors who were willing to back new enterprises. After the Second World War, taxation made it much more difficult for them to make and then retain such fortunes, encouraging them to relocate abroad or place their assets in a professionally managed portfolio.[95] In 1978, a pre-tax income of £50,000 translated into a post-tax one of £15,124, for example, making it difficult for investors to accumulate funds which they could put at risk through the purchase of corporate stocks.[96]

There was some residual post-war activity as the number of investors owning corporate stocks did rise, driven by post-war prosperity and a desire for capital gains in the face of the steady depreciation in the value of fixed-interest stocks. However, they were individually much less wealthy than their predecessors while legislation designed to prevent fraud circumscribed their investment opportunities. There were an estimated 3 million investors by 1970, or more than double the number at the

---

[93] T.W.L. Fraser, 'Issuing Houses and the Raising of Long-term Capital in London', in *The Pattern and Finance of Foreign Trade, with Special Reference to the City of London* (London: Institute of Bankers, 1949) pp. 222–231.

[94] H.C. Cowen, 'The London Stock Exchange and Investment', in *Current Financial Problems and the City of London* (London: Institute of Bankers, 1949) p. 36.

[95] Rubinstein, *Wealth and Inequality in Britain*, pp. 73–83; Smith, *Robert Fleming*, pp. 67, 116, 139, 144; F. Carnevali, *Europe's Advantage: Banks and Small Firms in Britain, France, Germany, and Italy since 1918* (Oxford: 2005) pp. 100–101; W.D. Rubinstein, *Men of Property*, pp. 61, 222, 280.

[96] Rubinstein, *Wealth and Inequality in Britain*, pp. 87, 97, 128–129; R. Dallas Brett, *Usury in Britain* (London: 1945) p. 87.

end of the Second World War. As in the past, a number of these investors were attracted by the excitement that owing shares in certain companies could provide with takeover bids providing a sudden rise in prices.[97] However, there were no major speculative outbursts. Instead, what was taking place was the creeping collective ownership of shares and the employment of finance professionals to manage diversified portfolios. Clayton and Osborn observed in 1965 that since the war investors "have been willing to entrust an increasing proportion of their savings to a variety of financial intermediaries."[98] Taxation was a major influence as life assurance companies and pension funds could reduce the amount that had to be paid. By 1957, institutions already owned 19 per cent of UK shares and that reached 35 per cent in 1972 and 55 per cent in 1983. The replacement of individuals by institutions changed the nature of the investments made. Even after they switched to corporate stocks rather than bonds, from the 1950s, because of the need to match inflation, institutions favoured those issued by large companies, as they were safer and more liquid. Institutions were not willing to take the risks that went with smaller companies, new technology and mines. Even with the rapid rise in the number of individual investors in the 1980s due to privatisation, individual holdings were largely confined to the stocks of established companies that had previously been national monopolies supplying gas, electricity and telecommunications. This made that portion of investment that was conducted in public a rather dull affair. As a consequence the public perception of investment continued to be strongly influenced by past speculative booms, corporate failures or financial frauds, as they were much more spectacular.[99]

---

[97] Heinemann, *Popular Investment and Speculation in Britain*, pp. 53, 57–59, 63–68, 72, 95–97.

[98] Clayton and Osborn, *Insurance Company Investment*, p. 22.

[99] Heinemann, 'Investment, Speculation and Popular Stock Market Engagement', pp. 264–269; Macrae, *The London Capital Market*, pp. 102–103; Johnson and Murphy, 'The Growth of Life Assurance in the UK since 1880', p. 155; Paish, *Business Finance*, p. 96; Clarke, *The City in the World Economy*, p. 12; Clayton and Osborn, *Insurance Company Investment*, pp. 22, 27, 34–35, 49, 67, 68; Moyle, *The Pattern of Ordinary Share Ownership*, p. 7; Jenkins, *The Stock Exchange Story*, p. 178; Thomas, *The Finance of British Industry*, pp. 115–117, 145–147; Dennett, *The Charterhouse Group*, p. 146; Thomas, *The Big Bang*, p. 17; Fishman, *The Transformation of Threadneedle Street*, pp. 36–37; Clarke, *Citizens' Financial Future*, pp. 11–12, 179, 183; Gleeson, *People and*

Unlike the individual investor, that of the increasingly dominant institutional investor did not generate the same public interest. The rise of the institutional investor was largely a product of government intervention. At the beginning of the twentieth century, insurance companies and investment trusts were already significant investors but were far outweighed by individual investors, especially when it came to shares. These individual investors were particularly attracted to railway securities, especially bonds, because of their combination of yield and security. Holding them did not require the intermediation of financial institutions or even the advice of financial experts because of the reliability and regularity of their interest payments and dividends. It was for those reasons that the nationalisation of railways both in Britain and abroad was such a serious blow to individual investors because it forced them to choose either government debt, which had a lower yield, or the stocks and bonds of companies whose earnings were more variable and less dependable because of the nature of the business they were in. The attractions of all fixed-interest securities, whether issued by governments or companies, were further undermined by inflation as the value did not adjust in line with prices. In contrast, the value of corporate stocks reflected the ability of companies to pay dividends, and this rose in line with inflation as businesses could raise the prices they charged. With railways and utilities largely in government ownership after the Second World War, this left the stocks in a diverse collection of companies as the only option for investors. Institutions were best placed to undertake this type of investment as they could employ trained staff to monitor and manage the portfolios required to balance the risk and returns involved in holding the stocks of companies operating under competitive market conditions. Under the management of George Ross Goobey, Imperial Tobacco's pension fund switched from allocating 28 per cent of its funds to shares in 1953 to 96 per cent in 1961. He was then followed by all other institutional fund managers. By 1999, pension fund assets were 62 per cent in equities and those of insurance companies at 51 per cent. These institutions also enjoyed tax advantages over individuals. They could gain exemptions from taxes on both income and capital gains while individual investors often could not. The highest tax rate on dividends in the UK peaked at 98 per cent between

Their Money, pp. 1–2, 135; *The Stock Exchange Official Yearbook*, 1985/1986; Rubinstein, *Men of Property*, pp. 284–298; Blakey, *The Post-War History of the London Stock Market, 1945–1992*, pp. 155–116.

1974 and 1979, while capital gains tax had been set at 30 per cent in 1965. To capture these tax benefits, individuals placed their funds with institutional fund managers. The value of funds managed by unit trusts, for example, rose from £2 billion in 1962 to £222 billion in 2000. As a result, share ownership by individuals declined from 54 per cent in 1963 to 11 per cent by 2016, despite the boost delivered by privatisation.[100]

Conclusion

The two centuries between 1820 and 2020 witnessed a total transformation in the importance and status of the individual investor and then its complete reversal. In the first century, the individual investor rose in importance as businesses of all kinds adopted the joint-stock form and issued huge amounts of stocks and bonds. Beginning with the railways and then extending to other types of enterprise, these corporate securities met the needs of investors in terms of both amount and variety. The investor that wanted certainty opted for bonds issued by railways and utilities, as they were able to command a regular income stream and could pay a guaranteed rate of interest. This was ideal at a time when inflation was of little concern. In contrast, the investor that wanted to take a risk in return for a possible windfall gain opted for the shares of mining companies, especially those still at the exploratory phase, as success could deliver fabulous profits. In between those two extremes on the spectrum, investors could pick and choose to suit their individual requirements as well as mix and match to design a portfolio that met their needs, changing the composition as and when they wanted. It was this flexibility of stocks and bonds that was their great attraction and made them the most popular investment in the years before the First World War. However, to many observers, all they saw was the froth of fraud and the frenzy of speculation that accompanied the growth of joint-stock companies and the subsequent trading of stocks and bonds on the expanding number of stock exchanges that spread around the world. What went unrecognised was that corporate failures, corrupt practices and volatile prices were an inevitable accompaniment to a market-based financial system that had delivered railway systems and urban utilities, financed the exploration for minerals, oil and other natural resources, and paid for the development of new products and

---

[100]Rutterford and Hannah, 'The Rise of Institutional Investors', pp. 242–264.

services. The two elements existed in uneasy harmony up to the First World War and even into the 1920s and 1930s. That equilibrium then began to disintegrate in the 1930s when the working of the market-based financial system was blamed for the financial and monetary turmoil experienced between 1929 and 1932, and the world economic depression that followed. In contrast, government intervention appeared to offer a more attractive alternative during the 1930s and this was confirmed by the successful management of the allied economies during the Second World War. The vindication for such a view was then found in the decades of peace and progress that followed the Second World War, as that was a time when financial markets were suppressed and individual investors marginalised. It was only in the 1970s, with the return of instability, that doubts crept in about the ability of governments to manage the economy better than if it was left to the market. The result was a gradual return to market conditions both in Britain and internationally. Nevertheless, there was to be no recovery in the position of the individual investor to that occupied in the past. The second century had witnessed the eclipse of the individual investor and brought a return to a more distant past when governments and elites were in charge though they were more answerable to the population as a whole compared to the political rulers and business magnates of the past.

Chapter 4

Investment and Investors: Popularity and Perception

Contemporaries derived their views on the pattern of investment and the behaviour of investors based on what they believed to be true, according to their biases, prejudices and level of knowledge. Even among the best informed, the evidence they had available to them, mainly derived from the reporting of the sensational and the episodic, presented a distorted view of both investment and investors. That was the case, for example, when use was made of the detailed statistics listing the value and distribution of securities listed on the London Stock Exchange. That only covered one aspect of investment and the activities of a particular group of investors as so much was hidden from view, taking place on other exchanges or in the private sphere. Nevertheless, it was used as a proxy for all that took place in the absence of anything better. The overall effect was to make even the most knowledgeable and expert, among contemporary observers, unreliable witnesses, including politicians and economists, but they had the power to influence others through the speeches they made and the words they wrote. That which was committed to print achieved a permanence, being read and believed by later generations. Nevertheless, there was no universal truth among contemporaries. All views were contested by those with different beliefs and other sources of information, especially when driven by opposing political positions and ideologies. This can be seen from the debate over availability of finance for manufacturing industry, which developed in the late nineteenth century and was ongoing a century later. Regardless of the evidence produced on either side, it became an article of faith that finance was either adequate or inadequate. In turn, access to finance was linked to Britain's economic decline in the twentieth century, with argument and evidence drawn from contemporary views on the pattern of investment and the behaviour of investors. There existed a great reluctance to abandon previous views, even when presented with new and contradictory evidence, if they resonated with what later generations wanted to believe. The myths of the past became articles of faith for later generations, detached from the need to provide supporting evidence.[1]

Given the importance of contemporary views in influencing both current and future judgements, it becomes important to establish what was most widely believed, gaining a currency beyond the individuals that expressed them and becoming ingrained among the public. That is difficult as there was no attempt to measure public opinion on such matters as the pattern of investment and the behaviour of investors. However, these subjects feature in contemporary novels between the mid-nineteenth century and the nineteen 30s, before virtually disappearing after the beginning of the Second World War. From the excitement of speculative manias through the losing and gaining of fortunes through investment, the behaviour of investors presented novelists with dramatic possibilities that attracted the interest of readers. Those who wrote novels picked up on what people were thinking and saying about the pattern of investment and the behaviour of investors, both emotionally and factually. As with facts, the lens provided by fiction was not an unambiguous one, but novels do provide a series of snapshots that capture the public mood at a moment in time. Stereotypes of investors, their choices and behaviour, emerge, providing an insight into what people believed to be true.[2] Alex Preda, in an

---

[1]See Cairncross, *Home and Foreign Investment*, p. 95; Hall, 'A Note on the English Capital Market', p. 63; Cairncross, 'The English Capital Market Before 1914', pp. 143–146; Hall, 'The English Capital Market Before 1914: A Reply', pp. 340–343; Cairncross, *The British Economy Since 1945*, p. 24; Pollard, *The Development of the British Economy*, pp. 9, 85, 102; W.D. Rubinstein, 'The Victorian Middle Classes: Wealth, Occupation and Geography', *Economic History Review*, 30, 621 (1977); J. Eatwell, *Whatever Happened to Britain: The Economics of Decline* (London: 1982) p. 79, 159–160; P. Kennedy, *Strategy and Diplomacy* (London: 1983) pp. 94–96.

[2]See T.S. Wagner, *Financial Speculation in Victorian Fiction: Plotting Money and the Novel Genre, 1815–1901* (Columbus: Ohio State University Press, 2010).

article on "The Rise of the Popular Investor," has used novels to support his analysis, but relied on very few examples chosen to support the points being made.[3] What is presented here is a rigorous and comprehensive attempt to match the reality of the pattern of investment and the behaviour of investors with the public's perception, and draw conclusions based on what is discovered.

The Investor as Speculator

In the nineteenth century, it was the Railway Mania of the 1840s that first began to attract novelists to the subject of investment and investors. The South Sea Bubble of 1720 had embedded itself in the public mind, but it involved relatively few people. Throughout the rest of the eighteenth century and into the nineteenth, investors largely focused on the National Debt, especially 3 per cent consols, though there was a brief flurry with canal companies in the 1780s. With the establishment of the London Stock Exchange in 1801, trading in the National Debt became a much more organised and regulated affair. That was until the speculative mania of the mid 1820s when foreign government loans and overseas mining companies took centre stage and railway companies made their first appearance. The combination of speculative interest in British stocks and bonds and the mass participation of investors came to the fore with the Railway Mania, and it was this which captured the imagination of the public and, like the South Sea Bubble of more than 120 years previously, left an enduring legacy.[4]

In the early nineteenth century, there was little popular interest in investment or investors, judging from the limited references in contemporary fiction as in Surr's 1815 novel, *The Magic of Wealth*, and Walter

---

[3]A. Preda, 'The Rise of the Popular Investor: Financial Knowledge and Investing in England and France, 1840–1880', *The Sociological Quarterly*, 42, 213, 216 (2001).

[4]N. Russell, *The Novelist and Mammon: Literary Responses to the World of Commerce in the Nineteenth Century* (Oxford: 1986) pp. 24, 26, 29; P. Burke, B. Harrison and P. Slack (eds), *Civil Histories* (Oxford: 2000): Slack, p. 162; Hannah, p. 286; A. Pollard (ed.), *The Representation of Business in English Literature* (London: 2000): Speck, pp. 19–24. For general attitudes towards finance see S. Banner, *Anglo-American Securities Regulation: Cultural and Political Roots, 1690–1860* (Cambridge: 1998) and R.E. Wright, *One Nation under Debt: Hamilton, Jefferson, and the History of What We Owe* (New York: 2008).

Scott's 1818 novel, *Rob Roy*.[5] A poem published in 1819 did emphasise the losses experienced by speculators and this was a theme that Thomas Love Peacock expanded on in his poems written in the mid-1820s, after the bubble had burst.[6] The losses made by speculators also featured in Bulwer-Lytton's 1828 novel, *The Disowned*, and Peacock's 1831 novel, *Crotchet Castle*.[7] However, they were brief mentions indicating that the subject had yet to attract popular interest, and that was the situation for the rest of the 1830s. Charles Dickens made a passing reference to losses due to speculation in *The Life and Adventures of Nicholas Nickleby*, which appeared in 1838. "The run of luck went against Mr Nickleby. A mania prevailed, a bubble burst, four stockbrokers took villa residences at Florence, four hundred nobodies were ruined, and among them Mr Nickleby."[8] It was from the 1840s that the public's attention was increasingly drawn to the behaviour of investors and what they chose to invest in. One novelist who covered the subject was Thackeray. In his 1841 novel, *The History of Samuel Titmarsh and the Great Hoggarty Diamond*, those who bought shares in insurance companies lost their money.[9] In 1843, Mrs Gore, in *The Banker's Wife*, dwelt on the risks that investors were being forced to take if they wanted to improve their returns compared to that from the public funds.[10] The highly transitory nature of any profits to be made from speculating in stocks and shares was a theme that Reynolds dwelt on in a series of books, *The Mysteries of London*, which appeared during and after the Railway Mania, from 1844 to 1856.[11]

---

[5]T.S. Surr, *The Magic of Wealth: A Novel* (London: 1815) Vol. 1: pp. 101–105, 112; Sir W. Scott, *Rob Roy* (London: 1818) pp. 426–427.

[6]Anon., *The Financial House that Jack Built* (London: 1819); T.L. Peacock, *Paper Money Lyrics* (1825–1826).

[7]E. Bulwer-Lytton, *The Disowned* (London: 1828): see ch. viii, xli, lxxii, lxxxvii; T.L. Peacock, *Crotchet Castle* (London: 1831) pp. 127–128, 130–131, 145, 148, 164–165, 200, 248.

[8]C. Dickens, *The Life and Adventures of Nicholas Nickleby* (London: Chapman and Hall, 1838) p. 29.

[9]W.M. Thackeray, *The History of Samuel Titmarsh and the Great Hoggarty Diamond* (London: 1841) pp. 9, 32–33, 46, 50–51, 66, 74–75, 78–82, 91–94.

[10]Mrs Gore, *The Banker's Wife or Court and City* (London: Henry Colburn, 1843) pp. 57–59, 111, 142.

[11]G.M. Reynolds, *The Mysteries of London* (London: 1844–1856) (edited by T. Thomas, Keele University Press, 1996) pp. 26–29, 46, 66–67, 75, 132–133, 197, 234–237, 304–308, 323.

As early as 1845, Aytoun wrote a short story featuring the Railway Mania in Scotland.[12]

Reflecting its capture of the public imagination, the Railway Mania was made the subject of an entire 1850 novel, *The Ladder of Gold* by Robert Bell. The story begins with the aftermath of the 1825 speculative bubble which left some investors nursing large losses while others made substantial gains. It then moved on to the opportunities that railways presented to investors. "The whole country, from coast to coast, was to be traversed and dissected by iron roads." This then became a speculative frenzy. "Railways at that moment occupied more attention than any other topic, foreign or domestic, that was before the country, because everybody hoped to make money out of them." What followed was the inevitable bursting of the speculative bubble. "The crash was as instantaneous as the collapse of a balloon.... The mass of the speculators were ruined; and a few crafty hands had amassed enormous wealth." What emerges from Bell's novel was that the public were fascinated by the behaviour of investors being carried away by speculation and losing heavily as a result.[13] This subject was taken up by Robinson in her 1851 novel, *The Gold-Worshippers*. "The railway fever was at its height. Doctors deserted their patients, merchants their counters, lawyers their briefs, every man his proper business, to become railway speculators." Despite advice to "Leave railways alone," investors would not because they had heard stories that "The Duchess of B. made two hundred thousand pounds by a fortunate speculation." Mrs Sparkleton borrowed £9,000, on the mortgage of her estate in order to speculate in railway shares. "She sold out and bought in, transferred, speculated in entirely new lines — until at last, for the trifling sum of fourteen thousand pounds, paid in actual cash, she found herself in possession of scrip, debentures, and securities to the value, she was informed, of nearly ten times that amount!" When the price of railway shares collapsed, speculators could not repay their loans and were bankrupted as a result. Mrs Sparkleton fled to Paris to escape her creditors. It was those who had avoided speculation that prospered, such as the moneylender, Mrs Skinflintz, who foreclosed on Mrs Sparkleton

---

[12] W.E. Aytoun, *How We Got Up the Glenmutchkin Railway and How We Got Out of It* (1845) reprinted in W.L. Renwick (ed.), *W.E. Aytoun: Stories and Verse* (Edinburgh: 1964) pp. 1, 22, 28.

[13] R. Bell, *The Ladder of Gold: An English Story* (London: 1850) pp. 107, 129–131, 160–163, 171, 188, 195, 199, 201, 224–230, 256, 302–311, 315, 366–367, 437.

and took possession of her estate, Longacres.[14] Investors who lost, and a few who gained, also featured in other novels published in early 1850s, suggesting that the subject now associated investment with speculation.[15] Though novelists could point to successful investors, the overwhelming legacy of the recurring speculative manias was that investment in shares of all kinds was highly risky and best avoided.[16] In *Villette* by Charlotte Brontë, which was published in 1853, it was observed that "The handsome property of which she was left guardian for her son, and which had been chiefly invested in some joint-stock undertaking, had melted, it was said, to a fraction of its original amount."[17] Even worse was the fate of investors who had bought shares in companies without limited liability, such as those of banks. In *Cranford* by Elizabeth Gaskell, which appeared in 1853, Miss Matty had bought shares in the Town and County Bank because of their high yield, despite being advised against it. When it failed, not only were the shares worthless but there were further potential liabilities.[18] The collapse of a joint-stock bank, and the loss experienced by the shareholders, was also a central theme of Thackeray's novel, *The Newcomes*, which appeared in 1854.[19] Nevertheless, there was some understanding that risks had to be taken if investments were to be made. The 1857 story, *No Thoroughfare*, by Charles Dickens and Wilkie Collins, reveals the difficult choices facing an investor at that time. An investment of £20,000 was split between a direct stake in a business producing 12 per cent per annum, but with all the risks that entailed, and consols, which were safe but yielded only 3 per cent.[20] The attractions of corporate

---

[14]E. Robinson, *The Gold-Worshippers; or, The Days We Live in* (London: G. Routledge and Co., 1851) pp. 8–14, 51–54, 85–87, 95, 140, 194–189, 212–213, 225, 306.

[15]Kingsley, *Yeast*, pp. 113–114, 155–156, 158, 170–171, 180, 197, 211; C. Sinclair, *The Mysterious Marriage or Sir Edward Graham* (London: Clarke Beeton and Company, 1854) pp. 329–333; W.M. Thackeray, *The Diary of C. Jeames De La Pluche, Esq.* (London: 1854) in *The Works of William Makepeace Thackeray* (London: 1872) Vol. 8: pp. 311–312.

[16]Mulock (Mrs Craik), *John Halifax, Gentleman*, pp. 307–308, 311–312.

[17]C. Brontë, *Villette* (London: 1853) pp. 95, 109.

[18]E. Gaskell, *Cranford* (London: 1853) ch. 13 entitled 'Stopped Payment', pp. 119–127, 129.

[19]W.M. Thackeray, *The Newcomes: Memories of a Most Respectable Family* (London: 1854) Vol. 1: pp. 14–18, 41, 52, 55, 57, 106, 279, 314, Vol. 2: pp. 92, 124–125, 128–129, 165–166, 287–289, 295, 299, 301, 344–345, 358–363, 379, 399, 434.

[20]C. Dickens and W. Collins, *No Thoroughfare* (London: 1867) pp. 36, 65–69.

stocks and bonds were that they lay between a business investment and the National Debt in terms of risk and returns, and it was that which underpinned their appeal. In Mrs Gore's 1857 novel, *Men of Capital*, Mr Stanley had doubled the income produced from his inherited wealth, through a careful choice of investments, while Mr Mordaunt, a Lancashire cotton textile manufacturer, had also doubled his fortune through successful "railway speculation." What was to be avoided was speculation by those lacking Mr Mordaunt's knowledge and expertise. "Railway bubbles, and every other frantic speculation of the hour, affords sufficient evidence of the craving after capital superseding every better aspiration, whether for this world or the next."[21] For Anthony Trollope, in his 1857 novel *The Three Clerks*, inside information was the ingredient required for successful speculation, but even that could not guarantee success. Alaric Tudor, a London civil servant, and his friend, Undecimus Scott, the eleventh son of Lord Gabelunzie, were speculating in the shares of a Cornish tin mine, the Wheal Mary Jane. They had available to them information acquired by Alaric, as he had been commissioned to write an official report on the mine. They had bought shares in the mine for £205 and sold them for more than £500. As Undecimus Scott was an M.P., the Vice-President of an insurance company and the director of "one or two minor railways," he was also in a position to possess inside information on various investments as well as influence the decisions made by government. By constantly speculating in shares, Alaric and Undy believed they would emerge substantial winners. "If a man speculates but once and again, now and then, as it were, he must of course be a loser. He will be playing a game which he does not understand, and playing it against men who understand it. Men who so play always lose. But he who speculates daily puts himself exactly in the reversed position. He plays a game which experiences teaches him to play well, and he plays generally against men who have no such advantage. Of course he wins." The reverse turned out to be the case. Based on inside knowledge, they risked all their money in the shares in a company being promoted to build a bridge across the Thames. However, their expectation that the bridge would get government backing proved false and so it was never built, making their shares worthless.[22]

---

[21] Mrs Gore, *Men of Capital* (London: James Blackwood, 1857) pp. liii, 94, 100–113, 110–113.

[22] A. Trollope, *The Three Clerks: A Novel* (London: 1857) pp. 73, 81, 85–88, 98, 110–112, 156, 156, 165–166, 229, 247–248, 304–306, 311–312, 379, 399, 418–421, 472.

Judging from the references to investment and investors in contemporary novels, the subject was one of growing interest to the public by the 1850s, with the gains and losses from speculation being the principal message being conveyed. This was the legacy of the Railway Mania, combined with the passing of the Limited Liability Acts. Charles Lever was one of those writers who captured the excitement that drove speculators to take risks, as in his 1859 novel, *Davenport Dunn*. Lady Lackington was willing to associate with "horrid people" who were "very well versed in some speculation or other — mines, or railroads, or the like" because she had made money following their advice. Among her and her friends, speculation became the main topic of conversation. "In those gorgeous drawing-rooms...., all were eagerly bent upon lists of stocks and shares, and no words were heard save such as told of rise or fall." All suffered when the speculative mania finally subsided with "thousands brought to destitution and beggary ... the great fortunes of the rich and the hardly-saved pittance of the poor alike engulphed." However, there was little sympathy expressed for those who had speculated and lost.[23] A succession of novels published in the late 1850s emphasised that only the National Debt was a safe investment.[24] That continued to be the case into the 1860s. In the 1863 novel, *Hard Cash* by Charles Reade, the banker, Richard Hardie, resorted to defrauding his children, friends and customers to cover up the losses he had experienced from investing in railway shares. Conversely, he recovered his fortune through successful speculation in Turkish bonds.[25] What was beginning to emerge in the fiction of the early 1860s was that investments, such as consols, were no longer attractive and greater risks were required to produce better returns, though speculation was to be avoided.[26] In the 1864 book, *Commercial Tales and Sketches*, it

---

[23]C. Lever, *Davenport Dunn or The Man and the Day* (Leipzig: 1859) Vol. 1: pp. 22, 41–43, 55, 61, 243, Vol. 2: pp. 16–19, 101, 127–129, 152–155, 169, 174, 190–216, 238, Vol. 3: pp. 25, 29, 39–40, 84, 104–105, 118–120, 130–132, 150–154, 160–161, 329–330, 333–334, 352–361.

[24]C. Reade, *Love Me Little, Love Me Long* (London: Chatto and Windus, 1859) ch. xxiv; Mrs H. Wood, *The Channings: A Story* (London: Macmillan and Company, 1862) p. 148; M.E. Braddon, *Lady Audley's Secret* (London: 1862) p. 136.

[25]C. Reade, *Hard Cash; A Matter-of-fact Romance* (London: 1863) pp. 8–9, 93, 105, 126–132, 167, 213–228, 249–253, 358, 415–417, 549, 563, 569, 604–605, 610–613.

[26]M.E. Braddon, *John Marchmont's Legacy* (London: Downey and Company, 1863) p. 54; W.H. Ainsworth, *John Law: The Projector* (London: 1864) pp. 42, 280.

was observed that "The railroads, for instance, were a mere speculation when first begun; now they are so necessary a part of our social inter-course, that the only source of wonder is, how we did so long without them." It was recognised that investors had the difficult task of differenti-ating between those joint-stock company speculations that were sound and those that were not.[27] Providing a detailed account of the mood and motivation that lay behind the speculative bubble that broke out in the mid-1860s was Mrs Henry Wood in her 1864 novel, *Oswald Cray*. Lady Oswald "was persuaded by an evil counsellor to sell out a large sum from the funds and invest elsewhere, for the sake of higher interest.... She put it into some bubble scheme, and it burst." Similarly, her doctor, Mark Cray, invested in a Welsh lead mine, the Great Wheal Bang Mining Company, on the advice of a close friend, using £4,000 that his wife, Caroline, had inherited. He told her that "some of the mines yield fifty thousand pounds profit the first year of working.... Talk about an invest-ment for your money, Caroline, what investment would be equal to this?" The mine failed leaving Mark and Caroline ruined.[28]

What was apparent from the novels of the 1860s was that the public, while wary of speculation, were also attracted to the possibilities of care-ful investment. In Braddon's 1865 novel, *Only a Clod*, Oliver Tredethlyn, a small landowner and farmer in Cornwall, was a careful investor "dab-bling a good bit with funds and railway shares." The spinster, Dorothea Burnett, spread her money between houses and shares. "She watched her small investments with an intelligence, and nursed them with a tenderness which her stockbroker had admiringly declared to be a credit to the sex she adorned by her commercial acumen." She accumulated a portfolio of "first-preference bonds in flourishing railway companies." In contrast, the City merchant, Lionel Hillary, was a "reckless speculator," driven by a desire to leave his daughter, Maude, a large fortune. On the verge of bank-ruptcy, and contemplating suicide, Maude saved him by agreeing to marry a man she did not love in return for him investing £20,000 in her father's business.[29] The message conveyed was that careful investment generated

---

[27] Anonymous, *Commercial Tales and Sketches* (London: 1864) pp. 136–141, 160–161, 217.

[28] Mrs H. Wood, *Oswald Cray: A Novel* (London: 1864) pp. 150–151, 160–161, 250–252, 282–284, 294–295, 330–348, 416, 443–454.

[29] M.E. Braddon, *Only a Clod* (London: Downey and Co., 1865) pp. 14, 28–31, 70–71, 77–81, 89–90, 134–136, 187.

profits and happiness while speculation produced losses and misery. To Amelia Edwards, writing in 1865, there was nothing inherently wrong about investments in joint-stock companies, only with fraud and speculation. "Enterprise has made us what we are: speculation would have ruined us." This message comes across in her novel, *Half a Million of Money*. On inheriting £2 million currently in "Government Stocks and Funds," Saxon Trefalden was advised to invest his money where it would bring a higher rate of return. He left this to his cousin William who invested in "government stock in all the chief capitals of Europe; shares in great Indian and European railways; in steam navigation companies, insurance companies, gas companies, docks, mines, and banks in all parts of the civilized world.... He alone knew how difficult it had been to choose the safe and avoid the doubtful." William told his cousin Edward that "You will find the money excellently invested." That was after he had been forced to hand it over, as his intention had been to flee abroad taking it all with him.[30]

Edwards's novel was one among many in the 1860s that emphasised the benefits that came from careful investment in corporate stocks and bonds and the losses that came from speculation and risky ventures. In Yates's 1866 novel, *Kissing the Rod*, Robert Spreightley forgot "his cautious dealings" and was then destroyed by "speculation after speculation."[31] Also appearing in 1866 was Charlotte Riddell's novel, *George Geith of Fen Court*. This warned investors of "Mines, and railways, and speculations of all sorts," but its principal theme was the danger of holding shares in companies without limited liability.[32] That same year Charlotte Riddell published another novel, *The Race for Wealth*, which did contain an outright attack on joint-stock companies. "There were companies for everything — for banking, for dining, for diving, for drinking, for bathing, and burying, and clothing, and washing, and furnishing. No person who has not studied the statistics of companies can have the faintest idea of the deluge which came upon the earth for its wickedness when once Parliament opened the sluice gates by doing away with Unlimited Responsibility." Nevertheless, Riddell recognised the appeal of investing

---

[30]A.B. Edwards, *Half a Million of Money* (London: George Routledge and Sons, 1865) pp. 1–3, 7–11, 21–25, 125–126, 166–173, 370–375, 398–401, 430–431, 460–461.

[31]E.H. Yates, *Kissing the Rod: A Novel* (London: Tinsley Brothers, 1866) Vol. 2: pp. 126–127, 144, 280.

[32]Riddell, *George Geith*, pp. 25, 88, 139, 450.

in joint-stock companies when the alternative was consols or mortgages. The former was liquid but low yielding, while the latter was illiquid but high yielding. Joint-stock companies appealed not only to "country simpletons, and ambitious widows, and discontented governesses, but sound commercial men." The conclusion to be drawn was that "No legislation can protect fools against the results of their own folly" and all had to accept the risks to be taken if the higher return was to be achieved. "Any man who, in these days, chooses to invest his savings in business, whether on his own sole risk or in company with other adventurers, has no right to ask for pity if the project fail."[33] If Riddell can be taken as reflecting the views of her times, then there was an acceptance that investment now involved greater risks but that did not mean that speculation was acceptable.

With the bursting of the mid-1860s speculative bubble, forever associated with the collapse of the finance house, Overend and Gurney, and the losses inflicted on investors, novelists emphasised even more the dangers of speculation. Anthony Trollope in *The Last Chronicle of Barset*, which was published in 1867, suggested a return to consols and mortgages.[34] Examples of the losses made from speculating in the shares of joint-stock companies were presented in a succession of novels. In Joseph Hatton's *The Tallants of Barton*, which appeared in 1867, the contrast is made between Christopher Tallant and his son, Richard. Christopher Tallant was a "self-made man. … His riches were the result of his own ability and industry," and he survived the bursting of the speculative bubble even though he owned shares. However, his son Richard had been speculating extensively using borrowed money. Though successful initially, using inside knowledge acquired through his father's business interests and by spreading false rumours, he ended up bankrupt as he "had gone on playing for higher stakes."[35]

This message that speculation did not pay was emphasised in another novel of 1867, Mrs Braddon's *Rupert Godwin*. Godwin was a banker who "had been bitten with the mania of speculation … and had plunged wildly into all manner of schemes, many of which had ended in ruin." To cover

---

[33] C. Riddell, *The Race for Wealth* (Leipzig: 1866) Vol. 1: pp. 172–180, Vol. 2: pp. 107, 128–135, 160–162, 172, 430.

[34] A. Trollope, *The Last Chronicle of Barset* (London: 1867) p. 259.

[35] Hatton, *The Tallants of Barton*, pp. 2–9, 63–71, 79–81, 88, 98–99, 131–132, 142–143, 219–221, 292–293, 308–309, 314–315, 345, 348–349, 369.

his losses, he stole from the customers of his bank but was betrayed by his confidential clerk.[36] Another speculator who lost all was the stockbroker, Philip Sheldon, in Braddon's 1868 novel, *Charlotte's Inheritance*.[37] In another 1868 novel by Bracebridge Hemyng and James H. Graff, *Telegraph Secrets*, Edward Arden, the owner of Bramly Hall, lost his estate through losses incurred by speculating on the Stock Exchange.[38] With these warnings, it was not surprising that Mrs Margaret Oliphant, in her 1869 short story, *Mrs Merridew's Fortune*, had her character's £10,000 inheritance "excellently invested on landed security, and bearing interest at four and a half per cent."[39] Despite the signals from novelists about the dire consequences of speculation, it continued to grip those with money to invest, judging from Laurence Oliphant's 1870 novel, *Piccadilly*.[40] The degree to which speculation had taken a hold among the wealthy, and even infected their servants, was also a theme in Shand's 1870 novel, *Against Time*. This was set in the years leading up to the collapse of Overend and Gurney. "There's an absolute glut of money, and a perfect flush of credit; shoals of investors with their pockets running over, only waiting and praying for someone to show them where to empty them to the best advantage." The bubble eventually burst ruining numerous investors.[41] Frederick Robinson, in the 1870 novel, *True to Herself*, even suggested that Turkish Bonds were a better investment than speculating in "shares in companies or banks," even though the Ottoman government was a serial defaulter.[42]

Speculation was even more central to a novel Hemyng and Graff produced in 1871, entitled *Too Sharp by Half: Or, The Man Who Made*

---

[36]M.E. Braddon, *Rupert Godwin* (London: John and Robert Maxwell, 1867) pp. 4, 8–9, 13–15, 299–311.

[37]M.E. Braddon, *Charlotte's Inheritance* (London: Ward, Lock and Tyler, 1868) Book 6th: ch. 2, ch. 3, ch. 5, Book 7th: ch. 2, Book 8th: ch. 1, ch. 3, ch. 7, Book 9th: ch. 3, Book 10th: ch. 5, ch. 7, ch. 10.

[38]B. Hemyng and J.H. Graff, *Telegraph Secrets* (London: Chapman and Hall, 1868) pp. 15, 28–31, 65, 94–97.

[39]Mrs M. Oliphant, *Mrs Merridew's Fortune* (1869) in *Neighbours on the Green* (London: Macmillan and Company, 1889) p. 212.

[40]L. Oliphant, *Piccadilly* (London: 1870), pp. 38, 60–62, 67–69.

[41]A.I. Shand, *Against Time* (London: 1870) pp. 13, 38, 40–43, 46, 58–62, 88, 115–116, 122, 139–143, 149, 163, 166, 170, 174, 181, 189–190.

[42]F.W. Robinson, *True to Herself* (London: 1870) Vol. 1: p. 156, Vol. 2: p. 40, Vol. 3: pp. 79–80, 131, 188.

Millions. This involved the successful speculative activities of Isaac Moskins, a London grocer. After a very successful investment in the shares of the Grand Trunk of Bohemia Railway Company, he became a professional speculator, exploiting the fact that news of his buying sent shares up in price, as he then sold out at a profit, leaving other investors nursing losses.[43] The message was clear. Speculation in shares was gambling and most lost as a result though a select few did gain. What continued to resonate was the speculative boom and bust of the mid-1860s as in Mrs Oliphant's 1872 novel, *At His Gates*. Those involved ranged from the banker, Reginald Burton, who bet on the rise and fall of the Funds, to the artist and member of the Royal Academy, Robert Drummond, who invested his entire fortune in the shares of the Rivers's Bank when it was converted into a joint-stock company. However, the bank was but a shadow of what it had been and collapsed, with the investors losing all their money.[44] In another novel published in 1872, *Ready-Money Mortiboy* by Walter Besant and James Rice, the provincial banker, Francis Melliship "invested largely in foreign stocks, promising a high rate of interest; in land and Credit Companies; in South American mining speculations. This was gambling; but he learnt the truth too late." As was the usual fate of speculators, he lost his money.[45]

With these fictional examples widely displayed, it was surprising that investors were not dissuaded from speculating, but Charlotte Yonge touched on the reason in her 1873 novel, *The Pillars of the House*. She observed that a legacy of £1,000 would mean "£30 per annum in the funds, or £50 in some risky investment."[46] That differential was sufficient to act as an inducement to those willing to take the risk and novelists were picking up on that in the 1860s and 1870s. This was the point made in Meason's book, *Three Months After Date and Other Tales*. This mixed fact and fiction and was originally serialised in the magazine *All Year Round* in 1865/1866, before appearing as two books. *Bubbles of Finance* was published in 1865 and *The Profits of Panics* in 1866. It was then

---

[43] B. Hemyng and J.H. Graff, *Too Sharp by Half: Or, The Man Who Made Millions* (London: 1871) pp. 13–18, 49, 51, 94–97, 110.

[44] Mrs Oliphant, *At His Gates* [serialized in *Good Words*] (London: Strahan and Co., 1872) pp. 37–39, 177.

[45] W. Besant and J. Rice, *Ready-Money Mortiboy: A Matter-of-fact Story* (London: 1872) p. 123.

[46] C.M. Yonge, *The Pillars of the House* (London: Macmillan & Co., 1873) Vol. 1: p. 249.

revised for the publication in 1874 as a single book with the author postulating that "Is there amongst us one man or woman in twenty, getting from three-and-a half to five per cent for his or her money, who will not jump at an opportunity which offers 10, 12, and often 15 per cent?"[47] Even experienced investors succumbed to these temptations, according to Anthony Trollope in his 1875 novel, *The Way We Live Now*. The bankers, Todd, Brehgert and Goldsheiner, lost £60,000 through the collapse of a foreign railway project.[48] As with most novelists, the fate awaiting speculators was to experience losses, leaving suicide the only escape, which was the case in 1876 novel, *The Prime Minister*.[49]

A much less subtle attack on speculation than Trollope's *The Way We Live Now* was the novel *Ye Vampyres* by The Spectre, which appeared in 1875. This condemned speculating on the rise and fall of stocks and shares as it ruined respectable members of the community who would never normally gamble.[50] However, it was also recognised that investors were driven to speculate because of the lack of alternatives and the possibility of stupendous gains from the likes of mining shares. This can be seen in James Payn's 1876 novel, *Fallen Fortunes*. He compared two investors. On the one hand, there was George Campden, who "had shares in every description of property: in banks, in railways, and in ships; and taking them all round, his investments had been very fortunate." On the other hand, there was John Dalton, who speculated and lost not only his own money but also his wife's. "He had not thought such a catastrophe possible when he had commenced his speculative career; he would not even have admitted he was plunging into speculation; all had looked safe and smooth; nothing had seemed to be wanting but a little happy audacity to

---

[47] M.L. Meason, *Three Months After Date and Other Tales* (London: Ward, Lock and Tyler, 1874) [Originally published in *All The Year Round* then two separate volumes. One was *The Bubbles of Finance*, 1865. The other was *The Profits of Panics*, 1866. They were then revised for the 1874 publication] preface, pp. 6, 8, 39, 56, 69–73, 84–85, 104–105, 107, 109, 112–113, 136–141, 153, 164–168, 184–188, 228, 237–242, 254–262, 294, 297 plus ch.iii 'How we "floated" the Bank' and ch. xi 'Bank of Patagonia Limited'.

[48] A. Trollope, *The Way We Live Now* (London: 1875) Vol. 1: pp. 30–34, 48–49, 84, 268–269, 349, Vol. 2: pp. 26–27, 89, 91–92, 99, 140, 294, 304, 307, 319, 361, 400.

[49] A. Trollope, *The Prime Minister* (London: 1876) Vol. 1: pp. 1–15, 21, 26–27, 222, 228, 230–236, Vol. 2: pp. 173, 194.

[50] The Spectre, *Ye Vampyres, A Legend or The National Betting-Ring, Showing What Became of It* (London: 1875) pp. 17–18, 24, 44–45, 50–51, 81, 157, 176.

place a man of his ability and connections in the very first rank of businessmen." Through the advice of Richard Holt, a London stockbroker and another successful investor, he invested the remaining £15,000 in a Brazilian gold mine, the Lara. This turned out to be highly profitable, and made him a wealthy man, but that was luck not judgement.[51] In her 1876 novel, *Adam Granger*, Mrs Wood again raised the risks attached to mining companies as "They generally end in the ruin of all connected with them." In this case, it was a Cornish tin and copper mine, the Great Trebeddon, which failed.[52]

The year 1876 also saw the publication of a book that mixed fact and fiction to produce a critical account of the speculation that was then in vogue along with practical investment advice. This was Erasmus Pinto's *Ye Outside Fools!* The investment advice included the likes of, "If you value your peace of mind, touch not a Foreign Bond," "There is no investment so good as English Railways," "Never buy a share in a mine, English or foreign" and "Take no shares in industrial companies, unless fully acquainted with the concern." Above all, he considered that "Land is the finest investment to be had." This view was being expressed just as the agricultural depression was beginning, which resulted in a steady fall in the price of rural property. What does emerge is the difficult choices that investors had to make and why they were drawn to the likes of foreign loans and joint-stock company stocks and bonds despite all the warnings. "Just now, all good securities have been forced up by the continued dullness of trade, the great scarcity of good investments, the general collapse in foreign securities, and the ease of the money market." He also recognised that speculators were perpetual optimists sustained by a diet of mystery and excitement, greed and the gambling instinct. "Who when a market rises thinks that it will not cease to rise, and when it falls think there will be no limit to the fall." He cautioned investors not to "deal in anything you do not understand; don't deal in any new securities unless you're rich and can afford to lose." Above all, he recommended the stocks and bonds of British railways. "They are real property and indestructible.... The strife of politics, the panics of finance alike are powerless to damage

---

[51] J. Payn, *Fallen Fortunes* (London: Chatto and Windus, 1876) pp. 10, 24–25, 40, 55–57, 62–71, 79, 84–85, 88–89, 98, 161–166, 217, 231, 247, 279, 301, 352, 357, 362, 367–370, 382, 392–398.

[52] Mrs H. Wood, *Adam Granger and Other Stories* (London: Richard Bentley and Son, 1876) pp. 4–6, 44–67, 72–73, 105–106, 109, 114–116, 127–128, 172–173.

them or permanently affect the price.... The investor may hold the best English Railways with the greatest confidence.... English Rails are the only true field for sensible operations, whether for speculation or investment."[53]

Despite the revelations of the Committee into Foreign Loans, which fed into the novels of the day, British investors continued to flock to corporate stocks and bonds and the debt of foreign governments because of the better returns on offer compared to land and consols. This can be seen in the novel, *The Golden Butterfly* by Walter Besant and James Rice, which was published in 1877. The financier, Gabriel Cassilis, constructed portfolios for Phillis Fleming, who had inherited £50,000, all invested in 3 per cent consols, and Lawrence Colquhoun who was of the view that, "why not get eight and nine per cent, if you can?" His lawyer, who was trying to advise him replied, "Because it isn't safe, and because you ought not to expect it." Cassilis was investing their money in the shares of the companies he was promoting and speculating in the bonds issued by the Republic of Eldorado. This strategy would have proved successful if Cassilis had not become became distracted at a vital moment because he believed his wife was having an affair, and so missed the opportunity to sell out at a huge profit. As it was, they lost most their money.[54] Other novels of the 1870s also paint a picture of a society obsessed with finding investments that yielded a better return than consols and UK railway stocks and bonds and captivated by the possibilities of shares in mining companies and other speculative ventures. In 1877, William Powell Frith tried to capture the mood of the time in a series of paintings entitled "The Race for Wealth." "I wished to illustrate ... the common passion for speculation, and the destruction that so often attends the indulgence of it." The character chosen to represent the investor was a clergyman who could not understand what had happened when the mining company he had invested in collapsed. "The catastrophe is complete: the little fortune has been invested in the mine, and the whole of it lost."[55]

---

[53] E. Pinto, *Ye Outside Fools!: Glimpses Inside the Stock Exchange* (London: 1876), preface, pp. 1–2, 6, 11, 32–37, 40–41, 49–55, 145–150, 191, 225, 247, 297–298, 334–335, 374–378, 383, 386–387.

[54] W. Besant and J. Rice, *The Golden Butterfly* (London: 1877) pp. 47, 86–90, 130–132, 143, 153–154, 165, 175, 228–229, 264, 285, 333–339, 431, 486, 490, 498, 509, 519–526, 532–536, 560–573.

[55] W.P. Frith, *My Autobiography and Reminiscences* (London: 1888) pp. 295, 343, 356–359.

This contemporary fascination with speculation comes across in various novels.[56] Wilkie Collins tries to explain its popularity in his 1878 novel, *The Haunted Hotel*. "If you put your hundred pounds into the Funds, you will get between three and four pounds a year.... Three or four pounds a year? That won't do. I want more than that."[57] For those willing to take extreme risks, there was always the lure of mining companies as Joseph Hatton touched on in his 1878 novel, *Cruel London*. "The example of men who have made large fortunes is always before the dupe who has lost."[58] It was these examples of the successful investor, regardless of their rarity, that drew investors in as Hawley Smart picked up on in his 1881 novel, *The Great Tontine*, and Charlotte Riddell in her 1882 novel, *Daisies and Buttercups*.[59] One who was ideally placed to comment on investor behaviour at that time was Walter Stafford Northcote, the Earl of Iddesleigh, as he served as Chancellor of the Exchequer. In his 1882 novel, *Luck o'Lassendale*, he compared three brothers, whose family owned a small estate which was suffering financially because of declining rents and rising expenses. Sir Francis Lassendale was a risk taker and speculated in the shares of a mining company. Alfred Lassendale only invested "in absolutely safe securities." Robert Lassendale, a successful lawyer, followed a strategy of making "judicious investments, and then sell out at a good profit, and reinvest, and so on." Inevitably, the mining company collapsed leaving Sir Francis with huge debts and no option but to sell the estate. Finally, there was a group of female investors who managed their own investments, took professional advice and did well. What this novel reveals was that contemporaries were aware of the variety of investor experiences, ranging from the committed speculator to the ultra-cautious, with those who chose the middle road faring best.[60] They also reveal the difficult decisions that investors had to make. Though not published until 1903, Samuel Butler's novel, *The Way of all Flesh*, was written in 1883 and reflected the thinking about investments that was current

[56]R. Black, *Love or Lucre: A Novel* (London: George Routledge and Sons, 1878) p. 795.

[57]W. Collins, *The Haunted Hotel* (London: 1878) p. 151.

[58]J. Hatton, *Cruel London: A Novel* (London: Frederick Warne & Co. 1878) pp. 65, 79.

[59]H. Smart, *The Great Tontine* (London: 1881) pp. 38, 40–41, 141; C. Riddell, *Daisies and Buttercups: A Novel of the Upper Thames* (London: Sampson Low, Marston, Searle and Rivington, 1882) pp. 11, 186.

[60]W. Stafford Northcote, Earl of Iddesleigh, *Luck o'Lassendale* (London: John Lane, The Bodley Head, 1882) pp. 34, 64–65, 68, 74, 83, 86–87, 109–116, 125–129, 135, 150–151, 182, 192–193, 199–200, 266, 307, 321, 334–339, 346.

at that time. Edward Pontifex inherited £5,000 and, after experiencing losses through speculation, chose to invest in railway stocks, which generated a higher yield and gained more in capital than consols.[61]

For novelists, the problem was that the careful investor with a balanced portfolio generated little excitement for the reader, whereas the speculator, who made or lost a fortune, did. For that reason, the image of the investor that novelists perpetuated was the speculator, as in Walter Besant's 1883 story, *All in a Garden Fair*. "The British public is never tired of companies; sometimes there is a lull, but only for a short time, and then the game goes on again with undiminished vigour.... Companies for electric lights, for packet-boats, for tramways, for torpedoes, for telephones, for hotels, for newspapers, and a hundred other things." There was also the usual crop of mining companies, whether it was silver in South America or copper in Australia.[62] Mrs Oliphant suggested in her 1883 novel, *Hester*, that "there are no such wild speculators as women." What appealed to all speculators was "the idea of making a fortune in a few hours ... buy a thing when it is cheap, and hold it till it becomes dear, and then ... sell it again.... There is a great deal of excitement in it."[63] By the 1880s, investment and speculation were synonymous as in Bracebridge Hemyng's 1885 book, *The Stockbroker's Wife*. All engaged in speculation but with differing results. Captain Ramsden "speculated, as most men do nowadays when they have a little spare cash to play with." Another successful speculator was the retired Indian civil servant, Sir William Benson, who amassed "an enormous fortune on the Stock Exchange." In contrast, the Leicestershire landowner, Robert Groome, lost heavily through speculation. Another who lost money looking for a better return on her investments was the widow of a physician, Mrs Mary Haydon.[64] Even those investors who held back from speculation were

---

[61] S. Butler, *The Way of All Flesh* (London: 1903) pp. 264, 273–274, 316–317, 369–371, 381, 419.

[62] W. Besant, *All in a Garden Fair: The Simple Story of Three Boys and a Girl* (London: 1883) pp. 11–13, 199, 209.

[63] Mrs. M. Oliphant, *Hester: A Study in Contemporary Life* (London: Macmillan and Co., 1883) pp. 172, 188–191, 264–265, 285, 333–335, 341–343, 414, 420, 436–439, 458–459.

[64] B. Hemyng, *The Stockbroker's Wife and Other Sensational Tales of the Stock Exchange* (London: John and Robert Maxwell, 1885) pp. 8–14, 22–23, 37–38, 82–85, 92–95, 99, 113, 144–145, 150–153, 156, 159–161, 168–169, 175–176, 191–196.

being forced to take greater risks because of the continuing low returns from consols and mortgages, as noted in a variety of novels written in the mid-1880s.[65]

The difficulty faced by investors was one addressed by Alexander Shand in his novel, *Fortune's Wheel*, which also appeared in 1886, indicating the extent to which the subject had become one of popular interest within British society at the time. When Jack Venables inherited £10,000, "chiefly invested in consols," he sold the low-yielding debt and embarked on a series of successful speculations, including property development in Scotland and silver mining in the USA. Another successful investor was Wilfred Winstanley, who was "perpetually selling out and buying again." His investing career had begun through a friendship with "Isaacs, the great Jew financier." Less fortunate was Sir Stamford Scraper, a City financier, who lost money investing in electric lighting companies after large initial profits. There was also David Moray, who lived on an income safely invested in "sound bank stocks," until the failure of the Southern Counties Bank left him on the verge of bankruptcy because it had unlimited liabilities, which the shareholders would be required to meet. This had been the case with the collapse of the City of Glasgow Bank in 1878, but Moray escaped that fate because the bank's investments in US mines, railways and land turned out very profitably.[66] The complexity of managing a diversified portfolio was one touched upon by George Bernard Shaw in his 1887 novel, *An Unsocial Socialist*. "I have railway shares, mining shares, building shares, bank shares, and stock of most kinds; and a great trouble they are to me."[67] Contemporaries recognised that successful investment required the careful management of a diversified portfolio, and the avoidance of speculation for the latter led to losses, as in Muirhead Robertson's 1888 crime novel, *A Lombard Street Mystery*.[68]

---

[65]C. Riddell, *Mitre Court: A Tale of the Great City* (London: Richard Bentley and Son, 1885) Vol. 2: p. 204, Vol. 3: pp. 230–231; R.L. Stevenson, *The Dynamiter* (London: 1885) p. 17; W. Collins, *The Evil Genius* (London: 1886) p. 228.

[66]A.I. Shand, *Fortune's Wheel: A Novel* (Edinburgh & London: William Blackwood and Sons, 1886) Vol. 1: pp. 127, 234–235, 268–271, Vol. 2: pp. 70–73, 81–85, 117, 194–195, 210–211, 217–219, 236–239, 242–243, 248, 257, Vol. 3: pp. 70–71, 84–85, 102–107, 243.

[67]Shaw, *An Unsocial Socialist*, pp. 20–21, 63, 91–94, 98–99, 198–199, 209, 212, 264–267.

[68]M. Robertson, *A Lombard Street Mystery: A Novel* (London: W. Bartholomew, 1888) pp. 8, 75–76, 233–234.

The year 1890 witnessed a crop of novels that featured investors who experienced differing fortunes because "Shares rise and fall — and companies sometimes fail," according to Wilkie Collins in *Blind Love*, a novel which was completed by Walter Besant.[69] Edward Roscoe in *The Burnt Million* by James Payn was involved "in into enormous speculations, which had turned out ill, and involved him in liabilities which he had no means of meeting."[70] Conan Doyle's novel, *The Firm of Girdlestone*, presented the two faces of investors. The principal partner in the firm of African merchants, John Girdlestone, had speculated and lost in US railroad shares and Cornish tin mines. In contrast, his son Ezra, who was "a brilliant man of business, did not speculate in shares."[71] In *A Crooked Path*, Mrs Alexander featured John Liddell, who was a successful speculator because he devoted himself to the business after he "had lost both wife and son."[72] Similarly, in *By Order of the Czar* by Joseph Hatton, Samuel Swynford, a London stockbroker, claimed that "I have not a single losing investment," despite being a speculator. "The secret of Sam's success on the Stock Exchange lay in his never losing his head…. A true speculator, Sam, no whining, no despondency over losses, just the same keen firm grip of things whether he lost or won, just the same looking forward to the big fortune he meant to win, with the exception that losses were a sort of tonic to him." What attracted him to speculation was the poor return on safe investments compared to the promise of large gains from risk taking. "A niggardly Government will only give two and a half" compared to the 25 per cent promised on many share issues.[73]

Nevertheless, the risks were real and produced losses for many investors. In Curtis Yorke's *A Romance of Modern London*, Maxwell Fenwicke was advised to "steer clear of mines … they're risky things — infernally risky." Despite that advice, he financed the opening up of a tin mine in Cornwall only to be surprised "that mining was so confoundedly

---

[69] W. Collins and W. Besant, *Blind Love* (London: 1890) pp. 57, 91, 114, 127, 254, 295.

[70] J. Payn, *The Burnt Million* (London: Chatto and Windus, 1890) Vol. 1: pp. 1–3, 7–8, 11–13, 246, 266, 289, Vol. 3: pp. 77–79, 97, 140–142, 164, 169, 184, 259.

[71] A.C. Doyle, *The Firm of Girdlestone: A Romance of the Unromantic* (London: Collins, 1890) pp. 1–7, 77, 13–14, 42, 76–81, 166–168, 290, 335.

[72] Mrs Alexander, *A Crooked Path* (London: Hurst and Blackett, 1890) pp. 30–32, 65–66, 82, 93, 305, 310, 449.

[73] J. Hatton, *By Order of the Czar: The Tragic Story of Anna Klosstock, Queen of the Ghetto* (London: 1890) pp. 112, 118, 126–130, 187–188, 193–194, 204, 312, 391.

expensive. It swallows up coin like the very deuce." In this case, the mine prospered.[74] An investment in a mining company was the subject of Thomas Terrell's book, *The City of the Just*. "A lot of old women and parsons in the country" bought shares in the Silver Streak Gold Mining Company, because it promised dividends of at least 115 per cent per annum.[75] Another novel featuring a mining investment was Frederick Wicks's *The Veiled Hand*. When Amy married Geoffrey Delfoy, she was given a dowry of £250,000 in 3 per cent consols, representing the most secure of investments. In contrast, the Great Coradell Copper Mine was very speculative, with the respectable City banker, Morris Heritage, refusing to become involved. He regarded mining companies as "legalised larceny," with their shares having "taken the place in the public mind of the forbidden lotteries and roulette tables." Nevertheless, other investors were eager to participate. The bank handling subscriptions to the Great Coradell Copper Mine "was besieged by an eager crowd before its doors were opened; and all day long its ordinary business was reduced to the narrowest possible limits short of complete suspension, while the British investor poured his savings into the Great Coradell." Confounding its critics, the mine turned out to be a great success once a railway had been built.[76]

Supporting the view that not all investments turned out badly was Mrs Alexander's 1892 novel, *Mammon*, which featured a successful investor, Mr Tracey. Through successful investing and miserly habits, Mr Tracey had built up a fortune of over £100,000 when he died.[77] Conversely, George and Weedon Grossmith's *The Diary of a Nobody*, which also appeared in 1892, emphasised the risks of speculation.[78] A.C. Gunter's novel, *Miss Dividends*, published in England in 1892, suggested

[74] C. Yorke, *A Romance of Modern London: A Novel* (London: 1892) Vol. 1: pp. 211–212, Vol. 2: pp. 29, 119, 127, Vol. 3: pp. 21, 181.

[75] T. Terrell, *The City of the Just* (London: Trischler and Company, 1892) pp. 18, 22–24, 30–36, 79–87, 109, 117–118, 156, 229–231.

[76] F. Wicks, *The Veiled Hand: A Novel of the Sixties, the Seventies, and the Eighties* (London: 1892), preface, pp. 10–11, 53–54, 67–68, 117–118, 171–193, 200, 220–221, 237–240, 250–256, 264–265, 268–269, 275, 281–282, 306, 311, 314, 398, 413, 416.

[77] Mrs Alexander, *Mammon* (Leipzig & London: Heinemann and Balestier, 1892) pp. 3–9, 36–37, 70, 97–99, 108, 137, 147, 160, 205–206, 291, 314.

[78] G. and W. Grossmith, *The Diary of a Nobody* (London: 1892) pp. 19–20, 87, 93–94, 147–148, 163–165.

that among all investors "none have so rashly and so lavishly squandered their money as the speculators of merry England."[79] The publicity given to examples where investors lost their money after speculating in shares, especially of mining companies, had created the ingrained belief by the 1890s that all such investments were either fraudulent or, at least, of very high risk.[80] Nevertheless, such investment continued apace because of the necessity of a higher rate of return. Even an accountant could succumb to the temptations of speculation, because of the potential gains. The accountant, Cosmo Greig, in F.H. Mel's *The Accountant*, which was published in 1894, "took to speculation; was successful. Speculated again and again, winning beyond his wildest hopes. The mad ventures which brought so many others to ruin only yielded profit to him, at all events on paper." However, this did not last and when his luck turned against him, his response was to take greater risks. Eventually, he discovered that his investments were in "unmarketable securities, many of which had already lost, or were rapidly losing, such reputation as they had had, and dividends from which were growing steadily less and less." His son was then forced to devote himself to recovering the family fortune and rescuing those investors who been persuaded by his father to invest in companies without limited liability.[81] Though it was recognised that only land or consols could provide complete security, as in Walter Besant's 1895 novel, *Beyond the Dreams of Avarice*, the yield was now so low that alternatives had to be sought, while the guarantee that they would retain their value could no longer be relied upon.[82] In the mid-1890s, it seemed impossible to find investments that combined both security and a reasonable return judging from contemporary novels. In Marie Corelli's *The Sorrows of Satan*, which was published in 1895, Geoffrey Tempest lost most of the fortune he had inherited by investing in "various bubble

---

[79] A.C. Gunter, *Miss Dividends: A Novel* (London: 1892) pp. 8–12, 26, 39, 104, 168, 274.

[80] I. Zangwill, 'Cheating the Gallows' (1893) in M. Cox (ed.), *Victorian Tales of Mystery and Detection: An Oxford Anthology* (Oxford: Oxford University Press, 1992) pp. 242–243; A.S. Swan, *The Strait Gate* (London: 1894) pp. 1–3, 16–18, 23–24, 74–75, 102, 154–157, 161, 204, 232, 238–239; M. Pemberton, *The Impregnable City* (London: 1895) pp. 86, 92–93, 246–247, 306.

[81] Mel, *The Accountant*, pp. 18–19, 21, 30, 33–36, 58–61, 79, 110, 152, 193, 249–250, 253–254, 261, 346.

[82] W. Besant, *Beyond the Dreams of Avarice* (London: 1895) pp. 10–11, 47, 58–59, 148–149, 156–161, 309, 324.

companies."[83] Under these circumstances, it was no wonder that the subject of investment was such a popular topic of conversation among those with money, featuring in two hit plays of Oscar Wilde's performed in 1895, namely, *An Ideal Husband* and *The Importance of Being Earnest*.[84]

With the speculative boom and bust involving mainly South African gold mining companies that peaked in 1895, investment in stocks and shares became an all-consuming subject, with entire novels making it their central theme. One was Francis Gribble's *The Lower Life*, which came out in 1896. The novel captured the excitement of the speculative fever of those who became involved and the astonishment of those who watched the mania unfold. Though many were initially suspicious, the profits being made by speculators drew more and more in. "What prejudice she had against gambling had been, at bottom, a prejudice against losing money." Despite the bursting of the speculative bubble, the expectation was that it would return. "Just now people are frightened, and put their money in the bank. Presently they'll be tired of getting one and a half percent on their deposits, and nothing at all on their current accounts. That's what we call 'a revival of confidence' and when it comes all the fun will begin once again."[85] Another novel published in 1896 was Headon Hill's *Guilty Gold*. "I think the public are about ripe for a little flutter in gold mines." The Golden Kloof Mining Company was a swindle but attracted investors in the belief that it would make their fortune. Other investors were attracted to bucket shops where they could gamble on the rise and fall of shares.[86] Investment in shares was being described as gambling and there was a call for legislation to prevent it from taking place. However, once the boom was over, that call died away, becoming accepted that this was how it was. In Arthur Morrison's 1897 story, *The Affair of the 'Avalanche Bicycle and Tyre Company Limited'* the point was made that "Immense fortunes were being made in a few days and

---

[83] M. Corelli, *The Sorrows of Satan* (London: 1895) pp. 12, 63, 76, 98, 172–173, 264, 384–387.

[84] O. Wilde, 'An Ideal Husband and The Importance of Being Earnest', in Oscar Wilde, *The Major Works* (Oxford: 1989) pp. 404–409, 418–421, 456–457, 460, 529.

[85] F. Gribble, *The Lower Life* (London: 1896) pp. 1, 6, 8, 10, 14, 16, 20–21, 25, 30–32, 40–45, 53–55, 60–74, 92–93, 100, 108–109, 118–120, 131–133, 137, 149, 176, 190–191, 197, 238–239, 285, 294, 308–311.

[86] H. Hill, *Guilty Gold: A Romance of Financial Fraud and City Crime* (London: 1896) pp. 1–6, 10–19, 23, 27–69, 78–79, 115–117, 134–135, 209–214, 341, 347–354.

sometimes little fortunes were being lost to build them up. … Sometimes the shareholders got their money's worth, sometimes more, sometimes less — sometimes they got nothing but total loss; but still the game went on."[87] Though there were investors who were naïve and easily fleeced or ready to gamble on anything at every opportunity, there were others who used their experience, knowledge and connections to make difficult decisions and emerge with a profit. George Gissing recognised this in his 1897 novel, *The Whirlpool*. Carnaby knew what he was doing when investing in companies mining gold and manufacturing bicycles and emerged with a profit. In contrast, Morphew speculated on the advice of his stockbroker and lost. "Speculation isn't quite so simple as I imagined. I made a couple of hundred, though — yes, and lost nearly three." Finally, there was Rolfe, who was very cautious and not willing to take risks. He took the advice of his banker and received a safe but low return. "To study the money market gave him a headache."[88] In Grant Allen's series of short stories, *An African Millionaire*, which appeared in 1897, the portfolio approach was adopted with the risks of South African mines matched by the security of railroad stocks and consols.[89] This need for a diversified portfolio that balanced risk and return was emphasised in Benson's 1898 novel, *The Money Market*. The £3 million Percy inherited from his grandfather was in securities producing an income of £60,000 per annum, or a yield of five per cent, which was twice that obtainable from consols.[90]

Nevertheless, the main message being conveyed in novels by the end of the nineteenth century, reflecting that of society generally, was that investment in corporate stocks was risky but only to be avoided when it became speculation. There was a spate of novels that featured losses made by those who speculated.[91] In 1899, Benson's *Mammon and Co.* explored

---

[87]A. Morrison, 'The Affair of the "Avalanche Bicycle and Tyre Co. Limited"' (1897) reprinted in H. Greene, *The Penguin Complete Rivals of Sherlock Holmes* (Harmondsworth: 1970–1973) pp. 103, 106–107.

[88]G. Gissing, *The Whirlpool* (London: 1897) pp. 6–10, 17, 38, 40–44, 48, 52, 64, 85, 129, 166, 194–197, 204–205, 231, 249, 302, 377, 383, 416–418.

[89]G. Allen, *An African Millionaire: Episodes in the Life of the Illustrious Colonel Clay* (London: 1897): see 'The Episode of the Japanned Dispatch-Box and The Episode of the Bertillon Method'.

[90]E.F. Benson, *The Money Market* (London: 1898) pp. 218–219, 234.

[91]H.S. Merriman, *Roden's Corner* (London: 1898) p. 98; G. du Maurier, *The Martian: A Novel* (London: 1898) pp. 143, 302, 426–427; Oxenham, *Rising Fortunes*, pp. 221–223,

what motivated investors when all predicted that the results were, almost inevitably, a loss of the money invested. Lady Haslemere actively speculated in obscure mining shares because, "If you have never earned a penny all your life, you have no idea how extraordinarily interesting it is to do so. You may think that it can't matter to me whether I gain ten pounds or lose twenty. But to gain it oneself — oh, that is the thing!"[92] With the yield on consols so low, and the chance of a profit being made from shares appearing so high, many investors were attracted by the possibilities of speculation, as Conan Doyle observed in his 1899 novel, *A Duet with an Occasional Chorus*.[93]

Among the novels appearing after 1900, a number did capture the benefits enjoyed by those investors who practised portfolio diversification, such as Arnold Bennett's *Anna of the Five Towns* in 1902.[94] However, it was the gains and losses from speculation that continued to absorb most attention in Granville Barker's 1903 play, *The Vosey Inheritance*, where it was losses through speculation that led the lawyer to stealing from his clients.[95] Conversely, in Frank Danby's novel, *Pigs in Clover*, which was published in 1903, successful speculation in South African gold mining shares transformed the financial prospects of Karl Althaus. In turn, his advice on investments allowed the impoverished English aristocrat, Stephen Hayward, to clear his estate of debts and make himself a rich man, while bankrupting Francis Jones, a publisher whom he disliked.[96] The constant fluctuations in the price of mining shares were sufficient to make an investor a fortune or destroy them totally, and gripped the imagination of the public. Fred White, in *A Bubble Burst*, which also appeared

273–275; H. Frederic, *The Market-Place* (London: 1899) pp. 6–10, 44, 48–49, 157; H. James, *The Awkward Age* (London: 1899) pp. 40, 64, 71–72, 141–142, 172, 239; E.F. Heddle, *The Pride of the Family* (London: James Bowden, 1899) pp. 10–12, 150–151, 222–223, 287–288.

[92] E.F. Benson, *Mammon and Co.* (London: 1899) pp. 15, 60–61, 100–101, 172–179, 198–199, 271–273, 281–282, 285–288, 296–298.

[93] A. Conan Doyle, *A Duet with an Occasional Chorus* (London: 1899) pp. 10–12, 249–262.

[94] A. Bennett, *Anna of the Five Towns* (London: 1902) pp. 30–33, 41–45, 65–66, 109–111.

[95] G. Barker, *The Voysey Inheritance* (London: 1903) [play].

[96] F. Danby (Mrs Julia Frankau), *Pigs in Clover* (London: William Heinemann, 1903) pp. 56, 66, 71, 310–311.

in 1903, considered that during the speculative boom in South African mining shares, "All England was in the grip of the mania" and "Bona fide speculation and business had become gambling pure and simple." These conditions lent themselves to the manipulation of the market by those with inside information.[97] Nevertheless, the investors who lost out most, according to Cutcliffe Hyne, in his 1903 novel, *Thompson's Progress*, were those who "considered that Consols and Land were the only securities worth recognizing."[98] What the novels of the early twentieth century reveal is that the public were aware that there was no single investment strategy that was foolproof and investors had an entire spectrum open to them, including emerging opportunities in the entertainment industry, according to E. Phillips Oppenheim's 1904 novel *Anna, the Adventuress*.[99] Barry Pain covered many of these new investments in his 1904 novel, *Deals*. These ranged from the Anglo-Foreign Hotels Syndicate and Greasewell's House Paints to the Exploration and Enterprise Finance Association, which financed mining ventures.[100]

Some of these new investment opportunities were so fanciful that they attracted the mockery of novelists. Guy Thorne and Leo Custance, in their 1904 novel, *Sharks*, featured the Lost Continent Recovery Company, which intended to raise Atlantis from the seabed. It attracted investors "who are dying to get rich without working! The fools — the grasping fools deserve to be cheated! Most of them do at any rate!" The whole affair was a hoax.[101] However, the principal targets for novelists were not the obviously fraudulent companies but those investors who persisted in speculating as in Hilaire Belloc's 1904 novel, *Emmanuel Burden*. Burden, a successful merchant who did not speculate, was contrasted with the London banker, Barnett, and Lord Benthorpe, who did engage in risky

[97]F.M. White, 'A Bubble Burst', in F.M. White, *The Doom of London* (London: 1903) (originally published in *Pearson's Magazine*, May 1903) pp. 1–16.

[98]Cutcliffe Hyne, *Thompson's Progress*, pp. 125–127, 156, 200, 245–249.

[99]E. Phillips Oppenheim, *Anna, the Adventuress* (London: 1904) pp. 72, 94, 110, 139.

[100]B. Pain, *Deals* (London: Hodder and Stoughton, 1904) pp. 6–7, 28–30, 51, 56–57, 62–63, 82, 108–110, 115, 126–127, 131–132, 150, 172–178, 191–200, 258–259, 274–277.

[101]G. Thorne and L. Custance, *Sharks: A Fantastic Novel for Business Men and Their Families* (London: 1904) pp. 2–15, 20–23, 30–33, 50–55, 144–145, 156–157, 180–181, 188–189, 226–229, 232–235, 278–279, 298–299, 340–345.

investments.[102] Another who was criticised was the lawyer in H.G. Wells's 1905 story, *Kipps*, who "Speckylated every penny — lost it all — and gorn."[103] As in the past, it was mines that were the most frequent object of this speculation. Though regarded as the riskiest of all investments, they had the potential to deliver a fortune for a lucky few, as Frances Hodgson Burnett spelled out in *A Little Princess*, which was published in 1905.[104] It was this chance of landing a great prize that continued to entice the public to speculate, as George Gissing made clear in his 1905 novel, *Will Warburton*, while accepting that the usual result was a total loss.[105] In E. Phillips Oppenheim's 1906 novel, *Mr Wingrave, Millionaire*, the Royal Hardwell Copper Mine in Utah was a success.[106] Conversely, speculation was the downfall of George Barty, a bank cashier in John Oxenham's 1906 *Profit and Loss*.[107]

What emerges from the novels written before the First World War was a sense that investors were obsessed with speculation, and this brought both success and failure. Also recognised was the never-ending search for securities that provided the perfect combination of income and safety, whether it was shares or property. This can be seen in a number of 1907 novels including Galsworthy's *The Country House*, William Le Queux's *The Secret of the Square* and *In His Grip* by David Murray.[108] One message that emerged was that speculation could bring down anyone because all were at the mercy of external events, such as a financial crisis in the

---

[102] H. Belloc, *Emmanuel Burden, Merchant, of Thames St, in the City of London, Exporter of Hardware: A Record of His Lineage, Speculations, Last Days and Death* (London: 1904) pp. 54–61, 65–76, 82–91, 104, 113, 119, 121–122, 158, 170–171, 196–197, 206–207, 212, 223.

[103] H.G. Wells, *Kipps: The Story of a Simple Soul* (London: 1905) pp. 219, 223, 296, 306.

[104] F.H. Burnett, *A Little Princess* (London: 1905) pp. 81, 87, 150, 240–241.

[105] G. Gissing, *Will Warburton: A Romance of Real Life* (London: 1905) pp. 15–16, 91, 96, 100.

[106] E. Phillips Oppenheim, *Mr Wingrave, Millionaire* (London: 1906) pp. 15, 40, 104–107, 235–236.

[107] J. Oxenham, *Profit and Loss* (London: 1906) pp. 5–11, 48, 115, 262, 273, 295, 309–311.

[108] J. Galsworthy, *The Country House* (London: 1907) pp. 10–11, 183–184; W. Le Queux, *The Secret of the Square* (London: The London Book Company, 1907) p. 166; D.C. Murray, *In His Grip* (London: John Long Limited, 1907) pp. 1, 26–27, 30–31, 34, 72, 77–78, 100, 108, 163, 171, 187, 209, 239, 242.

USA. Conversely, in Fox-Davies's 1908 tale, *The Finances of Sir John Kynnersley*, it was speculation that restored his family's fortune. Sir John Kynnersley had inherited the title, but not the house and estate that went with it. After an initial failure through a series of successful speculations, he made a great deal of money, largely at the expense of a crooked financier, allowing him to buy back his estate.[109] In contrast to the reward that came from risk, Arnold Bennett showed in another 1908 novel, *Buried Alive*, how an apparently safe investment could result in a large loss. An investment in the shares of Cohoon's Brewery Company was rendered worthless by the growth of the temperance movement.[110] No investment was absolutely safe, and even the most risky could turn out well, was the message of the age.[111]

This theme of the sudden wealth to be acquired through speculative ventures, more through luck than ability, was one which also ran through the four Lord Stranleigh novels written by Robert Barr. The first of these was *Young Lord Stranleigh*, which appeared in 1908. Lord Stranleigh of Wychwood was a wealthy landowner who was persuaded to invest in a West African gold mine even though he knew the great risk involved. As chance would have it, this turned out to be very valuable, leaving Stranleigh, an even wealthier man with a fortune of £200 million in gold bars. He then used this wealth to buy stocks during a financial panic. In the following volume, *Stranleigh's Millions*, which appeared in 1909, it is reported that he had made another £250 million on the rise of stocks after the panic was over. He then used this wealth to invest in a series of other companies, all of which turned out successfully. One was in retailing, Bendale's Stores, as he was a friend of the owner and his wife, while another was the Great Southern Railway, whose share price had, temporarily, sunk to a low level. In contrast, he steered clear of the Honduras Central Rubber Company, which was a fraudulent scheme. In *Lord Stranleigh Philanthropist*, which was published in 1911, he invested in two banks and an Austrian gold mine, all of which, again, turned out well.

---

[109]A.C. Fox-Davies, *The Finances of Sir John Kynnersley* (London: The Bodley Head, 1908) pp. 4–5, 9–10, 15, 38–39, 53–55, 75, 113, 133, 152–156, 184–189, 210–221, 235.

[110]A. Bennett, *Buried Alive* (London: 1908) pp. 119–121.

[111]E. Phillpotts and A. Bennett, *The Sinews of War: A Romance of London and the Sea* (London: T. Werner Laurie, 1908) p. 1; H. Belloc, *Mr Clutterbuck's Election* (London: 1908) pp. 1–3, 11–13, 16–18, 20–24, 31–37, 39, 43–44, 46, 52–56, 58–59, 120, 152, 180–181, 193–198, 216–220, 273–276.

In the final novel, *Lord Stranleigh Abroad*, which was published in 1913, he travelled to the USA where he invested in automobile manufacturing in Detroit and mining in the West, and again found success.[112] The impression generated by these Lord Stranleigh novels was that, when it came to investment, the entire world was open to the British investor and all he touched turned to gold, sometimes literally, without a great deal of effort on his behalf.

The novels of this era convey an impression of the enormous wealth at the disposal of the British investor, and their ability to employ it indiscriminately around the world. In the 1909 book by Bram Stoker, *The Lady and the Shroud*, for Roger Melton, "wealth piled in so fast that at times I could hardly use it to advantage," leaving him with a fortune of "well over a 100 million."[113] Nevertheless, it was acknowledged that investment of this kind was a high-risk game that could involve losses as well as profits, as in two other 1909 stories, namely, J.S. Fletcher's *The Contents of the Coffin* and E. Phillips Oppenheim's *Jeanne of the Marshes*.[114] There was also the middle road as described in E.F. Benson's 1910 novel *The Osbornes*, where one of the family, a London stockbroker, had "amassed a fortune … by means of careful and studied speculation" as he had "an unrivalled habit of being right with regard to the future movements of the stock market."[115] By then, the careful selection of a portfolio of foreign securities was seen to be essential for the preservation of income and wealth in *Howards End* by E.M. Forster, which also came out in 1910.[116] In Arnold Bennett's *The Card*, published in

---

[112]R. Barr, *Young Lord Stranleigh* (London: Ward, Lock & Co., 1908) pp. 1, 7, 10–14, 14–27, 33–43, 58, 63, 162–163, 188–189, 231–255; R. Barr, *Stranleigh's Millions* (London: Eveleigh Nash, 1909) pp. 26, 52, 58, 62, 173–174, 178–179, 184–185, 190–191, 204–207, 210–211, 220–221, 232–233, 236–238, 324–329; R. Barr, *Lord Stranleigh Philanthropist* (London: Ward, Lock & Co., 1911) pp. 16–17, 75–81, 201–203, 212–214, 224–225, 232–233, 236–239, 242–243; R. Barr, *Lord Stranleigh Abroad* (London: Ward, Lock & Co., 1913) pp. 20–21, 76.

[113]B. Stoker, *The Lady and the Shroud* (London: 1909) pp. 32, 43.

[114]J.S. Fletcher, 'The Contents of the Coffin' (1909) in Greene', *The Complete Rivals of Sherlock Holmes*, p. 924; E. Phillips Oppenheim, *Jeanne of the Marshes* (London: 1909) pp. 5, 26, 46, 119, 174, 193, 251.

[115]Benson, *The Osbornes*, pp. 4–7, 14–17, 37–38, 68–71, 144–145, 154–155, 170–173, 259, 263–264, 272–274.

[116]E.M. Forster, *Howards End* (London: 1910) pp. 28–29, 58, 139–140, 168–169.

1911, it was a diversified portfolio of investments in local companies that achieved the same end.[117]

At the same time, there continued to be references to investors who lost their money through speculation in the shares of joint-stock companies. Such was the message in Grace Pettman's 1912 novel, *A Study in Gold*. When Mark St. Leonard inherited £100,000, it "was all carefully invested," but they were "bringing in little better than consols!" His daughter, Margaret, advised him to stick with them as "they are safe investments," but he ignored her because she was a woman. Attracted by the possibility of doubling or trebling his money, he started to speculate. "Elated by success, the lust of the speculator fired Mark St. Leonard's blood. He sold out a still larger number of the sound investments his distant kinsman had left him, and plunged madly into the whirlpool of speculation." As predicted by his daughter, the companies collapsed, and Mark lost most of his inheritance.[118] Conversely, a well-constructed portfolio managed by a trustworthy stockbroker could be relied upon to deliver a reasonable return. In *Havoc*, Stephen Laverick, a City stockbroker, was commissioned by the opera singer, Mademoiselle Louise Idaile, to handle her investments. "'Will you buy me some stocks, some good safe stocks, which will bring me in at least 4 per cent.?' 'I can promise to do that', Laverick answered." Due to the choice of stocks, the portfolio was showing a profit of nearly £1,600 in a few weeks.[119] Investors were forced to take risks not only to obtain a satisfactory income but also, according to Joseph Hocking in his 1912 novel, *God and Mammon*, because "Everything would stagnate but for speculation. — Every new newspaper, every new hotel, every new enterprise whatsoever, is in the nature of speculation."[120] Arnold Bennett even made a hero out of Edward Machin, who had mastered the art of successful investment.[121]

Speculation, both successful and unsuccessful, was accepted as a fact of life on the eve of the First World War.[122] In *The Admirable Carfew*, a

---

[117] A. Bennett, *The Card* (London: 1911) pp. 30, 99, 135, 154–156, 210–211.

[118] G. Pettman, *A Study in Gold* (London: 1912) pp. 9, 10, 15, 65, 70, 101–104, 116–117, 121–133, 146–150, 157, 165, 201–207, 210–222, 226–227, 241, 276, 284–286.

[119] E. Phillips Oppenheim, *Havoc* (London: 1912) pp. 62–68, 98–99, 105, 116, 118, 236, 289–290, 315, 320–321, 329–330, 342–345.

[120] J. Hocking, *God and Mammon* (London: 1912) pp. 48–49, 67–69.

[121] A. Bennett, *The Regent: A Five Towns Story of Adventure in London* (London: 1913) pp. 1, 28, 38–39, 49, 148–150, 252–253.

[122] J. Buchan, *The Power-House* (London: 1913, reprinted 2007) p. 57.

1914 novel by Edgar Wallace, Carfew speculated on shares, losing money on some deals while making a profit on others. His friend, Gelden, lost money speculating in the shares of Siberian oil companies but became a millionaire after dabbling in tin mines, rubber plantations and then oil again.[123] Also published in 1914 was Margaret de Vere Stacpoole's novel entitled, *London 1913*. It attempted to capture the mood of speculation that pervaded London at that time, with those who engaged in it ranging from the "fabulously wealthy" who had made money in South Africa to Mr Thomas, a ship's purser, who complained about the difficulty of finding safe and remunerative investments. "Consols aren't safe; they have been falling for years — never seem to do anything but fall; put it in a bank, you get next to no interest."[124] By then, the days of certainty over investment, that came from land, mortgages, consols, and British railway stocks and bonds, were a distant memory. In their place, investors were faced with a bewildering range of investment opportunities, none of which could be relied upon to produce a guaranteed return. This uncertainty encouraged a perception among some that investment in stocks and bonds was little better than gambling. Among others, it was recognised that all investment involved a degree of risk which could be moderated by the creation of a balanced portfolio. Even the safest of alternative investments, such as shares in breweries or the bonds issued by foreign railways or stable governments, could prove unreliable. All this was captured in the fiction of the age which explains why the criticism of investors, and their investments, made so little impact. Contemporaries could sympathise with the difficult decisions that investors had to make and understand the temptations that led some to buy shares in the hope of great profits. Difficult decisions had to be taken because the certainties of the past no longer existed while some of the gambles did pay off.

The world of investment and investors was then changed radically by the First World War, but this does not come across in the few novels published in the early years of the conflict that dealt with the subject. Edgar Wallace's novel, *The Melody of Death*, though published in 1915, did not suggest that the First World War had resulted in much change in the behaviour of investors and the nature of the investments they made. There continued to be those who were frittering away their money "on every

---

[123] E. Wallace, *The Admirable Carfew* (London: Ward Lock and Co., 1914) pp. 23–25, 30, 54–55, 62–65, 70, 77, 90–91, 134, 160–169, 182–190.

[124] M. de Vere Stacpoole, *London 1913: A Novel* (London: 1914) pp. 3–6, 11, 65, 71, 79, 85–86, 103, 173, 196, 271, 314, 342, 344–356.

hair-brained scheme which the needy adventurers of finance brought to him" or speculating successfully in Canadian Pacific stock and American rails.[125] However, George Birmingham's book, *Gossamer*, which was also published in 1915, did begin to capture the changes that the war brought, though not their magnitude and duration. "The declaration of war will not simply mean the ruin of a few speculators here and there."[126] By 1916, the consequences were becoming more evident as in H.G. Wells's *Mr. Britling Sees It*. Mr Britling and his wife had accumulated a portfolio of securities worth over £25,000 which was "shrewdly and geographically distributed." With the outbreak of war, some were sold at loss and others collapsed in value as they stopped paying interest and dividends. They were left with a War Loan and securities, facing further "possibilities of shrinkage of capital and income."[127] While investors in general did badly as the war progressed, some reaped huge profits, such as John Blake, a successful shipowner, in Rider Haggard's 1918 novel, *Love Eternal*.[128]

Bridging the First World War were Galsworthy's *Forsyte Saga* novels. The first volume, *The Man of Property*, was published in 1906 and the rest then appeared from 1920 until 1933. They provide a retrospective view of investors and investment over that period. What emerges is how central investment was to the Forsytes before the First World War, but then fades in significance. In the 1906 novel, the various members of the family are virtually defined by their attitude towards investment. Jolyon Forsyte was a tea merchant and had shares in joint-stock companies. James was a solicitor and also had shares in joint-stock companies. Swithin was an estate and land agent, and placed his money in property. Roger made a living out of owning house property. Nicholas also owned house property but also invested in the shares of mining and railway companies. In the 1930 volume, *On Forsyte 'Change*, Galsworthy refers to Nicholas Forsyte as "the cleverest man in London" when it came to investments in utilities, tramways, canals and railways. "As a judge of an investment he was

---

[125] E. Wallace, *The Melody of Death* (London: Allied Newspapers Ltd, 1915) pp. 41–42, 48–49, 58, 63, 72–75, 78–79, 91, 98, 122, 127, 144, 155, 187.

[126] G.A. Birmingham, *Gossamer* (London: 1915) pp. 9–10, 14, 20–22, 27, 30, 35, 45, 54, 99, 103, 107, 114, 138, 164–165, 198–199, 201, 220–221.

[127] H.G. Wells, *Mr. Britling Sees It Through* (London: Cassell and Company, 1916) pp. 16–17, 28, 131, 176, 190, 208, 267, 341.

[128] H. Rider Haggard, *Love Eternal* (London: Cassell and Company, 1918) pp. 2–3, 7, 15, 19–21, 176, 202–203, 210.

perhaps unique, so much so that his five brothers felt it almost a relief when one of his investments went wrong." Finally, Timothy was a publisher and confined his investments to consols. "By this act he had at once assumed an isolated position, no other Forsyte being content with less than 4 per cent for his money." None of them succumbed to speculation. The person who did speculate in shares was Montague Dartie, who married James Forsyte's daughter, and he suffered losses as a result. The second volume in the Forsyte Saga, In *Chancery*, appeared in 1920, and suggests how successful their investments had turned out to be before the war. "They've turned 30,000 pounds into a cool million between them in the course of their long lives." In Book 3, *To Let*, which came out in 1921, and was set after the First World War, that success appears to continue as a result of the diversified nature of their portfolios. Though none of the Forsytes considered land a sound investment, they were attracted to it in the 1920s because, "after all was said and done there was something real about land, it didn't shift." Soames Forsyte, in particular, is praised for practicing sound investment. "He had always been so safe." In Book 6, *Swan Song*, which came out in 1928, it was said of Soames Forsyte that there was "no better judge of an investment, except his uncle Nicholas." By then, tax had become a serious issue for investors, but there was still no thought given to the risks posed to fixed-interest securities by inflation. What Galsworthy presents is a picture of a highly successful investing elite who spread their interests across the world and into different enterprises, all of which generated substantial profits for them, and this was the case both before the First World War and into the 1920s and 1930s.[129]

Other novelists of the immediate post-war era and into the 1920s also suggest continuity for the perception of investors and investments. Speculation remained a feature, for example, as in the detective stories of

---

[129] J. Galsworthy, *The Forsyte Saga:* [book 1] *The Man of Property* (London: William Heinemann Ltd., 1906) Forsyte Family Tree, pp. 13, 15, 20, 29–31, 36, 55, 63, 67, 86, 145–146, 175, 178, 186, 217, 225, 238, 289, 313, 316; [book 2] *In Chancery* (1920) pp. 442, 447, 474, 512, 525, 544, 569, 601, 646, 687, 721; [book 3] *To Let* (1921) pp. 795, 953–955, 1008–1010, 1044, 1066, 1080, 1096, 1101; [book 4] *A Modern Comedy: The White Monkey* (1924) pp. 45–47, 50–51, 100, 263, 284–285; [book 5] *The Silver Spoon* (1928) p. 661; [book 6] Swan Song (1928) pp. 752, 880, 913, 921, 992, 1068, 1071; [book 7] *End of the Chapter: Maid in Waiting* (1931) pp. 77–78, 289; [book 8] *Flowering Wilderness* (1932) pp. 629–630; [book 9] *Over the River* (1933) pp. 803, 806, 873, 941; *On Forsyte 'Change* (1930) pp. 71–72, 82, 91, 166–168, 259, 277.

J.S. Fletcher.[130] Edgar Wallace's 1921 novel, *Bones in London*, contained a series of stories about Augustus Tibbetts, known as Bones, whose speculations proved profitable but more though luck than judgement. These ranged widely from shipping and the foreign exchange market to companies engaged in manufacturing and producing oil. He also dabbled in companies making films, publishing a newspaper, selling shoes, running a detective agency and owning theatres, though he was convinced that "all new companies were founded on frauds and floated by criminals." These tales were little different from those circulating before the war.[131] The same was true of William Le Queux's 1922 novel, *The Stretton Street Affair*, with the stock market being seen as a way to both lose money and to make it because of the way shares rose and fell in price.[132] Connington's 1923 novel, *Nordenholt's Million*, also featured an investor who made himself wealthy through speculation in wheat and cotton as well as industrial and railway stocks.[133] Even the objects of speculation were the same as those in evidence before the war with Agatha Christie featuring the Burma Mines Ltd in her 1924 collection of stories in *Poirot Investigates*.[134] In 1925, Hilaire Belloc also returned to the theme of fortunate speculations in his novel, *Mr Petre*.[135] What this suggests is that the public continued to regard investment and investors in much the same way in the 1920s as they had before the war. One change was the use of the foreign exchange market as a means through which a speculator could become rich very quickly, as C.S. Forester did in his 1926 novel, *Payment Deferred*.[136] In Henry Wade's *The Verdict of You All*, which also appeared in 1926, there were references to the consequences of the war, with

---

[130] J.S. Fletcher, 'The Tobacco Box', in J.S. Fletcher (ed.), *Paul Campenhage, Specialist in Criminology* (London: Ward, Lock & Co., 1918) p. 132; J.S. Fletcher, 'The Magician of Cannon Street', in J.S. Fletcher (ed.), *Paul Campenhage*, pp. 290–293; J.S. Fletcher, *The Herapath Property* (London: 1920) pp. 10, 20, 246–253, 318.

[131] E. Wallace, *Bones in London* (London: Ward, Lock & Co., 1921) pp. 7–8, 11–13, 17, 66, 70, 83, 86, 103, 119, 128–130, 191, 225–229, 233, 244–245.

[132] W. Le Queux, *The Stretton Street Affair* (London: 1922) pp. 18, 23, 267, 283, 289–290, 319–320.

[133] J.J. Connington, *Nordenholt's Million* (London: 1923) pp. 79–81.

[134] A. Christie, *Poirot Investigates* (London: Bodley Head, 1924) 'The Lost Mine'.

[135] H. Belloc, *Mr. Petre: A Novel* (London: Arrowsmith, 1925) pp. 41, 48, 51, 59, 79–82, 104–106, 148, 159–161, 218–219, 257, 264–265, 271.

[136] C.S. Forester, *Payment Deferred* (London: The Bodley Head, 1926; reprinted London: Penguin, 2011) pp. 43–47, 62–68, 82.

Sir John Smethurst experiencing losses as a result of Russia defaulting on its debts and the collapse in the value of the German mark. However, the main story was of the evils of speculation with it driving one person to murder and another to suicide.[137] One change that had taken place was that investment in the National Debt had become an attractive option in the 1920s, according to Kitchin's 1929 novel, *Death of My Aunt*. Malcolm Warren's aunt had invested £500,000 in gilt-edged stocks which "had increased by about twenty per cent." In contrast, corporate shares were difficult to sell and fell in value.[138]

Speculation continued to offer the possibility of both gains and losses. The latter appeared in Edgar Wallace's 1928 novel, *The Twister*, while the *Red Aces*, in 1929 featured "an inveterate speculator" who "'had made considerable monies from his operations on the Stock Exchange.'"[139] In Vernon Loder's 1929 novel, *Whose Hand*, investors had been persuaded to buy shares in an experimental chemical company on the promise of dividends of 50 per cent per annum, which were never to be realised, while his 1931 novel, *Red Stain*, referenced losses on the Stock Exchange.[140] All this was standard fare for pre-1914 novels, while the 1930 poem, *About John*, by Hilaire Belloc, was suggestive of the diversified portfolio that any experienced investor would have constructed before the First World War, apart from the omission of securities from the USA. The portfolio had "a lot of stocks and shares/and half a street in Buenos Aires/a bank in Rio, and a line/of Steamers to the Argentine,/and options more than I can tell,/and bits of Canada as well./He even had a mortgage on/the house inhabited by John."[141] It was not until the aftermath of the collapse of the speculative boom in Britain and the Wall Street Crash in USA, which both took place in 1929, that a changed sentiment towards investors and investment appears to have begun, judging from two novels by Edgar Wallace, which appeared in 1932, the year of his death. In *The Guv'nor*, the oil shares that were a focus of speculation turned out to be worthless, while in *Mr J.G. Reeder Returns*, John Lane

---

[137]H. Wade, *The Verdict of You All* (London: 1926) pp. 7–32, 46–48, 89, 104–105, 128–129, 131–133, 168–170.

[138]C.H.B. Kitchin, *Death of My Aunt* (London: Hogarth Press, 1929) pp. 10–16, 33, 247.

[139]E. Wallace, *The Twister* (London: 1928) p. 31; E. Wallace, *Red Aces* (London: 1929) pp. 55, 77, 89, 160.

[140]Loder, *Whose Hand?* ch. 1, 3, 4, 14, 15; V. Loder, *Red Stain* (London: 1931), ch. x.

[141]H. Belloc, *New Cautionary Tales* (London: Duckworth, 1930) pp. 119–126.

Leopard was "a man who had no faith in the stability of stock markets" and so he had converted his money into gold which he kept in a vault in Sevenways Castle in Kent.[142]

In the book by Donald Stuart, *The Man Outside*, which was published in 1934, the portfolio of William Grant comprised investments that "were of the soundest." What this meant was that he "had property everywhere, a block of flats here; a row of shops there. Whole streets of houses in prosperous suburbs; a large interest in a Welsh coal mine and innumerable holdings in substantial companies."[143] This preference for safe domestic securities was evident in another 1934 novel, *The Bank Manager* by E. Phillips Oppenheim. Sir Julian Bott, who managed the Windsor Trust, complained that investors had become too risk averse, focusing on immediate returns and unwilling to finance long-term projects such as mining, oil wells or forestry in far-off countries.[144] Nevertheless, there continued to be investors willing to take such gambles, according to John Creasey's 1935 novel, *First Came a Murder*. One was Hugh Carruthers who "had gambled, under assumed names, through various brokers, until he lost pretty well a quarter of a million." One of his investments was shares in a tin mining company, the Marritaband Development Company. "The unfortunates who had bought shares had lost everything they had invested."[145]

In contrast, in Macdonell's 1936 novel, *Lords and Masters*, James Hanson gave his children preference shares and government bonds when they came of age so they could be financially independent.[146] With no hint of inflation, fixed-interest securities were the safe option for investors. Nevertheless, there remained investors always ready to take risks in exchange for higher returns. In Neville Shute's 1938 novel, *Ruined City*, it was a vicar, Canon Ward-Stephenson, who had bought shares in an oil tanker company and a bankrupt shipbuilding company, and then complained about the outcome.[147] At that time, according to Kitchin, in the *Death of his Uncle*, published in 1939, a War Loan was the safe option

---

[142]E. Wallace, *The Guv'nor* (London: Hodder and Stoughton, 1932) pp. 134–135, 149; E. Wallace, *Mr J.G. Reeder Returns* (London: 1932) pp. 1–3, 12–15, 24, 29–33, 40, 76–77.

[143]D. Stuart, *The Man Outside* (London: 1934) pp. 1, 4–5, 216–217, 255.

[144]E. Phillips Oppenheim, *The Bank Manager* (London: Hodder and Stoughton, 1934) pp. 7, 32, 39, 65, 70–75, 137, 159, 165, 219–222, 244–247, 297, 314, 317, 303.

[145]J. Creasey, *First Came a Murder* (London: 1935) ch. 1, 2, 4, 12, 13, 19, 20, 23, 24.

[146]A.G. Macdonell, *Lords and Masters* (London: 1936) p. 42.

[147]N. Shute, *Ruined City* (London: Heinemann, 1938) pp. 213–219, 228–229, 234–235.

while mining shares remained the choice of gamblers like Mrs Molyneux-Brown, who "was fond of a flutter."[148]

The impression generated by the novels written between the wars was that nothing much changed until the 1930s in terms of the public's attitude to investors and investment. The momentous events that took place between 1929 and 1939 shattered investor confidence in a way that neither the First World War nor the global pandemic had done. In the aftermath of the Wall Street Crash and Britain's forced departure from the Gold Standard in 1931, amidst a developing global financial crisis, there was a collapse in trust among investors. Safety and security during a world depression became the mantra for British investors, not a balancing of risk and return in a globally diversified portfolio and a willingness to take risks in overseas mines or new technology. War Loan, the stocks and bonds of major British companies, and domestic property became the assets of choice. The silence on investment and investors in the novels of the 1930s indicates that it was no longer a topic worth consideration. What this silence left was the indelible impression of past criticisms, when the activities of individual investors were seen as little better than gambling resulting in a wasteful investment at a time of national need.

The outbreak of the Second World War brought government controls and heavy taxes, with investment becoming a state-directed affair in which individual investors were marginalised. Investment and investors hardly rated a mention in the novels of the 1940s, as the public had far greater subjects to contend with. As controls and taxation continued into the post-war years, there was no return to the environment of the past in which individual investors had flourished and investment decisions were left to the free play of the market. Even Henry Wade's 1954 novel, *Gold was our Grave*, which did little more than replicate his inter-war work, acknowledges the impact made by taxation. Though some continued to speculate, investors mainly concentrated their holdings on "equities — and very sound ones. Breweries, textiles, rubber, mines, oil, engineering ... a smattering of investment trusts."[149] This focus on sound investments, and the need to construct a tax-efficient portfolio, was one that emerged in the 1950s as in L.P. Hartley's *A Perfect Woman*, which was published in 1955. Harold was an accountant who specialised in giving tax advice

---

[148] C.H.B. Kitchin, *Death of His Uncle* (London: Constable & Co., 1939) pp. 33, 83, 89, 108, 136–139, 145–146.
[149] H. Wade, *Gold Was Our Grave* (London: Constable and Co., 1954) pp. 155, 186, 205.

to investors. One was Lord Haverfordwest, who complained about "the miserable pittance that a robber Government still allows us to call our own."[150] This concern with the effects of taxation on investment and investors also came out in Clark Smith's 1956 novel, *The Deadly Reaper*.[151]

Apart from references to the effects of taxation, the fiction of the post-war years largely ignores investment and investors. One exception was John Boland's 1961 novel, *The Golden Fleece*, which featured a group of bank employees who speculated in shares. The staff of the Kensington branch of the London Counties Bank formed a syndicate to buy shares in a defunct African gold mine, the M'Gonii Mining Company, spread rumours that uranium had been discovered and then sold out at a large profit. This they succeeded in doing. Speculation on the Stock Exchange was seen as getting "money the easy way."[152] Another novel that took up the theme of stock exchange speculation was Jeffrey Archer's *Not a Penny More, Not a Penny Less*, which appeared in 1976. This also involved spreading false rumours and selling out at a profit.[153] The rarity of novels in the 1960s and 1970s taking up the theme of investment and investors suggests that the subject no longer interested the British public. Heavy taxation and the suppression of speculation through regulation removed the conditions which had supported the speculative manias of the past, reducing the process to the routine work of investment professionals or internalising it within the decision-making found within government departments, public authorities, public corporations and large businesses.

In the series of novels written between 1976 and 1993 by David Williams, and featuring the banker Mark Treasure, individual investors make only a rare appearance. In *Treasure Preserved*, which came out in 1983, it was mentioned that Lady Brasset "liked to play the stock market … made thousands, tens of thousands.… She was into commodities." What she did was referred to as "gambling."[154] There were a few more references to investors in the series of novels by John Malcolm, between

---

[150] Hartley, *A Perfect Woman*, pp. 14, 33–34, 193.

[151] Smith, *The Deadly Reaper*, pp. 198–199.

[152] J. Boland, *The Golden Fleece: A Slightly Criminous Novel* (Crowborough: Forrest House Books, 1961) pp. 8–9, 12–14, 20–21, 52, 57–60, 85, 153–161.

[153] J. Archer, *Not a Penny More, Not a Penny Less* (London: Jonathan Cape, 1976) pp. 50–51, 78–79, 254.

[154] D. Williams, *Treasure Preserved* (London: Collins, 1983) p. 156.

1984 and 2005, which featured another banker, Tim Simpson. What Tim Simpson ran was an art investment fund that operated as a tax-efficient vehicle for wealthy investors. In the 1984 book *A Back Room in Somers Town*, he helped provide "personal investment advice for those who have a problem of coping with too much money." In another 1984 book, *The Godwin Sideboard*, it was explained that the art investment fund was designed "to keep the taxman's hands off" the savings of their wealthy clientele. This aversion to paying tax was emphasised again in the 1986 novel, *Whistler in the Dark*, leading to "ways of thwarting the Inland Revenue." Being tax efficient also meant taking risks despite a preference for "bricks and mortar, blue chips and government stocks," as expressed by the accountant, Geoffrey Price, in the 1991 novel in the series, *Sheep, Goats and Soap*.[155] The overriding imperative for the investor of avoiding tax was also evident in Peter Robinson's novel, *Dry Bones that Dream*, which came out in 1995. Rothwell was "a damn good accountant. He saved me a lot of money from the Inland Revenue — all above board."[156] Tax was hardly of consequence for the late Victorian investor whereas 100 years later it was an essential consideration. By then, exotic investments that were also high risk, such as works of art, were only acceptable because of the tax advantages.

Conclusion

Investment and investors captured the public imagination during the nineteenth century, beginning in the 1820s, developed further during the Railway Mania of the 1840s, and then became a popular topic of conversation until the First World War. All this can be deduced from the numerous novels that dealt with the subject and the way it was treated. Investment and investors remained in the public eye between the wars, though the level of interest dropped, being squeezed out by economic, political and social instability, sandwiched between the aftermath of one world war and the beginning of another, and interrupted by the Wall Street Crash. Investment and investors then virtually disappeared from public

---

[155]Malcolm, *A Back Room in Somers Town*, pp. 11, 16, 21–25; Malcolm, *The Godwin Sideboard*, pp. 10–11; Malcolm, *Whistler in the Dark*, p. 12; Malcolm, *Sheep, Goats and Soap*, p. 22.
[156]Robinson, *Dry Bones that Dream*, pp. 33, 139.

debate after the Second World War, judging from their rare appearance in post-war novels. What this meant was that there was a real depth to the public understanding of investment and investors in the 50 years before the First World War, which was absent both before and after. Prior to the Railway Mania and then after the First World War, the popular understanding of investment and investors was often reduced to the image of the speculator and the stock exchange, with little appreciation of the magnitude and complexity of the process that was taking place. Under these circumstances, there was a preference for the central direction of the state or the professional guidance that came from a bank. Either of these was considered better than leaving the results to the preferences of individual investors lacking knowledge and experience, and easily swayed by the prospects of incalculable gain. Supporting such conclusions were the views expressed by contemporaries, especially during speculative booms and busts and subsequent corporate failures, which were then embedded in the work of novelists. Those novels then influenced the views of others both at the time and later, especially those whose work long remained in print. The views found in these novels often depicted the investor as a reckless gambler who should not be trusted with the disposal of their own money, let alone the savings of the nation. Such a conclusion resonated with those pressing for greater state intervention in order to reverse the flow of funds abroad or to direct finance to projects deemed more socially or economically deserving.

However, that judgement, based on a reading of contemporary views on investment and investors, misrepresents those held in the 50 years before the First World War. There were numerous examples of negative imagery, especially as speculation was equated with gambling. What was different about the period between the Railway Mania of the 1840s and the First World War was that the public also had a positive image of investors and their achievements as it was being conducted at the time. This even included the results of speculation. What those at that time had visible to them was a tangible product of the results of investment carried out by individuals unguided by either the state or the banks. That was in the shape of the railway system. The railway symbolised economic progress and delivered a greatly superior transport system not only for Britain but also the world. Under the circumstances, it was not possible to regard speculation as universally evil and totally wasteful. That attitude then changed from the First World War onwards. During the First World War, the government sequestered the US$ holdings of British investors, so as to finance purchases in the USA, as well as pressurising the London Stock Exchange not to provide a market for certain securities. At the same time, the London Stock Exchange became much more responsive to government influence as well as modifying the way its markets operated so as to make speculation much more difficult to conduct.[157]

These created precedents for the post-war world as they provided evidence of how certain practices could be outlawed, suppressed or curtailed through governmental and institutional intervention.[158] The experienced financial journalist, Hartley Withers, had noted as early as 1916 that attitudes towards investor protection were changing.[159] Driving the change was the fact that the war had made Britain a nation of investors as the public at large subscribed to the successive issues of war loan, believing it was their patriotic duty to do so. Writing in 1918, Comyns Carr, an expert on company law, was in no doubt that the result was "a remarkably widespread diffusion of money, and a wonderful growth in the habit of investment, among classes of the population to whom both are a novelty. It is computed that no less than 13,000,000 people are directly interested in various forms of Government war securities. After the war it is expected that a large number of people who never were investors before will be willing to entrust their savings to commercial companies, but will not be very well equipped to select those which are worthy of their confidence. Simultaneously, there will be a large crop of new schemes appealing for public support, mostly bona fide, but offering unique opportunity to the fraudulent and over-sanguine."[160] His warning was ignored, but events were to prove him right. Many of these new investors were soon drawn towards joint-stock company shares between the wars. By the mid-1930s, a company such as ICI had a total of 124,690 shareholders while Imperial Tobacco had 94,690, while numerous investors had been drawn into smaller and more speculative concerns. As many of these showed substantial losses after the Wall Street Crash, pressure grew for a fundamental reform of investor protection, either through legislation or intervention by the Stock Exchange. This was to come after the Second World

---

[157] See Michie, *Stock Exchange*, ch. 4.
[158] See H.B. Samuel, *Shareholder's Money: An Analysis of Certain Defects in Company Legislation with Proposals for Their Reform* (London: 1933) pp. 4–5, 9, 14, 67, 111, 329.
[159] H. Withers, *International Finance* (London: 1916) pp. 169–170.
[160] Report of the Company Law Amendment Committee (London: 1918) Reservation by Mr A.S. Comyns Carr, pp. 13–14.

War.[161] Thus, it was a fundamental change in the size and composition of the investing public, as a result of the First World War, that changed the public's attitude towards investors, creating the belief that they were innocent victims of financial insiders. Combined with a sudden transformation in the balance between laissez faire and state intervention, that also took place as a result of the war, the result was to modify the past practice of both governments and financial institutions and take steps to protect the investor from the consequences of their own actions. The maxim *caveat emptor* gradually ceased to operate when applied to investors, with consequences for the opportunity for investors to take financial risks. This had consequences for the British economy after the Second World War.[162]

---

[161] Michie, *Stock Exchange*, pp. 174–177.

[162] G. Robb, *White-Collar Crime in Modern England: Financial Fraud and Business Morality, 1845–1929* (Cambridge: 1992) pp. 156–157.

Chapter 5

Banks and Bankers: Power and Trust

Introduction

In the aftermath of the financial crisis of 2007/2008, the reputation of British bankers experienced a sudden reversal. Prior to the crisis, British bankers had been among the most respected individuals in Britain, custodians of the nation's savings, responsible for the functioning of the payments system and relied upon to provide credit and capital for all. They were trusted individuals, admired for their expertise in a globally competitive business and envied because of the wealth that success brought. That was all very different from their reputation after the financial crisis. In 2012, Patrick Jenkins observed that, in the eyes of many, bankers "epitomise the worst aspects of capitalism, breaching laws willy-nilly and exploiting profit opportunities with no moral compass."[1] Caroline Binham and Marin Arnold reflected in 2015 that "Since the financial crisis, Britain's bankers have been vilified, fired and mocked."[2] The impression these comments suggest is that stretching as far back as it was possible to go, British banks and bankers were numbered among the most trusted institutions and individuals within British society. Such an impression is wrong. Banks and bankers were always regarded with a degree of suspicion by the British public, being long associated with moneylending, and

---

[1] P. Jenkins, *Financial Times*, 11th December 2012.
[2] C. Binham and M. Arnold, 'Season of Goodwill to Bankers Began Soon After Tory Victory', *Financial Times*, 23rd December 2015.

the practice of usury, which was condemned in Christian society.[3] That suspicion did not disappear in Britain during the nineteenth and twentieth centuries but it was greatly moderated as banks gained a reputation for efficiency and stability.[4] Nevertheless, the intangible nature of banking, involving the use and manipulation of money, meant that the business of banks and bankers was never fully appreciated.[5] The close relationship between bankers and money also meant that those leading the principal banks were seen as a small, coherent and wealthy group, not only able to determine the direction of the economy through their control of finance but also influence government and thus the political and social life of the country. The results were considered detrimental by many.[6] Writing in 1984, Michael Moran suggested that British banking was "dominated by an elite selected by birth and united by kinship, common education and economic interests."[7] The historian, Neil Ferguson, picked out the banker, Nathan Rothschild, as one of the most powerful figures of the nineteenth century, with another banker, Siegmund Warburg, playing a similar role in the twentieth century.[8]

The problem with such generalisations is that the banking sector was both large and diverse and in a continuous state of flux throughout the nineteenth and twentieth centuries. Old banks disappeared, new ones were formed, and a process of mergers and disposals took place. There were

---

[3]T. Mortimer, *Every Man His Own Broker* (London: 1761); cf The Usury Act of 1660.

[4]P. Johnson, 'Civilizing Mammon: Laws, Morals and the City in Nineteenth Century England', in Burke, Harrison and Slack, *Civil Histories*, pp. 302–303, 319.

[5]A. Simmons, 'The Early Twentieth Century: Uniformity, Drudgery and Economics', in A. Pollard (ed.), *The Representation of Business in English Literature* (London: IEA, 2000) p. 99.

[6]A few examples include Haxey, *Tory MP*; V. Sandelson, 'The Confidence Trick: Sir Norman Tullis and Partners', in H. Thomas (ed.), *The Establishment* (London: 1959); R. Spiegelberg, *Power Without Accountability* (London: 1973); M. Lisle-Williams, 'Beyond the Market: The Survival of Family Capitalism in English Merchant Banks', *British Journal of Sociology*, 35 (1984); M. Lisle-Williams, 'Merchant Banking Dynasties in the English Class Structure: Ownership, Solidarity and Kinship in the City of London, 1850–1960', *British Journal of Sociology*, 35 (1984).

[7]M. Moran, *The Politics of Banking: The Strange Case of Competition and Credit Control* (London: 1984) p. 27.

[8]N. Ferguson, *World's Banker. The History of the House of Rothschild* (London: 1998); N. Ferguson, *High Financier: The Lives and Time of Siegmund Warburg* (London: Penguin, 2010).

also fluid boundaries between different types of banks and between banks and non-banks. Reflecting this situation was the inability to define a bank in English law.[9] Collectively, banks were the most important businesses within the financial system. Banks collected savings from the many and lent to the few, handled the investments of the wealthy, provided credit for trade, financed large and small businesses, supplied mortgages for the purchase of houses, arranged corporate loans, issued stocks and bonds, and traded securities and derivatives. There were banks that provided the full range of financial services while others took a specialist approach. Some banks operated from a single office while others had multiple branches either in one country or throughout the world. Ownership of banks included individuals, partnerships, public companies, governments and mutual organisations. All banks had, as a priority, the need to preserve the trust of those who used them as they stood between lenders on the one hand and borrowers on the other. This made banks vulnerable to both solvency and liquidity risks. A solvency crisis occurred when a bank made a loan which was not repaid, and so was unable to repay those to whom it owed money. A bank was also exposed to a liquidity risk. A bank lent money it had borrowed from others, such as those who made deposits or held its notes, promising that they would be repaid on demand or on a specified date. A bank was a business that borrowed short and lent long, paying less for the former than it received from the latter. This placed a bank at the mercy of rumours which could encourage mass redemptions by those to whom it owed money.

Acquiring a Reputation

Over the course of the nineteenth century, British banks and bankers appeared to have discovered the secrets that lay behind successful banking. One example was in retail banking where the numerous individual banks were replaced by a few, organised as companies, each operating a

---

[9]See Memorandum by the Committee of London Clearing Bankers to the Company Law Amendment Committee, *Journal of the Institute of Bankers*, 65 (1944); G. Blunden, 'The Supervision of the UK Banking System', *Journal of the Institute of Bankers*, 96 (1975). For an authoritative discussion of what defines a bank and an attempt to count the number of UK banks, see the chapter by I. Bond in M. Hollow, F. Akinbami and R. Michie (eds), *Critical Perspectives on the Evolution of American and British Banking* (Cheltenham: Edward Elgar, 2015).

large network of branches from a central head office. Aided by the rapid communications and transport provided by the telegraph and railway, a retail bank could constantly monitor the balance between assets and liabilities, and so maximise returns and minimise risks. In addition, a large bank could employ, train and supervise its staff in such a way that their behaviour could be monitored and controlled, so avoiding both excessive caution and excessive risk taking, as well as eliminate decisions based on sentiment, familiarity and connections rather than evaluation and calculation. It was the emergence of these large retail banks that established British banking's reputation for conservative behaviour as they adopted a cautious approach when making loans. That reputation for caution was also applied to the London-based merchant banks. Acting through networks of contacts, they provided the credit that underpinned global trade and issued stocks and bonds on behalf of governments and companies from around the world. With reputations to protect in order to command the trust of those with whom they did business, these banks were very careful in selecting the business that they engaged in, gaining them a very conservative reputation. Finally, the Bank of England also acquired a reputation in the nineteenth century for stability unmatched by any other in the world, because of its ultra-conservative approach to lending.

What that generalisation ignored, based as it was on a few retail and merchant banks, was the constant challenge posed by the shadow banking sector. Also ignored were the enormous differences that existed between the established banks, and the degree of competition that existed. At the beginning of the twentieth century, for example, among the large retail banks, the Union Bank of London was run by a German-born Jewish merchant banker, Felix Schuster, whose family bank had been absorbed into it. In contrast, the Midland Bank was managed by the British-born Methodist, Edward Holden, who had begun as a clerk and trained as an accountant. A further contrast could be made with Barclays Bank which long retained the Quaker ethos that had motivated the individual banks that had amalgamated for mutual protection. Furthermore, there were enormous differences in terms of structure, organisation and the way they conducted their business.[10] A similar problem existed when generalising about the merchant banks. There was a constant stream of entries and exits

---

[10]See J.A.S. Leighton-Boyce, *Smiths the Bankers, 1658–1958* (London: 1958); Ackrill and Hannah, *Barclays: The Business of Banking*; R.S. Sayers, *Lloyds Bank in the History of English Banking* (Oxford: Oxford University Press, 1957); W.E. Crick and J.E. Wadsworth,

among Britain's merchant banking community before the First World War, as well as fluctuating fortunes among those who stuck the course. While the Kleinworts, Schroders and Morgans were rising, the Barings, Rothschilds and Raphaels were in decline.[11]

Even greater differences existed between the established retail and merchant banks, on the one hand, and their numerous competitors from the shadow banking sector, on the other hand. There were always new types of financial enterprises appearing, ready to exploit emerging opportunities, meet new challenges or experiment with novel ways of conducting banking. In the 1860s, for example, there were a spate of universal banks formed in Britain that combined retail and investment banking using short-term deposits to finance long-term investment, relying on the liquidity of stocks and bonds as a way of covering the risks. Most of these failed as they were vulnerable to both liquidity and solvency crises.[12] That did not prevent others being tempted to repeat the exercise, time and again, of using short-term funds to finance long-term investment, because of the potential profits to be made. One example was the numerous land and mortgage companies that borrowed short term in Britain and lent long term abroad, with land and property as collateral. These faced difficulties whenever a liquidity crisis occurred as they could not realise their assets sufficiently quickly to repay those from whom they had borrowed.[13] When the full range of British banks is surveyed, it becomes clear that

---

A 100 Years of Joint-Stock Banking (London: Hodder and Stoughton, 1936); J. Clapham, *The Bank of England: A History* (Cambridge: Cambridge University Press, 1944).

[11] Mikkelsen, *The Market Practice and Techniques of London Issuing Houses*, pp. 33–36, 40–42, 56–57, 77–82, 94–96, 161, 190–196, 231–236, 246; P. Ziegler, *The Sixth Great Power: Barings 1762–1929* (London: 1988) pp. 199–200, 283–285, 302–304, 324, 345, 359, 361; R.W. Hidy, *House of Baring in American Trade and Finance, 1763–1861* (New York: Russell and Company, 1949) pp. 123, 419; J. Lepler, '"There is No Need for Anyone to Go to America": Commercial Correspondence and Nineteenth-century Globalisation', *The Rothschild Archive: Review of the Year 2007/2008*, pp. 16–19; Y. Cassis, 'The Banking Community of London, 1890–1914: A Survey', *Journal of Imperial and Commonwealth History*, 13, 109–126 (1984–1985).

[12] Cottrell, *Investment Banking in England*, pp. 176–178, 405, 443–444, 449, 463, 479–480, 491–492, 506, 510, 524–527, 849; Cottrell, 'London's First "Big Bang"'? pp. 71–73, 90; A.S.J. Baster, *The International Banks* (London: 1935) p. 40.

[13] F. Larkworthy, *Ninety-One Years* (London: Mills and Boon, 1924) [The memoirs were edited for publication by Harold Begbie] pp. 282, 306–309, 319–340, 354, 402–407. See Magee and Thompson, *Empire and Globalisation*, p. 202.

there was no stereotypical British bank or banker but an enormous depth and diversity that waxed and waned over time.[14] In 1911, an estimated 242,446 worked in financial services in Britain and that doubled to 435,121 in 1951 and doubled again by 1971, when it reached 952,170. These included not only the large retail banks and

[14]Magee and Thompson, *Empire and Globalisation*, pp. 200–202; Y. Cassis, 'Bankers in English Society in the Late Nineteenth Century', *Economic History Review*, 38, 314, 329 (1985); Wainwright, *Henderson: A History of the Life of Alexander Henderson, First Lord Faringdon, and of Henderson Administration*, pp. 14, 15, 18, 23, 59, 72, 92, 95; S.D. Chapman, *Raphael Bicentenary, 1987* (London: 1987) pp. 19–31, 36, 43; D. Wainwright, *Government Broker: The Story of an Office and of Mullens & Co.* (East Molesey: 1990) pp. 30, 55, 58; W.J. Reader, *A House in the City: A Study of the City and of the Stock Exchange Based on the Records of Foster and Braithwaite, 1825–1975* (London: 1979) pp. 10, 27, 37–39, 89, 91, 98, 106–107, 117, 125–128, 134, 148–153; The Editors of Institutional Investment, *The Way It Was: An Oral History of Finance, 1967–1987* (New York: William Morrow & Co., 1988) p. 493, 496, 502; S. Chapman, 'British-Based Investment Groups Before 1914', *Economic History Review*, 38, 238–239 (1985); A.C. Drury, *Finance Houses: Their Development and Role in the Modern Financial Sector* (London: 1982) pp. 18–21, 32, 41–42, 76, 89, 94–109; J. Armstrong, 'Hooley and the Bovril Company', *Business History*, 28, 18–20 (1986); R.P.T. Davenport-Hines and J.J. van Helten, 'Edgar Vincent, Viscount D'Abernon, and the Eastern Investment Company in London, Constantinople and Johannesburg', *Business History*, 28, 35 (1986); Turrell and van Helten, 'The Rothschilds', pp. 182–191; S. Diaper, 'Merchant Banking in the Inter-War Period: The Case of Kleinwort, Sons and Company', *Business History*, 28, 55–56, 59–60, 73–74 (1986); I.F. Jones, *The Rise of a Merchant Bank: A Short History of Guinness Mahon* (Dublin: 1974) pp. 22, 31–32, 36–38; J. Ayer, *A Century of Finance, 1804–1904: The London House of Rothschild* (London: 1905): list of loans; A. Ellis, *Heir to Adventure: The Story of Brown, Shipley and Company, Merchant Bankers, 1810–1960* (London: 1960) pp. 95, 111, 121, 141; A.J. Murray, *Home from the Hill: A Biography of Frederick Huth, Napoleon of the City* (London: 1970) p. 166; Lisle-Williams, '"Beyond the Market"', 35, 249–257 (1984); Lisle-Williams, 'Merchant Banking Dynasties', 35, 340–347 (1984); S.D. Chapman, 'Aristocracy and Meritocracy in Merchant Banking', *British Journal of Sociology*, 37, 181–183, 194 (1986); J. Harris and P. Thane, 'British and European Bankers, 1880–1914: An Aristocratic Bourgeoisie?' in P. Thane, G. Crossick and R. Floud (eds), *The Power of the Past* (Cambridge: 1984) p. 228; Adler, *British Investment in American Railway*, p. 149; C.A. Jones, *International Business in the Nineteenth Century: The Rise and Fall of a Cosmopolitan Bourgeoisie* (Brighton: 1987) pp. 68, 130, 140; 155–157, 160–162; H. Raymond, *B.I. Barnato: A Memoir* (London: 1897) pp. 33–34; Y. Cassis, *City Bankers, 1890–1914* (Cambridge: Cambridge University Press, 1994) pp. 35–37, 57–59.

leading merchant banks, that the public regarded as synonymous with banking, but also numerous building societies, mortgage companies, asset managers, finance houses, savings banks and investment banks.[15] As a consequence, it becomes impossible to justify generalisations over a period of 200 years about the origins, race, religion, class, politics, connections or behaviour of bankers, however attractive that may be, or identify a bank that could be described as typical. Snapshots taken at different times produce different results.[16]

A Century of Change, 1825–1914

During the nineteenth century, the composition, structure and operation of the British banking system was transformed. In the first two-thirds of the century, British banking remained exposed to the frequent financial crises that took place, resulting in numerous failures which were blamed on excessive risk taking by individual bankers, if not outright fraud. The journalist, D. Morier Evans, for example, wrote a series of books in the mid-nineteenth century that emphasised the fragile nature of the British financial system, and the recurrence of crises and criminality, including many involving banks.[17] In 1856, Seton Laing observed that "Numerous cases of fraud have come before the public within the last two years — in which opulent bankers, widely-dealing merchants, and trusted men of high station have so conspicuously figured."[18] Though some of these frauds were by bankers, undermining the degree of trust they could command, many were committed against banks, as Seton Laing's own account of *"The Great City Frauds of Cole, Davidson and Gordon"* showed.

---

[15] These statistics cover banking, insurance, finance and business services. Those for 1851–1971 are taken from C.H. Lee, British Regional Employment Statistics, 1841–1971 (Cambridge: 1979). These significantly undercount service occupations, especially for the earlier years. Those for 2009 are taken from the data produced by the Office of National Statistics. For an alternative count see S. Broadberry, *Market Services and the Productivity Race, 1850–2000: British Performance in International Perspective* (Cambridge: 2006).

[16] Keynes, 'The Prospects of Money', p. 633; UK International Financial Services, The Future, p. 19.

[17] See D. Morier Evans, *The Commercial Crisis of 1847* (London: 1848), *Facts, Failures and Frauds* (London: 1859), *The History of the Commercial Crisis, 1857–1858* (London: 1859), and *Speculative Notes, and Notes on Speculations, Ideal and Real* (London: 1864).

[18] S. Laing, *The Great City Frauds of Cole, Davidson and Gordon* (London: 1856) p. 181.

Nevertheless, after studying British banking in the nineteenth century, George Robb concluded that "For most of the Victorian period, the English banking system was riddled with fraud and mismanagement. Each wave of bank failures brought new revelations of criminal conduct. The financial crises of 1857 and 1866 and the collapse of the City of Glasgow Bank in 1878 were but the high-water marks in an age of widespread commercial dishonesty. By the late nineteenth and early twentieth centuries, improvements in bank management and accountancy had reduced the level of fraud, though by no means had eliminated it." However, even on his own evidence, the peak of bank failures and bank fraud was in the first half of the nineteenth century, and then there was a dramatic decline especially after the 1860s.[19] Among the changes was the emergence of the Bank of England as the lender of last resort to the banking system.[20] It was after the Overend and Gurney crisis of 1866 that the Bank of England established its reputation as the most trusted and respected bank in the world, and the British banking system developed resilience to both crises and fraud. At the retail level, that was accomplished through the conversion of the thousand small privately owned banks into a small number of large joint-stock banks. Through diversification and geographical spread, these large banks possessed the resilience to cope with recurrent liquidity crises while experience and training reduced the likelihood of a solvency crisis as well as preventing embezzlement, whether by owners or staff. This transformation was recognised at the time. F.E. Steele wrote in 1897 that "A banking system which consisted for the most part of a large number of comparatively small and unconnected institutions, each applying its limited resources to the service of a narrow area, may have answered very satisfactorily the requirements of previous generations, but the altered commercial conditions of the present day have both demanded a re-adjustment and rendered it inevitable." The result of this readjustment was "a banking system composed of a few homogenous institutions of world-wide reputation, conducted on a

---

[19] Robb, *White-Collar Crime in Modern Britain*, pp. 9, 16, 19, 23, 31, 53–55, 59–63; I.P.H. Duffy, *Bankruptcy and Insolvency in London during the Industrial Revolution* (Oxford D.Phil 1973), pp. 235, 255; T.L. Alborn, *Conceiving Companies: Joint-Stock Politics in Victorian England* (London: 1998) p. 168.

[20] Sir F.C. Knowles, *Monetary Crisis Considered* (London: 1837) pp. 9, 53, 78–80; See J. Keyworth, 'The Old Lady of Threadneedle Street', *Bank of England Quarterly Review* (2013).

comparatively uniform system, efficiently and economically worked and rigidly inspected." This new system was "likely to prove at least as stable when the time of trial comes as the ruinous and heterogeneous mixture of banks, large and small, private and joint-stock, of good and indifferent repute, which served a previous generation, but, which, mainly as a result of the impact of amalgamation, is rapidly becoming extinct."[21] The result was a great deal of professional and national pride in the achievements of the retail banking system which continued into the years before the First World War. The 1907 crisis, which shook the US banking system to its foundations, left British banks largely undisturbed. Though British banks and other financial institutions continued to fail, the banking system remained resilient.

This stability also extended to British merchant banks, though it was shaken by the near-death experience of Barings Bank in 1890, as it had been one of the largest and most established among their number. It had got into difficulties over loans to Argentina and only the support from other British banks, coordinated by the Bank of England, saved it from collapse. Through a process of trial and error, the British banking system learnt how to cope with crises and to provide the credit and capital required by a modern and open economy without locking up funds in excessive reserves. The combination of banks that were trusted counter-parties, the facilities provided by the London money market and the role of the Bank of England as lender of last resort made the British banking system both efficient and stable without the need to look for government support, even in a crisis. It appeared that the British had discovered the

---

[21] F.E. Steele, 'Bank Amalgamations', *Journal of the Institute of Bankers*, 18, 115, 123 (1897); See J. Dick, '*Accounting, Business and Financial History*, Compared with Former Years', *Journal of the Institute of Bankers* (1892); J.B. Attfield, 'The Advantages, or Otherwise, of the Establishment of Branches by Bankers, from the Point of View (a) of the Bankers; and (b) of the General Interests of the Community', *Journal of the Institute of Bankers*, 13 (1892); J.F. Dunn, 'Banking in 1837 and in 1897 in the United Kingdom, India and the Colonies: A Comparison and a Contrast', *Journal of the Institute of Bankers*, 19 (1898). See also R.W. Barnett, 'The History of the Progress and Development of Banking in the United Kingdom from the Year 1800 to the Present Time', *Journal of the Institute of Bankers*, 1 (1880); R.W. Barnett, 'The Effect of the Development of Banking Facilities upon the Circulation of the Country', *Journal of the Institute of Bankers*, 2 (1881); R.W. Barnett, 'The Reign of Queen Victoria: A Survey of 50 Years of Progress', *Journal of the Institute of Bankers*, 6 (1887).

secrets of successful banking which other countries had still to learn, including the USA. The British banker was universally valued and many emigrated, taking their skills, experience and patterns of behaviour with them. There was even a group of British banks that provided banking services to different countries around the world.[22]

Despite the success achieved by British banking in the years between 1866 and 1914, it did generate a degree of criticism at the time. That criticism focused particularly on the centralisation of control in London where the Bank of England had its head office, the money market was located, from where most British banks were run and foreign banks had their offices. This led to complaints from British businesses, especially when their applications for loans were refused, that they no longer received the financial support that they had been used to in the past. The large banks were portrayed as huge bureaucratic organisations that fostered an overly conservative culture among their staff and ignored the needs of the manu-facturing industry in the North. Similarly, the merchant banks were seen as conducting a largely international business to the detriment of domestic industry, especially as so many were of foreign origin and retained strong connections abroad.[23] What those criticising the banks ignored was not only the constraints that banks, reliant on volatile deposits, were under but also the competitive environment in which they all operated, forcing them to explore new ways of generating profits. This included the large retail banks facing competition from savings banks and building societies and the merchant banks experiencing an influx of rivals from abroad, attracted by the prospects of operating out of London, which was the world's finan-cial centre. Restrictions in Germany, for example, drove German bankers to relocate to London from where they could serve their customers by providing them with trade credit or access to foreign stocks and bonds.

---

[22]Magee and Thompson, *Empire and Globalisation*, p. 202; E. Green, 'Export Bankers: The Migration of British Bank Personnel to the Pacific Region, 1850–1914', in O. Checkland, S. Nishimura and N. Tamaki (eds), *Pacific Banking, 1859–1959: East Meets West* (London: 1994) pp. 79, 97; M. Pohl and K. Burk, *Deutsche Bank in London, 1873–1998* (Munich: 1998) pp. 24, 41, 97, 101.

[23]R.J.S. Hoffman, *Great Britain and the German Trade Rivalry, 1875–1914* (Philadelphia: 1937) p. 75; B.L. Anderson, 'The Social Economy of Late-Victorian Clerks', in G. Crossick (ed.), *The Lower Middle Class in Britain, 1870–1914* (London: 1977) pp. 127–130; Joseph, 'Industrial Finance', pp. 6–18; M. Anson and T. Gourvish, *Leopold Joseph: A History* (London: 2002) pp. 5–7.

That included British customers. There was remarkably little evidence to suggest that British banks, either individually or collectively, were failing to provide their customers with the finance they required despite the criticisms made by some contemporaries. Other contemporaries were equally ready to contradict such claims.[24]

Coping with Crises, 1914–1945

The outbreak of the First World War caught the British banking system completely unprepared. Only prompt action by the banks themselves, the Bank of England and the Treasury averted a crisis that threatened the entire financial system with collapse. This spirit of cooperation set a precedent for the years to come.[25] The British banking system faced enormous challenges between the end of the First World War in 1918 and the end of the Second World War in 1945. The environment within which British banks operated became increasingly complicated compared to the past, whether it was in the domestic economy, overseas countries or international finance. The UK, for example, was forced to suspend participation in the gold standard between 1919 and 1925 and then again from 1931 onwards, with implications for the standing of the UK£ as an international currency. Domestically, this period was one in which Britain's traditional industries experienced very difficult trading conditions, pushing many businesses into losses in the 1920s and 1930s. Throughout, the large British retail banks consolidated their position, dominating the domestic market. Writing in 1926, Sykes welcomed the result as it provided a banking system that was not only more stable and efficient but also increased the supply of credit, because a larger bank could operate on the basis of lower reserves. However, he was conscious that it made banks more conservative in their lending though he attributed this to the prevailing

---

[24] F.W. Hirst, *British Capital at Home and Abroad: An Examination of Recent Statements as to Exports of Capital Abroad* (London: 1910) [revised articles reprinted from the *Economist*. Hirst was the editor] pp. 9, 13, 19, 21; F.W. Hirst, *The Six Panics and Other Essays* (London: 1913) pp. 227–228; J.A. Hobson, 'Foreign Investments and Home Employment', *Financial Review of Reviews*, 10 (October 1910); H.H. Bassett, *British Commerce* (London: 1913) p. 33. See Lenfant, *British Capital Export*, pp. 104–105, 136, 462.

[25] See R. Roberts, *Saving the City: The Great Financial Crisis of 1914* (Oxford: Oxford University Press, 2013).

economic conditions in the 1920s. "On the whole, amalgamation has increased the capacity to make loans; but the mechanical and impersonal control imposed by the organisation necessary in great concerns has tended to reduce the initiative of smaller entrepreneurs and business men, and is an obstacle to quick recovery from acute trading depression."[26]

Building on pre-war criticism of the banking system, an official investigation during the war had suggested that the banks were not providing British industry with adequate financial support. That criticism was then widely accepted as providing an explanation for Britain's economic difficulties between the wars.[27] Writing in 1931, S.E. Thomas observed that banks "have been blamed for refusing necessary long-term finance for industrial purposes, while affording every facility to the short-term borrower.... They have been accused of catering for the financial needs of ... the financier ... the speculator ... the large capitalist."[28] The collapse of banking systems around the world, including those of Germany and the USA, reduced the level of that criticism, as the British banking model had proved resilient in the wake of the Wall Street Crash. H.E. Evitt wrote in 1931 that "None other than the British banking system could have withstood so successfully such a financial upheaval as we have recently witnessed, and this undoubtedly has been due to the deeply-rooted belief in the integrity and prudence of our banks."[29] This self-congratulation continued throughout the 1930s, as with C.W. Taylor in 1935. "The strength of the British banks has been amply demonstrated during the last few years of crisis and depression. During that period there has not at any time been any hint of failure or even of real anxiety for their safety."[30] One American expert, J. Philip Wernette, admired the way that British banks were able to balance risk taking and risk avoidance. "Competition is very

---

[26] J. Sykes, *The Amalgamation Movement in English Banking, 1825–1924* (London: 1926) pp. 152–157, 186.

[27] *Financial Facilities for Trade*: Report 1st July 1916, Cd 8346, pp. 4–6; A. Marshall, *Industry and Trade* (London: 1919) p. 346; Kirkaldy, *British Finance During and After the War*, pp. 115–120.

[28] S.E. Thomas, *British Banks and the Finance of Industry* (London: 1931) pp. 14, 94–96.

[29] H.E. Evitt, 'Exchange Dealings under Current Conditions', *Journal of the Institute of Bankers*, 52, 456 (1931).

[30] C.W. Taylor, 'The Case against the Nationalisation of the Banks', *Journal of the Institute of Bankers*, 56, 374, 385–386 (1935).

keen but it does not lead to unsound practices in order to get business."[31] However, he did consider that British banks had become too detached from manufacturing and that criticism remained commonplace in the 1930s.[32]

There remained the enduring belief, for example, that the merchant banks ignored the needs of manufacturing. Writing in 1933, J.R. Jarvie complained that "These Anglo-Foreign private banks have rarely any interest in the financing of British industries. They are out all the time for foreign loans."[33] What this criticism failed to take on board were the difficulties that the merchant banks faced and the efforts they made to build up a domestic business, particularly in the 1930s. Faced with radically different conditions, many merchant banks failed or changed their strategy. The type of business that the merchant banks carried out, combining short-term finance through bills and long-term investment with the issue of stocks and bonds, was being squeezed at home by a combination of retail banks and new finance houses, and internationally by US banks, as they could access abundant finance in New York, denominated in US$s. In the 1920s, merchant banks had responded by taking greater risks, such as engaging in the expanding foreign exchange market. This left them vulnerable in a crisis, which took place between 1929 and 1932, including Britain leaving the Gold Standard. Among those that remained, many switched to a lower-risk business model, taking on advisory roles. Beneath the veneer of stability and permanence that appeared to characterise British merchant banking between the wars, generated by a focus on the largest and most established, there was considerable change and turmoil, but that went unnoticed at the time. As merchant banks were partnerships, and often restricted to a few individuals and limited staff, their disappearance and retrenchment passed largely unnoticed. What was most noticeable for merchant banks between the wars was their growing involvement in domestic finance, which expanded in the 1930s as other business opportunities contracted, especially foreign ones.[34]

---

[31] J.P. Wernette, 'The English Banking System', *Harvard Business Review*, 366–379 (1935).

[32] A. Vallance, *The Centre of the World* (London: 1935) pp. 122–124, 234–235, 239–240.

[33] J.R. Jarvie, *The Old Lady Unveiled: A Criticism and an Explanation of the Bank of England* (London: 1933) p. 44.

[34] See B. O'Sullivan, *From Crisis to Crisis: The Transformation of Merchant Banking, 1914–1939* (London: Palgrave Macmillan, 2018).

However, the main criticism of banks between the wars was directed at the large retail banks. These had been singled out for attack in the inquiry into finance and industry, by the Macmillan Committee that reported in 1931. This inquiry followed an earlier one, into Industry and Trade, that had exonerated the banking system from responsibility for the difficulties being experienced by British manufacturing.[35] The negative verdict passed on banks by the 1931 inquiry was despite ample evidence to the contrary. On the 30th of May 1930, Sir Roland Nugent, the Director of the Federation of British Industry, told the inquiry that "We came across no evidence of anybody not having credit from the bank when they ought to have had it. We did have evidence the other way, that the banks had been rather over-generous." He was supported in that view by the Glasgow shipbuilder, Sir James Lithgow, who was Chairman of the Federation of British Industry. "It is totally wrong to look for a scapegoat in the banking institutions. It is not anything that they have done or left that has made industry unprofitable. Any deficiencies in the banking system today are due, in my opinion, to the fact that there is not a sufficiently prosperous industrial system on which to build the credit." However, the chairman of the inquiry, Lord Macmillan concluded on the 8th of May 1930, after hearing the evidence of the Cambridge economist, D.H. Robertson, that "We have had a considerable amount of evidence that there is a gap in the credit machinery of this country and that some organisation is required to fill the gap." It was the evidence of economists, and the influence of another, J.M. Keynes, who was a member of the inquiry, that swayed the committee and led to the criticism of the banks.[36] A reason for the critical stance the Macmillan Committee adopted was its unwillingness to acknowledge that the banks faced very difficult conditions, which they had to surmount in order to survive.[37] It was this belief that the banks neglected manufacturing, regardless of mounting evidence to the contrary, that prevailed throughout the 1930s.[38] One reason it did

---

[35]Committee on Industry and Trade: Final Report, Cmd 3282 (1929), section iv/3 access to Capital and Financial Facilities, pp. 43–58.

[36]Committee on Finance and Industry: Report, Cmd 3282 (1931), Minutes of Evidence: Sir Roland Nugent, Director of the Federation of British Industry Q3261 20th March 1930, Sir James Lithgow, chairman FBI; Q8494 Lord Macmillan, chairman of the Committee Q475 8th May 1930.

[37]Committee on Finance and Industry, 1931 Report.

[38]P. Arnold, *The Bankers of London* (London: 1938) pp. 54, 102; R.S. Sayers, *The Bank of England, 1891–1944* (Cambridge: 1976) pp. 253, 530–531.

was that it fitted into a general criticism of capitalism that was widespread at the time.[39] In reality, the depressed state of the economy made all banks reluctant to continue lending to businesses that faced difficult conditions.

The outbreak of the Second World War was long anticipated in financial circles, giving banks ample time to prepare, including the Bank of England. During the war, banks were quickly converted into agents of the state. Rather than operate as businesses, competing for customers and making judgements on whether to grant loans or not, banks were used to distribute cash, make and receive payments, collect savings and to provide loans to approved borrowers. There was little scope for discretionary behaviour in an economy involving the central direction of labour; rationing of essential food, clothing and other material; compulsory savings; state control of production; and the use of currency and capital controls to govern international financial transactions. As was observed in *The Banker* in 1941, "For the time being, commercial banking as it is normally understood has ceased to exist and in all important matters the banks must now be regarded largely as the agents of the Treasury. Banking has joined the Civil Service."[40] It was this pattern of behaviour that was carried into peacetime, especially as the election of a Labour Government in 1945 raised the real prospect that all banks would be taken into state ownership, as happened to the Bank of England.[41]

Frozen in Time, 1945–1979

What followed the end of the Second World War in 1945 was a unique period in global financial history because of the absence of major crises until the 1970s. The British government also intervened to insulate the country from international competition and to neutralise domestic fluctuations in economic activity. This extended to the banking system where, through the Bank of England, the government imposed a policy of control and compartmentalisation. Externally, the use of exchange controls and restrictions on foreign investment created barriers between British-based banks and international finance, greatly to the detriment of the global role they were still able to play. The result was to freeze the

---

[39] A. Citizen, *The City Today*, pp. 19–23.
[40] 'Bankers as Civil Servants' in 'The City in War', *The Banker*, lix August 1941, p. 77.
[41] Brett, *Usury in Britain*, pp. 20, 31, 87–92.

structure of banking into the pattern that had emerged before the Second World War, despite the challenges and opportunities of the post-war years dictating a need for change. Competition was limited as collusion and cartels were encouraged, being considered beneficial to the exercise of control. It was in this period that previous criticisms accusing British banking of being conservative and even complacent had a degree of justification. Conversely, the banking system was remarkably stable, with no significant crises or failures even at the individual level. This was not attributed to the benign environment within which banks operated, and the controls and compartmentalisation imposed by the government, but to the inherent strengths possessed by the banks.[42] As a consequence, the stability and resilience of the banks were taken for granted. Instead, the banks were accused of being slow to modernise and failing to provide the finance that manufacturing required, as the conclusions of the Macmillan Committee were widely accepted. The post-war complaints from business, about the poor service from banks and the periodic shortages of finance, were blamed on the banks, not on the government policies which dictated the environment within which they had to operate.[43] These criticisms grew in the 1970s when British industry faced serious difficulties for the first time since the end of the Second World War. That led to the government appointing another inquiry to investigate the links between finance and the economy. In their submission in 1979 to the Committee to Review the Functioning of Financial Institutions, the banks hit back. "The banks believe that the onus of responsibility rests with critics of the financial system to show that it has in fact been a major impediment to economic progress; and they suggest that no such case has yet been made."[44] This lack of evidence was no barrier to the continued belief that the banks bore a heavy responsibility for Britain's relatively poor economic performance since the end of the Second World War, especially in manufacturing.

---

[42] C.N. Ward-Perkins, 'Banking Developments', in G.D.M. Worwick and P.H. Ady (eds), *The British Economy, 1945–1950* (Oxford: Oxford University Press, 1952) p. 223.

[43] D.F. Channon, *The Service Industries: Strategy, Structure and Financial Performance* (London: 1978) pp. 72–79; P. Scott, *The Triumph of the South: A Regional Economic History of Early Twentieth Century Britain* (London: 2007) p. 265.

[44] Committee to Review the Functioning of Financial Institutions (1979): Minutes of Evidence: Clearing Banks, p. 177.

Ignoring the Lessons of History

Towards the end of 1979, the newly elected Conservative government of Mrs Thatcher abandoned exchange controls. No longer could British banks shelter behind government-imposed barriers that restricted the international lows of credit and capital. The result in the 1980s was much greater competition both internationally and domestically. In the face of the onslaught from US investment banks and European universal banks, the British merchant banks largely succumbed and were taken over. The opening up of the membership of the London Stock Exchange to banks in 1986, known as Big Bang, was but one stage in the eventual triumph of the US investment banks over their British rivals. Among the many changes affecting the retail banks, one of the most momentous was the end to the division between them and the building societies. Throughout, however, the British banking system remained stable, weathering crises and individual bank failures. That contributed to the ingrained belief that, whatever its faults, the British banking system had discovered the secrets of stability and resilience. What was ignored was that these lessons were a product of a unique set of circumstances, and so needed to be adjusted and refined in order to meet new challenges. That had happened in the past but not after the 1970s. After 1979, British banks increasingly operated in a global economy largely free from exchange controls, and were forced to compete against the ex-building societies at home and US and European banks abroad. In addition, with the demise of the UK£ as an international currency, and the switch to the US$, the Bank of England lost part of its ability to act as lender of last resort as British banks conducted so much of their business in dollars. The Bank of England also lost its banking supervisory role in 1997, becoming, increasingly, little more than a manager of the payments system and a monetary policy institute acting on behalf of the government. Unbeknown to contemporaries, the basis on which the stability of the British banking system rested was being undermined.[45]

What developed between 1979 and 2007 was a banking system that was unstable at many levels. It was unstable at the regulatory level through the creation of the tripartite system in 1997/1998, as this left no

---

[45] See Dimsdale and Hotson, *British Financial Crises*; F. Capie and G. Woods, *Money over Two Centuries: Selected Topics in British Monetary History* (Oxford: Oxford University Press, 2012).

single agency with overall authority ready to act immediately and decisively in a crisis. The result was delay and indecision in the crisis of 2007. Though it retained the obligation to act as Lender of Last Resort after 1997, the Bank of England lost its responsibility for banking supervision. This destroyed its ability to anticipate emerging problems in banking, formulate a speedy and targeted response, and then execute that strategy before a liquidity crisis affecting a single bank became one infecting the entire system, and then metamorphosed into a solvency crisis. That is what had happened in the past. The banking system was also unstable at the market level as the Bank of England's role as Lender of Last Resort had been eroded through the switch to the use of the US$ as a basis for interbank lending and borrowing. This deprived it of the ability to provide the liquidity required in an emergency when it was US$s not UK£s that were required. Only the US Federal Reserve Bank could provide liquidity in the form of US$s. Finally, at the level of individual banks, the system had also become unstable as a result of two separate developments. The first was the merging of commercial and investment banking and retail and investment banking, symbolised by the event known as Big Bang in 1986. This blurred the distinction between different types of banking during which bankers lost sight of the importance of liquidity. The imperative of preserving liquidity had become a cornerstone of British banking since the Overend and Gurney crisis of 1866, but it was now being ignored in favour of products and processes imported from the USA. The second development was that banking became increasingly competitive. The retail banks and the ex-building societies competed aggressively for business, whether it was attracting the deposits of savers through high rates of interest or the borrowing of home buyers with low rates of interest. Building societies were converted from mutually owned financial institutions, specialising in providing mortgages to home owners using retail deposits, into profit-maximising companies seeking business across a wide spectrum of financial activities, ranging from funding through wholesale markets to the repackaging and resale of home loans. Added to that was the aggressive expansion of the two Scottish banks into England, as this introduced a new competitive element into the British financial system.

It was in these years after 1979 that British banks and bankers acquired their new reputation as risk takers. British banks indulged in a frenzy of lending that generated large profits for their shareholders and huge bonuses for their staff. New financial products, investment vehicles and trading systems were adopted that appeared to provide depositors and investors with high and safe returns while simultaneously giving borrowers abundant loans at low interest rates, regardless of their credit rating or business model. When the crisis did eventually happen, the government was forced to intervene to prevent a systemic collapse so saving the banks, their depositors and their employees, though not their shareholders, from the consequences of their risk taking. The cumulative effect of the crisis of 2007/2008, and the subsequent revelations of unscrupulous behaviour and market manipulation, was to transform the reputation of British banking that had been built up over the previous 150 years. No longer were British banks seen as conservative guardians of the nation's savings. No longer was the standard of behaviour, maintained by British bankers, regarded as being the highest in the world. No longer was the British system of financial regulation held up as the model to be copied by others. No longer did the Bank of England symbolise central banking competence.[46]

During the second half of the nineteenth century, British bankers had worked hard at cultivating an image of total reliability, which they appeared to have achieved by the end. As Dunn noted, when comparing British banks in 1837 with those in 1897, "A large bank, conducted on the principle of limited liability, with vast resources, issuing audited balance sheets and subjected to a rigorous system of inspection, inspires confidence and support."[47] According to Perry, writing in 1908, "The prudence with which our joint-stock banks are now managed, and their long freedom from failures, has induced the public to regard them with implicit confidence."[48] They not only retained that reputation throughout the rest of the twentieth century but built upon it as they surmounted one crisis after another, while other banking systems had to be rescued from collapse by government intervention. That ended with the failure of the Northern Rock Bank in 2007 and then the more general crisis of 2008, when only government intervention prevented a complete collapse. Revelations since that event further tarnished the collective reputation of

---

[46]F. Capie, *The Bank of England, 1950s–1979* (Cambridge: Cambridge University Press, 2010) pp. 1, 524–529.

[47]Dunn, 'Banking in 1837 and in 1897', p. 380.

[48]S.E. Perry, 'The History of Companies' Legislation in England in its Practical Aspect, and its Effect upon Our Industrial and Banking Development', *Journal of the Institute of Bankers*, 29, 496 (1908).

British banks and bankers. In 2012, the *Financial Times* gave its review of British banking the headline, "Scandals dominate the Bank Sector."[49] For most of the twentieth century, British banks and bankers had a reputation for being risk averse. It was this behaviour that was believed to underpin their stability through events as tumultuous as world wars and global financial crises. There was a collective pride in the achievements of British banks and bankers, led by the Bank of England, but shared with the largest retail banks and leading merchant banks. Unfortunately, the lessons of the past, that had underpinned the reputation of British banks and bankers, were ignored because the assumption was made that stability was built into the system and nothing could disturb it. As Sayers wrote in 1957, "The banking system appears to have become immune to the troubles that used to lead to suspension of business."[50] It was that assumption that was shattered in 2007/2008.[51]

The Perception of Power

One element of banks and bankers that most interested the public was the belief that with money went power. In turn, that power was concentrated in the hands of banks and bankers. As the writer, H.S. Merriman put it his 1904 novel, *The Last Hope*, "There is only a certain amount of money in

---

[49] *Financial Times*, 29th December 2012.

[50] Sayers, *Lloyds Bank in the History of English Banking*, p. 204. See M. Ackrill and L. Hannah, *Barclays: The Business of Banking, 1690–1996* (Cambridge: Cambridge University Press, 2001) pp. 70, 93, 99, 103–104, 105, 109, 117–121, 139, 160–165, 207–209, 213, 226, 233; Capie and Woods, *Money over Two Centuries*, pp. 333–334; Dimsdale and Hotson, *British Financial Crises*: (introduction, pp. 7, 21, British Financial Crises in the Nineteenth and Twentieth Centuries (F. Capie) p. 11; Some Shareholding Hazards (N. Dimsdale and A. Hotson) pp. 21, 26, 40–44, 53; Holding Shareholders to Account: British Banking Stability and Contingent Capital (J. Turner) pp. 139, 151–152; Narrow Banking, Real Estate, and Financial Stability in the UK, c. 1870–2010 (A. Offer) p. 158); J.D. Turner, *Banking in Crisis: The Rise and Fall of British Banking Stability, 1800 to the Present* (Cambridge: Cambridge University Press, 2014) pp. 5, 50–51, 88, 93; M. Billings and F. Capie, 'Financial Crisis, Contagion and the British Banking System between the World Wars', *Business History*, 53, 197 (2011).

[51] C.P. Kindleberger and R.Z. Aliber, *Manias, Panics, and Crashes: A History of Financial Crises* (London: Palgrave, 2011) pp. 302–311; R.S. Grossman, *Unsettled Account: The Evolution of Banking in the Industrialized World since 1800* (Princeton: Princeton University Press, 2010) p. 190.

the world — and we bankers usually know where it is."[52] The control that banks exercised over the means of payment and the ability of bankers to grant or refuse loans gave them a power that was visible to all. In the late nineteenth century, the radical economist, J.A. Hobson, suggested that it was bankers, acting in concert, that had taken Britain into a war in South Africa. In his 1902 book, Imperialism, he broadened this out to suggest that bankers had the power "to manipulate the policy of nations," and he continued to hold these opinions during and after the First World War.[53] Such views were widely shared by those contemporaries of Hobson, and many later scholars, who saw banks and bankers as providing the evidence they sought linking money and power.[54] However, that evidence was lacking when the views and actions of banks and bankers themselves were examined. The conclusion that Cassis reached for the 1890–1914 period, for example, was that bankers were "very rarely driven by circumstances into making overtly political actions."[55] Due to the changing structure of British banking, the power of the individual banker was in decline from the mid-nineteenth century onwards. Banking became dominated by companies employing trained staff, and their focus was on their own careers and the success of the business, not political power or social advancement. Nevertheless, the public continued to attribute bankers with a degree of power they did not possess, especially in the twentieth century when it was the apparatus of the state that became dominant.

Evidence for this perception can be found in the output of novelists throughout the nineteenth and twentieth centuries. The exercise of power was something that they and their readers could appreciate and understand while the intricacies of banking practice were not, judging from a comment made by one. In the 1910 novel, *Psmith in the City*, P.G. Wodehouse, who had worked in a bank, admitted that "The whole system of banking was a horrid mystery to him."[56] Instead, the link between bankers and

---

[52] H.S. Merriman, *The Last Hope* (London: 1904) pp. 149–150.

[53] J.A. Hobson, *The War in South Africa: Its Causes and Effects* (London: 1900) pp. 189–194, 197, 207, 224; Hobson, *Imperialism*, pp. 51–53, 56, 94, 357, 368; Hobson, *The Evolution of Modern Capitalism*, ch. x: The Financier.

[54] See R.E. Dumett, 'Exploring the Cain/Hopkins Paradigm: Issues for Debate; Critique and Topics for New Research', in R.E. Dumett (ed.), *Gentlemanly Capitalism and British Imperialism: The New Debate on Empire* (London: Longman, 1999).

[55] Cassis, 'The Banking Community of London', p. 1223.

[56] P.G. Wodehouse, *Psmith in the City* (London: 1910) pp. 5–6, 11, 19, 21, 26, 30, 37, 71, 128, 131–132.

power seemed obvious. As early as the beginning of the nineteenth century, Lord Byron wrote in his poem, *Don Juan*, produced between 1818 and 1824, "Who hold the balance of the world? Jew Rothschild and his fellow-Christian, Baring."[57] Following on from Byron, using the Rothschilds as symbols of the power of bankers, Benjamin Disraeli gave it substance in two 1840s novels, namely, *Coningsby* in 1844 and *Tancred* in 1847. The banker, Sidonia, "was lord and master of the money market of the world, and of course virtually lord and master of everything else."[58] In Thackeray's novels, dating from the 1840s and 1850s, bankers were also credited with political and social power as well as financial.[59] To Mrs Gore, in her 1854 novel, *The Money Lender*, bankers were the "real potentates of modern times who sway the destinies of nations and individuals with a rod of gold."[60] Money gave bankers entry into the top level of British political and social life, as in Emma Robinson's 1856 novel, *The City Banker*.[61] For Sala, in his 1862 novel, *The Seven Sons of Mammon*, it was a banker who "was a power in the state and a prince in the land,"[62] and the same conclusion was drawn in 1869 by Charles Lever in *That Boy of Norcott's*.[63] However, this close association between bankers and power in the mind of the public appears to have faded away in the 1870s and 1880s. It was not until the 1890s that the link between bankers and power was revived, judging from the novels produced at those times.[64] This belief in the power of bankers before the First World War is most apparent in the novels of Hilaire Belloc, published between 1904 and 1910. Belloc's series of novels tell the story of I.Z. Barnett, a German-born Jewish banker who achieved great success in Britain. He became Lord Lambeth and then the Duke of Battersea, having made a fortune running the Anglo-Moravian Bank. By the 1910 novel, he was able to dictate

---

[57]Lord Byron, *Don Juan*, 1818–1824.

[58]B. Disraeli, *Coningsby* (London: 1844), pp. 230–238, 242, 258, 278, 357; B. Disraeli, *Tancred or the New Crusade* (London: 1847) pp. 112–115, 124–126, 132, 165, 212, 254.

[59]W.M. Thackeray, *Vanity Fair* (London: 1847/1848) p. 538; Thackeray, *The Newcomes*, Vol. 1: p. 279.

[60]Mrs. Gore, *The Money Lender* (London: 1854) pp. 31, 134–137.

[61]E. Robinson, *The City Banker or Love and Money* (London: 1856) pp. 8–9.

[62]G.A. Sala, *The Seven Sons of Mammon* (London: Tinsley Brothers, 1862) pp. 3–7.

[63]C. Lever, *That Boy of Norcott's* (London: 1869) pp. 172, 192, 196–197, 222.

[64]Wicks, *The Veiled Hand*, p. 67; Alexander, *Mammon*, pp. 36–37, 98–99, 108; Ouida, *The Massarenes: A Novel* (London: 1897) pp. 69, 81, 134–136, 200–201, 217, 534–535.

policy to the British government and it was only by turning to another banker, the American, G. Quinlan Smith, that they were able to escape his clutches.[65] In contrast, other novels, while recognising that British bankers were respected and well connected, suggest they no longer had the power possessed by the Rothschilds in the past or the European and American bankers of their day.[66]

After the First World War, financiers, including British bankers, were again portrayed as powerful individuals. In Dorothy Sayers's novel, *Whose Body?*, the wealthy financier, Wintrington, "controlled the finances of five countries."[67] Agatha Christie also suggested that bankers possessed immense power as in the 1925 novel, *The Secret of Chimneys*,[68] and then again in the 1940 novel, *One, Two, Buckle My Shoe*. In the later novel, the banker, Alastair Blunt, was "a man in whose hands lay supreme power."[69] To the Labour Member of Parliament, Ellen Wilkinson, in her 1932 novel, *The Division Bell Mystery*, power was found in "Lombard Street or perhaps even across the Atlantic Ocean."[70] To Anthony Wynne, in his 1934 novel, *Death of a Banker*, there continued to exist a global conspiracy of bankers. "All you international money-lenders work together. You have offices and branches in every country. Most of you are related by blood. It is a closed corporation, a ring, if you like.... You have the world

---

[65]Belloc, *Emmanuel Burden*, pp. 55–58, 70–76, 104, 113, 119, 121–122, 158, 170–171, 206–207, 212; Belloc, *Mr Clutterbuck's Election*, pp. 20–22, 193–198, 206–207; H. Belloc, *A Change in the Cabinet* (London: 1909), pp. 232–233; H. Belloc, *Pongo and the Bull* (London: 1910) pp. 1–4, 13–14, 33, 71–80, 88, 93, 102–103, 178–179, 237, 305; Belloc, *Mr. Petre*.

[66]Merriman, *Roden's Corner*, pp. 122–129, 240; W. Besant, *The Alabaster Box* (London: 1900) pp. 4–13; E.W. Hornung, 'The Black Mask' (1901), in *The Collected Raffles Stories* (Oxford: Oxford University Press, 1996) pp. 324–325; Wodehouse, *Psmith in the City*, pp. 11, 19, 26, 30; E.C. Bentley, *Trent's Last Case* (London: 1913) pp. 1–7.

[67]D.L. Sayers, *Whose Body?* (London: T. Fisher Unwin, 1923) pp. 16–17, 40–42, 56–59, 69, 79, 171.

[68]A. Christie, *The Secret of Chimneys* (London: John Lane, The Bodley Head, 1925, reprinted by Pan Books) pp. 18, 23–24, 77, 81, 97, 100–101, 165; A. Christie, *One, Two, Buckle My Shoe* (London: 1940) pp. 10–11, 15–16, 18, 42–43, 56–57, 86–87, 132–133, 155, 180–181, 185.

[69]Christie, *One, Two, Buckle My Shoe*, pp. 10–11, 15–16, 18, 42–43, 56–57, 86–87, 132–133, 155, 180–181, 185.

[70]Wilkinson, *The Division Bell Mystery*, p. 194. See E. Bramah, *The Bravo of London* (London: Cassell & Co., 1934).

parcelled out among you and you keep to your own pitches."[71] This was an echo of the earlier views expressed by Hobson. Nevertheless, the power possessed by bankers was seen to be limited as they were unable to prevent the outbreak of another world war, according to Macdonell in his 1936 novel, *Lords and Masters*, and Ronald Fraser's 1942 one, *Financial Times*.[72] What the novels written between the wars appear to suggest was that there was an underlying belief that banks and bankers possessed power which was not necessarily used for the benefit of society as a whole, and that this contributed to the economic and political problems being experienced.

During and long after the Second World War, novelists were largely silent on the question of the power of bankers and their ability to influence governments. This is surprising as it was a subject of much debate in academic circles and among socialist politicians. What this suggests was that the public were little interested in the subject of the powerful bankers dictating policy to successive governments, compared to greedy ones intent on making money for themselves, as in Caryl Churchill's 1987 play, *Serious Money*.[73] It was only at the end of the century, in the wake of Big Bang in the City, that the issue of powerful bankers came to the fore. Until then, the high levels of personal taxation, the supervision of state-owned central banks and the existence of a strong regulatory system suppressed the power that could be exercised by individual bankers. In the 1997 novel by Grant Sutherland, *Due Diligence*, a close relationship between a London merchant bank and the British government is hinted at, but this was insufficient to prevent them being taken over by a US bank.[74] Paul Kilduff's novels between 1999 and 2003 also suggest a connection between financial power and political power through the banking system.[75] However, in the 2001 novel, *The Frontrunner*, it is made clear that the real power lay with the world's central banks, whose coordinated

---

[71] A. Wynne, Death of a Banker (London: 1934) pp. 129, 184.

[72] Macdonell, *Lords and Masters*; R. Fraser, *Financial Times* (London: Jonathan Cape, 1942) p. 177.

[73] C. Churchill, *Serious Money: A City Comedy* (London: 1987).

[74] G. Sutherland, *Due Diligence* (London: Hodder Headline, 1997) pp. 245–245. See N. Marsh, *Money, Speculation and Finance in Contemporary British Fiction* (London: 2007) pp. 1, 8, 12–16, 35, 45, 70–71, 96, 108–110, 115, 131, 143.

[75] P. Kilduff, *Square Mile* (London: Coronet Books, 1999), *The Dealer* (London: 2000), *The Frontrunner* (London: 2001), *The Headhunter* (London: 2003).

intervention prevented the collapse of the global financial system.[76] It was only with the financial crisis, which began in Britain in 2007 with the collapse of Northern Rock Bank, that the ability of individual bankers to influence governments comes, once more, to the fore. In Sebastian Faulks's *A Week in December*, which appeared in 2009, it was the combination of bankers' greed and inadequate supervision by politicians that was blamed for the crisis, which only government intervention could prevent from becoming an economic disaster.[77] For Ben Elton in *Meltdown*, which was also published in 2009, the financial crisis was a result of bankers persuading a newly elected Labour government to adopt policies that favoured their interests. These bankers were then richly rewarded and given titles. One of those was Rupert Bennett, later Lord Bennett, who was a trusted advisor to the Prime Minister. "You knighted me for services to British banking. You made me a Labour peer. How can you possibly pretend that you didn't know what I was doing and that you didn't support it 100 per cent? If it turned out I was wrong then you were wrong too. We were all wrong. ... The money men had created massive wealth for themselves and given back nothing to society but resentment and fear."[78] Placing the blame on a few powerful bankers was an attractive and plausible explanation for crises and catastrophe when the likes of the Rothschilds and J.P. Morgan played a prominent role in the financial world. However, it was steadily less believable when banking became a highly regulated business conducted by public companies, as was the case in Britain after the Second World War. It was only in the wake of the financial crisis of 2007/2008 that the image of the powerful banker re-emerged, and then only briefly and to a mild degree. For the public at large, it was much easier to believe in bankers being driven by greed not power, and banks taking excessive risks in the pursuit of profit, disregarding the interests of their customers or the wider community. Power was a much more intangible concept than greed and so it was the latter not the former that most interested the public. Those who linked banks and bankers to the exercise of power were those whose interest was in economics and politics as they dealt in the world of the abstract not that of individuals.

---

[76] Kilduff, *Frontrunner*, pp. 1–2, 17, 198–199, 212–215, 462, 469–471.

[77] S. Faulks, *A Week in December* (London: Hutchinson, 2009) pp. 125, 309, 375–377.

[78] B. Elton, *Meltdown* (London: Bantam Press, 2009) pp. 21, 78–79, 211, 213, 236–237, 262, 270, 362, 390, 442–443, 457–461.

The Changing Perception of Banks and Bankers

Prior to the Financial Crisis, the public perception of banks and bankers appears to have been based on complete trust in their stability. After the crisis, that changed to mistrust with bankers becoming some of the most despised members of society. Such was the degree of "banker bashing" that the government was empowered to impose punitive fines on banks and introduce legislation to control the way they did business. What this indicates is that perception matters. When banks were trusted, they could be left to regulate themselves. With trust gone, the calls for legislative intervention became unstoppable, leading to a financial system placed under government control and even ownership. A key determinant in the public perception of banks and bankers were the number and severity of bank failures taking place. These had devastating consequences not only for those who had deposited money in the bank or held its notes, as they could lose all, but also for the wider community suddenly deprived of credit and the means of payment. For those reasons, a bank failure quickly brought banks and bankers into disrepute, destroying the trust and respect that had been built up over the years. Bank failures regularly featured in contemporary fiction, exaggerating the public's fears about their stability, but they were less able to do it in the absence of systemic crises.[79]

The lack of trust in banks and bankers at the beginning of the nineteenth century was evident in Surr's 1815 novel, *The Magic of Wealth*; Lord Byron's poem, *Don Juan*; and Thomas Gaspey's 1821 novel, *Calthorpe*.[80] It was a running theme in the work of Thomas Love Peacock, dating from the 1820s and 1830s, with bank notes being labelled "fools gold."[81] Bank failures followed by absconding bankers were also common themes. Harriet Martineau, in the early 1830s novel, *Berkeley the Banker*,

---

[79]P.E. Smart, 'Bankers in Fiction', *Journal of the Institute of Bankers*, 82, 93 (1961). For more on this see R.C. Michie, 'Bursting the Bubble: The 2007 Northern Rock Crisis in Historical Perspective', in A.T. Brown, A. Burn and A. Doherty (eds), *Crises in Economic and Social History: A Comparative Perspective* (Woodbridge: The Boydell Press, 2015) pp. 303–321 (with Matthew Hollow) and Michie, 'Nature or Nurture', pp. 60–84.

[80]Surr, *The Magic of Wealth*, Vol. 1: pp. 132–133, 151–153, 168, 200–204, Vol. 2: pp. 72, 129, 168, 170–175, 249; Lord Byron, *Don Juan*; T. Gaspey, *Calthorpe, or Fallen Fortunes: A Novel* (London: Longman, Hurst, Rees, Orme and Brown, 1821) Vol. 1: p. 267.

[81]Peacock, *Paper Money Lyrics*: 'Pan in Town', 'The Three Little Men'); Peacock, *Crotchet Castle*, pp. 127–128, 130–131, 145, 148, 164–165, 200, 248.

contrasted the solvent and carefully managed Berkeley's Bank with the insolvent and fraudulent Cavendish's Bank, but both failed after experiencing a run. The one exception was the Bank of England, which she described as "the greatest bank of deposit and circulation in the world."[82] In her 1837 novel, *The Man of Business*, Mrs Gore, observed that "Many will be ruined," as a result of the Westerton Bank failure.[83] The subject in her 1843 novel, *The Banker's Wife*, was the banker, Richard Hamlyn, who had plundered the accounts of his customers in order to maintain a lavish lifestyle. What followed, once rumours spread that "Hamlyn and Co were insolvent, bankrupt, ruined, lost," was a bank run that brought it down and spread to other banks. "If they were insecure, who was solid? If the painstaking, virtuous, exemplary Hamlyn was a knave, whose honesty was to be trusted? More than one banking-house, of the highest reputation, had cause to rue the discoveries of that day!" As it was, the family were ruined and Richard Hamlyn had to be buried in secret in an unmarked grave to avoid a public uproar because of the money the depositors had lost.[84] Mrs Gore's graphic story of the collapse of a leading London private bank followed on from another by Horace Smith, *The Moneyed Man*, which was published in 1841. There it was recognised that a bank was "the most fragile and destroyable thing in existence-a thing that may be annihilated by a whisper!" Once trust was lost, the bank could not be saved, though it was solvent, despite support from other banks, who were "ever anxious to prevent the stoppage of any of their brotherhood, because it generates a distrust which may extend to the whole fraternity."[85] In Robert Bell's 1850 novel, *The Ladder of Gold*, the bank, Sarkens Brothers, only survived because of public support from the local landowner.[86] For Mrs Craik, in her 1856 novel, *John Halifax, Gentleman*, it was a wealthy mill owner who saved a solvent bank from collapse by making a public deposit of

---

[82] H. Martineau, *Berkeley the Banker* (London: 1832–1834) Vol. 1: pp. 2, 8, 13–14, 38–39, 65–67, 82, 132–141, 156–157, Vol. 2: pp. 24–25, 131, 138–139.

[83] Mrs Gore, *The Man of Business, or Stokeshill Place* (London: J. and C. Brown, 1837) pp. 120, 185, 264–269, 294–299, 326–327, 394–396.

[84] Gore, *The Banker's Wife or Court and City*, pp. 1, 8, 19, 22, 29, 54–59, 74–75, 90–94, 104, 111–115, 119, 121, 128–142, 167.

[85] H. Smith, *The Moneyed Man or the Lesson of a Life* (London: Darton and Company, 1841) pp. 1, 21, 28–29, 87, 104–105, 123, 160–161, 168–169, 181, 186, 190–191, 200–201, 290, 376–377.

[86] Bell, *The Ladder of Gold*, pp. 104–107.

£5,000. "A few who had come to close accounts, changed their minds, and even paid money in. All were satisfied."[87] Without that type of support, a bank could not survive a run, as happened to Smith, Brown, Jones, Robinson and Co in Charles Kingsley's 1851 story, *Yeast*.[88] Elizabeth Gaskell also included a bank collapse in her 1853 novel, *Cranford*.[89] In Thackeray's novel, *The Newcomes*, which was serialised between 1853 and 1855, the conservatively run bank, Newcome Brothers, proved resilient in a crisis while the risk-taking one, the Bundlecund Bank, collapsed.[90] The importance of trust in banking was also emphasised in Christian Le Ros's short story, *Christmas Day*, which was published in 1854. The long-established London private bank of Fograss, Fograss, Mowton and Snorton was almost forced to close because of a robbery, as a run would quickly develop once the news broke. Luckily, the stolen money was recovered in time.[91]

In two novels published in the late 1850s, Charles Dickens captured the divided views that the public had of British banks and bankers by then. In the 1857 novel, *Little Dorrit*, Merdle's bank collapsed, while in the 1859 novel, *A Tale of Two Cities*, Tellson's bank was stable and trustworthy.[92] However, it was the former that most attracted novelists, because of its dramatic possibilities, and so bank failures were given central billing in their stories. Charles Lever's 1859 novel, *Davenport Dunn*, told the story of the owners of the Ossory Bank in Kilkenny, who staged a run, for which they were ready, by spreading false rumours, in order to forestall a real one when news broke that they were insolvent.[93] In the 1850s, the

---

[87] Mulock (Mrs Craik), *John Halifax, Gentleman*, pp. 308–324.
[88] Kingsley, *Yeast*, pp. 113–114, 155–156, 158, 170–171, 180, 197, 211.
[89] Gaskell, *Cranford*, ch. 13 'Stopped Payment', pp. 119–127, 129.
[90] Thackeray, *The Newcomes*, Vol. 1: pp. 14–18, 41, 52, 55, 57, 106, 279, 314, Vol. 2: pp. 92, 124–125, 128–129, 165, 266, 288–289, 295, 299, 301, 344–345, 358–359, 362–363, 379, 399, 414.
[91] C. Le Ros, *Christmas Day; and How It Was Spent by Four Persons in the House of Fograss, Fograss, Mowton and Snorton, Bankers* (London: George Routledge & Co., 1854) pp. 1–2, 119–120, 137–143.
[92] C. Dickens, *Little Dorrit* (London: 1857) pp. 445, 628, 772, 777; C. Dickens, *A Tale of Two Cities* (London: Chapman and Hall, 1859) pp. 22, 36–37, 67–68, 266–267. The London private bank, Child & Co. is believed to have provided the model for Tellson's Bank: *Child & Co: A History* (Royal Bank of Scotland Group Publication, 2002) p. 11.
[93] Lever, *Davenport Dunn*, Vol. 1: pp. 42–43, Vol. 2: pp. 169, 174–175, 190–206, Vol. 3: pp. 130–131, 150–151, 160–161, 328, 336–337, 358–360.

only bank that commanded the absolute trust of the public was the Bank of England.[94] All other banks were vulnerable to rumour and collapse as Charles Reade showed in his two linked novels, *Love Me Little, Love Me Long* in 1859 and *Hard Cash* in 1863. When rumours spread that Hardie's Bank was insolvent, it was "beleaguered by a weeping, wailing, despairing crowd" and his house was stoned by a mob, many of whom had been ruined.[95] Judging from the novels of Mrs Henry Wood in the 1860s, there was a general lack of trust in banks and bankers.[96] A bank collapse was a principal feature in her 1863 novel, *The Shadow of Ashlydyat*. Once rumours spread that the banking house of Godolphin, Crosse and Godolphin was in difficulties, the attitude among its customers was that, whether the reports might be true or false, there would be no harm just to draw their money out and be on the safe side.[97] Only a benefactor could save a bank once it lost the trust of the public, as Amelia Edwards explained in her 1865 novel, *Half a Million of Money*.[98] Constant vigilance was required if a bank was to avoid failure as Edmund Hodgson Yates observed in his 1866 novel, *Kissing the Rod*. Before he got married, Robert Streightley "was in his office at 10 o'clock, and never left it, save on some business errand until six. He never took a holiday except on Christmas-day and Good Friday." That changed when he married as he neglected his business. That left him poorly prepared to meet the losses when a financial crisis broke. The bank collapsed.[99]

---

[94]W. Collins, 'The Biter Bit' (1859) in R.C. Bull (ed.), *Great Tales of Mystery* (London: Weidenfeld and Nicholson, 1960) p. 38; W. Pickersgill, *Washington Grange: An Autobiography* (London: 1859) pp. 281–291, 304–305, 321–322, 442–443.

[95]Reade, *Love Me Little, Love Me Long*, ch. xxx, xi and xii; Reade, *Hard Cash*, pp. 8–9, 93, 126–132, 167, 213–218, 249–253, 358, 415–417, 549, 563, 604–605, 610–613.

[96]Mrs H. Wood, *A Life's Secret: A Story* (London: Richard Bentley and Son, 1862) pp. 412–413; Wood, *The Channings: A Story*, pp. 351, 443; Mrs H. Wood, *Roland Yorke* (London: Richard Bentley and Son, 1869) pp. 94–95, 123.

[97]Mrs H. Wood, *The Shadow of Ashlydyat* (London: Richard Bentley and Sons, 1863) pp. 9, 17, 66–67, 135, 170, 181, 202–204, 226, 236–237, 243, 256–257, 273, 294–295, 302, 328–331, 376–379, 474–475.

[98]Edwards, *Half a Million of Money*, pp. 1–3, 7–15, 21–25, 97–102, 125, 143, 166–173, 242, 247, 370–375, 398–402, 430–431, 460–461.

[99]Yates, *Kissing the Rod*, Vol. 1: pp. 1–16, 54–57, 62–64, 90–93, 195, 217, 222, 337, Vol. 2: 87, 104–106, 114–115, 144, 212, 235, 280–281, Vol. 3: 39, 41, 73–77, 82–89, 132–133, 162, 166–168, 260, 268.

The 1860s witnessed a spate of novels featuring bank failures both before and after the Overend and Gurney crisis of 1866, but that event brought the subject to the forefront of public attention.[100] This was acknowledged by Joseph Hatton in his 1867 novel, *The Tallants of Barton*. The Eastern Banking Company was brought down by the failure of Overton, Baker & Co. despite being solvent and assistance provided by the industrialist, Christopher Tallant.[101] Mrs Braddon also featured another bank failure in her 1867 novel, *Rupert Godwin*, but this time the cause was the banker's "reckless speculation" and "unjustifiable extravagance" that had brought it down. "He knew that an hour's run upon his bank would demonstrate the fact of his insolvency."[102] All banks were vulnerable to a run as Charles Reade and Dion Boucicault pointed out in their 1868 novel, *Foul Play*.[103] These runs could be the product of unfounded and malicious rumours, as Bracebridge Hemyng and James H. Graff indicated in their 1868 novel.[104] In Alexander Shand's 1870 novel, *Against Time*, "Childersleigh, the great banking establishment in Lombard Street," which was "respected everywhere," was only saved from collapse through the introduction of new partners with additional capital. Even the Bank of England was not considered immune.[105] Though published in 1872, Mrs Oliphant's novel, *At His Gates*, took its storyline from the Overend and Gurney episode of 1866, as it featured a joint-stock bank that had only recently been converted from a private banking house. "Rivers's has a name like the Bank of England" but it failed after three years. "It was said the manager had absconded. Rivers's was at an end."[106] In another 1872 novel, *Ready-Money Mortiboy*, Walter Besant and James Rice

---

[100]Anonymous, *Commercial Tales and Sketches* (London: 1864) pp. 72–73, 217; Sala, *The Seven Sons of Mammon*, pp. 3–7, 30, 53, 75–76, 159, 172–179, 200–202; Riddell, *George Geith*, pp. 247–248, 255, 339, 349, 361.

[101]Hatton, *The Tallants of Barton*, pp. 2–9, 16–17, 36–37, 63–71, 79–81, 88, 98–99, 142–143, 131–132, 219–221, 292–293, 308–309, 314–315, 345, 348–349, 369, 565.

[102]Braddon, *Rupert Godwin*, pp. 8–9, 13–15, 20–28, 42, 111, 299–311.

[103]C. Reade and D. Boucicault, *Foul Play* (London: 1868) pp. 1–3, 36–37, 53, 106–113, 310–311, 408–412.

[104]Hemyng and Graff, *Telegraph Secrets*, pp. 94–109.

[105]Shand, *Against Time*, pp. 13–17, 38–43, 46, 58, 61–62, 73–74, 88, 116, 122, 155–156, 139–142, 149–153, 163, 170–171, 174, 181, 189–192, 199–200.

[106]Oliphant, *At His Gates*, pp. 33–41, 112, 177–184, 250–251, 260–261, 473–474, 476, 593–595, 738–741, 797, 808, 814–815.

distinguished between the fates of two rival bankers in the face of a crisis. Whereas Richard Mortiboy was a hard and calculating banker, disliked by all, Francis Melliship was a kind and accommodating man. "Mr Melliship advanced his customers at five per cent. Old Mortiboy at six or seven per cent;... Mr Melliship took the bad business; old Mortiboy the good-or none.... Mr Melliship never pressed a man, never turned a deaf ear to a tale of distress." The result was that Melliship's collapsed under the weight of bad debts, once rumours spread that it was in difficulties and a run developed, while Mortiboy's survived and flourished.[107] Reflecting the long shadow cast by the Overend and Gurney crisis, in 1874, Joseph Hatton was still referring to businesses "ruined by a great bank failure" in his novel *Clytie*.[108] He brought it up again in his 1877 novel, *The Gay World*, which traced the downfall of the banker, Loftus Kennett, "a name to conjure with both in social and financial circles." An inspection of the bank's accounts exposed that he had been stealing from his customers. "Defalcations of an enormous amount had been discovered in the management of the Kennett Bank."[109] Writing in 1878, Robert Black, in *Love or Lucre*, described a banker as someone "who takes your money into his hands and coolly settles it on his wife, to make his family secure at your expense, when he goes smash."[110]

Anthony Trollope's *The Way We Live Now*, which was published over the years 1874–1875, moved beyond the world of retail banking that the public were familiar with to deal with those engaged in international finance. Here, he made a distinction between established bankers doing a sound business and the new ones operating at the high-risk end. Representing the latter was Augustus Melmotte, recently arrived from Paris, while in the former camp was the firm of Todd, Breghert and Goldsheiner. "Mr Breghert was considered to be a very good man of business, and was now regarded as being, in a commercial point of view, the leading member of the great financial firm of which he was the second partner." In contrast, "it was said of Melmotte that 'His business was quite irregular, but there was very much of it, and some of it immensely

---

[107]Besant and Rice, *Ready-Money Mortiboy*, pp. 1–2, 117–118, 121–124, 143, 192–193, 318, 323, 394, 423, 444.

[108]J. Hatton, *Clytie: A Novel of Modern Life* (London: 1874) p. 139.

[109]J. Hatton, *The Gay World* (London: S. Blackett, 1877) pp. 54–55, 67, 77, 98, 147–149, 212–214, 264, 268–269, 288, 300, 304–305, 320, 370, 398–399.

[110]Black, *Love or Lucre*, p. 497.

profitable. He took us in completely.'" Melmotte's bank collapsed while Todd, Breghert and Goldsheiner survived, despite suffering some large losses.[111] However, it was stories concerning the failure of retail banks that continued to resonate most with the public. Mrs Oliphant's 1883 novel, *Hester*, dealt with a bank on the verge of failure, and was only saved by female intervention. "The Banking House of the Vernons was known through all the Home Counties as only second to the Bank of England, the emblem of stability, the impersonation of solid and substantial wealth." Its future was put in doubt when rumours spread that it was in difficulties, as that would lead to a run. "Everybody will rush upon us with our notes in their hands: and all the people who have deposit accounts will withdraw their money. It means Ruin." A wealthy cousin, Catherine Vernon, stepped in and saved the bank, staying on to run it.[112] One of the last novels in the nineteenth century to feature a major bank failure was George Sims's *Rogues and Vagabonds*, which was published in 1885. This had a chapter devoted to the failure of the Great Blankshire Bank. "The Great Blankshire Bank had been established for years, and was looked upon as a model of stability and sound finance. It was one of those old-fashioned banks, in which liability is unlimited, but its shares were reckoned as good as Bank of England notes. People would as soon have expected to hear of a Rothschild pawning his watch to get a dinner as that the Great Blankshire Bank had come to grief. The liabilities were enormous, but the first thought was for the unhappy shareholders. The depositors were safe. They would be paid to the uttermost farthing. The loss would strip the shareholders to the skin, and their garments would be divided among the creditors. No wonder the unhappy people on whom the blow fell reeled beneath the force of it. It was so sudden, so crushing, that it wrung something like a cry of agony from the victims. Men, who in the morning were prosperous citizens, sought their couches that night with bankruptcy staring them in the face."[113] By then, the business of retail banking was passing out of the hands of individuals and families and into those of companies, run by trained and experienced professionals and able to command large resources provided by numerous shareholders enjoying

---

[111]Trollope, *The Way We Live Now*, Vol. 1: pp. 30–34, 48–49, 84, 87, 268, 349, 368, Vol. 2: pp. 26–27, 89–92, 99, 272, 276, 294, 302–304, 307, 359–361.

[112]Oliphant, *Hester*, pp. 1–8, 15–17, 20–21, 136–139, 154–155, 285, 420, 436–439, 458–459.

[113]G.R. Sims, *Rogues and Vagabonds* (London: Chatto and Windus, 1885) ch. xliii.

the benefits of limited liability. Bank runs became a relic of the past and bank failures increasingly rare, and this resonated with the public and its perception of banks.

That left novelists to focus on the dwindling band of banks that remained private and with unlimited liability for the owners, as in the 1892 Sherlock Holmes story, *The Adventure of the Beryl Coronet* by Conan Doyle. Holder and Stevenson was "a large private bank" and that created uncertainty about its future, because the father had doubts about his son succeeding him. "He was not of a business turn. He was wild, wayward, and, to speak the truth, I could not trust him in the handling of large sums of money."[114] In contrast, a joint-stock bank recruited from a wide pool, put its staff through a training programme and then policed their behaviour. Archibald McIlroy explained, in the 1901 novel, *A Banker's Love Story*, that "A country manager's first duty is, not to bid for popularity" but "to look well after the Bank's interests." Failure to do so would result in dismissal or downgrading to a less responsible post.[115] That meant refusing credit to major customers who had exceeded the limit set, as in David Murray's 1907 novel, *In His Grip*.[116] In the 1911 novel, *Lord Stranleigh Philanthropist*, Robert Barr contrasts an old established private bank, Selwyn's, and a recently formed joint-stock bank, the Southern Counties. The experienced Scottish-trained banker, Alexander Corbitt, complained about the way Sir George Selwyn did business. "Selwyn's was the bank of the country gentlemen, presided over by Sir George, a country gentleman, for the benefit of country gentlemen. We lent money on landed property, which, as you know, cannot be turned quickly into cash if there is an urgent need for money ... I predicted disaster and disaster came." After the merger with the Southern Counties Bank, which had taken much of Selwyn's country business, Corbitt was allowed to run the bank as he wanted. "I know the intrinsic value of the chief securities in the market, so, by lending conservatively and keeping an eye on the Stock Exchange, I can realise at once in case of a decline if sufficient margin is not instantly placed in my possession to protect

---

[114]Sir A. Conan Doyle, 'The Adventure of the Beryl Coronet' (1892) in *The Complete Illustrated Sherlock Holmes* (Ware: 1986) pp. 238–240.

[115]A. McIlroy, *A Banker's Love Story* (London: T. Fisher Unwin, 1901) pp. 1–2, 124, 145–147, 172, 211, 228.

[116]Murray, *In His Grip*, pp. 1, 77–78.

the loan."[117] Banks became the trusted custodians of the nation's savings exposed to criminals who wanted to steal from them from 1890 onwards.[118] By then, the large joint-stock banks and the established City merchant banks were increasingly regarded as safe, stable and conservative, possessing a corporate culture that made them highly resilient. As early as the 1889 novel, *Three Men in a Boat*, Jerome K. Jerome, described the banker, George, as going "to sleep at a bank from ten to four each day, except Saturdays, when they wake him up and put him outside at two."[119] In the 1904 novel, *Teresa of Watling Street*, Arnold Bennett went much further. "Nothing is more marvellous than the rapid growth of our banking system, which is twice as great now as it was 20 years ago — and it was great enough then."[120] Only the rumour of an earthquake in South Africa, flooding the gold mines, could threaten the stability of the British banking system, according to Fred M. White in a 1903 story, *A Bubble Burst*.[121] For Robert Barr, in his 1908 novel, *Young Lord Stranleigh*, the threat came from a gigantic plot, orchestrated from Wall Street, to manipulate the global gold market.[122] In William Le Queux's invasion novels, it took a war to precipitate a run on the banks, and then their collapse following looting.[123]

Reflecting the trust placed in British banks by the public, novelists were forced to switch to the shadow banking sector for examples of bank failure. Credit and loan institutions attracted their attention, especially

[117]Barr, *Lord Stranleigh Philanthropist*, pp. 78–81, 201–203, 212–214, 224–225.

[118]H. Hill, 'The Sapient Monkey' (1893) in Cox, *Victorian Tales of Mystery and Detection*, pp. 234–235, 239–240; Zangwill, 'Cheating the Gallows', pp. 241–242, 245, 252; A. Morrison, *The Case of Laker, Absconded* (1895) in Greene, *The Complete Rivals of Sherlock Holmes*, pp. 45, 47–54, 66–67, 72; H. Keen, 'The Tin Box' (1896) in Cox, *Victorian Tales of Mystery and Detection*, pp. 425–426; J. Hatton, *The Banishment of Jessop Blythe: A Novel* (London: 1895) pp. 28–30; Mrs Oliphant, 'The Strange Adventures of John Percival' (1896) in Mrs Oliphant, *A Widow's Tale and Other Stories* (London: 1898) pp. 93, 96, 108; B. Orczy, 'The Theft at the English Provident Bank' (1901) in B. Orczy (ed.), *The Old Man in the Corner* (London: 1909); McIlroy, *A Banker's Love Story*, p. 103; W. Scarborough Jackson, *Nine Points of the Law* (London: 1903).

[119]J.K. Jerome, *Three Men in a Boat* (London: 1889) p. 17.

[120]A. Bennett, *Teresa of Watling Street: A Fantasia on Modern Times* (London: 1904) pp. 7–8.

[121]White, 'A Bubble Burst', pp. 1–16.

[122]Barr, *Young Lord Stranleigh*, pp. 231–255.

[123]Le Queux, *The Great War in England in 1897*; Le Queux, *The Invasion of 1910*.

after the collapse of the Liberator Building Society in 1892 and the flight of its chairman, Jabez Balfour. The popular journalist, W.T. Stead, wrote a short story, "Two and Two Make Four," in 1893, which included a character called Spencer Balfour and a company named the Emancipator.[124] The George Gissing novel, *The Whirlpool*, which was published in 1897, featured the Britannia Loan, Assurance, Investment and Banking Company, built up by Bennet Frothingham. It suffered a run and collapsed as rumours spread that it was in trouble. "The name of Bennet Frothingham stood for criminal recklessness, for huge rascality; it would be so for years to come."[125] A similar institution was described in Margaret de Vere Stacpoole's novel, *London 1913*, which was published in 1914. The Battersea Building Trust collapsed after rumours led to a run. "All over the country ... defenceless folk ... have been tempted to part with their money on the promise of big dividends, on one pretext or another. Of course, it's their own fault, their own greed. And there is no limit to their gullibility."[126] Conrad's novel, *Chance*, also appeared in 1914, and told the story of the Orb Deposit Bank and the Sceptre Trust, both of which failed after rumours led to a run.[127]

Public trust in banks and bankers was further enhanced during the First World War and in the 1920s and 1930s, when other countries experienced banking failures. British joint-stock banks were regarded as safe havens in difficult times, if the impression generated by novels is to be believed.[128] As before the war, those banks that failed came from the shadow banking sector as in J.S. Fletcher's 1920 novel, *Middle Temple Murder*. It was the Hearth and Home Mutual Benefit Society that

---

[124] W.T. Stead, "'Two and Two Make Four,' A Christmas Story for the Times', in *The Review of Reviews*, viii July-December (London: 1893) pp. 550–555.

[125] Gissing, The Whirlpool, pp. 14–15, 38, 40–44, 48, 52, 64, 118. See also Belloc, *Emmanuel Burden*, pp. 54–61, 65–76, 82–91, 104, 113, 119, 121–122, 158, 170–171, 196–197, 206–207, 212, 223.

[126] Stacpoole, *London 1913*, pp. 3–7, 11, 32–34, 38, 65, 71, 79, 85–86, 103–106, 109–110, 173, 196, 203–205, 271, 286, 297, 314, 333–334, 342, 344–356.

[127] J. Conrad, *Chance* (London: 1914) pp. 6, 68–71, 78–81, 84–5209, 228–229, 362, 377, 385, 433–434.

[128] M.A. Hamilton, *Dead Yesterday* (London: 1916) p. 234; Birmingham, *Gossamer*, pp. 9–10, 14, 20, 45, 54, 76, 103, 107, 138, 114, 164–165, 198–200, 220–221; J.S. Fletcher, *The Chestermarke Instinct* (London: 1921) pp. 10–13, 16, 22, 26, 28, 32, 106–107, 288, 293–295, 300, 307; G.U. Ellis, *Every Man's Desire* (London: Duckworth, 1925) pp. 9–11, 22, 35, 40; J. Hilton, *Ill Wind: Contango* (London: 1932) ch. 2: Florence Faulkner.

collapsed, after its manager disappeared with its funds, while the Market Milcaster Banking Company survived a similar occurrence.[129] Judging from the behaviour of the London banker, Henry Warren, in Nevil Shute's 1938 novel, *Ruined City*, British bankers exercised great caution when making loans, despite the pressure to assist customers in financial difficulty. "This is a bank ... of good repute ....We take in money on deposit, and it is my business to keep that money safe. We lend it out again at small interest on good security. It is no part of our business to take risks, or to make speculations with the money deposited with us. That is not our understanding with our depositors, and that is not our policy."[130] When a novel did feature a bank collapse, it was set in the distant past, which was the case with Stanley Weyman's *Ovington's Bank*. Though published in 1922, the story was set a century before. Even then, the country bank was saved through the intervention of the local landowner, as it was solvent.[131] Nevertheless, novelists were aware that bank stability was always at risk and that bankers needed to ensure that their behaviour did not threaten it. In Anthony Wynne's 1934 novel, *Death of a Banker*, it was noted that "No bank on earth can stand a run by its customers."[132] In John Creasey's 1935 novel, *First Came a Murder*, no bank was completely secure, even Bleddon's. "If once Bleddon's credit was publicly doubted, there would be a tremendous rush on all branches of the bank. Every depositor would clamour for his money-and even Bleddon's would be able to pay little more than a 10 per cent of the total call for ready cash."[133] In contrast, a finance house could fail without causing a systemic crisis, as was the case in Cyril Hare's 1937 novel, *Tenant for Death*.[134] With examples of banking crises all over the world in the 1930s, the British public was well aware of how precarious a bank was if not properly managed. Under the

---

[129] J.S. Fletcher, *The Middle Temple Murder* (London: Ward, Lock and Co., 1920) pp. 126–137, 198–200, 247.

[130] Shute, *Ruined City*, pp. 1, 4, 9–10, 27, 86–88, 187, 213–219, 228–229, 234–235, 242.

[131] S.J. Weyman, *Ovington's Bank* (London: John Murray, 1922) pp. 8–22, 30–31, 36, 44–45, 60–64, 68–69, 90–91, 136, 142–143, 205, 232, 250, 256, 276–277, 294–295, 306, 327, 350, 391–392, 414–415, 457, 461–482, 486, 509–510.

[132] Wynne, *Death of a Banker*, pp. 10–11, 50–53, 61–71, 84–85, 61, 85, 107, 118–119, 128–129, 182, 185, 188–189, 206–207, 230–231, 252.

[133] Creasey, *First Came a Murder*, chs. 4, 12 and 23.

[134] C. Hare, *Tenant for Death* (London: Faber and Faber, 1937) (reprinted by Penguin) pp. 14–15, 42, 66–67, 72, 84–85, 130–217.

circumstances, it was only natural that the public sided with the bank against those who tried to rob it. Edgar Wallace wrote numerous stories featuring J.G. Reeder, who was retained by the Bankers' Association to investigate cases of embezzlement, robbery and forgery.[135] J.S. Fletcher also featured thefts from banks in his stories, whether they were committed by partners and staff or robbery with violence by outsiders.[136] Agatha Christie featured two attempted thefts by managers of different banks in her 1924 collection of stories, *Poirot Investigates*.[137] In Henry Wade's *The Duke of York's Steps*, which was published in 1929, a City banker, Sir Garth Fratten, was murdered because those involved in an attempted fraud believed he would expose them.[138] In the 1926 novel, *Payment Deferred* by C.S. Forester, a bank clerk was dismissed for insider trading, which was not a criminal offence at the time.[139] Vincent Seligman, himself a banker, wrote in his 1934 novel, *Bank Holiday*, that "The British Public stolidly continue to place unlimited confidence in their financial institutions, no doubt because they enjoy that reputation for sound and conservative finance."[140]

Individual bankers were also seen as trusted figures in the 1920s, as in Dorothy Sayers's 1923 novel, *Whose Body?*, Agatha Christie's *The Secret of Chimneys* in 1925, Arnold Bennett's *Lord Raingo* in 1926, and

---

[135] Wallace, *The Melody of Death*, pp. 60–61, 78–79, 137; Wallace, *Red Aces*, pp. 55, 77, 89, 160; Wallace, *The Guv'nor*, pp. 70–76; Wallace, *Mr J.G. Reeder Returns*, pp. 9–10, 17, 84, 130–135, 149.

[136] Fletcher, 'The Tobacco Box'; J.S. Fletcher, 'The Murder in the Mayor's Parlour' (1922) in *The Secret of the Barbican and Other Stories* (London: 1925); J.S. Fletcher, 'Blind Gap Moor' (1918) in *The Secret of the Barbican and Other Stories* (London: Hodder and Stoughton, 1925); Fletcher, *The Middle Temple Murder*, pp. 126–137, 198–200, 247; Fletcher, *The Chestermarke Instinct*, pp. 10–13, 16, 22, 26, 28, 32, 106–107, 288, 293–295, 300, 307; J.S. Fletcher, *The Mystery of the London Banker: Being Entry Number Seven in the Case-Book of Ronald Camberwell* (London: George G. Harrap and Co., 1933) pp. 9, 38–39, 83, 160, 224.

[137] Christie, *Poirot Investigates*. See 'The Million Dollar Bond Robbery' and 'The Disappearance of Davenheim'.

[138] H. Wade (pseudonym of Sir Henry Aubrey Fletcher), *The Duke of York's Steps* (London: 1929) pp. 9–12, 15, 31–34, 36, 63, 71, 94, 174, 249, 263–265, 331, 348–349.

[139] Forester, *Payment Deferred*, pp. 43–47, 62–68, 82.

[140] V. Seligman, *Bank Holiday* (London: 1934) pp. 1–2, 9–13, 26–28, 41, 46–49, 62–67, 76, 92–93, 104, 216–218, 296–300.

Henry Wade's 1929 novel, *The Duke of York's Steps*.[141] An element of doubt did creep in after the Wall Street Crash. This left a legacy of mistrust in the USA which was transmitted to the UK, as can be seen in Anthony Wynne's 1934 novel, *Death of a Banker*. Despite acknowledging that "Our banking system is the soundest in the world," he launched an attack on it, with his focus being the London merchant bank, Hall and Company.[142] In John Creasey's *First Came a Murder*, which appeared in 1935, the banker Sir Basil Riordan and, especially, his son, Marcus, had resorted to murder in order to cover up their attempt to rob their own bank and flee with the proceeds.[143] Another merchant banker willing to commit murder was Alastair Blunt in Agatha Christie's 1940 novel, *One, Two, Buckle My Shoe*.[144] In Anthony Berkeley's *The Silk Stocking Murders*, which was published in 1941, the merchant banker, Pleydell, also turned out to be a murderer though he had an excuse as he had gone mad. However, none of this was directed towards the men as bankers. Pleydell and his father "were scrupulously honest, they were behind no shady deals."[145] Similarly respected was the merchant banker, Henry Warren in *Ruined City*, the 1938 novel by Nevil Shute. This was despite him ending up in prison as his actions had been motivated by a desire to reopen a shipbuilding yard and so bring prosperity back to an entire town.[146] This suggested that even British merchant bankers did not retain in the 1930s and 1940s the stigma attached to their US counterparts.

What stigma there was attached to bankers did not extend to those running the large joint-stock banks. In the 1931 novel by W. Stanley Sykes, *The Missing Moneylender*, the local bank manager was described as "a staid and prosaic individual, as befitted his occupation. His habits

---

[141] Sayers, *Whose Body?* pp. 16–17, 40–42, 56–59, 69, 79, 171; Christie, *The Secret of Chimneys*, pp. 18, 23–24, 77, 81, 97, 100–101, 165; A. Bennett, *Lord Raingo* (London: 1926) pp. 1, 38–41, 72, 124; Wade, *The Duke of York's Steps*, pp. 9–12, 15, 31–34, 36, 63, 71, 94, 174, 249, 263–265, 331, 348–349.

[142] Wynne, *Death of a Banker*, pp. 10–11, 50–53, 61–71, 84–85 61, 85, 107, 118–119, 128–129, 182, 185, 188–189, 206–207, 230–231, 252.

[143] Creasey, *First Came a Murder*, chs. 4, 12 and 23.

[144] Christie, *One, Two, Buckle My Shoe*, pp. 10–11, 15–16, 18, 42–43, 56–57, 86–87, 132–133, 155, 180–181, 185.

[145] A. Berkeley, *The Silk Stocking Murders* (London: Penguin, 1941) pp. 32–35, 51–52, 55–56, 107, 121, 165, 180–181.

[146] Shute, *Ruined City*, pp. 1, 4, 9–10, 27, 86–88, 187, 213–219, 228–229, 234–235, 242.

were clock-like in their precision."[147] It was these joint-stock banks that were in the ascendancy as Henry Wade observed in his 1929 novel, *The Duke of York's Steps*. "The position of the private banks is anything but secure these days-half a slip, and the big five swallow them."[148] There was even a degree of nostalgia in the 1920s for days when banks were local and personal rather than branches of national organisations, with trained staff obeying rules laid down in London. This can be seen in Mottram's three novels based on Gurney's Bank in Norwich, which became part of Barclays. Published between 1927 and 1931, these novels told the story of a retail bank from the eighteenth to the twentieth centuries. The message throughout was that bankers were trusted. Even after the conversion of banks into companies, which brought greater efficiency and professionalism, that trust remained, but with a loss of the personal touch.[149] In E. Phillips Oppenheim's 1934 novel, *The Bank Manager*, it was said about James Huitt, who managed the Aldwych branch of Barton's Bank, that "I cannot imagine anyone ever making him act upon impulse, saying or doing an incorrect thing." It thus came as a great shock that he had been murdering customers after robbing their accounts.[150] In a series of articles for *Lloyds Bank Staff Magazine*, republished in 1937 as *The Adventures of Mr. Pitkin*, Basil Boothroyd described a local bank manager as "a kind-hearted and loyal clerk who knew his place."[151] The same impression was generated by Clifford Witting in his 1941 novel, *Measure for Murder*. The bank clerk, Walter Tudor, observed that "The work was easy, but deadly monotonous."[152]

---

[147] W.S. Sykes, *The Missing Moneylender* (London: 1931) (reprinted by Penguin) pp. 7–8, 11–12, 17, 44–46, 159.

[148] Wade, *The Duke of York's Steps*, pp. 9–12, 15, 31–34, 36, 63, 71, 94, 174, 249, 263–265, 331, 348–349.

[149] R.H. Mottram, *Our Mr Dormer* (London: Chatto and Windus, 1927) pp. 24, 29, 118–119, 160, 216, 269, 272–273, 278, 289, R.H. Mottram, *The Boroughmonger* (London: Chatto and Windus, 1929) pp. 76–81; R.H. Mottram, *Castle Island* (London: Chatto and Windus, 1931) pp. 162, 147, 218, 245–246, 260–263, 268, 291–296, 301–303, 404, 414.

[150] Phillips Oppenheim, *The Bank Manager*, pp. 39, 65, 70–75, 137, 159, 165, 219–222, 244–247, 297, 303, 314, 317.

[151] B. Boothroyd, 'The Adventures of Mr. Pitkin, Bank Manager', *The Dark Horse* (Lloyds Bank Staff Magazine) (London: 1937) p. 7.

[152] C. Witting, *Measure for Murder* (London: Hodder and Stoughton, 1941) pp. 9–13.

That did not mean that bankers were liked by the public, as the description of Titian Woollacombe in Ronald Fraser's 1941 novel, *Financial Times*, reveals. Woollacombe became a banker because he was "not fit for anything else. A duller Boy, a Boy more exquisitely unfitted for any of the higher branches of human activity, I have never seen."[153] This perception of bankers as dull but trustworthy continues into the post-war years, as in the novels of George Bellairs, a bank manager himself. These were published in the late 1940s and into the 1950s.[154] This continuing trust in bankers was evident In Anderson's 1977 novel, *Death in the City*, Sir Geoffrey Gillington had worked his way up to become chairman of Britain's biggest bank, the London Metropolitan. He was described as "wholly sincere and a very decent sort." To him, trust was a two-way relationship and essential for the successful functioning of the bank. "The most important bank loans are made to people-determined by the banker's judgement of the personality of the man he's dealing with."[155] Guaranteeing the trust placed in banks was the degree to which they were policed by annual audits carried out by trained accountants belonging to the professional institutes. As Bruce Marshall wrote in his 1958 book, *The Bank Audit*, "The whole point about British Chartered Accountants is that they never sign a Balance Sheet unless they know it is correct."[156] The banks were also very careful when making loans, employing chartered accountants to carry out special investigations when required. The central character in *The Barbary Light* by P.H. Newby, which was published in 1962, was Owen Hanner who "goes round shutting up businesses when they don't give the bank a big enough return on the money they've borrowed."[157] In the 1977 novel by J.R.L. Anderson, *Death in the City*, the well-respected chartered accountant, James Henniker of Pooley, Handyside and Henniker, was called in by the London Metropolitan Bank

---

[153]Fraser, *Financial Times*, pp. 9, 41–43, 46, 58, 84, 113–115, 120, 128, 150–151, 156–158, 160–161, 177, 211–213, 218, 222.

[154]G. Bellairs, *Calamity at Harwood* (London: 1945); G. Bellairs, *Dead March for Penelope Blow* (London: The Thriller Book Club, 1951) pp. 13, 143, 146–147.

[155]J.R.L. Anderson, *Death in the City* (London: Victor Gollancz, 1977) pp. 39–43, 43, 46–47, 50–51, 58–59, 62, 65, 71, 106, 111–112, 116, 164–167, 191–195, 242–243, 256, 277.

[156]Marshall, *The Bank Audit*, pp. 3–58, 87, 123, 126–127, 368–373.

[157]Newby, *The Barbary Light*, pp. 32, 40, 50–51, 67, 80–81, 128, 138–141, 178–187, 192–193, 202–203, 224–227, 280–281, 286.

to conduct a special audit of one of its customers suspected of being in serious financial difficulties.[158] There were novels about thefts from banks but few featured crooked bank staff because, "Bank staffs, almost without exception, are law-abiding folk," according to Howard Davis in the 1960 novel, *Trouble in the Bank*.[159] In John Boland's novel, *The Golden Fleece*, which appeared in 1961, the honest and hardworking staff of the Kensington branch of the London Counties Bank did use the bank's money to speculate but no losses resulted.[160] Instead, it was mainly outsiders who attempted to rob banks, but those in the 1959 novel by John Brophy and the 1969 one by R.F. Delderfield were both set in the past, suggestive that they were unlikely to succeed because of the preventive measures now being taken. In the Delderfield novel, it was noted that, by 1969, "Bank security is good and getting better all the time."[161]

Ken Follett's *Paper Money*, which was published in 1977, does feature a bank robbery, but the target was a van transporting cash. It also included the near failure of bank, the Cotton Bank of Jamaica, but this was a small operation and received no publicity because that "would be enough to cause that collapse."[162] With the failure of a major British bank being considered so unlikely in the late twentieth century, Ken Follett set his 1993 novel, *A Dangerous Fortune*, in the years between the Overend and Gurney crisis of 1866 and the Baring Crisis of 1892.[163] The perception in the post-war years was that the large retail banks could not fail, and so stability could be taken for granted. This was unlike the position in the past where such banks were trusted, but it was accepted that any bank could fail, either because of individual circumstances or a global crisis. The British public also had confidence in merchant bankers, judging from

---

[158]Anderson, *Death in the City*, pp. 39–43, 43, 46–47, 50–51, 58–59, 62, 65, 71, 106, 111–112, 116, 164–167, 191–195, 242–243, 256, 277.

[159]H.C. Davis, *Trouble in the Bank* (London: Ward, Lock and Co., 1960) pp. 7–8, 16–17.

[160]Boland, *The Golden Fleece*, pp. 8–9, 12–14, 20–21, 52, 57–60, 85, 153.

[161]J. Brophy, *The Day They Robbed the Bank of England* (London: Chatto and Windus, 1959); R.F. Delderfield, *Come Home Charlie and Face Them* (London: Hodder and Stoughton, 1969) pp. 8–11, 7.

[162]K. Follett, *Paper Money* (London: 1977) [writing as Zachary Stone] pp. 14–16, 88–89, 185, 212, 218–220, 241–243, 247.

[163]K. Follett, *A Dangerous Fortune* (London: Macmillan, 1993) pp. 218, 252, 464, 513, 522–526, 594–595.

William Haggard's 1981 novel, *The Money Men*.[164] Beginning in the 1970s, there were a series of "banker-sleuth" novels in which merchant bankers were cast as individuals trusted by all to solve complex crimes. David Williams published seventeen novels over the 1976–1993 period, featuring Mark Treasure, the chief executive of the merchant bank, Grenwood, Phipps & Co. "Treasure combined the attributes of the traditional, inspired amateur in merchant banking with latter-day tutored professionalism," and these remained with him even though "Merchant banks are a dying breed."[165] The other "banker-sleuth" series was written by John Malcolm, and extended to 15 novels published between 1984 and 2005. It starred Tim Simpson, who managed the art investment fund for the family-owned merchant bank, White's. The world of merchant banking was seen as largely closed to outsiders. "You could never join them, except by birth or equivalent wealth." White's Bank was one of a diminishing band of privately owned merchant banks, as most had "disappeared or have been swallowed up by the big clearing banks and others." The public "have no idea what a merchant banker really does. ... If he is young, he is bound to be something of a cad....If he is old, he is bound to be disgustingly rich and something of a twister. Otherwise, they have no concept of him. How he actually spends his time is a mystery. ...They are not very popular." Nevertheless, they were trusted.[166]

Reflecting the trusted status of merchant banking in society by the 1980s, Dick Francis also published, in 1984, a "banker-sleuth" novel, *Banker*. Though providing a positive view of the merchant banker, it did

---

[164] W. Haggard, *The Money Men, a Novel* (London: Hodder and Stoughton, 1981) pp. 28–29, 64, 166.

[165] D. Williams: *Unholy Writ* (London: Collins, 1976), *Treasure by Degrees* (London: Collins, 1977), *Treasure up in Smoke* (London: Collins, 1978), *Murder for Treasure* (London: Collins, 1980), *Copper, Gold and Treasure* (London: Collins, 1980), *Treasure Preserved* (London: 1982), *Advertise for Treasure* (London: 1984), *Wedding Treasure* (London: Macmillan, 1985), *Murder in Advent* (London: Macmillan, 1986), *Treasure in Roubles* (London: 1987), *Divided Treasure* (London: 1988), *Treasure in Oxford* (London: 1989), *Holy Treasure* (London: 1989), *Prescription for Murder* (London: 1991), *Treasure by Post* (London: 1992), *Planning on Murder* (London: 1992), *Banking on Murder* (London: Harper Collins, 1993).

[166] Malcolm: *A Back Room in Somers Town*; *The Godwin Sideboard*; *The Gwen John Sculpture*; *Whistler in the Dark*, *Gothic Pursuit*; *Mortal Ruin*; *The Wrong Impression*; *Sheep, Goats and Soap*; *A Deceptive Appearance*; *The Burning Ground*; *Hung Over*; *Into the Vortex*; *Simpson's Homer*; *Circles and Squares*; *Rogues' Gallery*.

point out the risks they ran. "We gamble here on shipbuilders, motors, textiles, you name it, and all of those can go bust."[167] It was this risk-taking element of merchant banking that increasingly came to the fore in the 1980s, as in Peter Robinson's 1995 novel, *Dry Bones that Dream*, "Banks are basically run on greed."[168] Williams ceased to produce his "banker-sleuth" novels in 1993 though Malcolm went on to 2005. By then, a new type of banking novel was appearing, written by people who knew the business from the inside.[169] What these novels picked up on was the growing realisation among the British public that since Big Bang in 1986 British banking was an integral part of a global industry led by the Americans, and so featured British bankers working for US investment banks, British banks engaged in global financial markets or American bankers operating out of London. The British term, merchant banker, was largely abandoned in preference to the US one, investment banker. The central character in Linda Davies's 1995 novel, *Nest of Vipers*, was an American banker working in London, for example.[170] The series of novels written by Michael Ridpath between 1995 and 2006 largely focused on the activities of US investment banks in London. In the 2003 novel, *Fatal Error*, the comment was made that "We're all called investment bankers now."[171] Paul Kilduff was another who wrote a series of novels between 1999 and 2003 that placed British banks and bankers in the context of the global financial system.[172] What these novels drew upon were recent events in world financial history such as the actions of rogue traders, the risks posed by hedge funds and the Dot.Com speculative bubble. These were then mixed into global politics to produce transatlantic financial thrillers that appealed to an international audience. In 2012, Aifric Campbell wrote a novel, *On the Floor*, set in a US investment bank in

---

[167]D. Francis, *Banker* (London: Michael Joseph, 1982) pp. 3, 6, 10, 21, 30–31, 83–84, 98–99, 130, 186–187, 303, 392.

[168]Robinson, *Dry Bones that Dream*.

[169]S. Rustin, 'New Style Crime Wave in the City', *Financial Times*, 1st January 2000.

[170]L. Davies, *Nest of Vipers* (London: Vigliano, 1995, reprinted 2014) pp. 3, 21, 39, 50.

[171]M. Ridpath, *Free to Trade* (London: Heinemann, 1995), *Trading Reality* (London: Heinemann, 1996), *The Market Maker* (London: Michael Joseph, 1999), *Final Venture* (London: Michael Joseph, 2000), *The Predator* (London: Michael Joseph, 2001), *Fatal Error* (London: Michael Joseph, 2003), *On the Edge* (London: Michael Joseph, 2005), *See No Evil* (London: Michael Joseph, 2006).

[172]Kilduff, *Square Mile, The Dealer, The Frontrunner, The Headhunter.*

London, which conjured up an unpleasant and highly competitive environment which corrupted all those involved.[173]

Though British merchant banks had long been in decline, it was the collapse of Barings in 1995 that made the British public recognise finally what was happening, judging from the novels published subsequently. What also made its appearance in these novels was the recognition that rumours alone could destroy a bank. In the 1997 novel by Grant Sutherland, *Due Diligence*, the family-owned British merchant bank, Carlton Brothers, was brought to the brink of collapse by rumours spread by the US bank, American Pacific, to make it easier and cheaper for them to buy it. The owner, Lord Belmont, agreed to sell out. "The world has moved on, and away from our kind of banking. London's no longer the financial centre of gravity.... More than a century and a half after our arrival, the time has come for the Carlton family to make its unceremonious exit from the City."[174] Mark Cohen's *The Butchers' Ball*, which was published in 1999, also focused on a family-owned merchant bank, *Butcher's Bank*, being destabilised by false rumours. "There are few prospects more succulent to the world's media than that of a merchant bank facing imminent extinction, apparently through its own folly."[175] What was missing was any suggestion that one of the big retail banks could be brought down by rumours. The public's trust in these banks appeared undiminished despite the major changes they were experiencing with a much more competitive trading environment.

British banks and bankers came under the spotlight again in the wake of the financial crisis of 2007/2008. In 2009, Sebastian Faulks set a novel, *A Week in December* in the years between the failure of Northern Rock and the collapse of RBS. It centred on the activities of John Veals, a hedge fund manager, who targeted the Allied Royal Bank, hoping to make a large profit by "shorting" the bank's shares. This involved selling shares that he did not own, spreading rumours that it was in trouble, buying the shares when the price fell and delivering them to those to whom he had

---

[173] A. Campbell, *On the Floor* (London: Serpent's Tail, 2012).

[174] Sutherland, *Due Diligence*, pp. 7, 26–29, 33, 74–75, 90, 126, 251, 254–252, 264–265, 284–285, 340–341, 358–360, 410–411, 470.

[175] M.B. Cohen, *The Butchers' Ball* (London: Hodder and Stoughton, 1999) pp. 3, 14, 22, 61, 69–73, 81–83, 88–93, 106, 126–127, 182–183, 133, 160–161, 218, 356–357. For a similar storyline see J. McLaren, *Black Cabs* (London: Simon and Schuster, 1999) pp. 10–13, 27, 46, 50–3, 91, 123, 171, 388.

sold shares. He was unconcerned that his actions would cause the bank to fail as the government would intervene to save it: personal greed among bankers was the cause of the financial crisis.[176] That was also the storyline in Ben Elton's 2009 novel, *Meltdown*. Banks "had been lending money and investing in expansion at an insane rate and there was no real money to cover these reckless transactions." His principal character was Rupert Bennett who joined the Royal Lancashire Bank, where he became Chief Executive Officer and masterminded the takeover of the National City Bank. He was knighted and then given a title for his services to banking but was forced to resign after the financial crisis. "Lord Bennett was a ruthless man, there was no doubt about that, for his entire adult life he's been creating disasters and then escaping the consequences. In this case he couldn't." "The bank was broke. He knew it and shortly so would the world." He had also used inside knowledge to speculate in shares in another bank, the ex-building society, Caledonian Granite. Having been told it was going to be rescued by the government, he bought shares before they rose in value once the announcement was made. As this was a criminal offence, he fled abroad to escape punishment.[177] Another novel dealing with the aftermath of the banking crisis was *This Bleeding City*, by Alex Preston, which came out in 2010. This concentrated on the complex financial products which banks had invested in prior to the crisis, but then could not be sold, leaving them with huge losses and facing bankruptcy. "The banks were writing off billions in bad debts, and companies were unable to issue new bonds."[178] No longer did the public trust the big retail banks as that had ended with the collapse of Northern Rock in 2007, destabilising the entire British banking system as a consequence.

---

[176] Faulks, *A Week in December*, pp. 8–13, 32–37, 62–69, 102–104, 125, 190, 231–233, 268–269, 309, 371, 375–377, 390.

[177] Elton, *Meltdown*, pp. 21, 29, 59, 78–81, 88–89, 211, 236–237, 262, 270–272, 277, 281, 296–299, 304–308, 310–311, 320–321, 336, 343–344, 358–362, 390–391, 442–443, 457–461, 472, 477–480. In the real world Northern Rock was taken over by the government without compensation for the shareholders — I have personal experience of this as I was a shareholder. This is an illustration of novelists changing the facts to fit the plot but generating a false impression as a result.

[178] A. Preston, *This Bleeding City* (London: 2010) pp. 7–9, 14–17, 63–67, 112–113, 116–117, 132–134, 173–175, 186–187, 192–193, 225–226, 238–239, 250–251, 277–283, 303, 307–311, 320–325, 328–329.

As the experience of the 2007/2008 crisis faded, and the public understanding moved beyond a search for scapegoats in the shape of greedy bankers, a narrative developed that linked Big Bang in 1986, the collapse of Barings Bank in 1995, the disappearance of British merchant banks and the takeover of the City of London by Americans. Ignored in this narrative were the wider issues involving the transformation of the global financial system since the 1970s and the role played by central banks and international regulators. This comes across in Justin Cartwright's *Other People's Money*, published in 2011, which was about a long-established merchant bank, Tubal and Company, brought down by investing in new American-style financial products. "Even Tubal's fell for it." Until then, British banks had been conservatively managed.[179] John Lanchester, in *Capital*, which came out in 2012, followed a similar line. His focus was the collapse of a British merchant bank, Pinker Lloyd, in the financial crisis, due to the losses of a rogue trader and the spread of rumours. "People began to wonder about Pinker Lloyd's exposure to short-term loans and its reliance on borrowing money cheaply, easily and quickly on the international money market. Credit dried up overnight: lenders withdrew their loans. Clients withdrew their money, they had to ask the Bank of England for help, the Bank dithered and bingo, Pinker Lloyd was out of business. The bank had gone into receivership; its assets were being parcelled out and sold off; and everybody lost their jobs."[180] The legacy of the banking crisis of 2007/2008 was that rumours could bring down any British bank, no matter how large or established. British banks and bankers were no longer to be trusted, leading to a demand for government intervention.

Conclusion

It is almost as if the perception of banks and bankers came full circle over the course of 100 and 50 years. With the sole exception of the Bank of England, in the first half of the nineteenth century, banks and bankers were not trusted, being easily destabilised by rumours, whether they were true or false. These bank collapses had devastating consequences,

---

[179] J. Cartwright, *Other People's Money* (London: Bloomsbury, 2011) pp. 71, 182, 238–239.

[180] J. Lanchester, *Capital* (London: Faber and Faber, 2012) pp. 15–25, 192–194, 337, 345–347, 445–449, 509, 466–467, 476–477, 576.

imposing huge losses on those who had deposited their savings in the bank, held the notes that it had issued and were its owners either as partners or investors. For those reasons, bank failures were feared and this was evident in the novels written in the mid-nineteenth century, with runs providing action and drama in many stories. Much less evident was an interest in the power of individual bankers, though the wealth and influence of the Rothschilds in particular, magnified by contemporary writers, did attract public attention from time to time. There was then a long period in which banks emerged as trusted institutions able to withstand both individual shocks, as with robberies, and wider events ranging from crises to wars. This period extended from the late nineteenth century until the financial crisis of 2007, and it was during these years that British banks built up a reputation for resilience and British bankers as safe custodians of the nation's money. In addition, what power individual bankers possessed was used for the public good as exhibited during two world wars and in the era of government control that extended from the 1950s into the 1970s. It was that reputation of both banks and bankers that was shattered in the crisis of 2007. No longer were banks stable financial institutions that could be trusted, while bankers were exposed as individuals motivated solely by greed. Those shattered reputations were the legacy of the events of 2007/2008.

Over the course of the nineteenth century, British banking became increasingly resilient through a number of separate developments. One was the emergence of a small number of very large banks, which spread their risks through the management of an extensive branch network and the central balancing of assets and liabilities. Another was the role played by the Bank of England as lender of last resort to the financial system. Finally, a highly efficient money market grew up in London that allowed banks to borrow and lend among themselves, and so reduce the possibility of a liquidity crisis while operating on low reserves of cash. Between 1866 and 2007, the British banking system was able to cope with successive crises. However, the perception of banking within Britain took time to reflect this reality and then only partially. For much of the nineteenth century, the image of British banks was that they remained fragile institutions perpetually on the edge of collapse. This image was fuelled by the earlier crises such as that of the bank failures of 1866, associated with Overend and Gurney. These crises left a lasting impression which long coloured the perception of British banks, despite the absence of major systemic banking crises.

This stability of British banking did gradually influence perception. The British public increasingly recognised that the failure of a major bank was unlikely and that the collapses of a small one did not mean that they had to rush to withdraw funds from all, and so provoke a liquidity crisis. Instead, the criticism of banks switched to a belief that they had become highly conservative institutions, unwilling to take any risks, and this contributed to the decline of the British economy. Based on this perception, the solution devised was either greater state intervention, as practised in the 1950s to 1970s, or the promotion of much greater competition in banking, which was the policy pursued in the 1980s and 1990s. While the former policy accentuated the natural conservatism of many bankers, the latter one undermined the stability of the British baking system. However, as the perception was so firmly established that British banks could withstand any crisis, and a collapse in public trust was impossible, the emerging risks faced by the entire system from the 1980s onwards were ignored. The eventual outcome was the banking crisis of 2007/2008. Perception then continued to drive attitudes towards banks and bankers as it were they, rather than the environment created by government policy, that were blamed for the crisis. Fuelled by such perceptions, the government intervened to drive through changes in the structure and practice of British banking. These changes owed much more to conditions in the USA, even though there were fundamental differences between the two countries' banking systems, than to the reality of a British experience that had delivered almost 150 years of stability.

Chapter 6

The Company Promoter: Finding the Missing Link

Introduction

One of the greatest contributions to the transformation of economic life over the last two centuries has been the development of the joint-stock company. Until the nineteenth century, most business was conducted on a small scale by individuals. A sole enterprise or partnership was indivisible from the individuals who owned and ran it. That meant its finance and success were dependent upon them alone. Most did not survive successive generations as few closed groups, such as families, could constantly generate those with the ability, interest and commitment to sustain a business over the long term. Death, retirement and the lack of a male heir, when few women took on managerial roles, drained the pool of talent. In contrast, the organisation of a business as a company offered many benefits compared to sole enterprises or partnerships. Ownership and management were separate in companies, making it easy to bring in talented outsiders and create a meritocratic structure. Companies also had an identity of their own, which gave them both permanence and flexibility, and so could evolve over time. The result was that it was companies that increasingly dominated the way economic activity was organised and the provision of all types of goods and services. Before the widespread use of the corporate form, for example, finance was raised informally and there was heavy reliance on short-term credit, as supplied by banks, rather than long-term capital. The few exceptions were companies used in either spreading the burden of risk taking, as in long-distance trade and deep-level mining, or in raising large amounts of capital, which was the case with canals and urban utilities. In a company, risk could be spread and capital raised by selling stocks and bonds to a wide circle of investors. Those who bought the bonds were attracted by the greater liquidity of the asset they held compared to a loan. Purchasers of stocks did so for a variety of reasons, but all included the ability to buy and sell them. For some investors, stocks were akin to participating in a lottery, producing huge gains if the venture was successful. For others, the attractions of stocks lay in the higher yield compared to a bond, and one which had the possibility of rising in value over time while accepting the risk of a loss if the company failed. The major advance in the popularity of joint-stock companies came in the nineteenth century with the development of railways. Other types of business increasingly adopted the corporate form either because it provided access to capital or allowed owners to sell out. The securities issued as a result of the conversion of established businesses into corporate enterprises brought in investors looking for safe and remunerative assets, while those from new companies exploring for minerals and oil or developing a new technology attracted those willing to take high risks in exchange for high returns.[1]

This transformation of economic life through the growing reliance on the company required specialist intermediaries who could connect those requiring finance, or the vendors of existing businesses, with investors willing to purchase corporate stocks and bonds. These intermediaries were found among Britain's large shadow banking sector, and they became known as company promoters during the nineteenth century. The company promoter occupied a position between owners of a business, whether embryonic or established, seeking to sell out on the most favourable terms for themselves, and investors focused solely on profiting from the interest and dividends paid and the appreciation in stock and bond prices. The company promoter had to balance these opposing interests in such a way that both were satisfied. Occupying this intermediary position meant that company promoters were accused by vendors for underpaying and investors for overpricing. Investors were also quick to blame company promoters when a company failed, rather than accept that the vendors had been greedy and untruthful and that their own expectations had been unrealistic. The company promoter also took risks that made them vulnerable to failure. They had to borrow money

---

[1] See Michie, 'Financial Capitalism', in Neal and Williamson, *The Cambridge History of Capitalism*, Vol. 2: pp. 230–263.

from banks to meet their expenses and to pay the owners of a business. In return, they provided collateral in the form of the shares of the company they hoped to float. If the company was not floated, they were left with shares they could not sell, loans they could not repay and expenses they could not recoup. Even if the company was floated, there was the risk that the shares would fall in price, forcing them to sell out at a loss, leading to their own bankruptcy once banks called in their loans. Nevertheless, despite the criticism they received and the risks that they ran, company promoters flourished in Britain from the mid-nineteenth century until the 1930s. This suggests that not only was the role they performed a necessary one but it was also profitable for those who carried it out. When the demand for the services provided by company promoters revived after a long hiatus caused by the Second World War and government-imposed controls, the separate occupation of company promoter had largely disappeared. Instead, the task was undertaken by the merchant banks from the 1950s onwards. Increasingly, the activities once performed by the company promoter were attached to the occupation of investment banker, which had long been the situation in the USA, being referred to in the Money Trust Investigation of 1912.[2] Investment banks then became the leading symbols of the casino capitalism that was blamed for the banking crisis of 2007/2008, when they were considered a recent import from the USA, and not in the tradition of British banking. This reflected an ignorance of the earlier existence of company promoters and the role they had played, as they were not considered an integral part of the British banking system.[3] However, it is only by rediscovering company promoters that it becomes possible to take a holistic view of the entire British banking system.

The Rise of the Company Promoter

What the traditional view of British banking fails to recognise was the increasingly important role being performed by company promoters from

---

[2] V.P. Carosso, *The Morgans: Private International Bankers, 1854–1913* (Cambridge Mass.: 1987) pp. 271, 396, 403, 461–464, 499–503, 514; *Money Trust Investigation*: Investigation of financial and monetary conditions in the United States under House Resolutions numbers 429 and 405 before the subcommittee of the Committee on Banking and Currency (Washington, 1912).
[3] See Michie, 'Nature or Nurture', pp. 1–334.

the mid-nineteenth to the mid-twentieth century, before they disappeared as a separate profession. There is ample evidence to indicate that a growing number and variety of company promoters were filling the voids in corporate finance.[4] By 1892, Montagu Williams identified company promoters as a specific group within the financial system. "The successful company promoters are enormously wealthy.... Quick at figures, cool-headed, and gifted with a retentive memory, the company promoter is an excellent business man. There is a good deal of variety in his work. He transforms all manner of going concerns from private enterprises into share investments for the public,... He also finds capital for ... mines, valuable and valueless. His ability in placing an undertaking before the public in an alluring form is marvellous."[5] It was this variety attached to the nature of company promoters and the activities they engaged in that meant that they were difficult to classify. Napier observed in 1901 that "It is not always easy to determine whether a particular person is or is not a promoter of a certain company, or is an independent director and not a mere nominee of the promoter."[6] The distinct group of company promoters that appeared in the nineteenth century began with the numerous railway companies formed from the 1820s onwards. These had been promoted by a combination of local entrepreneurs and London-based lawyers, stockbrokers and bankers. The former were in touch with those who would benefit directly from the line, while the latter could steer legislation through Parliament, raise short-term funds and recruit investors nationally. That culminated in the Railway Mania of the 1840s, from which emerged individuals experienced in the promotion of companies and what it took to attract investors. These early companies required specific Acts of Parliament in order to have the legal status required to operate as companies. Legislation from the 1850s onwards then made it relatively easy to form joint-stock limited-liability companies.[7]

---

[4] Essex-Crosby, *Joint-Stock Companies in Great Britain*, pp. 34–35, 88; Ayres, *Fluctuations in New Capital Issues*, pp. 188–189; J. Armstrong, 'The Rise and Fall of the Company Promoter and the Financing of British Industry', in J.J. van Helten and Y. Cassis (eds), *Capitalism in a Mature Economy: Financial Institutions, Capital Exports and British Industry, 1870–1939* (Aldershot: Edward Elgar, 1990) pp. 115–126; P.L. Payne, 'The Early Scottish Limited Companies, 1856–1895: An Historical and Analytical Survey', *California Institute of Technology Working Paper*, 222, pp. 26, 40, 92 (1977).

[5] Williams, *Round London, Down East and Up West*, pp. 257–258.

[6] Napier, 'The History of Joint-Stock and Limited Liability Companies', p. 407.

[7] See Robb, *White-Collar Crime in Modern Britain*.

The result of that legislation was to put company promotion on a permanent footing rather than the occasional pursuit it had been in the past.[8] Company promoters fulfilled a growing need from the mid-nineteenth century onwards in two ways. One was to mobilise finance for highly speculative ventures, including bringing the products of new technology to the market and exploiting recently discovered mineral deposits. For this, the company promoter had to gain the trust of investors, for the outcome was as much a gamble as a calculation. Most such enterprises ended in failure, as was the nature of experimental work or geological exploration, but a few produced spectacular results enriching all involved. The other aspect of the work of a company promoter was to convert an existing private business into a public company and so make it accessible to investors. Here, the company promoter had an existing track record to work with and so could convince investors to participate through a forward projection of earnings. As individual businesses increased in scale and outgrew personal ownership, the company promoter came to play an important role in transforming private enterprise into public corporations. They provided businesses with a permanent structure that outlasted those who had founded them and investors with a range of assets beyond government debt, land mortgages and physical property. Company promoters became an integral part of a financial network that included retail banks, merchant banks, brokers, jobbers, lawyers and accountants, through which businesses raised finance and investors were supplied with a wide range of investment opportunities.[9] Increasingly, it was only London that possessed the breadth and depth of talent and

[8]B.C. Hunt, *The Development of the Business Corporation in England, 1800–1867* (Cambridge, Mass.: 1936) pp. 54, 72, 105; For some examples see Watson, *Industrial Finance in the UK*; Harrison, *Growth, Entrepreneurship and Capital Formation*; Du Cross, *Wheels of Fortune.*

[9]P.S. Manley, 'Gerard Lee Bevan and the City Equitable Companies', *Abacus: A Journal of Accounting and Business Studies*, 9, 107–108 (1973); P.S. Manley, 'Clarence Hatry', *Abacus: A Journal of Accounting and Business Studies*, 12, 49 (1976); Jefferys, *Trends in Business Organisation in Great Britain since 1856*, pp. 119, 133, 272, 278, 295–300, 320, 325–333, 343–345, 359, 363–364; Jefferys, 'The Denomination and Character of Shares, p. 45; H.J. Habakkuk, 'Fluctuations and Growth in the 19th Century', in M. Kooy (ed.), *Studies in Economics and Economic History* (London: 1972) p. 264; F.W. Paish, 'The London New Issue Market', *Economica*, n.s. xviii, 2, 13 (1951); E. Nicholls, *Crime Within the Square Mile: The History of Crime in the City of London* (London: 1935) pp. 122–133, 141–160.

facilities to support the activities of these company promoters, especially when it came to businesses that were large, complex or operated abroad. In 1898, the Scottish entrepreneur William Hector asked his friend, the Glasgow stockbroker, W.J. Anderson to help him promote a railway in Brazil. Anderson replied that "I would recommend your friend to try London as companies of this kind are more readily taken up there than here."[10] Glasgow had been an important centre for company promotion in the mid-nineteenth century but then increasingly left the business to London.[11]

Despite the visible presence of company promoters, the difficulty of the tasks they had to perform went largely unrecognised by contemporaries. Sir Henry Drummond Wolff in 1908 was one of the exceptions.[12] Much more typical was the view expressed in *The Bailie*, in 1898, where it was stated that all the company promoter had to do was "wave his hand and investors shovelled their hard-earned sovereigns into his lap."[13] Some insight into the work of a company promoter can be found in the autobiography of H. Osborne O'Hagan, who operated as one from the 1860s to the 1890s, working closely with the solicitors, Ashurst, Morris and Crisp, and the stockbrokers, Panmure Gordon. He began his career with a firm of engineers, drumming up local support for the companies that would construct and operate tramways in different localities. Based on that experience, he set up as a company promoter on his own account in the 1880s accepting the risks involved. "The financier must be prepared to spend many thousands of pounds in his investigations of concerns he may have to reject. Even when the greatest care is taken, most promising-looking companies will sometimes come to grief from various causes — the change of fashion, the retiring of those in whom the management rested without satisfactory substitutes, incompetent management, etc." He encountered few problems promoting well-established companies enjoying strong local support or during a speculative boom, as with those involving electric lighting in the 1880s or mining gold in South Africa in the 1890s. However, in most cases, a lot of work was necessary if the promoter was to bring a company to the market. That involved persuading the vendor to agree terms that would satisfy investors

---

[10] W.J. Anderson to William Hector in Rio de Janeiro 15th June 1898.

[11] Checkland, *The Mines of Tharsis*, pp. 16–18, 105–106, 111–113, 123–124, 126–127, 132, 138, 186.

[12] Sir H.D. Wolff, *Rambling Recollections* (London: 1908) p. 59.

[13] *The Bailie*, 24th August 1898.

and then convincing investors that the company was an attractive investment. "A financier of any standing has, as a rule, a large clientele ready to follow him, knowing that in any deal he will probably have lowered the purchase price first asked beyond the amount he puts on to cover his profit and expenses, and further, that he will not have taken up and introduced the concern unless he believes that thereafter it would reflect credit on him."[14]

The main role of the company promoter was knowing what investors would buy and how much they would pay; selecting those people who would act as directors, inspiring confidence in the business; and persuading banks and others to provide sufficient funds to bridge the gap between the inception of the project and the sale of shares. When the enterprise to be floated as a company was entirely new, there was a pre-stage involving the use of a syndicate to establish it as a going concern before an appeal to outside investors was made. Those involved in the syndicate, including the promoters, expected to be richly rewarded if the enterprise proved to be a success because of the risks that they took, as there was a high failure rate among such companies.[15] It was this high failure rate that generated much adverse publicity regarding company promoters because they were blamed for the outcome, rather than the risky nature of the enterprise or the difficulty of forecasting future earnings. The few company promoters that were prosecuted, and ended up in prison, gave credence to accusations that all were corrupt. This negative image belied the fact that company promoters were behind numerous solid enterprises, which meant they retained a loyal following among investors.[16] The negative image of the company promoter was a longstanding one, dating from past speculative manias. D. Morier Evans

---

[14] See H.O. O'Hagan, *Leaves from My Life* (London: John Lane, The Bodley Head, 1929) two vols.

[15] J.G.D. Nye, *The Company Promoter in London, 1877–1914*, Kings College London Ph.D. (2011), pp. 15, 23–26, 111–113, 123, 143, 187, 201–202, 244–249, 257–258, 267, 304, 352, 364, 369–371, 378, 383; Taylor, *Creating Capitalism*, pp. 11, 177, 187, 201–203; Taylor, *Boardroom Scandal*, pp. 11, 21–23, 43–49, 90, 94, 97, 103, 108–116, 122, 126, 136–150, 169, 177–184, 187, 194–205, 215, 223–223, 239, 241; *Economist*, 21st February 1880, 10th July 1880.

[16] Johnson, *Making the Market*, pp. 225–228; G. Elliot, *The Mystery of Overend Gurney: A Financial Scandal in Victorian London* (London: 2006) pp. 129–140; Taylor, *Boardroom Scandal*, pp. 22–25, 40–42, 50, 59, 82–84, 71–75, 97, 103, 108–116, 126–128, 133–148, 160–169, 177–178, 187, 192–205, 215–223, 239–241, 251, 255, 260.

wrote in 1852 that "The man who assumes as a calling the constitution of joint-stock associations, is most frequently looked upon as a doubtful character, who, if even to be trusted, requires looking after."[17] In 1881, the *Scottish Banking and Insurance Magazine* warned its readers to be very wary of any enterprise involving company promoters as "Promoting companies is not a business or profession, and no one is therefore specially trained for it."[18] W.R. Lawson claimed in 1884 that "Three-fourths of the fraud practised on the public is done by promoters. They get hold of worthless properties and foist them on investors at an exorbitant price."[19] Writing prior to the First World War, the radical politician, L. G. Chiozza Money, claimed that it was due to company promoters that "Hundreds of millions of capital have been wasted in the last twenty years through the dangling of fancy baits before the possessors of unearned investment."[20] The First World War appeared to have changed nothing. In the preface to Thomas Johnson's *The Financiers and the Nation*, which was published in 1934, Sydney Webb, dismissed all company promoters as "swindlers," with Johnson listing the few who were prosecuted as evidence, rather than the many who were not.[21]

This perception of company promoters mattered because it discouraged the participation of established merchant banks. Nevertheless, a number were tempted to enter the field when attractive opportunities arose. These included Barings, Rothschilds, Morgans, Hambros and Speyers. What merchant banks did was restrict the degree to which they became involved, often preferring to act through others rather than directly.[22] One British merchant banker who got involved in company promotion was Arthur Grenfell. He was a partner in the established merchant bank, Chaplin, Milne and Grenfell, and was very well connected within the London banking community. In 1906, he established the Canadian

---

[17] Morier Evans, *City Men and City Manner*, p. 62.

[18] *The Scottish Banking and Insurance Magazine*, September 1881.

[19] Lawson, *The Scottish Investors' Manual*, p. 36.

[20] Chiozza Money, *Riches and Poverty*, p. 166.

[21] T. Johnson, *The Financiers and the Nation* (London: 1934) pp. 42–46, 55, 69–70, 79–86, 94–96, 121–133, 137–138, 143, 183–193. Preface by Sydney Webb, p. v.

[22] J. Rutterford, 'The Merchant Banker, the Broker and the Company Chairman: A New Issue Case Study', *Accounting, Business and Financial History*, 16, 57, 64 (2006); Ball and Sunderland, *An Economic History of London*, pp. 245, 256–261; Barker and Robbins, *A History of London Transport*, Vol. 2: p. 70.

Agency in London, which specialised in issuing the stocks and bonds of smaller Canadian companies. All went well initially, but in 1914 the business collapsed as it had borrowed extensively to finance a portfolio of securities, and these could not be sold to repay his debts. The collapse of the Canadian Agency also brought down Chaplin, Milne and Grenfell. Grenfell tried to explain what had happened in a letter to Earl Grey, written in May 1914. "I was and am a fool. I could easily have retired in comfort and luxury. But some fatal impulse has driven me on and on, and I stuck too long to my guns." Here was the confession of a risk taker from among banking's elite, who had been attracted by the prospects of company promotion.[23] Outside the realms of banking, company promoters were recruited from a wide variety of professions and occupations. Lawyers had long been involved with the promotion of railways, utilities, banks and insurance companies and some City solicitors made a speciality of the business.[24] Ashurst, Morris and Crisp took up the business in the 1860s and were involved with 145 different companies by 1895. Two of their clerks, Slaughter and May, left to form their own legal partnership, and they also took up company promotion. The City solicitor, Frederick Gordon, became a successful company promoter in the late nineteenth century, focussing on companies engaged in hospitality, retailing and property. He was responsible for the Gordon Hotels Company which, by 1900, had become the largest hotel company in the world with a chain of 15 hotels in the UK and Europe. Accountants also took up company promotion. David Chadwick, a Manchester accountant, was responsible for promoting at least 47 companies, most of which were conversions of existing family-owned businesses, in the 1860s and 1870s. Between 1878 and 1900, another accountant, Henry Seymour Foster, promoted 66 companies, most of which only enjoyed a brief existence.[25] With a membership of over 5,000 by the First World War, the London Stock Exchange also provided a fruitful recruiting ground for company promoters, with many becoming involved, including major firms such as

---

[23] Arthur Grenfell to Earl Grey. 26th August 1906, 29th November 1906, 30th May 1914; Memorandum by Arthur Grenfell on the Canadian Agency, 1914; Smith St. Aubyn & Co. Ltd, Discount Company, Business Diary Showing Day-to-Day Business, 6th June 1914.

[24] Ball and Sunderland, *An Economic History of London*, pp. 245, 256–261; P. Matthias, *Retailing Revolution* (London: 1967) p. 125; Barker and Robbins, *A History of London Transport*, Vol. 2: p. 25.

[25] Johnson, 'Civilizing Mammon', p. 317.

Foster and Braithwaite, in the 1880s and 1890s. Having built up a successful business promoting companies, the brokers Helbert, Wagg & Co. resigned from the London Stock Exchange in 1912 to pursue it on a full-time basis.[26] Merchants and mining engineers also became involved in promoting companies, operating in those parts of the world with which they were most familiar, whether it was nitrate mining in Chile in the 1880s or gold mining in West Africa in the 1890s. The result was to make London the hub of the international mining industry with thousands of companies being promoted there between 1870 and 1914.[27]

[26] Duffy, *Bankruptcy and Insolvency in London*, pp. 150–151; H. Pollins, 'The Marketing of Railway Shares in the First Half of the 19th Century', *Economic History Review*, 8, 239 (1954–1955); W. Vamplew, 'Banks and Railway Finance: A Note on the Scottish Experience', *Transport History*, 4, 1164 (1971); L. Mackinnon, *Recollections of An Old Lawyer* (Aberdeen, 1935) pp. 182–183; *Aberdeen Free Press*, 3rd November 1881.

R. Kettle, *Deloitte and Company, 1845–1956* (Oxford: 1958) pp. 13, 17, 40–44; A.B. Richards, *Touche Ross and Company, 1899–1981: The Origins and Growth of the United Kingdom Firm* (London: 1981) pp. 1–5; Cottrell, *Industrial Finance*, pp. 113–117, 139–140, 154, 164, 167, 179–180; C.A. Jones, *British Financial Institutions in Argentina, 1860–1914*, University of Cambridge Ph.D. 1973, pp. 106, 118, 175, 302–306; D. Edwards, M. Edwards and D. Matthews, 'Accountability in a Free-Market Economy: The British Company Audit, 1886', *Abacus* 33 1997, pp. 4–8, 12, 22–23; M. Anderson, J.R. Edwards and D. Matthews, 'A Study of the Quoted Company Audit Market in 1886', *Accounting, Business and Financial History*, 6, 381 (1996); R.H. Parker, 'Regulating British Corporate Financial Reporting in the Late 19th Century', *Accounting, Business and Financial History*, 1, 60, 64, 67–69 (1990); D. Matthews, *A History of Auditing: The Changing Audit Process in Britain from the 19th Century to the Present Day* (London: 2006) pp. 9–11, 23, 68, 85, 141; T.A. Lee, 'Bankrupt Accountants and Lawyers: Transition in the Rise of Professionalism in Victorian Scotland', *Accounting, Auditing and Accountability Journal*, 24, 882, 884, 886, 895 (2011); J. Maltby, 'A Sort of Guide, Philosopher and Friend: The Rise of the Professional Auditor in Britain', *Accounting, Business and Financial History*, 9, 29, 33–34, 38–42 (1999); London Stock Exchange: Sub-Committee on the Limitation of Members: Report 6th May 1904; R. Roberts, *Schroders: Merchants and Bankers* (London: 1992) pp. 312–313, 342, 364, 373, 389–390, 399; Reader, *A House in the City*, pp. 96–100; J. Orbell, *Baring Brothers & Co: A History to 1939* (London: 1985) pp. 43, 51–53, 79–85.

[27] J. Schneer, *London 1900: The Imperial Metropolis* (New Haven: Yale University Press, 1999) p. 72. For examples see the chapters in R.E. Dumett (ed.), *Mining Tycoons in the Age of Empire: Entrepreneurship, High Finance and Territorial Expansion* (Farnham: Ashgate, 2009) (E. Cade and F. Gordon, 'British Imperialism and the Foundations of the Ashanti Goldfields Corporation, West Africa', pp. 64–74, 82; M. Monteen, 'John T. North,

Such was the prominence and success of company promoters that they were singled out for a mention in Bassett's listing of British businessmen in 1912. This provides a snapshot of their background and activities just before the First World War. Among their number was the Canadian, J. R. Bartlett, who promoted the British Oil and Cake Mills Company, while the German, William Mendel, specialised in retailing, with the department stores of Harrods and D.H. Evans. Nathaniel Spens from Glasgow and Walter de Frece from Liverpool both gravitated to London, but M. Stevens continued to be active in Manchester, with the Manchester Ship Canal Company and Trafford Park Estates to his name.[28] In addition to those singled out by Bassett, there were numerous other company promoters active in the years before the First World War. These included Moreton Frewen, who brought back to London many promising opportunities, most of which were failures, though they did include the very successful Broken Hill Proprietary Mining Company from Australia.[29] Conversely, there were those whose interests were very local such as Arthur Burr, who was obsessed with promoting companies mining coal in Kent, bankrupting himself in the process.[30] H. Jameson Davis experienced great success by promoting Marconi's Wireless Telegraph and Signal Company in 1897, after the government had

---

the Nitrate King, and Chile's Lost Future', p. 115; J. Mouat, 'Whitaker Wright, Speculative Finance, and the London Mining Boom of the 1890s', in R.E. Dumett (ed.), *Mining Tycoons in the Age of Empire, 1870–1945: Entrepreneurship, High Finance, Politics and Territorial Expansion* (Farnham: 2009) pp. 129–144, J. Phillips, 'Alfred Chester Beatty: Mining Engineer, Financier and Entrepreneur, 1898–1950', pp. 217–234); Marchildon, *Promotion, Finance and Mergers in Canadian Manufacturing Industry*, pp. 63–66; F.M.L. Thompson, 'Britain', in D.S. Spring (ed.), *European Landed Elites in the 19th Century* (Baltimore: 1977) p. 35; W. Hunt, *Heirs of Great Adventure: A History of Balfour, Williamson and Company, Ltd* (London: 1951, revised 1960) Vol. 1: pp. 15–16, 90, 95, 150, Vol. 2: pp. 28–32, 71, 78, 80, 108, 116, 120, 132–133, 191–193; Barker and Robbins, *A History of London Transport*, Vol. 2: pp. 25, 41, 71, 113; A. Lentin, *Banker, Traitor, Scapegoat, Spy? The Troublesome Case of Sir Edgar Speyer* (London: Hans Publishing Ltd, 2013) pp. 13, 39; Camplin, *The Rise of the Plutocrats*, pp. 46–60; Max Aitken to F.C. Clarke 21st August 1903; Aitken to E. Mackay Edgar 27th June 1903, Aitken to W.G. Gordon 22nd December 1903.

[28] Bassett, *Business Men at Home and Abroad.*

[29] Leslie, *Mr Frewen of England*, pp. 53–55, 86, 145.

[30] A.E. Ritchie, *The Kent Coalfield — Evolution and Development* (London: Iron & Coal Trades Review, 1919) pp. 1–7.

refused to support it.[31] The years from the 1860s to the First World War witnessed an explosion in the activities of company promoters, and their collective achievements far outweighed the frauds and failures singled out for media attention, but the perception was otherwise.

The company promoter then continued to flourish after the First World War, encouraged by new opportunities, a lack of competition and an absence of legislative restrictions. There were an increased number of businesses seeking outside finance, to compensate for the shrinkage in that available through informal channels because of high taxation and low profitability. For owners of businesses, there were also tax advantages in converting into a public company. The number of investors had also been swollen through purchases of government debt for patriotic reasons during the war, and they were searching for better returns and potential capital gains in the 1920s. Established merchant banks remained reluctant to commit themselves to company promotion because of its poor reputation, though a lack of business increasingly forced them in that direction, especially in the 1930s. The rules of the London Stock Exchange also became more restrictive after the First World War, increasingly forcing members to either abandon company promotion on a part-time basis or leave and take it up full time. The result was a host of new entrants to the field of company promotion in the 1920s. Among these was Clarence Hatry who moved into company promotion from a background in insurance and money broking, and became one of the most high-profile company promoters. His real breakthrough came once he began issuing local authority loans in the mid-1920s. These provided him with a source of short-term finance to meet the expenses involved in company promotion. He was one among many who became involved in the conversion of established smaller businesses into companies. Despite the important role played by company promoters between the wars, they continued to be regarded as marginal figures with a poor reputation. The speculative boom of 1919–1920 left a legacy of overcapitalised and poorly performing companies, and this was blamed on company promoters, especially as many small investors had lost money. A number of company promoters were also arrested and prosecuted following the collapse of the speculative boom creating the impression that all were crooks. That poor reputation was then confirmed with the corporate collapses that followed the bursting of the speculative boom of the late

---

[31] S.G. Sturmey, *The Economic Development of Radio* (London: 1958) pp. 18–19.

1920s, especially as this one brought down Clarence Hatry. By 1929, he was suffering a liquidity crisis as he had overextended himself by promoting too many companies at ever finer margins because of the growing competition in the business. To cover a shortfall in funds, he overissued securities, intending to repay when conditions improved. As they did not, he was unable to do so and his crime was exposed, leading to arrest, trial and conviction in 1930, with a blaze of publicity.[32] His fall confirmed, in the eyes of the public, the perception of company promoters as crooks.[33] Paul Einzig wrote in 1933 that "Domestic industrial issuing activity was handled almost entirely by second-rate, third-rate and the generally lesser-known financial houses; none but the largest industrial concerns could arrange their issues to be brought out under the auspices of one of the first-class issuing houses." However, he added the comment that "this state of affairs has undergone a complete change," and this was confirmed by himself and others in the 1930s.[34] With the collapse of international business after the 1931 financial crisis, the leading merchant banks switched their attention to the domestic market, invading the territory once occupied by the company promoters. Among those were Barings and Flemings. Though there was another

---

[32] Swinson, *Regulation of the London Stock Exchange*, pp. 1–5, 11, 18, 36–40, 45–47, 50–55, 98–100, 107, 111–113, 121–122, 130–137, 140–141, 156, 158, 164–165, 171–172, 179–182, 189–192, 194–198, 200–202, 213–215, 220–223, 227; C. Swinson, *Share Trading, Fraud and the Crash of 1929: A Biography of Clarence Hatry* (London: Routledge, 2019) pp. 7–9, 15–17, 21, 24, 34–35, 40, 42, 45, 53, 61, 68–69, 94, 109, 115, 118, 134–137, 140; O'Sullivan, *From Crisis to Crisis*, pp. 3, 21; M. Hollow, *Rogue Banking: A History of Financial Fraud in Inter-war Britain* (Basingstoke: Palgrave Macmillan, 2015) pp. 62–63; Thomas, *The Finance of British Industry*, pp. 24, 48–50, 91–92, 115–117; Kinross, *50 Years in the City*, pp. 37, 43, 60, 45, 66, 73, 78, 122; F.W. Paish, *Business Finance* (London: 1961) p. 105; Hannah, *The Rise of the Corporate Economy*, p. 76; Dennett, *The Charterhouse Group*, pp. 14–32, 36, 45–46, 57–59; Hoffman, *Great Britain and the German Trade Rivalry*, p. 75; Anderson, 'The Social Economy of Late-Victorian Clerks', pp. 127–130; Anson and Gourvish, *Leopold Joseph*, pp. 5–7; Board of Trade, *Share Pushing*.

[33] Hirst, *Wall Street and Lombard Street*, pp. 80–82. See H.W. Paulet, *Statesmen, Financiers and Felons* (n.p.: 1934).

[34] P. Einzig, 'Internal and International Banking', *The Banker*, xxviii, 98 (1933); J.G. Jarvie, 'Finance for Small Industries', *The Banker*, xxxii, 95–96 (November 1934); Political and Economic Planning, *Report on the Location of Industry* (London: 1939) pp. 97–98.

speculative bubble in 1936, the quality of the companies promoted was a considerable improvement over those of the late 1920s, and there were no high-profile failures or prosecutions.[35]

After the Second World War, the established merchant banks found that much of their traditional business remained closed to them because of government controls at home and abroad, and so focused on the business of corporate finance, including company promotion. At the same time, legislation had been introduced which prevented many of the most flagrant abuses while the London Stock Exchange was much more assiduous in policing the new issue market. All this made the business of promoting joint-stock companies more respectable though it lost much of its dynamism in the process. The result was an increasing convergence of traditional merchant banking and the business of the company promoters until the two became branches of the same integrated business. In 1954, the internationally orientated merchant bank, S. Japhet and Company, merged with the domestically oriented industrial finance house, the Charterhouse Group. In 1962, the long-established merchant bank, Schroders, merged with the ex-stockbrokers, Helbert, Wagg & Co.[36] Company promotion continued to attract adverse publicity whenever a venture failed and investors lost money, with past examples of fraudulent behaviour trotted out for inspection. However, the stigma once attached to company promoters had been greatly reduced through its association with the established merchant banks before the business eventually ended up in the hands of the US investment banks.[37]

The Public Perception of Company Promoters

The Macmillan Committee Report of 1931, on which Keynes was such an influence, provided authoritative support for a belief that a gap existed

---

[35]Orbell, *Baring Brothers & Co.*, pp. 43, 51–53, 79–85; Smith, *Robert Fleming*, pp. 100–114, 121–138; Hollow, *Rogue Banking*, pp. 26, 36, 46–50, 54–55, 62, 72–74.

[36]C.E. Steffenburg, 'Merchant Banking in London', in *Current Financial Problems and the City of London*, p. 64; W. Maude, *Anthony Gibbs & Sons, Merchants and Bankers, 1808–1958* (London: 1958) pp. 52, 77; Roberts, *Schroders*, pp. 312–313, 342, 364, 373, 389–390, 399; Dennett, *The Charterhouse Group*, p. 69. See W.L. Fraser, *All to the Good* (London: 1963) and S. Japhet, *Recollections from My Business Life* (London: privately printed, 1931).

[37]As example see R. Lambert, 'Charlatans: Financial Scandals of the 20th Century', *Financial Times*, 1st January 2000; D. McKie, 'The Fall of a Midas', *The Guardian*, 2nd February 2004.

in the financial system, and its conclusion has been applied to the periods before the First and after the Second World War. That structural gap was unique to corporate finance because others were quickly filled by new entrants, like the building societies and savings banks.[38] What went unrecognised was that the structural gap in corporate finance was filled by company promoters, and that omission supported the criticism being made that banks were overly conservative.[39] Though the existence of company promoters was recognised, they were dismissed as swindlers and their role marginalised. As Keynes famously said in *The General Theory of Employment, Interest and Money*, which was published in 1936, "When the capital development of a country becomes a by-product of the activities of a casino, the job is likely to be ill-done."[40] This perception of company promoters is confirmed by the way they were depicted in contemporary novels. There were always authors ready to weave stories around figures and events in the news, and company promoters were no exception. This can be seen in the Sexton Blake stories that appeared in their thousands between the 1890s and the 1960s from the pen of hundreds of different writers.[41] A study of novels over the long-term provides not only a means of capturing changes in the perception of the company promoter but also the message that was being conveyed to the public. What the appearance of company promoters in fiction did was to constantly blur fact and fiction. In this battle for the public imagination, it was the latter that triumphed because there was very little understanding of what company promoters did, even among experts, while a novelist could present a simplified version that focused on the more dramatic aspects.

There were occasional mentions of promoters, sometimes called projectors, in fiction before the nineteenth century but they were not

---

[38] See Michie, 'Nature or Nurture'; R.C. Michie, *British Banking: Continuity and Change from 1694 to the Present* (Oxford: Oxford University Press, 2016) pp. 1–334.

[39] Carnevali, *Europe's Advantage*, pp. 16, 24.

[40] Keynes, *The General Theory of Employment*, ch. 12 'The State of Long-term-Expectation'.

[41] See M. Hodder, *Sexton Blake Internet Archive,* in particular, *The Sexton Blake Timeline* and *The Sexton Blake Bibliography.* These contains various articles and lists, titles of stories and novels, which include the activities of crooked financiers and titles such as 'The Great Bank Smash' (1910), 'The Great Bank Fraud' (1912), 'The Banker's Trust' (1916), 'The Case of the Two Financiers' (1917), 'The Case of Two Bankers' (1918), 'The Case of the Blackfriars Financier' (1918).

common.[42] One of the earliest references in the nineteenth century was in the poems of Thomas Love Peacock, written during the speculative mania of the 1820s. "Now curst be the projects, and curst the projectors/and curst be the bubbles before us that rolled/which bursting, have left us like desolate spectres/bewailing our bodies of paper and gold." In his 1831 novel, *Crotchet Castle* companies failed and promoters were either bankrupted or fled the country.[43] In the 1838 novel by Charles Dickens, *Nicholas Nickleby*, the villain of the piece, Ralph Nickleby was one of the promoters of the United Improved Hot Muffin and Crumpet Banking and Punctual Delivery Company.[44] Thackeray featured a company promoter, Mr Brough, in his 1841 novel, *The History of Samuel Titmarsh*. After a brief period of success, his companies collapsed, the investors lost heavily and he fled to France "with a million of money."[45] Dickens extended his treatment of company promoters in *Martin Chuzzlewit*, which appeared in 1843–1844. The Anglo-Bengalee Disinterested Loan and Life Assurance Company failed, with one promoter murdered while the other fled the country.[46] Prior to the Railway Mania, neither company promoters nor their creations were regarded as other than marginal and dubious.

The Railway Mania then led to a spate of stories that featured company promoters, with readers left in little doubt that they were not to be trusted and the schemes were of little value.[47] However, once the speculative bubble surrounding railways subsided, and the lines were completed and working, a deeper and more reflective view emerged, as in Robert Bell's 1850 novel, *The Ladder of Gold*. Richard Rawlings promoted railway companies and he was depicted as both able and trustworthy.[48] The legacy of the Railway Mania was a mixed one when it

---

[42]Taylor, *Creating Capitalism*, pp. 11–15, 42, 54–56, 63, 80, 122, 177, 182, 187, 201–203.

[43]Peacock, *Paper Money Lyrics*; Peacock, *Crotchet Castle*, pp. 127–131, 145–148, 164–165, 248.

[44]Dickens, *Nicholas Nickleby*, pp. 35–37.

[45]Thackeray, *The History of Samuel Titmarsh*, pp. 9, 32–33, 46, 50–51, 66, 74–75, 78–82, 91–94.

[46]C. Dickens, *The Life and Adventures of Martin Chuzzlewit, 1843–1844* (London: Chapman and Hall, 1842) pp. 507, 510–511, 528–529, 524–527, 752, 792, 893, 950.

[47]Aytoun, 'How We Got Up the Glenmutchkin Railway', pp. 1, 22, 28; Reynolds, *The Mysteries of London*, pp. 27, 132–133, 234–237, 304–308, 313.

[48]Bell, *The Ladder of Gold*, pp. 98, 100, 107, 171, 188, 195–199, 201, 224–230, 256, 302–315, 366–367, 437.

came to company promoters. The public appreciated the improvement to transport but remained sceptical of the methods used to promote the companies. It was this scepticism that triumphed as can be seen in Emma Robinson's 1851 novel, *The Gold-Worshippers* which featured Mr Humson, "the Napoleon of Steam." As a company promoter, he was considered a "false god" who resorted to "fraud and deception."[49] Charles Lever's 1859 novel, *Davenport Dunn*, had a company promoter as its central character. He was described as "the most crafty and unprincipled knave of all Europe," being "a schemer and a swindler, unprincipled and unfeeling."[50] Despite the achievements of the Railway Mania, company promoters continued to be seen as unprincipled rogues in the 1850s. That perception continued into the 1860s though they were now seen as playing a more central role in the financial system.[51] This can be seen in Mrs Henry Wood's 1864 novel, *Oswald Cray*. Mr Barker and Mark Cray were the promoters of the Great Wheal Bang Mining Company, which failed and the investors lost all their money, including Barker and Cray. "This much must be said for the Great Wheal Bang Company-that its projectors were at least honest in their belief of its genuineness. In that they differed from some other companies we have heard of, which have turned out to be nothing but a swindle."[52]

Another popular novelist who took up the theme of company promoters at this time was Charlotte Riddell. In her 1866 novel, *The Race for Wealth*, Lawrence Barbour, an industrialist, became a company promoter, teaming up with the merchant, Mr Alwyn. "These were the palmy days of limited liability and unlimited speculation....There were companies for everything.... At last he had found the true El Dorada — the alchemist's secret. Under his touch, the most unpromising ventures became perfect mines of gold." The inevitable then happened as the companies all failed, leaving Lawrence Barbour penniless.[53] Charlotte

---

[49]Robinson, *The Gold-Worshippers*, pp. 8–14, 25, 51–55, 71, 103–105, 140, 194–199, 300.

[50]Lever, *Davenport Dunn*, Vol. 1: 42–43, 55, 61, 243, Vol. 2: 16–19, 101, 104–105, 118–120, 127–129, 150–160, 169, 166–167, 175–177, 190–196, Vol. 3: 25–30, 34, 39, 52–53, 84, 329–330, 333–334, 339, 352–353, 358–361.

[51]Anonymous, *Commercial Tales and Sketches* (London: 1864) pp. 151, 160–161, 166–168.

[52]Wood, *Oswald Cray*, pp. 250–251, 281–284, 294–295, 330–348, 416, 442–456.

[53]Riddell, *The Race for Wealth*, Vol. 1: pp. 14–15, 22, 56–57, Vol. 2: pp. 55–56, 62, 83–87, 123–126, 172–173, 174–181, 257, 287, 308–313.

Riddell followed that novel with *Far Above Rubies* in 1867, which featured another company promoter, Peter Black. Unlike Lawrence Barbour, he was a crook as he embezzled money from the companies he promoted before they collapsed.[54] The same year that *Far Above Rubies* came out, Joseph Hatton published *The Tallants of Barton*, which also featured a company promoter. Richard Tallant induced "Honest and industrious people … to invest hard-earned savings in rotten schemes made to look safe by the names of the gentlemen who figured as directors." He was eventually shot by an associate whom he had double-crossed.[55] The following year, Mary Braddon also published a novel involving a company promoter, Philip Sheldon. He was a man willing to commit fraud and murder. His schemes ended in failure, and he died a pauper, shunned by family and friends.[56] Though the public considered that punishment and an early death were the fitting end for a company promoter, Wilkie Collins, in his 1868 novel, *The Moonstone*, had an alternative suggestion. Those "that gets up Companies … and robs from thousands" escaped punishment.[57]

Reflecting the position they now occupied among the panoply of financiers, by 1870, company promoters had become regular characters in contemporary novels. Laurence Oliphant, in his 1870 novel, *Piccadilly*, featured no less than three of them. They spent their time trying to persuade friends and relatives to buy shares in highly dubious companies, which inevitably failed, with all losing their money.[58] However, by then, there was some recognition that not all company promoters were crooks, and some companies were sound. This can be seen in Alexander Shand's *Against Time*, which also appeared in 1870. Hugh Childersleigh, an impoverished landowner, and Robert Hempriggs, a solicitor, decided to become company promoters. "There's an absolute glut of money, and a perfect flush of credit; shoals of investors with their pockets running over, only waiting and praying for someone to show them where to empty them

---

[54]C. Riddell, *Far Above Rubies* (London: 1867) pp. 100–101, 107–108, 112–119, 222, 258–261, 430–441.

[55]Hatton, *The Tallants of Barton*, pp. 2–9, 16–17, 36–37, 79–80, 99, 219–221, 292–293, 308–309, 314–315, 345, 348–349.

[56]Braddon, *Charlotte's Inheritance*, Book 6th ch. 3, Book 6th ch. 5, Book 7th ch. 2, Book 9th ch. 3, Book 8th chs. 1, 2, 3 and 7, Book 10th chs. 5, 7 and 10.

[57]W. Collins, *The Moonstone* (London: 1868) pp. 54, 300, 507.

[58]Oliphant, *Piccadilly*, pp. 15, 61, 68–70, 82, 91.

to the best advantage." They floated the Credit Foncier and Mobilier of Turkey, which was well received and proved to be a great success. Though Childersleigh proved himself both capable and honest, Hempriggs got caught up in the speculative fever, and fled with money stolen from the Credit Foncier. This brought it down, despite being a "flourishing business." That was in contrast to those companies where "promoters and managing directors chuckled over the pilfered booty they had hid away in snug marriage settlements and quiet foreign investments, and liquidators rubbed their hands over the corpse of credit."[59] This negative view of company promoters was widespread in the 1870s.[60] Meason reprised in 1874 the stories he had published in 1865/1866, with a new preface claiming that "Hardly a day passes without a case of joint-stock company swindling being investigated by one or other of our metropolitan magistrates." Nevertheless, he acknowledged that "An experienced promoter takes care, as a general rule, not to bring forward a joint-stock company unless he is pretty sure that the shares will be taken up."[61]

Anthony Trollope featured a firm of company promoters, Fisher, Montague and Montague, in *The Way We Live Now*, which appeared in 1874/1875. "The object of Fisher, Montague and Montague was not to make a railway to Vera Cruz but to float a company." Once that was done, they would walk away with the money they had made.[62] Trollope also dismissed the work of company promoters in his 1876 novel, *The Prime Minister*, referring to the San Juan Mining Association as "one of those sham things that melt away like snow and leave the shareholders nowhere."[63] Reflecting the low regard in which they were held, company promoters were subjected to a full frontal attack in the 1875 fantasy novel *Ye Vampyres* by The Spectre, being accused of "legalized robbery."[64] In James Payn's 1876 novel, *Fallen Fortunes*, the company promoter, Richard Holt, was willing to do anything to force the woman he desired to marry him, including reducing her father to penury. Having failed in his

---

[59] Shand, *Against Time*, pp. 13–15, 38–46, 58–62, 115–116, 139–142, 149–153, 181, 200.

[60] Hatton, *Clytie*, pp. 139–141.

[61] Meason, *Three Months After Date*, pp. liii, lv, 6, 38–40, 56, 69–73, 84–85, 104–113, 188, 237–243, 253–262, 294, 297.

[62] Trollope, *The Way We Live Now*, Vol. 1: pp. 30–33, 77, 84, 368, 349, Vol. 2: pp. 26–27, 91–92, 99, 226–227, 276, 294, 302–304, 307, 359–361.

[63] Trollope, *The Prime Minister*, Vol. 2: pp. 110, 117, 126–129.

[64] The Spectre, *Ye Vampyres*, pp. 22–24, 44–45, 50–51, 190, 230.

object, he killed himself, after which it was discovered that he had been very successful in the business, making money not only for himself but those who invested in his companies.[65] In the 1870s, the work of novelists suggests that the public were willing to give company promoters some credit for their achievements, while still regarding them and their creations with a great deal of suspicion.[66] This image led the artist, William Powell Frith, to choose a "promoter of bubble companies" as representative of his times in a series of five paintings, The Race for Wealth, which he completed in the late 1870s. Frith had the company promoter end up in prison, but a fellow artist, J.F. Sullivan, considered that so unlikely that he produced an alternative set of cartoons in 1880, in which the company promoter escaped punishment.[67]

The novels of the 1880s continued to depict company promoters as dubious financiers, engaged in high-risk gambles. In *The Great Tontine* by Hawley Smart, which came out in 1881, the company promoter, Anthony Lyme Wregis, committed suicide when it was discovered that not only had his schemes collapsed and the investors lost all their money but he was also bankrupt.[68] In Anstey's 1882 novel, *Vice Versa*, Marmaduke Paradine was a shady individual involved "with the promotion of a series of companies of the kind affected by the widow and curate, and exposed in money articles and law courts."[69] Mrs Riddell's 1882 novel, *Daisies and Buttercups*, made the passing comment about one company promoter that "There is not a swindling company-a good dashing swindling company, I mean-established since the Limited Liability Act came in, but Frank Field has had a finger in the pie." He eventually overextended himself and

---

[65]Payn, *Fallen Fortunes*, pp. 10, 24–25, 40, 55–57, 62–66, 69–71, 161–166, 231, 247, 279, 352, 357, 362, 367–370, 380, 392, 395.

[66]Wood, *Adam Granger*, pp. 44–55, 66–67, 72–33, 105–106, 105–106, 109, 114–116, 127–128, 172–173; Besant and Rice, *The Golden Butterfly*, pp. 87, 130, 333–339; Hatton, *Cruel London*, pp. 6–8, 13, 17–19, 47, 99–104, 173–175, 199, 390.

[67]Frith, *My Autobiography and Reminiscences*, pp. 295, 343, 356–359, 354, 461, 469; *The Times*, 22nd April 1880; *Fun*, 23rd June 1880. See C. Wood, *Victorian Panorama: Paintings of Victorian Life* (London: 1976); L. Lambourne, *Victorian Painting* (London: 1999); A. Noakes, *William Frith: Extraordinary Victorian Painter* (London: 1978); C. Wood, *William Powell Frith: A Painter and His World* (Stroud: 2006); M. Bills and V. Knight (eds), *William Powell Frith: Painting the Victorian Age* (New Haven and London: 2006).

[68]Smart, *The Great Tontine*, pp. 15, 40–41.

[69]F. Anstey, *Vice Versa* (London: 1882) pp. 16–17.

ended up bankrupt.[70] Another 1882 novel involving company promoters was that of Stafford Northcote, who had served as Chancellor of the Exchequer and became the Earl of Iddesleigh. In the *Luck o' Lassendale*, the landowner, Sir Francis Lassendale, became a company promoter as a route to restoring the family fortunes that were suffering because of falling rents and rising expenses. The mining company he was involved with eventually ran out of money and had to be wound up, leaving him with nothing.[71] In contrast, Walter Besant, in *All in a Garden Fair*, which was published in 1883, suggested that company promoters managed to acquire sufficient wealth to live on comfortably, even after all their companies failed. "The British public is never tired of companies; sometimes there is a lull, but only for a short time, and then the game goes on again with undiminished vigour."[72] These were no isolated examples because company promoters popped up in various novels in the 1880s and early 1890s, indicating that the public now accepted them as a fixture. Though there was some appreciation of the role they played, the more common view remained that they were too ready to promote any scheme if it offered the prospect of personal gain.[73] Novels simply reflected what the public believed, based on real events, according to Thomas Terrell in *The City of the Just* and Frederick Wicks in *The Veiled Hand*, both of which appeared in 1892.[74] Investors were being forced to diversify their portfolio, and include corporate stocks and bonds in their holdings, because of a lack of alternatives, which placed them in the hands of the company promoter. Such was the high profile of company promoters that Gilbert and Sullivan even featured one in their 1893 operetta *Utopia,*

---

[70] Riddell, *Daisies and Buttercups*, pp. 60–61, 185–186, 372–373.

[71] Stafford Northcote, *Luck o' Lassendale*, pp. 86–87, 109–116, 125–129, 135, 182, 192–193.

[72] Besant, *All in a Garden Fair*, pp. 8–13, 86, 125, 133–139, 147, 150–153, 156–157, 196–197, 200–203, 262–56, 284, 295–296.

[73] Hemyng, *The Stockbroker's Wife*, pp. 9–13, 175–176; Shand, *Fortune's Wheel*, Vol. 2: pp. 236–239, 242–243, 257; Vol. 3: pp. 70–71, 84–85; Robertson, *A Lombard Street Mystery*, pp. 77–78; L. Merrick, *Violet Moses* (London: Richard Bentley & Son, 1891) pp. 44–45, 44–48, 78, 99, 122, 142, 165; C. Riddell, *The Head of the Firm* (London: William Heinemann, 1892) pp. 117–118, 192–194, 282.

[74] Terrell, *The City of the Just*, preface, pp. 22–24, 35–36, 79–87, 109, 113–116, 155–156, 229–231; Wicks, *The Veiled Hand*, preface, pp. 177–186, 189–193, 239, 250–269, 275–281.

Limited.[75] However, the acceptance that company promoters had a role to play in the financial system was not accompanied by any change in their reputation. In the 1895 novel by Max Pemberton, *The Impregnable City*, the company promoter, Jacob Dyer, was described as a man "who had never known an honest thought nor done an unselfish action."[76]

The reputation of the company promoter took a further hit in the mid-1890s in the wake of the speculative boom in the shares of South African gold mines. In the 1896 novel by Francis Gribble, *The Lower Life*, the company promoter, Benjamin Cohen, was an "ignorant, unmannerly vulgarian," but others were more respectable and trustworthy, such as Arnold Brabant, who was "cautious as well as bold, he never risked too much upon a single venture, so that he never made a loss that seriously checked his progress." Regardless of the quality of company promoters, investors were driven to buy the shares of the businesses they brought to the market when they got "tired of getting one and a half percent on their deposits, and nothing at all on their current accounts."[77] Another 1896 novel, Headon Hill's *Guilty Gold*, painted company promoters in an even worse light. Horace Vardon was promoting a South African gold mining company, the Golden Kloof, and was willing to commit kidnap and murder in order to prevent the public being made aware that it was a complete fraud. "All the gold there is ever likely to be in this company will come from the pockets of your deluded victims!" He was eventually exposed, captured, tried, convicted and hanged for his crimes while his associates were rounded up and given long gaol sentences for fraud.[78] Other novels published in 1896 were less extreme in their condemnation of company promoters but still depicted them as the unacceptable face of finance.[79] Nevertheless, it was accepted that some companies were a success, even mining ones.[80] In the 1897 tale of *"The Affair of the 'Avalanche Bicycle and Tyre Company Limited'*," Arthur Morrison observed that "Sometimes the shareholders got their money's worth,

---

[75] W.S. Gilbert and A.S. Sullivan, 'Utopia, Limited; or, the Flowers of Progress' (London: 1893) in *The Complete Plays of Gilbert and Sullivan* (New York and London: 1976).

[76] Pemberton, *The Impregnable City*, pp. 86, 92–93, 246–247, 306.

[77] Gribble, *The Lower Life*, pp. 1–2, 6, 8, 10, 14, 16, 20–22, 32, 53–55, 73–74, 61–93, 101, 108–109, 118–120, 131–133, 285, 294, 308–311.

[78] Hill, *Guilty Gold*, pp. 1–17, 23, 27–69, 78, 115–117, 149, 346–354.

[79] F. Warden, *The Wharf by the Docks: A Novel* (London: 1896) p. 64.

[80] Mrs A. Gowing, *Gods of Gold* (London: 1896) pp. 8, 231–233, 294–295, 298–299.

sometimes more, sometimes less — sometimes they got nothing but total loss; but still the game went on."[81] The popular view was that most companies failed as in Merriman's novel, *Roden's Corner*, published in 1898.[82] To Olive Schreiner, in the 1899 novel, *Trooper Peter Halket of Mashonaland*, the quickest route to wealth was not by buying shares in a company but by promoting a company and selling out as soon as possible.[83]

By the end of the 1890s, there was some revision in the hostility with which company promoters were regarded. Not all company promoters were crooks, some companies had proved very profitable, alternative investments were hard to find and shares in high-risk ventures appealed to those who wanted to gamble. Nevertheless, company promoters remained the least trusted members of the financial community.[84] The public was not blind to the fact that companies exploring for minerals or developing a new technology were a gamble, and for every one that produced spectacular profits there were numerous others that disappeared without trace. That made an investment in their shares equivalent to a lottery. An example of this more balanced assessment is in the 1900 novel, *Ford's Folly* by Major Arthur Griffiths. Even though the company promoters, Pettifer and Mandeville, were exposed as crooks, the company they were promoting was "a great and enduring success."[85] Such was the success of a number of the South African gold mining companies that, by 1903, Frank Danby was able to paint a positive picture of the company promoter, Karl Althaus, in his 1903 novel, *Pigs in Clover*. "There's only one way of doing big business, if you want to go on doing it, and that is to do it straight."[86]

By 1903, Fred White could claim, in *A Bubble Burst*, that this was the "golden hour of the promoter" and "for the most part, the schemes

---

[81]Morrison, 'The Affair of the "Avalanche Bicycle and Tyre Co. Limited"', pp. 103, 106–107.

[82]Merriman, *Roden's Corner*, p. 138.

[83]O. Schreiner, *Trooper Peter Halket of Mashonaland* (London: 1899) pp. 27–36, 83.

[84]Benson, *Mammon and Co.*, pp. 15–16, 27, 31–33, 60–61, 86–89, 93–94, 100–101, 172–179, 198–199, 209–217, 268–269, 272–277, 281–282, 285–286, 296–298, 300–302, 310–311; Frederic, *The Market-Place*, pp. 6–11, 20–22, 26–27, 36, 44, 48–49, 81–82, 157, 183–184, 197, 202–205, 214, 217, 218–219, 236, 230, 282–285, 293–294.

[85]Major A. Griffiths, *Ford's Folly, Ltd.* (London: George Bell and Sons, 1900) pp. 9, 34–39, 46, 58–66, 75–77, 80–87, 90–94, 100, 103, 111–112, 142–144, 223–225, 242–244, 253, 265, 306, 314, 318–319.

[86]Danby, *Pigs in Clover.*

promised well" but there was "an enormous amount of rubbish."[87] It was this "rubbish" that continued to give company promoters such a bad name.[88] In the 1904 novel, *Sharks*, by Guy Thorne and Leo Custance, the company promoters, Slynge and Company, brought out the Lost Continent Recovery Company which was completely fraudulent. It intended to raise the lost city of Atlantis from the seabed, but Slynge and his associates fled with the money they had made before it was exposed.[89] Though most company promoters remained crooks in the eyes of the public, it was also recognised that they provided a useful function, and took risks themselves when bringing companies to the market.[90] In the years before the First World War, no longer were all company promoters condemned as crooks, nor were the companies they brought to the market dismissed as worthless. Nevertheless, the risky nature of many of the companies they promoted, especially the mines, and the high-profile nature of the business they conducted, continued to place them at the margins of the financial world. This more nuanced portrayal of company promoters was captured in 1905 in William Le Queux's thriller, *Sins of the City*. Among the company promoters featured, there was Sir Charles Olcott and an Italian, Guiseppe Guelfo, both of whom were considered untrustworthy. In contrast to them was the stockbroker, Roland Kenrick, who made clear that when he promoted a company he was "going to run this show as I've run everyone with which I've had anything to do-on the square. It will stand on its own merits, and, as far as I am concerned, the public shall see that there is at least some honesty in the City."[91] These mixed signals regarding company promoters and their companies come

---

[87] White, 'A Bubble Burst', pp. 1–16.

[88] S. Kuppord, *A Fortune from the Sky* (London: 1903) pp. 16–17, 20–21; C. Hyne, *Thompson's Progress*, pp. 245, 249; E. Phillips Oppenheim, *A Prince of Sinners* (London: 1903) pp. 81, 120, 136, 165–166, 168–169, 176–177.

[89] Thorne and Custance, *Sharks*, pp. 2–15, 20–23, 30–33, 50–55, 144–145, 156–157, 180–181, 188–189, 226–229, 232–235, 278–279, 298–299, 340–345.

[90] Bennett, *Teresa of Watling Street*, pp. 13, 140–142, 159–160, 207; Pain, *Deals*, pp. 6–7, 28–30, 51, 56, 131–132, 150, 172–175; H. Hill, *The One Who Saw* (London: 1905) pp. 74, 79; E. Wallace, *The Four Just Men* (London: 1905) p. 28; Belloc, *Emmanuel Burden*, pp. 54–58, 70–76, 82–91, 104, 113, 119, 121–122, 158, 170–171, 196–197, 206–207, 212. See Belloc, *Mr Clutterbuck's Election*; Belloc, *A Change in the Cabinet*; Belloc, *Pongo and the Bull*.

[91] W. Le Queux, *Sins of the City: A Story of Craft, Crime and Capital* (London: 1905) pp. 5–12, 28, 34, 54–57, 71, 78–79, 83, 93–101, 108, 119–124.

across in different novels.[92] In 1906, Florence Warden took a sympathetic view of a company promoter in *The Financier's Wife*. Under the influence of his wife, "William Dixon, the brilliant financier, whose exploits were causing the City to hold its breath," abandoned the "dirty work" he had been engaged in. As a result, he escaped prosecution when his companies collapsed, as he had done nothing wrong. "There are no worse things to be said of company-promoting than there are of any other sort of enterprise … only it is work which is done on a big scale, and so the ups and downs are great, and the noise is great at the rise and fall. Companies have to be formed, to be pushed; men who can do the work are as necessary as men who can hoe potatoes or carry a hod.... It's the bigness of the profits and the losses in City enterprises that makes people talk so much louder about them than about others."[93]

Despite the recognition among the public that company promoters served a necessary function in the financial system, they remained among the most disliked of all financiers. What appealed to the public was when company promoters were foiled in their attempt to defraud investors or punished when they did. This was the case in Fox-Davies's 1908 novel, *The Finances of Sir John Kynnersley*, in which Sir John Kynnersley outwitted the company promoter, Moses Ikestein.[94] Taking revenge on crooked company promoters was also a theme in the first two of Robert Barr's novels featuring Lord Stranleigh, which came out in 1908 and 1909. Conversely, Robert Barr praised another company promoter, Peter MacKeller, who could be relied upon to deliver "an honest estimate of the real value of any distant mining property which is offered for sale in London."[95] Edgar Wallace also recognised the diversity among company promoters and the companies they promoted in his pre-war novels.[96]

---

[92] A. Bennett, *The Loot of Cities: Being the Adventures of a Millionaire in Search of Joy (a fantasia) and Other Stories* (London: 1905) pp. 7–10, 18–26; Oxenham, *Profit and Loss*, pp. 262, 273–274, 309–311.

[93] F. Warden, *The Financier's Wife* (London: T. Werner Laurie, 1906) pp. 1, 17–18, 23, 35–36, 69, 141, 145–148, 205–206, 240.

[94] Fox-Davies, *The Finances of Sir John Kynnersley*, pp. 4–5, 9–10, 15, 38–39, 53–55, 75, 113, 133, 152–156, 184–189, 210–214, 235.

[95] Barr, *Young Lord Stranleigh*, pp. 1, 7, 10–27, 33–43, 58, 63, 162–163, 188–189, 208, 237, 242–246; Barr, *Stranleigh's Millions*, pp. 58, 173–174, 178–179, 190–191, 204–207, 210–211, 220–221, 232–233, 236–238, 324–329.

[96] E. Wallace, *The Nine Bears* (London: Ward Lock, 1910) pp. 25–27, 31–32, 42–47; Wallace, *The Admirable Carfew*, pp. 23–25, 54–55, 90–91, 162–169, 182–190.

Increasingly, however, company promoters were being depicted as stereotypical crooked financiers, as was the case with Rider Haggard in his 1909 novel, *The Yellow God*.[97] Another popular author of the time who used the stereotype of a company promoter in a 1909 novel, *Tono-Bungay*, was H. G. Wells, though he was doing so as an attack on the capitalist system. "I cannot claim that a single one of the great businesses we organized added any real value to human life at all. Several like *Tono-Bungay* were unmitigated frauds by any honest standard."[98]

In contrast, Grace Pettman's 1912 novel, *A Study in Gold*, was an attack on greed. It featured Caleb Otto-Smith, "the most successful company promoter and financier of the day." When his financial empire got into difficulties, he staged a fire at his house, so that he could claim the insurance. That plot failed, and his sister was killed as a result, and so he fled the country, creating a panic among investors. "The bubble had burst. The companies floated by Otto-Smith were hopelessly bankrupt; his affairs had been placed in the hands of the official receiver, and a warrant was out for the great financier's arrest for conspiracy and fraud." Eventually, Otto-Smith was traced, apprehended aboard an American liner bound for New York, extradited to Britain, made to stand trial and then sent to prison.[99] Others were more willing than Pettman to credit the company promoter with some positive features, such as E. Philips Oppenheim in *A Millionaire of Yesterday*, which featured Scarlet Trent, who was promoting the Bekwando Land and Mining Company. "You're never quite dishonest and you're never quite honest. You come out on top, and afterwards you hate yourself. It's a dirty little life."[100] Another 1912 novel that also shone a more positive light on company promoters was Joseph Hocking's *God and Mammon*. Sir William Pilken was a company promoter about whom there has "never been a breath of scandal.... His money is clean, as far as money can be clean. He has done it all by brains, push, pluck, perseverance.... London gives a cold welcome to the mediocre man, but it opens its arms to the man of real ability — the man

---

[97] H. Rider Haggard, *The Yellow God: An Idol of Africa* (London: 1909) pp. 1–40, 42, 48–52, 67, 89.

[98] H.G. Wells, *Tono-Bungay* (London: 1909) pp. 81–82, 128–129, 180–183, 241, 297, 304.

[99] Pettman, *A Study in Gold*, pp. 101–104, 115, 121–137, 165, 171, 204–207, 210–215, 219–222, 226–227, 276–286, 294.

[100] E. Philips Oppenheim, *A Millionaire of Yesterday* (London: 1912) pp. 53, 60–71, 114, 117, 121–3134, 146, 170–172, 264, 273, 278, 298–302, 314.

who means to succeed and never gives up trying. And when London opens its arms, nothing is impossible." One who tried to emulate him was George Tremain, but he became disillusioned with the life of "a mere company promoter" and gave it up. "Have I not been trading on credulity and ignorance.... I have lost my soul."[101] This negative opinion of company promoters is revealed by a remark in another 1912 novel, *Mightier than the Sword* by Alphone Courlander. "Collard's arrested. ... The company promoter — reg'lar crook."[102]

Conversely, others praised company promoters, suggesting that the public had come round to appreciating their achievements in the years before the First World War, while never entirely forgiving them for the way it was done or the type of people they were.[103] In the 1914 novel, *Chance*, Joseph Conrad even painted the company promoter, de Barral, more as a victim of a poor choice of investments rather than crook. After the collapse of his companies, the Orb Deposit Bank and the Sceptre Trust, he was sentenced to seven years penal servitude, stripped of all his assets by his creditors and forced to leave his daughter unprovided for. When released from prison, he emerged as a bitter and troubled man who eventually committed suicide.[104] More representative of the public perception of company promoters and their projects on the eve of the First World War was Margaret de Vere Stacpoole's 1914 novel, *London 1913*. This acknowledged that the company promoter, Archdale "had not set out to ruin folk.... His real criminality lay in the fact that he had no care at all for others.... He's just a man who sells rubbish to the public.... He buys an old business and tells lies about it, and inflates it and gilds it and sells it for 40 times what he paid for it-that's his business in life, the sale of rubbish to fools.... It's useless to warn people against Archdale ... people like to be swindled by him-it's a new sort of pleasure, like cocaine-taking." Nevertheless, Archdale was "The prince of crooks" and "The

---

[101] Hocking, *God and Mammon*, pp. 6–8, 25–26, 48–49, 71–75, 79–80, 90–94, 101, 107–109, 123–127, 143, 152–158, 164212, 216, 219, 232–233, 245, 257, 263–279, 289–292, 298–299, 301, 306, 313.

[102] A. Courlander, *Mightier than the Sword* (London: T. Fisher Unwin, 1912) p. 236.

[103] A. Blackwood, *A Prisoner in Fairyland* (London: Macmillan & Co., 1913) pp. 1–6, 15–19, 55, 221, 227, 229, 318, 402, 432, 458–459; G. Parker, *The Judgement House* (London: 1913) pp. 39–43, 52, 66, 86, 92–93, 117, 259–260, 269; M. Rittenberg, *Swirling Waters* (London: 1913) pp. 1–3, 7–11, 18, 29, 150–151, 273–277, 292, 308–309.

[104] Conrad, *Chance*, pp. 6, 68–71, 78–81, 84–5209, 228–229, 362, 377, 385, 433–434.

master money magician" because he "had ruined thousands and thousands and will ruin more." Such were his crimes that "The extinction of Archdale would be a boon to society ... Archdale deserved social destruction, just as a murderer deserves hanging."[105] With those parting words, the company promoter virtually disappeared from view for the duration of the First World War, apart from a few mentions in Sexton Blake stories set before 1914.[106]

The disappearance of company promoters from contemporary novels during the war indicates the degree to which public opinion was driven by events. It was not until the speculative boom following the end of war that they reappeared, generating much the same perception as they had in the past. In Edgar Wallace's 1921 novel, *Bones in London*, Augustus Tibbetts outwitted various fraudulent company promoters. "He had the firm conviction that all new companies were founded on frauds and floated by criminals."[107] In his 1928 novel, *The Twister*, Edgar Wallace featured a crooked company promoter, Julian Reef, who resorted to kidnap and murder in order to cover his tracks. As in pre-war novels, Wallace did recognise that not all company promoters were crooks. Anthony Braid, who specialised in promoting South African diamond mining companies, was described as honest and trustworthy.[108] Even Hilaire Belloc recognised that not all companies were fraudulent though company promoters themselves bordered on criminality, as in the 1925 novel, *Mr Petre*.[109] In his 1926 novel *Lord Raingo*, Arnold Bennett painted a positive picture of a company promoter, but suggested that he had little interest in the enterprises he brought to the market. "Although he had bought and sold vast undertakings, he had learnt little about any of them beyond what might emerge from a ruthless, critical examination

[105] Stacpoole, *London 1913*, pp. 6, 11, 65, 71, 79, 85–86, 103–104, 173, 196, 203–204, 271, 314, 333, 342, 344–356.

[106] 'The Mystery of Room 11', *Union Jack,* January 1910; 'The Meeting with Marsh', *The Pluck Library,* 22nd May 1915; 'The Scotland Yard Scandal', *The Pluck Library*, 29th May 1915. These 1915 stories were set before the First World War; 'The Third Shot', *The Pluck Library*, 10th April 1915.

[107] Wallace, *Bones in London*, pp. 7–8, 11–13, 17, 66, 70, 82–83, 86, 103, 128–130, 119, 130, 191, 225–229, 233, 244–245.

[108] Wallace, *The Twister*, pp. 10–13, 16–21, 24–25, 29, 31–33, 73, 92–93.

[109] Belloc, *Mr. Petre*, pp. 41, 48, 51, 59, 79–88, 104–106, 148, 159–161, 218–219, 257, 264–265, 271.

of their books of account."[110] In another 1926 novel, *The Verdict of You All* by Henry Wade, the company promoter, Sir John Smethurst, who specialised in reconstructing ailing industrial companies, was also viewed sympathetically, having a reputation for "straight dealing."[111] Conversely, in his 1929 novel, *The Duke of York's Steps*, the featured company promoters were capable of fraud and murder, indicating that writers adjusted their story lines to reflect the public mood. This was the year in which the Hatry scandal broke.[112]

Lying behind the increased negative perception of company promoters by the late 1920s was the poor performance of a number of enterprises floated in that decade, as indicated by Kitchin in his 1929 novel, *Death of My Aunt*.[113] The reputation of company promoters fell even further that year and subsequently with the collapse of the speculative boom in Britain and the prosecution and conviction of Clarence Hatry. It was also wrapped up with the Wall Street Crash in the USA. A number of the novels published in 1929 and during the 1930s took up the theme of crooked company promoters. One was Vernon Loder's *Whose Hand*, which came out in 1929. This was a tale of two City financiers, Cupolis and Mand, who promoted a company based on a flawed scientific process. "It had not mattered to the dead swindler whether the process was commercially valuable or not. He had merely used it as a lever to extract money from a selected public."[114] Loder followed that novel with two more which featured company promoters. The 1934 book, *Two Dead*, explored what happened to a company promoter after he had served his sentence and been released from prison. John Bulpin had promoted "a series of wild-cat companies" engaged in mining and new technology. All failed leaving investors with large losses but Bulpin rich. He was eventually arrested, prosecuted and sent to prison for twelve years. On release, he discovered that another company promoter, Robinson Voyle, had robbed him of all his money, and so he committed suicide.[115] However, Loder did put a positive spin on another company promoter, Jimmy Dansford, who rescued bankrupt

---

[110]Bennett, *Lord Raingo*, pp. 38–41, 124.

[111]Wade, *The Verdict of You All*, pp. 9–30, 89, 104–105, 128, 131–133, 168–170.

[112]Wade, *The Duke of York's Steps*, pp. 174, 249, 263–265, 331, 348–349.

[113]Kitchin, *Death of My Aunt*, pp. 5–6, 10–11, 33, 247.

[114]Loder, *Whose Hand?* chs. 1, 3, 4, 14, 15.

[115]V. Loder, *Two Dead* (London: 1934) chs. i, xii, xxv, xxvi, xxviii, xxix.

manufacturing companies by combining them into more efficient units and investing in new technology. He was regarded as a wealthy, respectable and successful financier. He appeared in the 1934 novel, *Murder from Three Angles*, suggesting that the public continued to have an ambivalent attitude towards company promoters and their creations.[116] E. Phillips Oppenheim even produced in 1934 a novel, *The Bank Manager*, that featured a respectable and successful company promoter. Sir Julian Bott, who "had sprung from the middle classes, had commenced life as a country stockbroker, inaugurated a Trust with an attractive name, bought up commercial undertakings one after the other, nearly every one of which had turned out to be successful. He had weathered two periods of depression and come out unscathed. The confidence which the British public is slow to give to a financier pure and simple had become his by right."[117] In his 1933 novel, *Business Is Business*, Basil Nicholson suggested that it was the gullibility of investors than encouraged company promoters to bring out schemes that had little chance of success.[118]

Nevertheless, company promoters continued to be regarded with suspicion because of either past or current examples, as in Kitchin's 1934 novel, *Crime at Christmas*. Axel Quisberg, was none other than the company promoter, Lowenstjierna, who in 1904 had been involved "in a series of wild-cat schemes in Africa" which had collapsed, while he disappeared with £250,000. "There is no doubt that he had committed a criminal offence in vanishing with the securities ... I dare say he sailed pretty near the wind."[119] Crooked company promoters also remained the stereotypical crooked financiers as in C. St. John Sprigg's *Death of an Airman*, which was also published in 1934.[120] They also took on starring roles in John Creasey's *First Came a Murder*, published in 1935. Marcus Riordon had promoted the Marritaband Development Company, which was "one of the biggest swindles we've had for a long time.... The unfortunates who had bought shares had lost everything they had invested." With his associates, he had promoted 76 different companies

---

[116]V. Loder, *Murder from Three Angles* (London: 1934) chs. 1, 3, 8, 9, 18, 19.

[117]E. Phillips Oppenheim, *The Bank Manager* (London: Hodder and Stoughton, 1934) pp. 70–74, 137, 219–222.

[118]B.D. Nicholson, *Business Is Business* (London: 1933) pp. 128–142, 152, 166–192.

[119]C.H.B. Kitchin, *Crime at Christmas* (London: Faber and Faber, 1934) pp. 1–5, 78–79, 115, 149, 182–185, 198–199, 234–235, 240–241, 248.

[120]C. St. John Sprigg, *Death of an Airman* (London: 1934) p. 15.

through which they "had defrauded a get-rich-quick public of close on two million pounds."[121] In another 1935 novel, *Death Round the Corner*, Creasey observed that in company promotion, "The border-line between honest dealing and fraud ... was so faint as to be decipherable only by those who knew the tortuous working of the Company Laws-and evading them."[122] A much more direct use of Hatry as an example of a crooked company promoter was in the 1935 novel by the Coles, *Big Business Murder*, even though the preface contained the claim that "All the characters in this story are entirely fictitious, and no one of them has any foundation in any living person." The novel featured Kingsley Manson whose mode of operation closely resembled the activities that had led Hatry to receive a long goal sentence. Manson had engineered "a vast swindle that involved the ruin of thousands of people, and perhaps a world financial crisis when the bubble burst." However, even the Coles recognised that investors were attracted to the corporate stocks marketed by company promoters because the rate of return was much higher than that from holding UK government debt.[123]

This labelling of company promoters as crooks continued throughout the 1930s, rising to the surface whenever events brought the subject to prominence. Cyril Hare's *Tenant for Death*, published in 1937, drew on the more prominent promoters of the inter-war years for his characters. Lionel Ballantine, the promoter of the London and Imperial Estates Company, was "One of those picturesque figures appearing from time to time in the financial world of London, whose activities lend colour to the ordinarily drab record of commerce.... More than once there had been unpleasant whispers as to his methods.... But each time the murmurs had died down, leaving Ballantine more prosperous than ever."[124] In another 1937 novel, Rupert Penny's *The Talkative Policeman*, the company promoter Jacob Welling was described as "A plausible rogue, familiar with the confidence trick in all its branches."[125] Even those financiers who tried to be honest were forced into fraudulent practices when it came to promoting companies, as was the case with Henry Warren in *Ruined City*

---

[121] Creasey, *First Came a Murder*, chs. 1, 2, 4, 12, 13, 19, 20, 23, 24.
[122] J. Creasey, *Death Round the Corner* (London: 1935) chs. 3, 5, 19, 20, 23.
[123] G.D.H. Cole and M. Cole, *Big Business Murder* (London: Collins, 1935) pp. 7–13, 16–25, 32–33, 85–89, 123, 138, 189–197, 230, 237–239, 248–250.
[124] Hare, *Tenant for Death*, pp. 14–15, 42, 66–67, 72, 84–85, 130, 216–217.
[125] R. Penny, *The Talkative Policeman* (London: 1937) pp. 135, 138, 195, 247–250.

by Nevil Shute, which appeared in 1938. Warren had lied in a prospectus and was sent to prison when the truth emerged.[126] Another company promoter who ended up in prison was Montague Thringle in Ngaio Marsh's 1940 novel, *Death at the Bar*.[127] There was a remarkable similarity between the perception of company promoters in the 1930s and their portrayal before the First World War. They continued to be regarded with suspicion, being the go-to stereotype for the crooked financier, but it was also recognised that they were an integral part of the financial system and performed an important role in providing finance to business and supplying investors with profitable investments.

During the Second World War, the public lost interest in company promoters as they were little in evidence and other events loomed much larger. That disappearance became permanent because either they no longer engaged in the business or did so in a way that failed to attract public interest. The few post-war novels that mention company promoters were largely a throwback to the pre-war era, judging from their subject matter,[128] and they became the forgotten figures of British finance. The company promoter in Jeffrey Archer's blockbuster novel of 1976, *Not a Penny More, Not a Penny Less*, was an American with a temporary office in London.[129] By the 1970s, the business previously done by company promoters was associated with the work of a merchant bank, judging from the novels of David Williams and John Malcolm, which appeared from the 1970s until the early 2000s, and the 1982 one, *Banker*, by Dick Francis.[130] Though still tinged with suspicion, the role of the company promoter became much more respected by being attached to merchant

---

[126] Shute, *Ruined City*, pp. 1, 4, 9–10, 86–87, 213–219, 228–229, 234–235.

[127] N. Marsh, *Death at the Bar* (London: 1940) pp. 67, 223, 255–256, 261, 277–278.

[128] Bellairs, *Calamity at Harwood*; G. Bellairs, *The Case of the Headless Jesuit* (London: John Gifford, 1950); Wade, *Gold Was Our Grave*, pp. 3–9, 20, 38, 42, 47, 119, 124–126, 155, 186–187, 302–305, 311.

[129] Archer, *Not a Penny More*, pp. 50–51, 78–79, 254.

[130] Williams, *Murder for Treasure*, pp. 16, 2–5, 153; Williams, *Advertise for Treasure*, pp. 18–19, 27; Williams, *Wedding Treasure*, pp. 12, 28–31; Williams, *Holy Treasure!* pp. 42–49; Williams, *Prescription for Murder*, pp. 7–9, 48, 50, 62, 88–89, 92–93, 98–99, 141, 148, 184–185; Williams, *Treasure by Post*, pp. 48–49, 56–57; Williams, *Planning on Murder*, pp. 17–19, 22–23, 177–178; Malcolm, *The Gwen John Sculpture*, pp. 12–15, 22–25, 32–33, 80–81, 195; Malcolm, *Whistler in the Dark*, pp. 10, 24–26, Malcolm, *A Deceptive Appearance*, pp. 10–13, 19; Malcolm, *The Burning Ground*, ch. 3; Francis, *Banker*, pp. 10, 21, 30–31, 83–84, 98, 186–187, 303, 392.

banking rather than remaining a standalone occupation. Most British merchant banks then disappeared after Big Bang in 1986, with US investment banks taking over their role, as in Grant Sutherland's 1997 novel, *Due Diligence*, and the 1999 novel by John McLaren, *Black Cabs*.[131] By then, the whole concept of company promotion had been submerged into the multinational/multifunctional activities of a small group of global banks largely from the USA. When Salema Nazzal wrote a novel, *The Folly Under the Lake*, in 2015, loosely based on the life of the British company promoter Whitaker Wright, who had flourished before the First World War, she did not give the character that occupation. She made him a financier who had made his money in the USA.[132] In place of company promoters, it was property developers that were perceived as the most dubious members of the financial community, as in Anderson's 1977 novel, *Death in the City*.[133]

Conclusion

In nineteenth century Britain, the title company promoter became widely used to describe the person responsible for converting established businesses into corporate enterprises as well as forming new ones that sought to attract the support of the investing public. The Companies Act of 1856, and subsequent revisions, made it relatively easy to form a company with the liability for any losses limited to the investment made by the shareholders. This greatly reduced the risks that investors were exposed to and so encouraged their mass participation in corporate enterprise. Nevertheless, investors continued to experience losses, because the risks associated with any business remained, but these were blamed on company promoters rather than the unrealistic expectations of investors, especially when fuelled by a speculative boom. It was the lottery associated with shares in companies, especially in high-risk areas like mining or new technology, that both generated public outrage when losses were made and encouraged investors to continue buying in the expectation of large gains. Company promoters had already attracted

---

[131] Sutherland, *Due Diligence*, pp. 33, 74–75, 90, 358–359; McLaren, *Black Cabs*, pp. 10–13, 27, 46, 50, 91, 388–390.

[132] S. Nazzal, *The Folly Under the Lake* (Dartford: Pneuma Springs Publishing UK, 2015).

[133] Anderson, *Death in the City*, pp. 43, 46–47, 50–51, 58–59, 71, 167, 191–195.

some attention from novelists in the middle of the nineteenth century, sparked by the Railway Mania in the 1840s and the first wave of companies formed under the Limited Liability Acts. Among the novels written in this period that featured company promoters were ones by Charles Dickens and Anthony Trollope, but many others were attracted to the dramatic possibilities of company promotion. By the late nineteenth century, the company promoter had become a stock figure in numerous novels, providing an insight into contemporary perception as they built upon real-life examples. These novelists included some of the most widely read of the era, such as the likes of Ouida, E. F. Benson, Arnold Bennett, H. G. Wells, E. Phillips Oppenheim, Rider Haggard and Edgar Wallace. Though the overriding message of these novels was that company promoters were the worst examples of the crooked financier, there was also the recognition that they now occupied a central role in the financial system. That recognition prevented any action being taken to outlaw them and their practices.

That negative imagery of the company promoter then continued into the inter-war years, benefitting from both a speculative boom in the early and late 1920s and the notoriety achieved by the most prominent among them. Company promoters then largely disappeared from the scene after the Second World War. Legislation, taxation and regulation combined to remove the opportunities open to company promoters during much of the 1940s and 1950s. As the demand for the services of company promoters gradually revived, their role was taken up by established merchant banks, who had been forced to retreat from their global business. The existence of a separate class of company promoters had ceased, and they disappeared from view. The role they had once performed was absorbed by banks, especially those from Wall Street who had long specialised in the business, where it was classed as investment banking. Forgotten was the existence of numerous company promoters in the UK who had long performed the same role.

The combination of the marginalisation and a predominantly negative image of company promoters had a lasting impact on the perception of the British financial system over the period from the mid-nineteenth to the mid-twentieth century, or a period of a hundred years. The effect was to distort the perception of British banks, suggesting that they did not cater to high-risk ventures at home especially in manufacturing, leaving a gap in the system to be exploited by crooked financiers. Ignored was the obvious explanation for the high failure rate, which was that company promoters were engaged in providing finance for high-risk ventures and early-stage businesses. Mineral exploration, for example, was an acknowledged gamble as was the development of any new technology, product or service, but the rewards for success could be enormous. Investors in the USA continued to be attracted to these gambles and their needs were met by the investment banks. Company promoters had done the same in Britain until the Second World War but their role was dismissed because of a perception that painted them as marginal players exploiting loopholes in the law and the gullibility of the public. This left the way clear for those demanding state intervention to rectify perceived failings in the financial system, especially between the wars when the British economy went through successive bouts of depression.

Chapter 7

The Jewish Presence: The Perpetual Scapegoat*

Introduction

The success of Britain's financial sector owed much to successive waves of immigrants who contributed skills, contacts and entrepreneurship. In 1870, *The Stock Exchange Review* observed that, "With very few exceptions, all those among us who have become millionaires by dealing in money were either aliens or of foreign extraction. The Barings came from Germany, the Thelussons from France, and the three most famous gatherers of millions — Rothschilds, Goldsmid, and Sampson Gideon — were Jews."[1] In 2006, it was noted by the *Financial Times* that "The people who work in the financial services industry operate in what is the nearest thing to a true meritocracy. Nationality and ethnic background are unimportant, and employees are as likely to have been educated in Paris, Bombay or St. Petersburg as in the UK."[2] Considering the involvement of Jews with finance, it was inevitable that they would be numbered among

---

*I have explored the presence of Jews in the City of London, and the public perception of their involvement in finance, for the century before the First World War. See R.C. Michie, 'Jewish Financiers in the City of London: Reality versus Rhetoric, 1830–1914', in C. Hofmann and M.L. Muller (eds), *History of Financial Institutions: Essays on the History of European Finance, 1800–1950* (London: Routledge, 2016) pp. 38–61. This chapter develops that analysis using additional material while taking it up to the present.

[1] *The Stock Exchange Review* (London: October 1870).

[2] 'The New City', *Financial Times*, 27–30th March 2006.

those immigrants.[3] However, the role played by Jews in Britain's financial sector went much further than a mere presence for it is claimed that they had a dominant influence. In 1852, Jewish financiers were a prominent feature in the City of London, the nation's financial centre, according to Morier Evans.[4] When the historian, David Kynaston, selected the leading figure for each period of his four-volume history of the City of London, three of them were Jews, namely, Nathan Rothschild (1815–1890), Ernest Cassel (1890–1914) and Siegmund Warburg (1945–2000).[5] Another historian, Niall Ferguson, also chose Nathan Rothschild and Siegmund Warburg as his key figures in British financial history, leading him to pose the question, "Why was it that bankers of Jewish origin played such a leading role in British financial history?"[6]

Making judgements about an entire sector of the economy, especially one as large and diverse as finance, based on a few individuals, is very hazardous as it is an easy task to provide examples where their contribution was minimal. Jews had a very limited presence in retail banking, for example, where the likes of Quakers or Scots would be chosen in their place. Even among international bankers, many of the most prominent were not Jewish even though they were foreign, as was the case with the Barings, Schroders and Kleinworts. Bearing a German name did not mean that they were Jewish, despite many believing that they were. Perception is an unreliable guide especially when influenced by latent anti-Semitism as was always the possibility with Jewish financiers. As the journalist Harley Withers observed in 1916, "Much of the prejudice against financiers is based on, or connected with, anti-Semitic feeling, that miserable relic of medieval barbarism. No candid examination of the views current about finance and financiers can shirk the fact that the common prejudice against Jews is at the back of them; and the absurdity of this prejudice is a very fair measure of the validity of other current notions on the subject of financiers."[7]

---

[3]C. Roth, *The Jewish Contribution to Civilization* (London: 1938) p. 227; J. Jacobs, *Jewish Ideals and Other Essays* (London: 1896) pp. 171, 178–179; A.M. Hyamson and A.M. Silberman (eds), *Valentine's Jewish Encyclopaedia* (London: 1938) pp. 391–393; W.D. Rubinstein, *A History of the Jews in the English-Speaking World: Great Britain* (London: 1996) pp. 54–55, 74; Rubinstein, *Men of Property*, p. 116.

[4]Morier Evans, *The City*, pp. 4, 17, 47, 101–104, 128, 170.

[5]D. Kynaston, *The City of London*, 4 vols (London: 1994–2001) Vol. 4 preface.

[6]See Ferguson, *The World's Banker* and *High Financier.*

[7]Withers, *International Finance*, p. 111.

Jews and Finance

Jews were always a tiny minority within Britain. In contrast, as the commercial and financial centre of Britain, and a major international hub for over three centuries, London was home to a significant number of Jews. The City of London acted as a magnet for Jews from around the world, attracted as they were by the opportunities it provided for dealing in money and conducting commercial transactions. Many came from Germany, whether arriving to represent family banking and mercantile firms or to work in the numerous offices in the City where their experience and technical and language skills were highly valued.[8] In addition, events such as the Franco-Prussian war of 1870/1871 drove German-Jewish financiers from Paris because of nationalist hostility, and they chose London as a convenient alternative location. Legislation in Germany in the 1890s, designed to curb speculation, also led to the migration of financiers from that country to London, where they could operate free from such restrictions while serving their existing customers. Similarly, US bankers, which included Jewish firms, set up business in London from the 1950s to evade the controls imposed on them domestically.[9] Nevertheless,

---

[8]T.M. Endelman, *The Jews in Britain, 1656–2000* (Berkeley/Los Angeles: University of California Press, 2002) pp. 4, 43, 47–49, 80–81; W.D. Rubinstein, M.A. Jolles and H.L. Rubinstein, *The Palgrave Dictionary of Anglo-Jewish History* (London: Palgrave Macmillan, 2011) pp. 96, 185, 448, 558, 612–614, 638, 729; H. Pollins, *Economic History of the Jews in England* (London: 1982) pp. 43–48, 56–58, 60, 108–109; 111–112; P.L. Cottrell, 'The Business Man and Financier', in S. and V.D. Lipman (eds), *The Century of Moses Montefiore* (Oxford: 1985) pp. 24–26, 30–31, 40; S. Brook, *The Club: The Jews of Modern Britain* (London: 1989) p. 16; J. Parkes, 'The History of the Anglo-Jewish Community', in M. Freedman (ed.), *A Minority in Britain: Social Studies of the Anglo-Jewish Community* (London: 1955) p. 42; S. Aris, *The Jews in Business* (London: 1970) pp. 49, Hoffman, *Great Britain and the German Trade Rivalry*, p. 75; G. Alderman, *Controversy and Crisis: Studies in the History of Jews in Modern Britain* (Boston: 2008) pp. 232–236; V.D. Lipman, 'The Victorian Jewish Background', in A. and R. Cowen, *Victorian Jews through British Eyes* (Oxford: 1986) pp. xi–xiv; D. Kessler, *The Rothschilds and Disraeli in Buckinghamshire* (Waddesdon: Rothschild Waddesdon, 1996) pp. 20–22, 27–28; Anderson, 'The Social Economy of Late-Victorian Clerks', pp. 127–130. In Rubinstein, Jolles and Rubinstein, *The Palgrave Dictionary of Anglo-Jewish History*, a Jew was defined Jewish as '...anyone who was or is regarded as Jewish or regarded themselves as Jewish', pp. vii.

[9]Alderman, *Controversy and Crisis*, pp. 232–236; Lipman, 'The Victorian Jewish Background', pp. xi–xiv; Kessler, *The Rothschilds and Disraeli in Buckinghamshire*, pp. 20–22, 27–28.

the number of Jews in the City also remained very small at all times. In 1883, Joseph Jacobs attempted to count the number of Jews occupying prominent positions in the City of London, and to document those businesses in which they played a key role. His calculations produced a figure of around 1,500, which was a small percentage of the City's working population. He also discovered that it was not finance but selected commodity trades that Jews dominated. No more than five per cent of the membership of the London Stock Exchange was Jewish, for example, and this probably reflected their contribution to the City of London as a whole at that time.[10]

What an examination of *The Palgrave Dictionary of Anglo-Jewish History* reveals is that a large number of Jews had engaged in the trading and distribution of commodities like sugar, tea, coffee, nuts, rubber, tin, copper, diamonds, fur, feathers, gold and silver before the First World War.[11] This was only to be expected as London was the commercial and communications hub of the world economy in those years. It hosted most of the world's main commodity markets and provided an excellent location from which merchants and brokers could direct operations, engage shipping, obtain insurance and credit, and maintain contact with buyers and sellers around the world. Typical of those Jews who came to London when it was the leading international commercial centre was Julius Czarnikow. He arrived from Germany in 1854 and became a commodity broker specialising in sugar, connecting consumers in Germany with producers in the British Empire. When the German government banned the use of futures contracts in 1896, much of the business once done there transferred to London, along with the staff, because they had become vital to the conduct of international trade.[12] London remained a global commercial centre between the wars, with the Empire playing an increasingly important role. According to Findlay in 1927, "As London is preeminently the centre of finance in Europe, both shippers and buyers find it absolutely necessary to establish themselves here.... The facilities, indeed, which London enjoys for buying and selling, chartering and

---

[10] See J. Jacobs, *Studies in Jewish Statistics: Social, Vital and Anthropometric* (London: 1891); J. Jacobs, 'The Stock Exchange', in *Jewish Encyclopaedia* (New York: Funk & Wagnalls, 1901–1906); J. Jacobs, *Jewish Contributions to Civilization: An Estimate* (Philadelphia: 1919) pp. 228–229, 235, 239, 241–242, 245.

[11] Rubinstein, Jolles and Rubinstein, *The Palgrave Dictionary of Anglo-Jewish History*.

[12] H. Jones and H.J. Sayers, *The Story of Czarnikow* (London: 1963) pp. 9–31, 40.

financing, are unique, and one cannot, therefore, see anything to disturb its importance as the commercial centre of Europe."[13] For these reasons, it continued to attract Jews from around the world. It was only with the disruption caused by the Second World War, followed by the loss of Empire, and then the growing importance of governments and multinational corporations in international trade, that led to the City of London's demise as a commercial centre. With that came its declining attraction for Jewish merchants and brokers, with a location such as Switzerland being increasingly favoured because of tax advantages.[14]

Important as trade was to the City of London, and the attractions that had for Jewish merchants and brokers, it was with finance that Jews were closely identified. This was epitomised by the Jewish banking family, the Rothschilds, who possessed enormous wealth and power. John Reeves gave his 1887 book about the Rothschilds the subtitle, "The Financial Rulers of Nations." "It is a name which conjures up in the imagination visions of untold wealth and unrivalled power, which appear so startling and amazing as to be more appropriate to romance than real life. It has become a household word synonymous with unbounded riches, and is as familiar to the ears of the struggling artisan as to those of the banker or trader."[15] Such was the success of a small number of Jewish financiers in the first three-quarters of the nineteenth century, led by the Rothschilds, that they gained admittance to the upper levels of British society.

---

[13] J.A. Findlay, *The Baltic Exchange* (London: 1927) p. 42.

[14] Jones, *International Business in the Nineteenth Century*, pp. 140, 155–157, 160–162; D.C.M. Platt, *Latin America and British Trade, 1806–1914* (London: 1972) p. 110; Maughan, *Markets of London*, p. 108; E. Van Cleef, *Trade Centers and Trade Routes* (New York: 1937) pp. 132, 244; J.W.F. Rowe, *Primary Commodities in International Trade* (Cambridge: 1965) pp. 44–45, 51–54, 155–158; J. Jonker and J.L. van Zanden, *A History of Royal Dutch Shell: From Challenger to Joint Industry Leader, 1890–1939* (Oxford: 2007) pp. 38–87; *British Warehouseman* (Summer 1908) p. 14; Economist Intelligence Unit, *The London Metal Exchange* (London: 1958) p. 93; G.L. Rees, *The History of the London Commodity Markets* (London: 1978) pp. 58–59; Findlay, *The Baltic Exchange*, pp. 17, 42, G.D. Hodge, *56 Years in the London Sugar Market* (London: 1960) pp. 13–14; H.G. Cordero and L.H. Tarring, *Babylon to Birmingham* (London: 1960) pp. 106, 182; P. Harley, *My Life in Shipping, 1881–1938* (London: 1938) pp. 75, 205; G.L. Rees, *Britain's Commodity Markets* (London: 1972) pp. 138, 180; R.J. Hammond, 'British Food Supplies, 1914–1939', *Economic History Review*, 16, 5–6 (1946).

[15] J. Reeves, *The Rothschilds: The Financial Rulers of Nations* (London: 1887) pp. 1, 6–8, 20, 208, 249–251.

They built grand houses in London's West End, owned large estates in the country, entered Parliament in the Commons and the Lords, and became closely allied to the aristocracy and the royalty.[16] Nevertheless, Jewish bankers continued to be viewed with a degree of suspicion not found among other financiers.

A few Jewish financiers were involved in floating loans for foreign governments that then defaulted and the promotion of companies which quickly failed, leaving investors with large losses and a deep sense of grievance. One was the Dublin-born Abraham Gottheimer, commonly known as Albert Grant or Baron Grant. He was associated with one of the most notorious frauds of the mid-nineteenth century, the Emma Silver mine, though it was non-Jewish Americans who were primarily responsible.[17] Another to whom the stigma of crooked financier was attached in the late nineteenth century was the London-born Jew, Barney Barnato, even though most of the companies he was involved with proved highly profitable. Much more high profile among the fraudulent financiers of the age were Jabez Balfour and Whitaker Wright, and neither of them was Jewish.[18] Also marking out Jewish financiers for a degree of hostility was their strong international connections. These had long existed, with the

---

[16]Lentin, *Banker, Traitor, Scapegoat, Spy?* pp. 3–11, 13, 24–28, 32–33, 39, 49, 34, 70, 174; P. Thane, 'Financiers and the British State: The Case of Sir Ernest Cassel', *Business History*, 28, 80–87 (1986); D. Sunderland, *Financing the Raj: The City of London and Colonial India, 1858–1940* (Woodbridge: Boydell Press, 2013) pp. 8, 92–98; *Hambros Bank Ltd, London, 1839–1939* (London: 1939) pp. 5–10, 27–28; S. Nicholson, *A Victorian Household* (London: 1988) pp. 137, 148, 170, 148–145; S. Nicholson, *An Edwardian Bachelor: Roy Sambourne, 1878–1946* (London: 1999) pp. 16–17, 20–21, 29, 34–35, 43–44, 68, 100–101, 106, 116–117; D. Sebag-Montefiore, *The Story of Joseph Sebag and Co. and its Founding Families* (London: 1996) p. 12; Camplin, *The Rise of the Plutocrats*, pp. 37, 46, 49, 59–60, 156–160, 223; Pollins, *Economic History of the Jews in England*, 60, 108–112, 168–169.

[17]O'Hagan, *Leaves from My Life*, Vol. 1: pp. 32–35.

[18]Robb, *White-Collar Crime in Modern Britain*, pp. 97–104; Elliot, *The Mystery of Overend Gurney*, pp. 129–140; Taylor, *Boardroom Scandal*, p. 165; D. McKie, *Jabez: The Rise and Fall of a Victorian Rogue* (London: 2004) pp. 15–19, 220, 256–258; Mouat, 'Whitaker Wright', pp. 129–134, 141–144; R.E. Dumett, 'Edwin Cade and Frederick Gordon: British Imperialism and the Foundations of the Ashanti Goldfields Corporation, West Africa', in Dumett, *Mining Tycoons*, pp. 64–74, 82; M. Monteon, 'John T. North, The Nitrate King, and Chile's Lost Future', in Dumett, *Mining Tycoons*, pp. 111–115; Nye, *The Company Promoter in London*, 2011, p. 113.

Rothschilds being prominent as they had branches in Frankfurt, Paris, Vienna and even Naples as well as London. There was a steady influx of more Jewish financiers, especially from Germany, in the 50 years before the First World War when London became the ideal base from which to conduct an international financial business. One such firm was Bonn & Co. a small bank established in London in 1910. According to Lionel Fraser, who worked for them at that time, "Max Bonn was a Jew to his fingertips, of German origin, naturalized British, guttural, sensitive, brilliantly intelligent, a trained international banker."[19] Another who arrived at this time was Saemy Japhet. He came from Frankfurt, opening a branch of his banking business in London in 1896 before making it the base for his international operations in 1900. "Now my head office was in London ... business developed splendidly, and we were busier than ever.... We were recognised as one of the leading arbitrage and commission houses."[20] The international nature of their business emphasised the foreign origins of Jewish financiers, suggesting that their allegiance lay more to their fellow Jews, wherever located, than to Britain, though the evidence to support such an accusation was absent. Japhet, for example, lost their valuable New York connection with Goldman Sachs, a Jewish firm of investment bankers, to Kleinworts, who were not Jewish, because they offered better access to London. Similarly, the Jewish stockbrokers Helbert, Wagg & Co. were cut out from their Rothschild business by the non-Jewish brokers, Panmure Gordon, because they offered to provide them with a Far Eastern connection.[21]

What appeared to intensify the antagonism towards Jewish financiers in the 25 years before the First World War was a large influx of poor Jewish immigrants. An estimated 120,000 Jews arrived in Britain between 1890 and 1914, coming mainly from the Russian Empire where they were experiencing persecution. Though none of them possessed the skills, knowledge, connections or capital to qualify them for employment in the financial sector, their arrival was associated with the small trickle of bankers and brokers coming from Germany, attracted to London because of its

---

[19] Fraser, *All to the Good*, pp. 30–35, 64–65, 77.

[20] Japhet, *Recollections*, pp. 7, 18–25, 35, 40–43, 60–62, 70, 72–78, 91, 96–97, 102–103, 112.

[21] Japhet, *Recollections*, pp. 7, 18–25, 35, 40–43, 60–62, 70, 72–78, 91, 96–97, 102–103, 112; Roberts, *Schroders*, pp. 355–390.

position as an international financial centre.[22] The lack of a connection between the mass immigration of Jews from Russia and the arrival of a few German financiers can be measured from the membership of the London Stock Exchange in 1914. In that year, a total of 218 members and 31 clerks had been foreign born. Of these, only one member and one clerk had been born in Russia. In contrast, 153 were German and a further 20 were from Austria, 18 from the Netherlands and 7 from Switzerland. Among clerks, a similar picture emerges with 27 from these four countries.[23] These arrivals from Germany, like the banker Sir Edgar Speyer, became prominent and respected figures in British public life before the outbreak of the First World War.[24] Despite rising tension between Britain and Germany after 1900, there were close economic, financial and commercial ties between the two countries, and many were convinced that war between the two countries was impossible.[25] What hostility there was towards German financiers before the First World War had much more to do with them being Jewish than German, aggravated by the mass immigration that was taking place.[26]

Though there was growing anti-Semitism directed at financiers in Britain from the 1890s onwards, it was quite mild compared to that in the USA. Of the 5 million Jews who left Eastern Europe between 1880 and 1914, two million went to the USA. A large number settled in New York

---

[22]C. Russell and H.S. Lewis, *The Jew in London: A Study of Racial Character and Present-day Conditions* (London: 1900) p. 12; L.P. Gartner, 'Notes on the Statistics of Jewish Immigration to England 1870–1914', *Jewish Social Studies*, 22, 99 (1960); J.A. Garrard, *The English and Immigration, 1880–1910* (Oxford: 1971) p. 213; D. Feldman, 'The Importance of Being English: Jewish Immigration and the Decay of Liberal England', in D. Feldman and G. Stedman Jones (eds), *Metropolis London: Histories and Representations since 1800* (London: Routledge, 1989) pp. 56, 62, 76; Alderman, *Controversy and Crisis*, pp. 230–231, 237; Lipman, 'The Victorian Jewish Background', pp. xii, xiv, xvi, xix; A. Godley, *Jewish Immigrant Entrepreneurship in New York and London, 1880–1914: Enterprise and Culture* (Basingstoke: Palgrave, 2001) pp. 20, 30, 54, 60.

[23]Data from R.C. Michie, *The London Stock Exchange: A History* (Oxford: 1999).

[24]D. French, *British Economic and Strategic Planning, 1905–1915* (London: 1992) pp. 68, 92–94; Kennedy, *Strategy and Diplomacy*, pp. 94–96; Lentin, *Banker, Traitor, Scapegoat, Spy?* pp. 27–28.

[25]C.J. Fuchs, *The Trade Policy of Great Britain and Her Colonies since 1860* (London: 1905) p. viii. See N. Angel, *The Great Illusion* (London: 1909).

[26]Schneer, *London 1900*, pp. 169, 182, 238, 251, 258.

but, as in London, they lacked the connections and skills required to enter finance, unlike those Jews who came from Germany. However, this rising anti-Semitism in the USA was attached to the long-standing hostility shown towards the bankers and brokers of Wall Street. They were blamed for the periodic monetary and financial crises that took place in the USA, because of their support for the Gold Standard. That hostility then merged into another over the power of the Wall Street investment banks and the New York Stock Exchange, that appeared to be growing in the late nineteenth century with the rise of a group of business leaders popularly known as Robber Barons. The conclusions drawn by many in the USA at the time was that the country was in the grip of a small number of international financiers who conspired to limit the supply of money, control access to finance, manipulate trading on the New York Stock Exchange and dominate the business of the country. This eventually crystallised into a belief in the existence of a powerful Money Trust in which the Jewish investment bank, Kuhn Loeb, was a major element.[27] As early as 1885, an American journalist resident in London, George W. Smalley, suggested that what he observed happening in the USA had parallels in the UK, by highlighting the influence of Jewish financiers. "English society, once ruled by an aristocracy, is now dominated mainly by a plutocracy. And this plutocracy is to large extent Hebraic in its composition. There is no phenomenon more noticeable in the society of London than the

---

[27] B.E. Supple, 'A Business Elite: German-Jewish Financiers in Nineteenth Century New York', *Business History Review*, 31, 143–178 (1957); V.P. Carosso, 'The Wall Street Money Trust from Pujo through Medina', *Business History Review*, xlviii, 437 (1973); V.P. Carosso, *Investment Banking in America: A History* (Cambridge, Mass.: 1970) pp. 78, 93; Carosso, *The Morgans*, pp. 333, 347; J. Hughes, *The Vital Few: American Economic Progress and its Protagonists* (New York: Houghton Mifflin, 1966) pp. 318–323, 403; S. Fraser, *Everyman a Speculator: A History of Wall Street in American Life* (New York: Harper Collins Publishers, 2005) pp. 44, 56–57, 59, 69, 73, 94, 101, 105–110, 129, 141–3, 157, 172, 175, 183, 189–190, 192, 197–198, 203–206, 213–229, 232, 261, 269–271, 286, 302–303, 316, 338; C.R. Geisst, *Wall Street: A History*, updated ed. (Oxford: Oxford University Press, 2012) pp. 118–126, 131; M. Josephson, *The Robber Barons: The Great American Capitalists, 1861–1901* (New York: Harcourt Brace, 1934) pp. 404–405; T.C. Cochran, *Business in American Life: A History* (New York: McGraw-Hill, 1972) pp. 155–157, 231; G. Myers, *History of the Great American Fortunes* (New York: The Modern Library, 1909, 1936) pp. 574–575. See *Report of Governor Hughes's Committee on Speculation in Securities and Commodities* (New York: 7th June 1909); *Money Trust Investigation*.

ascendancy of the Jews." The Rothschilds, in particular, were at the centre of a powerful international network.[28]

What united the various strands of anti-Semitism, whether home-grown or imported, and gave it a focus on finance, was the boom in South African gold mining shares in the mid-1890s. That was followed by the outbreak of a war in South Africa in 1899, in which the British fought for control of these gold deposits. This speculative bubble drew in both established Jewish financiers like the Rothschilds and those with an interest in the diamond and precious metals trade, like Barney Barnato. In 1886, the Rothschilds had formed the Exploration Company to finance mining developments around the world, and that included South Africa. Jewish banks, brokers and merchants from Germany were also attracted by the potential of diamonds and then gold mining in South Africa. The German/Jewish bank, Spiegel & Co. transferred its head office from Berlin to London in 1896, as it specialised in mining stocks. It was this mining boom that also persuaded Saemy Japhet to come to London.[29] Due to the diverse nature of the Jews who became involved in the South African gold mining boom of the 1890s, they could be viewed, simultaneously, as privileged individuals who occupied the highest levels of British political and social life, shadowy figures engaged in speculative transactions and dubious company promotions, and international financiers doing the bidding of their masters in Berlin or Paris. This left them open to attack from a variety of different quarters in the 1890s.

A link was then made between the activities of these Jewish financiers and the outbreak of the Anglo-Boer war in 1899. Many believed this war was fought in the interests of these financiers as it involved control of the South African gold mines. It was the radical economist, J.A. Hobson, who drew together the different strands of anti-capitalism, anti-imperialism and anti-Semitism through a focus on the activities of Jewish financiers in his 1900 book, *The War in South Africa*. "A few of the financial pioneers in South Africa have been Englishmen, like Messrs Rhodes and Rudd; but recent developments of Transvaal gold-mining have thrown the economic resources of the country more and more into the hands of a small group of international financiers, chiefly German in origin and Jewish in race."

---

[28] G.W. Smalley, *Society in London, by a Foreign Resident* (London: Chatto and Windus, 1885) pp. 85–87, 90, 94–95, 118.

[29] Turrell and van Helten, 'The Rothschilds', pp. 182–187, 191; Raymond, *Barnato*, pp. 33–34, 194; M. Karo, *City Milestones and Memories* (London: 1962) p. 1.

His claim was that "We are fighting in order to place a small international oligarchy of mine-owners and speculators in power in Pretoria."[30] Hobson then expanded his thesis linking finance and territorial expansion through Jewish financiers to explain the whole process of imperialism in 1902. "By far the most important economic factor in Imperialism is the influence relating to investments.... In large measure the rank and file of the investors are, both for business and for politics, the cat's-paws of the great financial houses, who use stocks and shares not so much as investments to yield them interest, but as material for speculation in the money market. In handling large masses of stocks and shares, in floating companies, in manipulating fluctuations of values, the magnates of the Bourse find their gain. These great businesses-banking, broking, bill discounting, loan floating, company promoting-form the central ganglion of international capitalism. United by the strongest bonds of organisation, always in closest and quickest touch with one another, situated in the very heart of the business capital of every State, controlled, so far as Europe is concerned, chiefly by men of a single and peculiar race, who have behind them many centuries of financial experience, they are in a unique position to manipulate the policy of nations."[31] There was no question that his target was Jewish financiers, as he made this explicit in the 1926 edition of *The Evolution of Modern Capitalism*.[32] The Hobson view was influential both at the time it was propounded and with subsequent generations looking for a link between finance and politics, though the explicit Jewish references were increasingly omitted.[33]

That leaves unanswered whether the facts that Hobson and others relied upon to build their case for an international Jewish financial

---

[30] Hobson, *The War in South Africa*, pp. 189–194, 197, 207, 224.

[31] Hobson, *Imperialism*, pp. 51–53, 56, 94, 357, 368.

[32] Hobson, *The Evolution of Modern Capitalism*, ch. x: The Financier.

[33] L.H. Jenks, The Migration of British Capital to 1875 (New York: 1927) pp. 5, 267, 271, 279–281, 335; P. Cain, 'J.A. Hobson, Financial Capitalism and Imperialism in Late Victorian and Edwardian England', *Journal of Imperial and Commonwealth History*, xiii, 20 (1985); P.J. Cain and A.G. Hopkins, *British Imperialism: Innovation and Expansion, 1688–1914* (London: 1993) pp. 123–129; P.J. Cain and A.G. Hopkins, *British Imperialism: Crisis and Deconstruction, 1914–1990* (London: 1993) pp. 167, 292–296; W. Hutton, *The State We're In* (London: 1995) p. 124; Alborn, *Conceiving Companies*, p. 10; J. Siegel, *For Peace and Money: French and British Finance in the Service of Tsars and Commissars* (Oxford: Oxford University Press, 2014) pp. 18, 213. See Dumett, 'Exploring the Cain/Hopkins Paradigm'.

conspiracy can bear the weight put upon them. As the most important financial centre in the world between 1890 and 1914, there were strong connections between financiers located in London and South African mining finance, but the same could be said of everywhere else in the world. Writing in 1911, Sir Theodore Morrison made clear that "India's indebtedness to England is not principally due to her political connection with the British Empire. It is due to the fact that London is the principal loan market of the world. Public as well as private loans are raised by foreigners in London, because money may be had more easily and more cheaply in London than anywhere else."[34] Conversely, New York increasingly provided Canada with financial services, because of the strong links to the US economy, even though that country was an integral part of the British Empire. As Anthony Julius concluded about the Hobson thesis, "This thesis omitted critical facts and falsified others." However, that did not prevent it being widely believed, especially when espoused by prominent politicians and leading intellectuals.[35] Central to the operation of the world economy in the 25 years before the First World War was a system for the multilateral exchange of goods, services and capital rather than one determined by imperial links, and that applied to Britain. It was with the introduction of controls over the movement of goods and money in the 1930s that an imperial network was substituted for a global one, being strengthened as a result of the Second World War. In the 1950s and 1960s, these economic ties between Britain and its Empire gradually unravelled to be replaced by those with Europe.[36]

---

[34] Sir T. Morrison, *The Economic Transition in India* (London: 1911) p. 229.

[35] A. Julius, *Trials of the Diaspora: A History of Anti-semitism in England* (Oxford: Oxford University Press, 2010) pp. 60–61, 65, 150, 268–285, 345, 367, 405–407.

[36] C. Newbury, 'Cecil Rhodes, de Beers and Mining Finance in South Africa: The Business of Entrepreneurship and Imperialism', in Dumett (ed.), *Mining Tycoons*, p. 106; Frankel, *Investment and the Return to Equity Capital,* tables 6, 9, pp. 28, 124; Newbury, *The Diamond Ring*, pp. 54, 80, 114, 127, 142; Kubicek, *Economic Imperialism*, pp. 50–54, Table 3.1; Blainey, 'Lost Causes of the Jameson Raid', p. 353; Kubicek, 'The Randlords of 1895', pp. 101–102; Richardson and van Helten, 'The Development of the South African Gold-Mining Industry, 1885–1918', pp. 334; van Helten, 'Empire and High Finance', pp. 529–548; Chapman, 'Rhodes and The City of London', pp. 647–666; Turrell and van Helten, 'The Rothschilds', pp. 181–205; B.R. Tomlinson, 'Economics and Empire: The Periphery and the Imperial Economy', in J.M. Brown and W.R. Louis (eds), *Oxford History of the British Empire* (Oxford: Oxford University Press, 1997) pp. 62–63;

What also undermined the Hobson thesis was the declining power and influence of the established Jewish financiers from the 1870s onwards. International finance was both risky and profitable and attracted numerous bankers whose success waxed and waned. This competition forced long-established Jewish bankers, the Raphaels, to concentrate on a few niche areas, while the Rothschilds were a declining force as they lacked a branch in New York, which was becoming increasingly important.[37] Even in his eulogy to the Rothschilds in the 1880s, Reeves admitted that they were also in retreat. "Their business is established on so firm a basis, and their wealth is already so immense, that their chief solicitude and care must be to discover safe and reliable investments by which their money may accumulate automatically, rather than to increase it by leaps and bounds through speculative and risky enterprise. …The cream of business invariably falls to them. Large and lucrative undertakings are submitted daily to them, and constantly declined, as they very properly refuse to entertain, or embark in any enterprises which do not come within the well-defined and strictly recognised sphere of business."[38]

There were two main developments in the late nineteenth century which worked against the interests of all individual financiers, whether Jewish or not. The first was the replacement of international trust networks, which had worked in favour of dispersed co-religionists like Jews, with formal networks and legally binding contracts.[39] The second was the

B.R. Tomlinson, 'Imperialism and After: The Economy of the Empire on the Periphery', in Brown and Louis (eds), *Oxford History of the British Empire*, pp. 358, 363, 364, 366.

[37] Diaper, *Merchant Banking in the Inter-War Period*, pp. 55–56; Ziegler, *The Sixth Great Power*, pp. 164, 283–285, 302–304; Carosso, *Investment Banking in America*, pp. 78, 93; Chapman, 'Aristocracy and Meritocracy in Merchant Banking', pp. 181–183, 194; Carosso, *The Morgans*, pp. 11–12, 47, 60, 147–150, 157, 220, 271, 278, 302–305, 318, 396, 403, 446–448, 461–464, 496–503, 509, 514, 583, 596, 613; Ferguson, *High Financier*, pp. 41–42; Lepler, 'There Is No Need for Anyone to Go to America', pp. 16–19.

[38] Reeves, *The Rothschilds*, pp. 208, 249–251.

[39] Y. Cassis, *Capitals of Capital: A History of International Financial Centres, 1780–2005* (Cambridge: Cambridge University Press, 2006) pp. 38, 104, 118, 138; N. Ferguson, *The Cash Nexus: Money and Power in the Modern World, 1700–2000* (London: 2001) p. 378; Cassis, *City Bankers*, p. 5; Cottrell, *Investment Banking in England*, pp. 176–178; P.E. Austin, *Baring Brothers and the Birth of Modern Finance* (London: Pickering and Chatto, 2007) pp. 21–28, 40, 47, 55, 61, 129, 141–142, 161, 173; S.D. Chapman, 'The Establishment of the Rothschilds as Bankers', *Transactions of the Jewish Historical Society*, 29, 177–193 (1988); L. Hannah, 'The Moral Economy of Business: A Historical

entry into international finance of joint-stock banks with a large capital base, access to the deposits of their customers and possessing extensive contacts spread around the world. Germany's Deutsche Bank, for example, opened a London office in 1873 from which it conducted a global business, with turnover rising from £7.7 million in 1874 to £1.1 billion in 1913.[40] The fact that Hobson could make his analysis so appealing, despite the weakness of the evidence, indicated the power of perception both at the time and subsequently. Once a climate of suspicion had been fostered, as it was from the 1890s, it was a relatively easy matter to blame almost any episode in finance on a Jewish conspiracy whenever a Jewish banker or broker was involved.[41] This is what happened, for example, over the alleged manipulation of shares in the Marconi Company in 1910 or the attempt to rig the silver market in 1912.[42]

Long before the First World War, international networks of individual financiers were being replaced by those operated by banking companies run by salaried officials.[43] That became even more the case between the wars because of the complexities caused by the First World War and government intervention. Within Britain, the era of the individual financier was waning, including those who were Jewish. Though there were

---

Perspective on Ethics and Efficiency', in Burke, Harris and Slack (eds), *Civil Histories*, p. 297; Scott and Hughes, *The Anatomy of Scottish Capital*, pp. 20, 34–37, 49; *Toronto Daily Star*, 21st November 1910.

[40] Pohl and Burk, *Deutsche Bank in London*, pp. 13, 19, 24, 41, 43, 55. I have explored this development in 'The City of London and International Banking in the 19th and 20th Centuries: The Asian Dimension', in S. Nishimura, T. Suzuki and R.C. Michie (eds), *The Origins of International Banking in Asia: The Nineteenth and Twentieth Centuries* (Oxford: Oxford University Press, 2012), pp. 13–54.

[41] Gartner, 'Notes on the Statistics of Jewish Immigration', p. 99; Garrard, *The English and Immigration*, p. 213; Feldman, 'The Importance of being English', pp. 56, 62, 76; Alderman, *Controversy and Crisis*, pp. 230–231, 237; Lipman, 'The Victorian Jewish Background', pp. xii, xiv, xvi, xix; Godley, *Jewish Immigrant Entrepreneurship*, pp. 20, 30, 54, 60.

[42] C. Holmes, *Anti-Semitism in British Society, 1876–1939* (New York: 1979) pp. 65–66, 77–79, 80–82, 108–109, 117; W.J. Baker, *A History of the Marconi Company* (London: 1970) p. 17; Camplin, *The Rise of the Plutocrats*, pp. 46, 49, 55, 156.

[43] U. Olsson, *Furthering a Fortune: Marcus Wallenberg, Swedish Banker and Industrialist, 1899–1982* (Stockholm: Ekerlids Forlag, 2001) pp. 137–139. See S. Pak, *Gentleman Bankers: The World of J.P. Morgan* (Cambridge, Mass.: Harvard University Press, 2013) ch. 2, 3, 7.

speculative bubbles in the 1920s and 1930s, the financiers involved were a mixed bunch with no major Jewish figure involved. Among the most prominent was Clarence Hatry. Though his father was a German Jew, he had immigrated to Britain in the 1870s, became a British citizen and converted to Christianity. This meant that Hatry had been born in Britain and brought up a Christian. His Jewish origins were not a feature of his financial career.[44] The Jewish financier had largely ceased to be singled out for special condemnation as it was capitalism itself, and the global financial system in particular, that was blamed by many, from across the financial spectrum, for the chaos that the world economy was in.[45] Nevertheless, a few continued to believe in an international Jewish financial conspiracy.[46] After the Second World War, government controls, and the activities of highly-regulated banks and markets, dominated finance, leaving little scope for the individuals to operate, including Jews, apart from in niche areas.[47] In response, Jewish entrepreneurs in Britain switched to property development, where they became major players in the post-war world.[48] However, there continued to be a lingering commitment to the Hobson line on the causes of imperialism, though omitting the explicit anti-Semitic element, as in Will Hutton's popular book, *The State We're In*, which was published in 1995.[49] Once in circulation, it was impossible to banish a myth that was simple and plausible.

The Perception of Jewish Financiers

There was a long-standing antipathy towards Jewish financiers because of their association with moneylending, and the negative imagery attached to

---

[44] C. Swinson, *Share Trading, Fraud and the Crash of 1929* (London: Routledge, 2019) pp. 7–9, 24, 34–35, 40, 42, 45, 53, 156, 172.

[45] A.J. Kushner, *British Anti-Semitism in the Second World War*, Sheffield University Ph.D. 1986, p. 388.

[46] Swinson, *Regulation of the London Stock Exchange*, p. 198.

[47] F.E. Cottier, 'London Representatives of Foreign Banks', *The Banker*, xvi, p. 27 (1930). (He was the London representative of Banque Nationale de Credit, Paris); P. Einzig, 'The Jews in International Banking', *The Banker*, xxviii, 29, 31 (October 1933); P. Einzig, 'Foreign Bank Branches During the War', *The Banker*, lix August 1941, p. 95.

[48] See the entries in Rubinstein, Jolles and Rubinstein, *The Palgrave Dictionary of Anglo-Jewish History*.

[49] Hutton, *The State We're In*, p. 124.

that pursuit.[50] However, this hostility towards Jewish financiers was not of constant intensity, but varied over time, while its basis also changed, widening beyond a simple accusation of usury. Measuring this intensity of hostility and identifying its changing basis are difficult, but novels provide a way of tracing both over the nineteenth and twentieth centuries. There was an element of casual anti-Semitism evident throughout in British fiction, reflecting that it was embedded in British culture. In the nineteenth century, Jews were regularly portrayed as avaricious moneylenders or as unscrupulous brokers. This can be seen from the outset as in Thomas Love Peacock's 1806 poem, *Levi Moses*, as he was a Jewish stockbroker who thought it acceptable to cheat his clients. In the *Paper Money* poems of 1825–1826, Jews were blamed for encouraging speculation.[51] The combination of a Jewish mother and a Scottish mother made Ebenezer MacCrotchet, in Peacock's 1831 novel, *Crotchet Castle*, perfectly fitted to enrich himself "at the expense of the rest of mankind, by all the recognized modes of accumulation on the windy side of the law."[52] In Thomas Surr's 1815 novel, *The Magic of Wealth*, Jews were among those who frequented Garraway's Coffee House to buy and sell anything that would make them a profit.[53] In Edward Bulwer-Lytton's *The Disowned*, which was published in 1828, Morris Brown's father was a Jewish broker, which meant that he was "a man who makes an income out of other people's funds."[54] As a result of their banking and broking activities, Jewish financiers became rich and powerful as in Lord Byron's poem, *Don Juan*, dating from the years between 1818 and 1824.[55] To him, as for so many others, the symbol of all Jewish financiers was the Rothschild family.

Throughout the nineteenth century, two central perceptions about Jewish financiers came to the fore time and again. The first was their willingness and ability to make themselves wealthy through the manipulation of money, whether it was lending at exorbitant rates of interest or

---

[50] E. Rosenberg, *From Shylock to Svengali: Jewish Stereotypes in English Fiction* (London: 1961) pp. 14, 27, 33–35, 140, 168–169, 297, 344; Withers, *International Finance*, p. 111; Rubinstein, *Capitalism, Culture and Decline*, p. 52; Brett, *Usury in Britain*, pp. 120, 139.

[51] T.L. Peacock, *Levi Moses* (1806); Peacock, *Paper Money*.

[52] Peacock, *Crotchet Castle*, pp. 127–128.

[53] Surr, *The Magic of Wealth*, Vol. 1: pp. 8, 102.

[54] Bulwer-Lytton, *The Disowned*, ch. viii.

[55] Byron, *Don Juan*.

buying and selling stocks and bonds. The second was the power that the control of money brought, whether it was to influence governments or ascend to the top of the social hierarchy. Many picked up on the first through the application of the term "moneylender" to all Jewish financiers, regardless of the business that they did. The second element grew as the public became aware of the role played by the Rothschilds in international finance. Mrs Gore, in her 1837 book, *The Man of Business*, referred to Baron Nebuchadnezzar Salfiore as one of the "great Jews of the Stock Exchange" where he was known as "the first Baron of Jewry."[56] Benjamin Disraeli then fleshed out the character of the Jewish financier on the international stage in his 1844 novel, *Coningsby*. This featured the financier, Sidonia, "one of the greatest capitalists in Europe. ... He had established a brother, or a near relative, in whom he could have confidence, in most of the principal capitals. He was lord and master of the money market of the world, and of course virtually lord and master of everything else." On his death, he left "the greatest fortune in Europe...it could only be calculated by millions." His son, young Sidonia, inherited both the fortune and the power.[57] Disraeli continued the story of Sidonia in the 1847 novel, *Tancred*. Sidonia was "immensely rich" and dealt "with the fortunes of Kings and Empires, and regulates the most important affairs of nations."[58]

Despite the positive view taken of Jewish financiers on the international stage, they continued to be classed as moneylenders when operating domestically, as in Robert Bell's 1850 novel, *The Ladder of Gold*.[59] Mrs Gore's 1854 novel, *The Money Lender*, captured both these elements in her character Abednego Osalez. He operated as moneylender in both the east end and west end of London but an international banker in the City. As an international banker, he was one of the "real potentates of modern times who sway the destinies of nations and individuals with a rod of gold, and issue their decrees in bank-notes and Exchequer bills — Money is indeed power." Conversely, as a moneylender, he was hated, because of the "detestable nature of his usury." Osalez's philosophy was that "I buy whatever I can buy cheap, and sell it whenever I can sell it dear.... Everything is to be had for money." He despised those to whom he lent money because their borrowing was driven by a desire to shine in

---

[56] Gore, *The Man of Business*, pp. 180, 254.
[57] Disraeli, *Coningsby*, pp. 230–238, 242, 258, 278, 357.
[58] Disraeli, *Tancred*, pp. 113–115, 124–126, 132, 164, 212, 254, 282.
[59] Bell, *The Ladder of Gold*, p. 167.

society, but it also gave him power over them, no matter how mighty they might appear in the eyes of the public. To Mrs Gore, Jewish financiers were "the master hands that move the wires of kingly puppets; the main-springs of aristocratic action; without whom, privy-councils and parliaments might mouth and gibber in vain; the veritable monarchs who make peace and war." Osalez was not Jewish as his grandfather had converted to Christianity when marrying a protestant. However, he was assumed to be Jewish and so acted as one, concentrating on making money by whatever means he could.[60]

This view of Jewish financiers as simultaneously wealthy and powerful because of their international role and unscrupulous moneylenders domestically was widespread in the 1860s, as in George Augustus Sala's 1862 novel, *The Seven Sons of Mammon*, and Braddon's 1863 book, *Aurora Floyd*.[61] It also comes through in the case of the Jewish financier, Mr Wesser, in Meason's collection of stories dating from the 1860s, and then republished in 1874. Wesser was an international financier, who "knew everybody and every establishment connected with monetary matters throughout Europe" and "knew every loan that had ever been contracted by any government in the civilized world, and was as familiar with the money-markets of the New as of the Old World." However, he was also behind the rumours that led to a run on the Arungabad and Hardiman's Bank, forcing it close, as that would make him a large profit even though those with deposits in the bank would lose their savings.[62] Judging from the work of Charles Lever, it was the perception of Jewish financiers as internationally powerful that was beginning to triumph. He had already hinted in his 1859 book, *Davenport Dunn*, that the international bankers, the Glumthals, were the real power in international finance.[63] Ten years later in *That Boy of Norcott's*, he described the Jewish financiers, the Nathanheimers, as the "great potentates of finance and trade." He added that "From one end of Europe to the other the whole financial system was in the hands of a few crafty men of immense wealth, who unthroned dynasties, and controlled the fate of nations with a

---

[60]Gore, *The Money Lender*, pp. 23, 31, 38, 46, 95, 98–99, 113, 134–139, 153, 162–133, 167–168, 181–190, 208–209, 226–227, 242.

[61]Sala, *The Seven Sons of Mammon*, p. 3; M.E. Braddon, *Aurora Floyd* (London: Downey and Company, 1863) p. 152.

[62]Meason, *Three Months After Date*, pp. 39, 241–242, 253–262.

[63]Lever, *Davenport Dunn*, Vol. 2: pp. 195, 238, Vol. 3: pp. 52–53, 84–86, 130, 336.

word."[64] This was accompanied by an admiration of the high standards followed by Jewish financiers. The Jewish stockbroker, Signor Nazzari, was more honest and trustworthy than his Christian rivals in Amelia Edward's 1865 novel, *Half a Million of Money*.[65] Yates suggested in his 1866 novel, *Kissing the Rod*, that the hostility towards Jewish financiers was both unjustified and in decline. The Jewish financier, Daniel Thacker, was widely accepted in London society.[66]

Nevertheless, the link between Jews and moneylending continued to influence public perceptions of Jewish financiers, and that extended to those engaged in international finance. This can be seen in a succession of Charlotte Riddell's books. Jews were the worst among moneylenders in her 1866 novel, *George Geith of Fen Court*. In *Joy After Sorrow*, which appeared in 1873, but was a reworking of an 1856, novel, she used the phrase "as avaricious as a Jew." The 1874 novel, *Mortomley's Estate*, featured two German Jews who were willing to go to any lengths, including fraud, in the pursuit of money. Riddell continued to describe Jewish financiers as moneylenders in her 1882 novel, *Daisies and Buttercups*.[67] This description of all Jewish financiers as no better than moneylenders was commonplace at the time, judging from the work of other writers, such as Sheridan Le Fanu in his 1871 novel, *Checkmate*, and Robert Black's 1878 novel, *Love or Lucre*.[68] Muirhead Robertson, in the 1888 novel, *A Lombard Street Mystery*, referred to Jacob Alldis as "a veritable Shylock in business transaction," indicating the persistence of that stereotype.[69] The novels of Anthony Trollope suggest a somewhat mixed perception of Jewish financiers by the 1870s. In *The Way We Live Now*, which was published in 1874/1875, the Jewish banker, Mr Breghert, "was considered to be a very good man of business." He "was absolutely a Jew — not a Jew that had been, as to whom there might possibly be a

---

[64] Lever, *That Boy of Norcott's*, pp. 172, 192, 196–197, 222, 313–317.

[65] Edwards, *Half a Million of Money*, p. 220.

[66] Yates, *Kissing the Rod*, Vol. 1: pp. 90–93.

[67] Riddell, *George Geith*, p. 348; C. Riddell, *Joy After Sorrow* (London: 1873) pp. 1–4, 10–11, 34, 134, 175, 187, 256, 266, 317, 327; C. Riddell, *Mortomley's Estate: A Novel* (London: 1874) Vol. 1: pp. 23–25, 152–153, 200–205, 217, Vol. 2: ch. 12, Vol. 3: chs. 6, 8 and 10; Riddell, *Daisies and Buttercups*, pp. 10, 418–419.

[68] J.S. Le Fanu, *Checkmate* (London: 1871) pp. 158, 216; Black, *Love or Lucre*, pp. 645–647.

[69] Robertson, *A Lombard Street Mystery*, p. 9.

doubt whether he or his father or his grandfather had been the last Jew of the family; but a Jew that was."[70] Conversely, Trollope followed up this novel with another featuring a dubious Jewish financier. The 1876 novel, *The Prime Minister*, featured Ferdinand Lopez, "half foreigner, half Jew," who "is what they call a speculator. Money is not safe with him."[71] The other image was of Jewish financiers possessing great wealth, as in Joseph Hatton's 1878 novel, *Cruel London*.[72]

Whereas Jewish bankers were being portrayed as increasingly respected and trusted by the 1870s, reflecting the established position occupied by the Rothschilds, other Jewish financiers were seen as much more dubious figures. That was apparent in Walter Besant's 1883 novel, *All in a Garden Fair*. It was never stated that the company promoter, Colliber, was Jewish but he was described as having a "hooked nose, and sharp eyes and quick savage manner."[73] The conversion of some Jewish financiers to Christianity made labelling based on religion more difficult. George Bernard Shaw acknowledged this in his 1887 novel, *An Unsocial Socialist*, because the Jewish banker, Mr Jansenius, had his children educated as Christians.[74] In James Payn's 1890 novel, *The Burnt Million*, Joseph Tremenhere, "the greatest moneylender that London has ever produced," begun life as a Jew but had ceased to practice and brought up his daughters as Christians. What tainted him was not being Jewish but his occupation as a moneylender. "Mr Tremenhere had made his fortune as a money-lender…. He might have been a good man for all that."[75] This more benign view of Jews was motivated by sympathy for them because of their persecution in Russia, as in Joseph Hatton's 1890 novel, *By Order of the Czar*.[76] In the 1891 novel by Leonard Merrick, *Violet Moses*, it was the Jewish stockbroker, Leopold Moses, who was honest while the

---

[70] Trollope, *The Way We Live Now*, Vol. 1: pp. 30–34, 48–49, 77, 84–85, 268, 368, 349, Vol. 2: pp. 26–27, 92, 99, 140, 272, 276, 294, 302–4, 307, 339, 359–361, 400.

[71] Trollope, *The Prime Minister*, Vol. 1: pp. 4–8, 12, 14, 27–31, 74, 120, 128–129, 155, 185, 191, 228–229, 235–238, 373, Vol. 2: pp. 31–32, 39–40, 73, 110–11, 117, 126–129, 134–136, 140–141, 194, 274–275, 320–321, 352, 379.

[72] Hatton, *Cruel London*, p. 278.

[73] Besant, *All in a Garden Fair*, p. 284.

[74] Shaw, *An Unsocial Socialist*, pp. 20–21, 63, 209.

[75] Payn, *The Burnt Million*, Vol. 1: pp. 1–3, 7–8, 11, 13, 6, 76, 111–119, 250, 289, Vol. 3: pp. 77–79, 97, 140–142, 164, 169, 184, 259.

[76] Hatton, *By Order of the Czar*, preface, p. 219.

Christian, Robert Dyas, was a crook.[77] There was even a light-hearted depiction of a Jewish company promoter in Gilbert and Sullivan's comic opera, *Utopia, Limited*, performed in 1893.[78]

However, in the 1890s, a more hostile attitude towards Jewish financiers developed in Britain, being imported from the USA. In the 1894 American novel by W.N. Harvey, *A Tale of Two Nations*, the English banker, Baron Rothe, a manipulator "of stocks, bonds and money," was behind a plot which would, once again, subjugate the USA to English rule. "England is a creditor nation. Her greatest rival of today is the United States. If things continue as they now promise, the great American republic will soon rival us as the creditor nation of the world. The only way to defeat this is to keep her in debt to us." Baron Rothe was a Jewish financier who had the power to "dictate to nations" because of his wealth. He was one of "The money kings of Europe" and could pay politicians to back his plans while control of a newspaper allowed him to influence public opinion.[79] This American account of the power of Jewish financiers played out well in the UK in the 1890s where there was a growing resentment of the wealth of Jewish financiers, as this allowed them to buy up the estates that the impoverished English aristocracy were having to sell and establish themselves in the upper reaches of British society. This is what happened to Outram Hall in Rider Haggard's 1894 novel, *People of the Mist*, as the purchaser was Mr Cohen, a Jewish bullion broker. The point was made that "If he is a Jew, what does it matter? He has a title, and they say he is enormously rich."[80] In Marie Corelli's *The Sorrows of Satan*, which was published in 1895, the reason that Lord Elton had to sell his ancestral home, Willowsmere, was because he had lost his money by borrowing from and investing through Jewish bankers and brokers.[81]

This renewed hostility towards Jewish financiers went far beyond the underlying anti-Semitism of the past. Jewish financiers were not only labelled greedy capitalists, fraudulent financiers and market manipulators but they were also a threat to the British state because of their lack of

---

[77] L. Merrick, *Violet Moses*, pp. 44–48, 78, 99, 122, 142, 165.

[78] Gilbert and Sullivan, *Utopia, Limited*. See the song of Mr Goldbury.

[79] W.N. Harvey, *A Tale of Two Nations* (Chicago: Coin Publishing Company, 1894) pp. 9–10, 12, 21, 32, 34, 51–52, 98, 102, 215–216, 219, 223, 232, 257–258.

[80] H. Rider Haggard, *People of the Mist* (London: Longmans, Green and Co., 1894) pp. 3, 7, 1, 334–337.

[81] Corelli, *The Sorrows of Satan*, pp. 98, 386–387.

232 The War on Wealth

patriotism. The collapse in the boom in gold mining shares in 1895 whipped up public hostility towards Jewish financiers, as they were seen to have played a major role in the speculative mania that had taken place. A spate of novels featured Jewish financiers who were painted as willing to do anything if it brought them the monetary rewards they craved, whether it was producing a false prospectus, manipulating share prices, insider trading and bribing journalists, or resorting to cheating, robbery, kidnap or murder if that was found to be necessary. They cared nothing for the consequences their actions had for investors.[82] Along with these attacks on Jewish company promoters, brokers, bullion dealers and their clerks, Jews continued to be described as unscrupulous moneylenders in numerous novels.[83]

To counter this avalanche of bad publicity, there were a few words of praise for Jewish financiers. In *The Grand Babylon Hotel* by Arnold Bennett, which was published in 1902, the Jewish financier, Sampson Levi, was described as "very rich and hospitable" as well as likeable, respected and trustworthy.[84] Another novel that took a more positive view of Jewish financiers was Elinor Glyn's *The Reason Why*, which was published in 1911. It concluded its debate on whether the rich and powerful financier, Francis Markrute, was Jewish or not with the statement, "If I like people, I don't care what is in their blood."[85] Margaret de Vere Stacpoole, in her 1914 novel, *London 1913*, described those financiers who had made their money in South Africa, as "excellent and amiable people."[86] For Edgar Wallace, in his 1914 collection of short stories, *The Admirable Carfew*, Jewish financiers were a mixed lot ranging from

---

[82]Gribble, *The Lower Life*, pp. 1–2, 6, 8, 10, 14, 16, 20–21, 25, 30–32, 40–45, 53–55, 60–74, 92–93, 101, 108–109, 118, 120, 131–133, 137, 149, 152, 176–179, 190–191, 206–209, 238, 278–279, 285, 294, 303, 307–311; Hill, *Guilty Gold*, pp. 1–14, 17, 23–41, 47–64, 78, 115–117, 149, 209–214, 341, 346–343; Warden, *The Wharf by the Docks*, p. 1.
[83]Gowing, *Gods of Gold*, pp. 20, 214, 302; Benson, *The Money Market*, pp. 56–69, 152–153, 255–258; G.R. Sims, *In London's Heart* (London: Chatto and Windus, 1900) p. 234; Besant, *The Alabaster Box*, pp. 4–13, 66, 220, 230; Griffiths, *Ford's Folly, Ltd.*, p. 100; J. Hocking, *The Man Who Rose Again* (London: 1906) p. 4.
[84]A. Bennett, *The Grand Babylon Hotel* (London: Chatto and Windus, 1902) pp. 52, 91, 96, 169–170.
[85]E. Glyn, *The Reason Why* (London: 1911) pp. 1, 58, 77, 266–271, 275, 378.
[86]Stacpoole, *London 1913*, pp. 3–7, 11, 52, 65, 71, 79, 85–86, 103–105, 109, 112–114, 173, 196, 206, 271, 286–287, 314, 333–334, 342, 344–356.

Lewis and Gobleheim, who brought out sound and profitable companies, through Lord Kullug, who stayed just within the law, to Swelliger and Friedman, who were crooks.[87]

What positive comments there were, however, were far outweighed by the negative. As Julia Frankau pointed out in the 1903 novel, *Pigs in Clover*, "It is the misfortune of the Jews that one of their community cannot misbehave without earning opprobrium for their whole body."[88] There was also a tendency to group all crooked financiers together and label them Jewish, especially if they had foreign names.[89] Reflecting the public's attitude towards Jewish financiers, a number of novels contained plots in which they were duped by those they had tried to cheat.[90] One was Frederic's 1899 novel, *The Market-Place*. The saving grace was that, having lost, the Jewish financiers "don't complain; they don't cry and say it's cruel: they know it's the rule of the game. They accept it and begin at once looking out for a new set of fools and weaklings to recoup themselves on.... They get hold of most of the things that are going, because they're eternally on the move. It's their hellish industry and activity that gives them such a pull, and makes most people afraid of them."[91] There were also novels in which Jewish financiers ended up bankrupt and in prison, after having tried to buy their way into the top level of Edwardian society. This emerges in Grace Pettman's 1912 novel, *A Study in Gold*, which featured the Polish Jew, Caleb Otto-Smith. "Men of his type who had accumulated wealth usually sought in marriage a girl of rank, who had the entrée of the very highest society, and was willing to exchange the prestige of her title and ancestry for a share of the millionaire's gold.... Most of these girls had been trained by ambitious mothers to believe that the

---

[87]Wallace, *The Admirable Carfew*, pp. 23–25, 30–31, 54–55, 64–65, 77, 90–91, 104–106, 134, 160–169, 182–190.

[88]Danby, *Pigs in Clover*, pp. 52–57, 80, 84, 85, 95, 99, 106–107, 140–147, 175, 244, 278.

[89]Ouida, *The Massarenes*, pp. 69, 81, 534–535.

[90]Fox-Davies, *The Finances of Sir John Kynnersley*, pp. 4–5, 9–10, 1538–1539, 53–55, 75, 113, 133, 152–156, 184–189, 210–221, 235; Philips Oppenheim, *A Millionaire of Yesterday*, pp. 53, 60–67, 71, 90–91, 102, 114, 117, 121–123, 134, 261–264, 146, 170–172, 273, 278, 298–302, 312; Barr, *Young Lord Stranleigh*, pp. 1, 7, 10–27, 33–43, 58, 63, 162–163, 188–189, 208, 229, 231–255; Barr, *Stranleigh's Millions*, pp. 26, 52, 62, 58, 173–174, 178–179, 184–185, 190–191, 204–207, 210–211, 220–221, 232–233, 236–238.

[91]Frederic, *The Market-Place*, pp. 6–10, 11, 20–22, 26–27, 36, 4, 48–49, 81–82, 127, 157, 181–184, 202–205, 214, 217–219, 236, 240, 282–285, 293–296, 306–309, 312, 358–359.

chief end of their lives was to make a brilliant match; possibly not one among them would have refused to bestow her aristocratic hand upon the grey-haired unprepossessing financier who had come to England as an alien, a young Polish Jew, a well-nigh penniless exile."[92] Jewish financiers were also cast as unlamented murder victims.[93] The 1912 novel, *God and Mammon* by Joseph Hocking, provides something of an assessment of the public perception of Jewish financiers in Britain in the years before the First World War. "I have no prejudice against Jews ... I know several who are among the straightest men in London. It has become the thing to malign them, but speaking as I find, they are quite as honourable as — other people. Of course, there are two classes among them; the desirable ones and, and the other sort.... You may be right about Jews; there are doubtless many straight, honourable men among them; but there's nothing under heaven worse than the shady members of the Semite race."[94]

In the years before the First World War, what was added to the traditional prejudice against Jewish financiers was a belief that they were also unpatriotic and could not be trusted. Hilaire Belloc articulated this in a series of novels beginning in 1904 with *Emmanuel Burden, Mr Clutterbuck's Election* in 1908, *A Change in the Cabinet* in 1909 and then culminating with *Pongo and the Bull* in 1910. These featured the German Jewish financier I. Z. Barnett, who had established himself in London as a rich and powerful banker, becoming Lord Lambeth and then the Duke of Battersea. His enemies continued to refer to him as the "Peabody Yid" who had "only got to wink and it's like a red-hot poker to the politicians." Such was his power that the Duke of Battersea believed he could lecture the Prime Minister on the state of national finances. The effect was to antagonise the Prime Minister as he recognised that "He was being bullied: his country was being bullied by the money-lenders.... He had never thought of England save as the ally and even contemptuous ally of the forces that were now opposed to him. He had watched with

---

[92] Pettman, *A Study in Gold*, pp. 9–10, 15, 65, 70, 100–101, 116–117, 121–123, 130–132, 146–149, 157, 165, 204–205, 210–222, 226–227, 276, 286, 294.

[93] J.S. Fletcher, *The Bartenstein Case* (London: John Long, 1913) pp. 19, 24–29, 35–36, 49, 56, 84, 106, 119, 131–132, 255; F.M. White, *The House of Mammon* (London: Ward Lock and Co., 1914) pp. 3–4, 13, 17–19, 59–60, 121–122, 139–140, 161–162, 177, 297–298, 344–345, 350, 353–356.

[94] Hocking, *God and Mammon*, pp. 6–8, 25–26, 48–49, 71–81, 90–94, 101, 107–109, 120–123, 158, 164, 265–279, 287–289, 289, 291–292, 298–299, 301–313.

indifference the intermarriage of the great families with these swine." As a result of the way he was treated, the Prime Minister turned to an American financier for a loan, suggesting that Belloc recognised that the era of the Jewish financiers like the Rothschilds was over and a new one with the Morgans had begun.[95] Belloc was not the only writer who picked up on a public mood which regarded Jewish financiers as unpatriotic because of their religion, foreign origins and international connections.[96] Judging from Gilbert Parker's 1913 book, *The Judgement House*, lying behind these views on Jewish financiers were the events in South Africa. The novel featured a financier called Wallstein, who "knew little and cared less about politics.... He was spoken of as a cruel, tyrannical, greedy German Jew, whose soul was in his own pocket and his hand in the pockets of the world."[97]

In the 20 years before the First World War, hostility towards Jewish financiers moved from being a product of casual anti-Semitism to become a concerted attack that overwhelmed the few positive views that circulated. The Hobson thesis built on an underlying current of anti-Semitism as found in contemporary novels. In turn, the wide acceptance of the Hobson thesis encouraged more writers to weave their stories around it, which gave further credence to the thesis. Fiction fuelled fact, which then fed fiction and so the sequence was repeated. It was only during the First World War, and then subsequent developments, that the cycle was broken, and, even then, not completely. Judging from George Birmingham's 1915 novel, *Gossamer*, the war had brought a realisation of the importance and fragility of international finance and the role played by Jewish financiers in maintaining it for the benefit of all. The key character in the novel was

---

[95] Belloc, *Emmanuel Burden*, pp. 55–61, 65–76, 82–91, 104, 113, 119–122, 158, 170–171, 196–197, 206–207, 212; Belloc, *Mr Clutterbuck's Election*, pp. 20–24, 39, 43–44, 180–181, 193–198, 216–220, 273–276; Belloc, *A Change in the Cabinet*, pp. 5–7, 16, 18, 21, 32, 68–69, 89, 99–104, 121, 232–235; Belloc, *Pongo and the Bull*, pp. 3, 13–14, 41–43, 71–80, 88, 102–103, 178–179, 237, 305.

[96] C. Stanton and H. Hosken, *The Sinners' Syndicate* (London: Hurst and Blackett, 1907) pp. 47–48, 58–59, 252–253, 317; Haggard, *The Yellow God*, pp. 1–42, 48, 51–2, 62, 67, 89, 116; A.E.W. Mason, *The Turnstile* (London: 1912) pp. 68–69, 82–84, 97, 180–181, 195–197, 209; Phillips Oppenheim, *Havoc*, pp. 62–68, 98–99, 105, 116–118, 289–290, 315, 320–321, 329–330, 342–345.

[97] Parker, *The Judgement House*, pp. 39–43, 52, 66, 86, 117, 259–260, 269, 310–311, 470–472.

Carl Ascher of Ascher, Stutz and Co. Ascher had been born in Hamburg. "My particular kind of banking, international banking, can best be carried on in England. That is why I am here, why my business is centred in London, though I myself am not an Englishman. I am a German." He was considered to be a Jew, but claimed not to be. Despite being German born, the British government turned to him for advice on how to manage the financial crisis caused by war.[98] What can also be noted is the absence of novels featuring Jewish financiers during the First World War, and for some years afterwards.

One of the first post-war appearances of a Jewish financier was in Dorothy Sayers's 1923 novel, *Whose Body?* This presented a much more positive picture compared to those of the pre-war era. Sir Reuben Levy was portrayed as a respectable, likeable, trustworthy, self-made banker loved by his wife and daughter. "The terrible fighter of the Stock Exchange, who could with one nod set the surly bear dancing, or bring the savage bull to feed out of his hand, whose breath devastated whole districts with famine or swept financial potentates from their seats, was revealed in private life as kindly, domestic, innocently proud of himself and his belongings, confiding, generous and a little dull. His own small economies were duly chronicled side by side with extravagant presents to his wife and daughter." Reuben Levy was murdered by an eminent sur-geon, Sir Julian Freke, who had never forgiven him for marrying the woman he loved.[99] Agatha Christie also featured a Jewish financier in her 1925 story, *The Secret of Chimneys*. This was Herman Isaacstein, who was "one of the strong silent yellow men of finance." He was called "Nosystein" behind his back but was trusted by the British government to act as their agent in secret negotiations over a financial deal in competi-tion with American interests.[100] What continued was the casual anti-Semitism of old, stressing the link to moneylending and trading, as in Ellis's 1925 novel, *Every Man's Desire*, Galsworthy's 1928 instalment of the Forsyte Saga, *Swan Song*, and his 1930 collection, *On Forsyte 'Change*.[101]

---

[98] Birmingham, *Gossamer*, pp. 9–10, 14, 20, 22, 27, 30, 35, 45, 54, 76, 99–103, 117, 164–165, 198–201, 220–221.

[99] Sayers, *Whose Body?* pp. 16–17, 36–39, 40–42, 58–59, 69, 79, 171.

[100] Christie, *The Secret of Chimneys*, pp. 18, 23–24, 77, 81, 97, 100–101, 165.

[101] Ellis, *Every Man's Desire*, p. 11; Galsworthy, *Swan Song*, pp. 880, 921; *On Forsyte 'Change*, p. 91.

The lack of a sustained attack on Jewish financiers between the wars can be seen from their treatment in different novels. In Henry Wade's 1929 novel, *The Duke of York's Steps*, the murderer was a Jewish financier of German origin, Leopold Hessel, who killed his partner, Sir Garth Fratten, to prevent him uncovering his fraudulent activities.[102] Conversely, in the 1931 novel, *The Missing Moneylender* by W. Stanley Sykes, it was a Jewish moneylender, Israel Levinsky, who was murdered with a doctor being responsible. Levinsky was described as a "a decent chap" who did not hide his Jewish identity under a different name or that of a company. "A Jew as a Jew is all right, but a Jew who pretends he is a Gentile is a nasty bit of work.' His brother and partner, Isaac Levinsky was 'a dapper little man of unmistakably Jewish appearance, neatly and quietly dressed." He was very upset by the disappearance and then murder of his brother. "In all things he avoided the ostentatious flashiness which is a failing of some of his race: heavy gold watch-chains and pointed, patent-leather boots were conspicuous by their absence." Instead, he was conservatively but expensively dressed. He combined both the emotion of a "lamenting Oriental" and the self-control of a "cool-headed Western business-man."[103] There was a brief return to the idea of a Jewish financial conspiracy in Anthony Wynne's 1934 novel, *Death of a Banker*. "All you international money-lenders work together. You have offices and branches in every country. Most of you are related by blood. It is a closed corporation, a ring, if you like…. You have the world parcelled out among you and you keep to your own pitches."[104] Unlike before 1914, these beliefs did not take root in Britain in the 1930s despite the difficult economic, financial and monetary conditions. There was also no sense that Jewish financiers were considered unpatriotic. In Macdonell's 1936 book, *Lords and Masters*, the Jewish financier, Amschel Wendelmann, attempted to prevent a war breaking out, rather than promoting one.[105] Nevil Shute's 1938 novel, *Ruined City*, reflected the mixed views on Jewish financiers with one, Sir John Cohen, pedalling shares in a dubious gold mine while another, Heinroth, was considered "a damn good chap … he never let me

---

[102] Wade, *The Duke of York's Steps*, pp. 8–12, 31–33, 36, 49, 63, 217, 263–265, 331, 337, 346–349.

[103] Sykes, *The Missing Moneylender*, pp. 7–8, 11–12, 17, 44–46, 158–159.

[104] Wynne, *Death of a Banker*, p. 129.

[105] Macdonell, *Lords and Masters*, pp. 125, 128–129, 231.

down," and helped to rescue an ailing shipbuilding company and so bring jobs back to a depressed region.[106]

During the Second World War, as in the First, Jewish financiers largely disappeared from public view, as there were few mentions in contemporary novels. One was in Ngaio Marsh's 1940 novel, *Death at the Bar*, where Jews continued to be associated with moneylending.[107] Adding a new twist to the image of Jewish financiers that same year, Agatha Christie featured a female in that role in *One, Two, Buckle My Shoe*. This was Rebecca Arnholt, whose mother was a Rotherstein, of the European financial dynasty. Her father was head of the American banking house, Arnholt. She was the sole heir to both sides of the business and joined her father in the bank, where she showed great ability. As she was Jewish, "the aptitude for it ran in her blood." After his death, she continued to be a powerful figure in the financial world with her immense holdings.[108] In 1941, Anthony Berkeley, in *The Silk Stocking Murders*, did feature a Jewish financier, Pleydell, as a murderer. However, it was made clear that he committed the crimes because he had become insane. He was viewed sympathetically both as a Jew and a financier. "Pleydell senior was of the financial rank that is known as 'the power behind the throne,' meaning, in these days, the power behind the party; Pleydell junior had been spoken of for some years as more than a worthy successor, with several exploits of sheer genius on the financial battlefield already to his credit. Father and son were outstanding for another reason also; they were scrupulously honest, they were behind no shady deals, and they never crushed unless they were unnecessarily attacked.... The real pure-blood Jew, like Pleydell, ... is one of the best fellows in the world. It's the hybrid Jew, the Russian and Polish and German variety, that's let the race down so badly.... The Jewish outlook.... They'd give up everything in the world to save the life of a dying friend, or even to ensure that he had a really luxurious funeral if he wanted one; but that doesn't prevent them from asking the undertaker for a cash discount. And why should it? We call it callous, but it's only practical. That's our trouble; we can't distinguish between real and false sentiment. And the Jews do."[109]

---

[106] Shute, *Ruined City*, pp. 9–10, 216, 242.

[107] Marsh, *Death at the Bar*, p. 114.

[108] Christie, *One, Two, Buckle My Shoe*, pp. 10–11, 15–18, 42–43, 56–57, 86–87, 132–133, 155, 180–181, 185.

[109] Berkeley, *The Silk Stocking Murders*, pp. 32–35, 51–52, 55–56, 107, 116, 121, 165, 180–181.

Written in 1945, in *Calamity at Harwood* by George Bellairs, a Jewish financier, Solomon Burt, was murdered because he was a patriot. He had discovered a gang of German spies operating in a property he owned, and they killed him before he could expose them.[110] In the years after 1945, references to Jewish financiers were scarce in British novels, suggesting that the topic had ceased to generate public interest. When it was raised, Jews were depicted a successful, trustworthy and ruthless but little different from others in the world of finance. One exception was Ken Follett in his 1977 novel, *Paper Money*, which featured a Jewish financier who was something of a throwback to those of the pre-First World War era. Felix Laski, originally from Poland, specialised in buying small undervalued companies and then selling off their assets. He used information obtained through blackmail and funded his purchases from the proceeds of robberies. Laski was regarded as "A man totally without integrity" by those who knew about his dealings, but he got away with it.[111] By 1993, in his historical novel, *A Dangerous Fortune*, Ken Follett, painted a more positive picture of the Jewish banking family, the Greenbournes.[112] Similarly, in the 1992 novel by David Williams, *Planning on Murder*, the Jewish financier and property developer, Julius Kuril, was ruthless but honest.[113]

In Paul Kilduff *Square Mile*, which appeared in 1999, the City investment bank Steen Odenberg, founded by a German Jew and a Swede, was considered to be no different from any of the others operating in London at that time.[114] In Sebastian Faulks's 2009 novel, *A Week in December*, which revolved round the financial crisis in Britain, the hedge fund manager, John Veals, was from a Lithuanian Jewish family. However, he had been brought up in London, where his father was an undertaker, and though "His family was Jewish ... he had no interest in their God or their traditions." What he lived for was "the acquisition of money.... He hated holidays because they kept him from the markets.... The only activity, the only aspect of human life, that interested John Veals was money." By the twenty-first century, the race or religion of a financier was irrelevant, even one whose obsession with making ever more

[110]Bellairs, *Calamity at Harwood*.

[111]Follett, *Paper Money*, pp. 14–16, 135–136, 164, 182, 185, 212, 218–220, 241–243, 247.

[112]Follett, *A Dangerous Fortune*, pp. 218, 252, 404, 513, 522–526, 594–595.

[113]Williams, *Planning on Murder*, pp. 17–19, 22–23, 177–178.

[114]Kilduff, *Square Mile*.

money could bring down a bank and cause a financial crisis.[115] The attitude to Jewish financiers by then can be seen in Justin Cartwright's *Other People's Money*, which was published in 2011. The book told the story of the downfall of a private bank, Tubal and Co. The founder of the bank was Jewish, Moses Tubal, and it was still run by the same family, but they had long ago converted to Christianity. Like other merchant bankers, Tubal was a relic of the past, and race and religion no longer mattered.[116]

Compared to the depth and breadth of hostility towards Jewish financiers a hundred years before, the subject ceased to resonate with the public after the Second World War. When added to the rather intermittent and casual anti-Semitism aimed at Jewish financiers for most of the nineteenth century, this leaves the 20 years before the First World War as an aberration. There was almost an open season of accusations made against Jewish financiers. This open season ended with the First World War and made only a rare appearance in the century that followed. As those years stand out in terms of the degree of hostility shown towards Jewish financiers in Britain, they cannot be explained away by reference to currents of anti-Semitism that waxed or waned over the centuries. Instead, they were a product of British credit and capital dominating international finance. Jewish financiers played an important role in this, with the arrival of successive cohorts from Germany in particular, though it was not individuals but banking companies, and their network of connections that spanned the globe, that were in the ascendancy. Nevertheless, when the activities of Jewish financiers were combined with the mass arrival of Jews from Russia, the bursting of a speculative boom involving the shares of gold mining companies and then a war in South Africa in which Britain fought to control gold deposits, the basis of a thesis involving an international financial conspiracy was born. The final catalyst in this thesis was the growing anti-Semitism in the USA and the particular focus on Wall Street investment banks run by Jews with international connections. This hostility was imported into the UK through both factual accounts and contemporary fiction, being taken up by likes of Hobson and Belloc and given wide currency through the popularity of their writings. It was this fusion of fact and fiction which made the idea of an international conspiracy of Jewish bankers believable because it could be attached to random but

---

[115]Faulks, *A Week in December*, pp. 8–13, 62, 231–233, 268–269.
[116]Cartwright, *Other People's Money*, pp. 71, 182, 238–239.

unconnected facts and woven into a coherent narrative. In this case, perception triumphed.

Conclusion

There existed an almost magical belief in the ability of Jewish financiers to make themselves wealthy or influence government policy. As recently as 1999, Peter Stormonth Darling, a veteran financier in the City of London, wrote, "There was another reason to stay with Warburgs, if the full truth was be told. I believed I would make more money in the business environment created by a team of brilliant Jewish financiers, who had already shown their competitive edge over the more conventional and longer-established City firms."[117] However, the perception of the power and influence of Jewish financiers is out of proportion with the reality. Jews were always a tiny minority not only in Britain but also in financial services and clustered in niche areas, even in the City of London. Their influence was also in decline from the 1870s onwards as international financial transactions increasingly flowed through market networks and global banks. This did not mean Jews were not important in finance. They brought expertise and connections. Without them, for example, the City of London would have been a less successful financial centre, especially in the conduct of international business. However, it is important not to exaggerate the power and influence of Jewish financiers, as that feeds into the belief in an international conspiracy. Conversely, they should not be written out of the history of British finance, especially the City of London, as their contribution was greater than their actual numbers would suggest. More specifically, the negative imagery attached to Jewish financiers, which intensified rather than diminished prior to the First World War, can be attributed to developments outside their control. The mass immigration of Jews had implications for those from the same racial or religious background, who had been long settled and become assimilated into society. It created antagonism that spread all the way to the wealthiest even though they commanded the respect of their peer group and were close personal friends of the most powerful in the land. The arrival of a mass of foreign Jews was perceived as a threat to British society and this fear led to Jewish

---

[117]P.S. Darling, *City Cinderella: The Life and Times of Mercury Asset Management* (London: 1999) p. 73.

financiers being targeted. This antagonism built upon the long-standing suspicion of Jews as moneylenders and usurers in a Christian community. Of equal importance, however, was the inspiration that novelists drew from developments in Wall Street, which were then given a British context. There was a transatlantic literary culture through a shared language and heritage that cross-fertilised novelists on each side of the Atlantic through regular visits and reading each other's work. In that way, activities and events in the City of London and Wall Street, for example, became mixed in the public mind even though conditions were radically different. The City of London was an international financial centre served by a functioning central bank and a stable banking system. In contrast, Wall Street was a domestic financial centre that lacked a central bank and was prone to banking crises. The former generated little of the excitement and personality beloved of novelists. In contrast, the latter provided ample material. This perception generated from fiction then fed into the work of people like Hobson, whose factual analysis gave plausibility to an anti-Imperial, anti-Capitalism, anti-Semitic rhetoric. In turn, that factual analysis then provided support for the fictional literature in which Jewish financiers became the hate figures of the pre-1914 world.

Chapter 8

The City of London: Jewel in the Crown or Cuckoo in the Nest

Introduction

Financial activity has long concentrated in a few locations, both within countries and internationally. A financial centre provides a place where payments are made and received, funds are borrowed and lent, assets and liabilities are matched and specialist services provided. This makes a financial centre a dense cluster of markets, services, facilities and expertise, all of which benefited from the interaction that came from proximity. A key feature of a financial centre was that, once established, it remained in place for long periods of time, only being dislodged by cataclysmic events such as wars and revolutions or major economic upheavals.[1] As a financial centre, the City of London not only served the United Kingdom but also the entire world. London hosted the world's dominant financial centre in the nineteenth century and vied for that position with New York over the twentieth century, but only retained that position over those centuries through undergoing considerable change. The City of London at the beginning of the twenty-first century was fundamentally different from

---

[1] Bank for International Settlements, Committee on the Global Financial System, *Long Term Issues in International Banking* (July 2010) p. 12S. See the collected articles in R. Roberts (ed.), *International Financial Centres: Concepts, Development and Dynamics* (Aldershot: Edward Elgar, 1994); R. Roberts (ed.), *Global Financial Centres: London, New York, Tokyo* (Aldershot: Edward Elgar, 1994); R. Roberts (ed.), *Offshore Financial Centres* (Aldershot: Edward Elgar, 1994).

that at the end of the eighteenth, even though it continued to occupy the same physical space and carry out similar functions, suggestive of continuity rather than change.[2]

The scale and scope of the City of London as a financial centre made it difficult for contemporaries to fully understand what took place there, leading them to generalise from those aspects with which they were familiar, while ignoring the rest. What many contemporaries were aware of was the changes taking place. In 1848, the historian, Macauley, was able to contrast how different the City was then from that of the seventeenth century.[3] Dunning and Morgan concluded in 1971 that the City had "evolved from being a general-purpose commercial and industrial centre to a highly-specialised supplier of a group of closely interrelated financial and trading services."[4] Whereas contemporaries could note that the City of London had experienced change in their lifetime, they had difficulty grasping long-term trends and so constantly underestimated its ability to adapt and thrive in the face of adversity.[5] The problem all contemporaries faced was that the City of London was never a single entity but a multi-layered and multifaceted one in a constant state of flux. This made generalisation impossible, with no single definition of the City of London capturing its entirety. For some, it was defined geographically as a particular part of London, others used it as term that encompassed Britain's entire financial sector, while some applied it to a particular set of activities wherever they took place.[6] As a result, the City of London came to be seen

---

[2]Cassis, *Capitals of Capital*, pp. 10, 19, 38, 67, 104, 118, 138, 154–155, 163–177, 185–193, 198, 202, 214–218, 220–225, 229, 233, 236; G. von Peter, 'International Banking Centres: A Network Perspective', *BIS Quarterly Review*, 2007; D. Thomas, 'UK Banks Push for Ambitious Financial Services Strategy', *Financial Times*, 22nd February 2021.

[3]T.B. Macauley (Lord Macauley), *The History of England* (London: 1848) Vol. 1: p. 272.

[4]J.H. Dunning and E.V. Morgan, *An Economic Study of the City of London* (London: 1971) pp. 31, 53.

[5]F. Welsh, *Uneasy City: An Insider's View of the City of London* (London: 1986) pp. 3–10; N. Roubini, 'Future of Finance', *Financial Times*, 2nd November 2009; J. Pickford, "London" in 'Big Hubs Keep the Wheels of Industry Turning', *Financial Times*, 9th May 2009; 'The Legal Impact of Brexit on the UK-Based Financial Services Sector', report by Freshfields Bruckhaus Deringer for The City UK (*Financial Times*, 9th May 2017); 'Omar Ali, UK Financial Services Leader, Ernst and Young', *Financial Times*, 9th May 2017).

[6]I have explored the City of London, in whole or part, over many years. This can be found in the following works: 'The London Stock Exchange and the British Economy, 1870–1930', in van Helten and Cassis, *Capitalism in a Mature Economy*, pp. 95–114;

as both a jewel in the crown of the British state, through its capacity to generate employment, incomes, profits and taxes, and a cuckoo in the nest, because of it was believed to destroy the economy of the country that provided it with a home. Before examining the validity of these opposing perceptions, it is necessary to establish some basic facts about the City, treating it from the perspective of that collection of activities that took place in a particular district of London. That perspective is the one that most people identified with, both at the time and with hindsight, and can best support an examination of change over two centuries.

Size, Composition and Change

During the nineteenth century, the City of London changed from being a densely populated residential area engaged in industrial and commercial activities to a business district serving the needs of both domestic and international trade and finance. The proportion of London's population living in the City fell from 25 per cent in 1700 to 11 per cent in 1837.[7]

R.C. Michie, *The City of London: Continuity and Change 1850–1990* (London: Macmillan, 1992) pp. xi, 1–238; 'The City of London and the British Government: The Changing Relationship', in R.C. Michie and P.A. Williamson (eds), *The British Government and the City of London in the Twentieth Century* (Cambridge: 2004); 'A Financial Phoenix: The City of London in the Twentieth Century', in Y. Cassis and E. Bussière (eds), *London and Paris as International Financial Centres* (Oxford: 2005); 'The City of London as a European Financial Centre in the Twentieth Century', in *Europäische Finanzplatze im Wettbewerb*, Bankhistorisches Archiv-Beiheft 45 (Stuttgart: Franz Steiner Verlag, 2006); 'The City of London as a Global Financial Centre, 1880–1939: Finance, Foreign Exchange and the First World War', in P.L. Cottrell, E. Lange and U. Olsson (eds), *Centres and Peripheries in Banking: The Historical Development of Financial Markets* (Ashgate Publishing Company, Aldershot, 2007); 'The City of London and the British Regions: From Medieval to Modern', in W. Lancaster, D. Newton and N. Vall (eds), *An Agenda for Regional History* (Newcastle upon Tyne: Northumbria University Press, 2007); 'The Emergence and Survival of a Financial Cluster in Britain', in Learning from Some of Britain's Successful Sectors: An Historical Analysis of the Role of Government (BIS Economics Paper No. 6, Department of Business Innovation and Skills, 2010); Michie, 'The City of London and International Banking'; R.C. Michie and S. Mollan, 'The City of London as an International Commercial and Financial Centre in the Twentieth Century', *Enterprise and Society*, 13(2) (2012).

[7] J. Innes, 'Managing the Metropolis: London's Social Problems and Their Control, c. 1660–1830', in P. Clarke and R. Gillespie (eds), *Two Capitals: London and Dublin*

What had begun as a relative decline then became an absolute one. As early as 1831, it was reported that the City of London's population was falling because "space is become more valuable for warehouses than human habitation."[8] In place of a residential workforce came a growing army of commuters employed on either a daily basis or regularly visiting the offices and markets located there. The effect was to transform the City into a specialist hub serving the British and global economy through the financial and commercial services it provided.[9] By 1911, only 19,657 lived in the City but 364,061 worked there.[10] A 1908 inquiry found that the City was "The scene of a great daily immigration, numbering on a conservative estimate a million persons" (a figure which included visitors). It concluded that its importance "is one derived wholly from the great part which it plays in the world's trade and finance."[11] An impression of the magnitude and complexity of the City does emerge from various contemporary accounts. To the journalist David Morier Evans, in 1851, the City was "a world within itself. ... a most mysterious and unfathomable labyrinth of lanes and alleys, streets and courts ... thronged with bustling multitude, whose various occupations, though uniting in one grand whole, seem to have no direct association with each other."[12] Scott in 1867 emphasised the commercial nature of the City. "The busiest, most enterprising and most wealthy emporium of either ancient or modern times."[13] Increasingly, it was identified solely with finance by contemporaries. In 1866, Henry Christmas described the City as "The financial

---

1500–1840 (Oxford: Oxford University Press, 2001) p. 63; D. Barnett, *London, Hub of the Industrial Revolution: A Revisionary History, 1775–1825* (London: I.B. Tauris, 1998) p. 13.

[8] Comparative Account of the Population of Great Britain in the Years 1801, 1811, 1821 and 1831, British Parliamentary Paper 348 (1831), p. 9.

[9] D.R. Green, *From Artisans to Paupers: Economic Change and Poverty in London, 1790–1870* (Aldershot: 1995) pp. 36, 58, 74–75, 83, 155, 173; D. Keene, 'The Setting of the Royal Exchange: Continuity and Change in the Financial District of the City of London, 1300–1871', in A. Saunders (ed.), *The Royal Exchange* (London: 1997) pp. 254–270; G. Norton, *Commentaries on the History, Constitution and Chartered Franchises of the City of London* (London: 1828) p. 195.

[10] City of London Day Census, 1911: Report (London: 1911).

[11] Report of an Enquiry by the Board of Trade into Working Class Rents, Housing and Retail Prices: London and Certain Outer Districts (London: 1908) p. 1.

[12] Morier Evans, *City Men and City Manners*, pp. 1–9.

[13] B. Scott, *A Statistical Vindication of the City of London* (London: 1867) p. 57.

metropolis of the world,"[14] and it was this description that stuck. To Escott in 1879, the City was also "the financial centre of the world," and he chose the Bank of England and the London Stock Exchange as its most representative institutions.[15] In 1888, the Glasgow banker, Charles Gairdner, noted that the City was the financial centre of Britain,[16] while in 1911 an American, Escher, concluded that it occupied that position for the entire world.[17] As with Escott, the most representative institutions of the City were the Bank of England and the London Stock Exchange. In 1909, Canada's Financial Post wrote, that "The London Stock Exchange is the greatest centre for investment and speculation in the world,"[18] while Walter Landells described it as "the nerve-centre of the world, hub of the universe."[19] Summing up these views in 1914 was Edgar Crammond, who told his audience at a meeting of the Royal Statistical Society that "The predominance of London in the international money markets has probably never been greater than it is at the present time."[20]

Despite finance crowding out commerce in the eyes of contemporaries before the First World War, the reality was different. The City remained a major commercial centre and those activities were expanding not contracting, though they were undergoing major changes that made them less visible to contemporaries. As international trade became increasingly complex, it was the City that met its needs for cheap and abundant short-term credit, access to a dense global communication network for the transmission of prices and orders, and a constant supply of ships to move commodities and manufactures around the world. The revolution in communications that had begun with the telegraph in the 1850s, and then extended to the telephone from the 1890s, permitted a growing separation

---

[14]H. Christmas, *The Money Market: What It Is, What It Does, and How It Is Managed* (London: Frederick Warne & Co., 1866) p. 94.

[15]T.H.S. Escott, *England: Its People, Policy, and Pursuits* (London: 1879) pp. 188–224.

[16]C. Gairdner, *The Constitution and Course of the Money Market* (Glasgow: 1888) p. 1.

[17]F. Escher, *Elements of Foreign Exchange* (New York: 1911) p. 146. See L.D. Wilgress, 'The London Money Market', *Journal of the Canadian Bankers Association*, 20, 210 (1912–1913).

[18]*Canadian Financial Post*, 10th April 1909.

[19]W. Landells, 'The London Stock Exchange', *Quarterly Review*, 1912, 106–107; cf. J.F. Wheeler, *The Stock Exchange* (London: 1913) pp. 82–83.

[20]E. Crammond, 'The Economic Relations of the British and German Empires', *Journal of the Royal Statistical Society*, lxxvii, 785 (1914).

between the physical movement of goods and the arrangements that underpinned international distribution. This allowed the City of London to emerge as an intermediary centre for international commercial transactions. The City was the only centre that possessed the range and depth of expertise, connections and markets necessary to support the functioning of the increasingly integrated world economy that was emerging before the First World War.[21] Enhancing the City's appeal as a commercial centre was the development of futures markets as these allowed buyers, sellers, merchants, brokers and bankers to cover the risks they were exposed to. German legislation banning futures trading in 1896 transferred much of this business to London.[22] The result was that of 357,361 who worked daily in the City in 1911, a total of 130,779 people were employed in commercial and related services, or 36.6 per cent. That was almost three times the size of those employed in financial services.[23] Contributions by different authors on separate aspects of the City, to George Sims's edited collection, *Living London*, did provide a glimpse of the depth and breadth of what took place there at the beginning of the twentieth century. "Day after day could you go there and find unsuspected centres of business in quarters that have a curious way of hiding themselves from the superficial sightseer. And each centre you would find represents an aggregation of

---

[21] Y. Cassis (ed.), *Finance and Financiers in European History, 1880–1960* (Cambridge: 1992) pp. 433–441; H. Withers, *Money-Changing: An Introduction to Foreign Exchange* (London: 1913) pp. 43–46; A.G. Ford, *The Gold Standard, 1880–1914: Britain and Argentina* (Oxford: 1962) p. 19; A.I. Bloomfield, *Short-Term Capital Movements under the pre-1914 Gold Standard* (Princeton: 1963) pp. 34–35, 43–44, 92; Cassis, *City Bankers*, pp. 5, 7, 17–23, 35–37, 57–59, 68–69, 93–94, 110, 144, 181, 208, 272, 315.

[22] F.H. Jackson (ed.), *Lectures on British Commerce, Including Finance, Insurance, Business and Industry* (London: 1912) pp. 14–17, 90–91, 125, 144. See Magee and Thompson, *Empire and Globalisation*, pp. 57–60, 114, 201; Platt, *Latin America and British Trade*, p. 110; R. Perren, *The Meat Trade in Britain, 1840–1914* (London: 1978) pp. 202–208, 211; S. Chapman, *Merchant Enterprise in Britain: From the Industrial Revolution to World War 1* (Cambridge: 1992) pp. 176–183, 202, 248, 289, 299–301, 304, 309, 312; S.B. Saul, *Studies in British Overseas Trade, 1870–1914* (Liverpool: 1960) p. 60; A.H. Beavan, *Imperial London* (London: 1901) p. 231; T. Critchell and J. Raymond, *A History of the Frozen Meat Trade* (London: 1912) pp. 102, 105–106, 172, 184; Rees, *Britain's Commodity Markets*, pp. 133, 138, 171–172, 280, 197, 241, 325, 351, 416–417, 437, 444; W.J. Loftie, *London City: Its History, Streets, Traffic, Buildings, People* (London: 1891) Vol. 1: pp. 179–181; Schneer, *London 1900*, pp. 7, 41–42, 64–65.

[23] City of London, *City of London Day Census, 1911: Report* (London: 1911), pp. 41–43.

allied interest ... the banks of Lombard Street; the shipping offices of Leadenhall and Fenchurch streets; the accountants of Old Jewry; the clothes and clothing interests of Wood Street. ... Each one of these is the scene of a multitude of busy men." Nevertheless, what impressed contemporaries most was the City of London as the financial centre of the world. "It is not possible to realise without much thought the industrial power that is wrapped up in money London. Railways through Africa, dams across the Nile, fleets of ocean greyhounds, great canals, leagues of ripening corn-London holds the key to all of these, and who can reckon on what besides?"[24]

It was inevitable that the First World War would have serious consequences for the City of London, considering the position it occupied in international trade and finance. The duration and extent of the conflict not only shattered the flows of money and goods that took place continuously between countries but also destroyed the trust upon which so much of the lending and borrowing, buying and selling, took place. Such activity shifted away from London to alternative financial and commercial centres, with New York being the greatest beneficiary, aided by the repatriation of the holdings of US investments held by British investors, as the British government acquired and sold these in its desperate search for dollars.[25] One illustration of the diminished importance of the City of London was the membership of the London Stock Exchange. This fell from 4,822 in 1914 to 3,884 in 1918, recovered to 4,035 in 1920, but then remained there for the rest of the inter-war years. The London Stock Exchange was no longer the dynamic international marketplace that it had

---

[24]G.R. Sims, *Living London* (London: Cassell, 1901–1903): (C.D. Lewis, The Bank of England; P.E. William Ryan, Going to Business in London; G.D. Ingall, London Stock Exchange; E. Pugh, Representative London Streets; R.A. Freeman, London Below Bridge; C.C. Turner, Scenes from Exchange and Office London; C.C. Turner, The City at High Noon; H. Leach, Railway London; Mrs Belloc-Lowndes, London's Drapers; C.D. Lucas, Scenes from Factory London; C.C. Turner, Money London; H. Thompson, Telephone Calls).

[25]Roberts, *Saving the City*, pp. 30–32, 45, 48–61, 67–68, 136, 141–143, 151, 167–169, 192, 227; S. Broadberry and M. Harrison (eds), *The Economics of World War 1* (Cambridge: Cambridge University Press, 1998): (S. Broadberry and M. Harrison, The UK during World War 1: Business as Usual? p. 220; H. Rockoff, 'Until It's Over, Over There: The US Economy in World War 1, p. 335); Sunderland, *Financing the Raj*, pp. 69–71; J. Inouye, *Problems of the Japanese Exchange, 1914–1926* (London: 1931) pp. 4, 174.

been before the First World War, with its once important US business lost.[26] Nevertheless, the City of London remained a financial centre of the first rank in the 1920s. No other centre could offer such a number and range of international connections, and depth of liquidity, as could London, and so it continued to act as a magnet for those needing access to the world's payments system, employ temporarily idle funds or obtain credit. It was in London that the world's largest and most active foreign exchange market developed. Despite the effects of the war, the problems experienced in the 1920s, and the competition from New York, Paul Einzig still maintained that the City of London was the dominant financial centre in the world in 1931.[27]

At this stage, there was little substantial change in the structure and composition of the City, for it remained both a commercial and financial centre, and one with a very pronounced international orientation.[28] These fed off each other as contemporaries acknowledged.[29] Nevertheless, in the eyes of most, the City was identified ever more closely with finance, to the annoyance of the ship broker, Percy Harley, in 1938. "It is remarkable how some country and even suburban folk think that the City is the Stock Exchange and the Stock Exchange is the City-and the chief occupation or indeed only occupation for City men-that is gentlemen-is stockbroking."[30] What also went unrecognised in the 1930s was the growing involvement of the City with domestic finance, whether in the form of the British Government's own greatly increased short- and long-term borrowing requirements, or the needs of British business to tap the London capital market because of the effects of low profitability and high taxation upon internal and informal sources of funds. This domestic business had begun growing in the 1920s, driving up the City's working population, as it continued to service the international economy. Employment in the City

[26]London Stock Exchange: Committee of Trustees and Mangers, Minutes 1914–1939.

[27]P. Einzig, *The Fight for Financial Supremacy* (London: Macmillan & Co., 1931) pp. 39–49.

[28]Maughan, *Markets of London*, pp. 107–108.

[29]R.J. Truptil, *British Banks and the London Money Market* (London: Jonathan Cape, 1936) p. 272; Royal Commission on the Geographical Distribution of the Industrial Population: Minutes of Evidence, 1938: Evidence of Sir David Owen, Port of London Authority.

[30]Harley, *My Life in Shipping*, p. 82. See H. Barty-King, *The Baltic Exchange: The History of a Unique Market* (London: 1977) pp. 351, 379.

reached 500,000 in the 1930s.[31] That domestic reorientation was accelerated by the 1931 financial crisis, when Britain abandoned the Gold Standard. That crisis represented a turning point for the City of London as an international financial centre for it destroyed much of the confidence that had continued to be placed in it by the international community after the First World War. Nevertheless, the City retained much of its international business because it remained the financial centre for not only the vast British Empire but also those numerous countries that tied their own currencies to the UK£.[32] Truptil's assessment in 1936 was that the City of London was still the dominant financial centre globally, though he accepted that it "can no longer lay claim to that absolute degree of financial supremacy which it held in the nineteenth century."[33]

During the Second World War, the City was subjected to large-scale aerial bombing which Holden and Holford estimated destroyed a third of the buildings, especially those connected to commerce.[34] A 1944 report on the destruction observed that "The areas intimately associated with certain trades have been practically razed to the ground."[35] The destruction, combined with the reduced access to cheap finance and the restrictions imposed on trade and finance by the government after the war, led to the decline of the City as a commercial centre, which was increasingly evident by the 1960s. It had been steadily losing its central position within the domestic supply chain since the late nineteenth century, but that had

---

[31] O.R. Hobson, *How the City Works* (London: 1940) pp. 36–38, 71, 126, 135; N. Dimsdale and N. Horsewood, 'The Financial Crisis of 1931 and the Impact of the Great Depression on the British Economy', in Dimsdale and Hotson (eds), *British Financial Crises*, p. 135; R. Roberts, 'The City of London as a Financial Centre in the Era of Depression, the Second World War and Post-War Official Controls" in A. Gorst, L. Johnman and W.S. Lucas (eds), *Contemporary British History, 1931–1961* (London: 1991) p. 68.

[32] Financial News, *The City, 1884–1934* (London: 1934) p. 64; W. French, *Port of London: Handbook of Rates, Charges and General Information* (London: 1937) p. 35; Van Cleef, *Trade Centers and Trade Routes*, pp. 132, 244.

[33] Truptil, *British Banks and the London Money Market*, pp. 1, 21–22, 79–80, 102, 107, 110, 125–128, 136, 142, 149, 155, 167, 176–180, 194, 199, 238, 242, 246, 265–266, 309, 320.

[34] C.H. Holden and W.G. Holford, *The City of London: A Record of Destruction and Survival* (London: 1951) p. 184.

[35] City of London Council, Report by the Improvements and Town Planning Committee on the Preliminary Draft Proposals for Post-War Reconstruction in the City of London (London: 1944) pp. 1–14, 15.

been compensated by becoming an essential link that connected producers with consumers globally. It was that position that was badly damaged by wartime destruction and post-war government restrictions, exchange controls and taxes. These favoured international agencies, multinational companies and global banks rather than the merchants, brokers and markets located in the City of London.[36] As Stahl warned in 1951, "There has been built up in London a highly-complex system of merchants, bankers, commodity markets and traders of various kinds to secure the growth of overseas trade under free terms of finance and commerce and free interplay of the market. The system was long in building but it may be quickly damaged."[37] What she prophesied happened over the next 20 years.[38]

It was not only the commercial side of the City of London that suffered during and after the Second World War. The financial side was also badly damaged as a special issue of the *Banker* magazine revealed as early as 1941.[39] Over the course of World War Two, British holdings of foreign assets were sold and could not be replenished because of government-imposed restrictions. This forced the City to concentrate upon cultivating its domestic business, as Steffenburg, from Hambros Bank, explained in 1949. "Since the closing of the London market to new foreign issues the merchant banks have turned towards participation in British issues of bonds and shares."[40] Combined with the disruption caused by the war, the

---

[36] K.M. Stahl, *The Metropolitan Organization of British Colonial Trade: Four Regional Studies* (London: 1951) pp. 4–7, 158, 218, 236–237, 244, 292–296; W. Malenbaum, *The World Wheat Economy, 1885–1939* (Cambridge, Mass.: 1953) p. 104; P.T. Bauer, *West African Trade: A Study of Competition, Oligopoly and Monopoly in a Changing Economy* (London: 1954) pp. 199–203, 265; R. Greenhill, 'Merchants and the Latin American Trades: An Introduction', in Platt (ed.), *Business Imperialism*, pp. 159, 175, 180; A. Coates, *The Commerce in Rubber: The First 250 Years* (Singapore: 1987) pp. 50–53, 117, 149, 180, 187, 255, 337, 351, 360, 367; Rowe, *Primary Commodities in International Trade*, pp. 44–45, 51–54, 155–158; Rees, *The History of the London Commodity Markets*, pp. 58–59, 86, 101; J.B. Jefferys, *Retail Trading in Britain, 1850–1950* (Cambridge: 1954) pp. 11, 22, 47, 143–144.

[37] Stahl, *The Metropolitan Organization of British Colonial Trade*, p. 293.

[38] See Dunning and Morgan, *An Economic Study of the City of London*; F. Duffy and A. Henney, *The Changing City* (London: 1989).

[39] 'The City in War', *The Banker* August 1941: articles by P. Bareau, 'Eclipse of the Merchant Banker; H.E. Wincott, The Stock Exchange Looks Ahead; P. Einzig, Foreign Bank Branches during the War; D.E. Erlebach, The Baltic Exchange.

[40] Steffenburg, 'Merchant Banking in London', in *Current Financial Problems and the City of London*, p. 64.

continuance of capital and exchange controls also made it difficult for the City to recover much of its international banking business, other than with those countries that continued to use the UK£. These controls were only gradually relaxed during the 1950s and 1960s, but that was accompanied by the disintegration of the Sterling area, which undermined the City's position as a global financial centre. New York was now the dominant financial centre in the world.[41]

However, the segmented capital and money markets, which government-imposed barriers created after the Second World War, did provide the City of London with the basis for its post-war recovery. Banks, for example, could operate in London free from the domestic restrictions they faced.[42] What developed in London from the 1960s were markets in US$s, but free from the controls imposed by the US government. The City of London made the transition from the UK£, that was in decline, to the US$, which had become the international currency of choice, and so attracted a large international business as a result, such as the Eurodollar and Eurobonds markets. Those were followed in the 1970s by a booming foreign exchange market, as the fixed exchange rate regime of the post-war years collapsed. Again, this was a market based on the US$. The removal of British exchange controls in 1979 and then UK restrictions on the operation of banks and financial markets in 1986 helped London attract even more business from abroad.[43] To many contemporaries, this post-war revival of the City was due to continuity not change, being a product of the English language, a convenient time zone and the long-established financial micro-structure.[44] To others, the City's success was

---

[41] W.C. Clarke, *The City's Invisible Earnings* (London: 1958) p. 22.

[42] Clarke, *The City in the World Economy*, pp. 83–85, 10, 143, 160, 213, 218–219; Dunning and Morgan, *An Economic Study of the City of London*, pp. 31, 34, 41, 53, 260, 265; E.R. Shaw, *The London Money Market* (London: 1975) p. 163; N. Sowels, D. James and I. Hunter, *Britain's Invisible Earnings* (Aldershot: 1989) p. 91; A. Leyshon and N. Thrift, *Money/Space: Geographies of Monetary Transformation* (London: 1997) pp. 133, 136, 145, 155; J.H. Wood, *A History of Central Banking in Great Britain and the United States* (Cambridge: Cambridge University Press, 2005) p. 296.

[43] See 'Bank of England, London as an International Financial Centre', *Bank of England Quarterly Bulletin*, 29 (1989); City Research Project, *The Competitive Position of London's Financial Services: Final Report* (London: 1995).

[44] P. Hall, *Cities in Civilization: Culture, Innovation, and Urban Order* (London: Weidenfeld and Nicholson, 1998) ch. 28: 'The City of Capitalism Rampant: London 1979–1993', pp. 897–928.

due to change as it reinvented itself in response to new challenges and opportunities.[45] What was recognised by most was that change did take place throughout the post-Second World War years. The *Sunday Times Magazine* in 2006 considered that "As recently as 30 years ago, the City was a very different place."[46] This willingness of the City to adapt over time impressed the *Financial Times* journalist, Patrick Jenkins, in January 2021. "The City has a long history of innovation and adaptive change. That is just as well-clinging to the status quo is not an option."[47] Consequently, when considering any of the views expressed about the City of London, it must always be recognised that they were based on a partial understanding of what took place there, and one conditioned by its structure and composition at a particular moment in time. The result was a highly flawed perception but one that carried conviction because evidence existed to support it at the time it was written.

The City Casino

Long associated with the City in the mind of the public was speculation, especially in shares. The City was where the London Stock Exchange was located and many regarded it as little better than a casino where investors gambled and lost. There was a fine line between speculation, as undertaken by professionals in support of their trading and investment strategies, and gambling on the rise and fall of prices, and so it was easy for the former to be classed along with the latter and condemned as a result.[48] An official inquiry into the London Stock Exchange in 1878 concluded that "The great facilities afforded by the Stock Exchange for the unlimited purchase or sale of all sorts of securities, coupled with the system of making bargains for the account, that is, for a future day, open a wide door to mere gambling as well as to legitimate speculation."[49] What prevented

---

[45]Spiegelberg, *Power Without Accountability*, p. 6; *The Economist*, 7th December 1985.

[46]'The World's Wallet', *Sunday Times Magazine*, 3rd December 2006, pp. 62–70.

[47]P. Jenkins, 'Brexit Can Mean London Loses Even If the EU Doesn't Gain', *Financial Times*, 11th January 2021.

[48]Heinemann, *Popular Investment and Speculation in Britain*, pp. 5–11, 23–30, 42–50; Heinemann, 'Investment, Speculation and Popular Stock Market Engagement', pp. 251–269.

[49]London Stock Exchange Commission: *Report of the Commissioners and Minutes of Evidence* (London: HMSO, 1878) pp. 3, 9–10, 14, 21, 24.

action being taken, until the mid-twentieth century, to control or ban speculation, despite calls for that to happen, was the recognition that it played a vital part in the operation of markets.[50] In 1852, for example, Morier Evans accepted that the Stock Exchange was regarded "with contempt" but also observed that "the greatness of its dealings is unequalled" and that "every endeavour" was made "to abolish all which tends to make it despicable."[51] Though incremental reforms took place, speculation went largely unchecked before the First World War, because the prevailing view was that markets worked best if left to regulate themselves. As the public remained convinced that speculation was no different from betting on cards, dice or horses, the City continued to be regarded as some kind of casino.[52]

This perception of the City as a giant casino extended into the years between the two world wars, being the focus of an attack by Sydney Webb in 1931.[53] In 1933, the stockbroker Sir Stephen Killik accepted that "The Stock Exchange is often looked upon simply as an institution carried on for the purpose of speculation and gambling."[54] Helping fuel this perception was the Wall Street Crash in the USA in 1929, coinciding as it did with the bursting of a speculative bubble in the UK, involving the exposure and imprisonment of the financier, Clarence Hatry. Further undermining the belief that markets were best left to regulate themselves in the 1930s was the attempt to rig the pepper market and the use of

---

[50] *The Bank-The Stock Exchange-The Bankers-The Bankers' Clearing House-The Minister, and the Public: An Expose* (London: 1821); Dot, *The Stock Exchange and Its Victims* (London: 1851); *Exposure of the Stock Exchange and Bubble Companies* (London: 1854); H. Roy, *The Stock Exchange* (London: 1860) p. 13; H. May, 'The London Stock Exchange', *Fortnightly Review*, 580 (1885); H.M., *On the Analogy between the Stock Exchange and the Turf* (London: 1885). See Banner, *Anglo-American Securities Regulation.*

[51] Morier Evans, *The City.*

[52] Select Committee on Loans to Foreign States, Report (London: 1875); London Stock Exchange Commission (London: 1878); *Economist*, 23rd November 1895; A.P. Poley and F.H. Gould, *The History, Law, and Practice of the Stock Exchange* (London: 1911) p. 86; J.E. Day, *Stockbroker's Office Organisation, Management and Accounts* (London: 1911) p. 1.

[53] Johnson, *The Financiers and the Nation*, preface by Sydney Webb. For a discussion of these issues see A. Cairncross, *Economics and Economic Policy* (Oxford: 1986) — especially the chapter entitled "The Market and the State."

[54] Killik, *The Work of the Stock Exchange*, p. 49.

high-pressure techniques to sell worthless shares. However, the biggest blow to the belief in self-regulated markets came with the breakdown of global markets in the 1930s and the world depression that accompanied it. Nevertheless, many cautioned that excessive government intervention could lead to a worse outcome.[55] A government inquiry of 1936–1937, for example, warned against "any undue interference with the smooth running of the delicate machinery of legitimate finance in the City of London."[56]

During the Second World War, speculation was little in evidence because of government controls but the popular view in 1947 continued to regard the London Stock Exchange, in the words of Oscar Hobson in 1947, as "a den of gamblers and a casino."[57] This belief that the City was a giant casino remained even though legislation continued to suppress speculation after the Second World War, and the London Stock Exchange became the semi-official regulator of the securities market. In 1987, a joint Confederation of British Industry/City Task Force found that the stock market continued to be compared to "a casino or race meeting, where companies are put into play" by speculators.[58] Those who used the London Stock Exchange to bet on the rise or fall of share prices provided the ammunition that critics of the City required, especially when they blamed their losses on a market rigged against them. Less powerful now were the voices that warned that the functioning of the market would be damaged if speculation was banned. The outcome was a situation in which speculation was tolerated but attempts were made to regulate it in such a way that it took place within acceptable limits. As long as the City contained markets where securities or commodities were bought and sold, and prices rose and fell, there would be those who would be critical of it. The strength of their attack, and the popular support it received, varied in line with speculative booms and bursts. With speculation being largely suppressed after the Second World War, especially with the declining importance of the retail investor, this criticism of the City as being no

---

[55]The Times, *The City of London* (London: 1928) pp. 182–183; A. Hooker, *The International Grain Trade* (London: 1936) pp. 1–2, 135–136; *Two Centuries of Lewis and Peat, 1775–1975* (London: 1975) p. 46; Hobson, *How the City Works*, p. 71.

[56]Board of Trade, *Share Pushing*, pp. 6, 17, 29, 35–38, 44–45.

[57]O.R. Hobson, 'The Stock Exchange and the Public', *The Banker*, July 1947, pp. 31–32.

[58]Confederation of British Industry, *Investing for Britain's Future: Report of the CBI City/Industry Task Force* (London: 1987) p. 9.

more than a large casino was much less strident but the perception remained.[59]

The City/Industry Divide

That did not mean that popular criticism of the City died away over the course of the twentieth century. Instead, it shifted to an attack on the City because of its perceived failure to support the British economy. Prior to the First World War, there had been complaints from various manufacturers that they could not obtain the finance they required. Some connected this to the vast outflow of funds from Britain to other countries, orchestrated through the City, and suggested that it deprived domestic industry of finance. This connection was dismissed by others who pointed out that British industry had no need to raise funds in the City because it possessed ample funds from other sources. There was a City/Industry Divide because Britain's large and diverse financial system met the nation's financial needs in numerous different ways, and that was understood and appreciated by most contemporaries.[60] During the First World War, there were renewed complaints that industry was having trouble raising finance, which was hardly surprising given the rival financial requirements from the unprecedented military effort taking place. These complaints again pointed to the City's lack of engagement with the finance of British

---

[59] See Heinemann, *Popular Investment and Speculation in Britain*; Samuel, *Shareholder's Money*; L.W. Hein, *The British Companies Acts and the Practice of Accountancy, 1844–1962* (New York: 1978).

[60] Hirst, *British Capital at Home and Abroad*, pp. 9, 13, 19, 21. See Hirst, *The Six Panics and Other Essays*, pp. 227–228; Hobson, 'Foreign Investments and Home Employment', p. 10; Bassett, *British Commerce*, p. 33; Joseph, 'Industrial Finance', pp. 6–10; A.G. Whyte, *The Electrical Industry: Lighting, Traction and Power* (London: 1904) pp. 22–25, 69–72; *The Times* 20th October 1905; W.E. Hooper, *The Motor Car in the First Decade of the 20th Century* (London: 1908) pp. 40, 57; Artifex and Opifex, *The Causes of Decay in a British Industry* (London: Longmans, Green and Company, 1907) p. 276; British Electric Traction (Pioneer) Company: Extraordinary General Meeting, Report of Proceedings, 5th November 1896, British Electric Traction Company: General Meeting, 14th December 1896, General Meeting, 7th April 1898, 18th March 1899, 18th June 1900, 4th July 1901, 16th June 1902, 11th July 1904, 15th June 1911, 20th June 1912; Lenfant, *British Capital Export*, pp. 104–105, 136, 462.

industry, as in a government inquiry of 1916.[61] After the war, the City was again blamed by British industry for failing to provide financial support, despite its involvement in the post-war speculative boom that had seen the flotation of numerous manufacturing companies. Lavington in 1921 took the view that "The English market for new Stock Exchange securities is much better adapted to supply capital to such bodies as foreign states, railways and other large undertakings than to meet the demands arising from small industrial ventures."[62] The complaint made was that smaller enterprises were ignored by the City. This was only to be expected as the amount each enterprise required did not justify the expense involved in raising it, and so had traditionally been provided from personal savings and informal networks. These alternatives were less plentiful after the war because of the high levels of personal taxation and the general lack of profitability throughout British business. Investors were also discouraged from buying the shares of industrial companies due to the underperformance of those promoted during the speculative boom.[63] A government inquiry, appointed in 1924, conducted an exhaustive inquiry into the problems of British industry, and largely exonerated the City from responsibility, concluding in its 1929 report that they had discovered no "defects on the part of the British banks or other financial institutions, which are undoubtedly able and willing to supply industry with all necessary facilities on reasonable terms of security." They added that those "industries as are earning good profits are able to secure all the capital they need." Instead, they reached the conclusion that the major problem faced by manufacturing was "the continued unprofitableness of so many industrial concerns, which makes them unable to give security to the banks or to offer an attractive investment to the public."[64]

This was not the conclusion that the government or the public wanted to hear, in the search for scapegoats to blame for the difficulties being experienced by the traditional manufacturing industry. In the frame as principal scapegoat was the City of London, located far from the country's northern industrial heartlands and with a tradition of having limited involvement with domestic manufacturing. The response from the government was the appointment of another committee which would

---

[61] *Financial Facilities for Trade*: Report, pp. 4–6.
[62] Lavington, *The English Capital Market*, p. 219.
[63] Hirst, *Wall Street and Lombard Street*, pp. 81–82.
[64] Committee on Industry and Trade: Final Report, 1929, pp. 47, 298–299.

investigate the connection between finance and industry. This new committee took evidence between 1929 and 1931, producing a report during a monetary crisis when Britain was forced to abandon the Gold Standard. That committee reached the conclusion that "There is substance in the view that the British financial organisation concentrated in the City of London might with advantage be more closely co-ordinated with British industry, particularly large-scale industry, than is now the case; and that in some respects the City is more highly organised to provide capital to foreign countries than to British industry." The chairman of the inquiry Lord Macmillan took the view that "We have had a considerable amount of evidence that there is a gap in the credit machinery of this country and that some organisation is required to fill the gap." This "Macmillan Gap" was then enshrined as official confirmation of the City/Industry Divide, especially as it was supported by the leading economist of the day, John Maynard Keynes, who had served on the inquiry and contributed to its conclusion. That the conclusion was at variance with the evidence presented to the inquiry, which had stressed the alternative explanations for traditional industry's difficulties, was ignored both at the time and subsequently.[65]

The public had found its scapegoat, as the conclusion of the committee confirmed what most already believed, and this belief trumped the many voices that continued to suggest that the prime causes of industry's difficulties did not lie with the City.[66] It became standard practice in all investigations to refer to the "Shortcomings of the present machinery of the City of London," as in a 1939 report on the location of industry.[67] Even when evidence was presented that the City was increasingly engaged in providing finance for industry in the 1930s, there remained a strong belief in a City/Industry Divide, especially among economists, who had long

---

[65] Committee on Finance and Industry: Report (London: 1931) pp. 171–174 (Minutes of Evidence: Sir Mark Webster Jenkinson 27th March 1930, Sir Roland Nugent, Director of the Federation of British Industry 20th March 1930; Sir James Lithgow, chairman FBI 18th July 1930; Lord Macmillan, 8th May 1930).

[66] Jarvie, *The Old Lady Unveiled*, p. 44–46, 92, 234; Thomas, *British Banks and the Finance of Industry*, pp. 14, 21, 94–96, 112, 222–223, 240–241, 258; H. Withers, 'The Work of the New Issue Market', in *Financial News, The City, 1884–1934* (London: 1934) p. 46.

[67] Political and Economic Planning, *Report on the Location of Industry*, pp. 9, 27, 28–29, 224.

been critical of the role played by the London Stock Exchange in domestic finance.[68] In Grant's 1937 study of the capital market, the point was made that "The Stock Exchange is primarily an institution for imparting marketability to securities; only very secondarily is it an institution for providing new money for enterprise."[69] That approach was then taken by economists after the Second World War, with Britain's economic decline blamed on the lack of City finance for manufacturing. Evidence supporting that view, dating as far back as before the First World War, was used in support, while the equally vociferous views of those, for example, suggesting the causes lay in the damaging effects of legislation and taxation were ignored. The post-Second World War generation, which could contrast the global depression of the 1930s with the military and economic achievements of the 1940s, was conditioned to see government intervention as a solution to industry's problems. That meant that they found no attractions in views that criticised the state while those that stressed market failings, as with the City/Industry Divide thesis, were very appealing.[70]

Despite the, at best, inconclusive evidence for a City/Industry Divide from either before the First World War or between the two world wars, it became an article of faith for many after the Second, accepted without qualification by most into the 1980s even as evidence mounted of the City's growing engagement with British industry.[71] A report

---

[68] Arnold, *The Bankers of London*, pp. 21, 28, 54, 97, 102; Haxey, *Tory MP*, pp. 39–42; Keynes, *The General Theory of Employment*, pp. 154–160; Killik, *The Work of the Stock Exchange*, p. 49.

[69] A.T.K. Grant, *A Study of the Capital Market in Post-War Britain* (London: 1937) p. 128.

[70] Joseph, 'Industrial Finance', pp. 22–25, 69–72; Whyte, *The Electrical Industry*, pp. 22–25, 69–72; *The Times*, 20th October 1905; Hooper, *The Motor Car in the First Decade of the Twentieth Century*, pp. 40, 57; Artifex and Opifex, *The Causes of Decay in a British Industry*, p. 276; British Electric Traction (Pioneer) Company: Extraordinary General Meeting, Report of Proceedings, 5th November 1896, British Electric Traction Company: General Meeting, 14th December 1896, General Meeting, 7th April 1898, 18th March 1899, 18th June 1900, 4th July 1901, 16th June 1902, 11th July 1904, 15th June 1911, 20th June 1912.

[71] Brett, *Usury in Britain*, pp. 87–92, 111, 119–121, 139; Labour Party, *The City: A Socialist Approach: Report of the Labour Party Financial Institutions Study Group* (London: 1982) pp. 6, 15, 19, 21–22, 36, 56–57; Cairncross, *Home and Foreign Investment*, p. 95; Hall, 'A Note on the English Capital Market', p. 63; Cairncross, 'The English Capital Market Before 1914', pp. 143–146; Hall, 'The English Capital Market Before 1914: A Reply', pp. 340–343; Cairncross, *The British Economy Since 1945*, p. 24;

commissioned by the City concluded in 1973 that it was not well regarded "by educated and professional people, or by the populace at large."[72] The existence of a City/Industry Divide was embedded in the work of Sydney Pollard, for example, who was the author of the most popular textbook on the development of British economy in the twentieth century.[73] To Pollard, as late as in 1982, the City/Industry Divide was alive and well, and all that was required was to spell out its consequences, "Industry has every time to be sacrificed on the altar of the City's and the financial system's primacy."[74] However, as the financial system became increasingly domestically focused after the Second World War, it was difficult to explain the continued decline of manufacturing as a product of a City/Industry Divide, whatever may have been the case in the past.[75] As early as 1963, Paul Einzig dismissed the City/Industry Divide thesis, and his conclusions were increasingly supported by those who examined the way business was financed in Britain from the late nineteenth century onwards, as that revealed a growing integration rather than separation.[76] In an attempt to

---

A.J. Taylor, 'The Economy', in S. Nowell-Smith (ed.), *Edwardian England* (London: 1964) pp. 117, 121, 137–138; W.D. Rubinstein, 'The Victorian Middle Classes', p. 621; Eatwell, *Whatever Happened to Britain*, p. 79, 159–160; Kennedy, *Strategy and Diplomacy*, pp. 94–96; G. Ingham, *Capitalism Divided? The City and Industry in British Social Development* (London: 1984) pp. 113, 131–133, 169, 227–242; Kennedy, *Industrial Structure*, pp. 8, 17–18, 56, 110, 115–125, 139, 148–149, 160–167. (This book was an attempt to provide the evidence for the City/Industry Divide which was lacking in his earlier work. See W.P. Kennedy, 'Foreign Investment, Trade and Growth in the United Kingdom, 1870–1913', *Explorations in Economic History*, 11 (1974)); D. Coates and J. Hillard (eds), *UK Economic Decline: Key Texts* (London: 1995) — see the chapters by Fine and Harris, Zysman, Radice; D. Goodhart and C. Grant, *Making the City Work* (London: Fabian Trust, 1988); D. Coates, *The Question of UK Decline: State, Society and Economy* (London: 1994); Hutton, *The State We're In.*

[72] Inter-Bank Research Organisation, *The Future of London as an International Financial Centre* (London: 1973) pp. 1–2.

[73] Pollard, *The Development of the British Economy*, pp. 9, 85, 102.

[74] S. Pollard, *The Wasting of the British Economy; British Economic Policy 1945 to the Present* (London: 1982) p. 87.

[75] Committee on the Working of the Monetary System: Report (London: 1959) pp. 80–81, 108–109, 162–163.

[76] P. Einzig, *Why London Must Remain the World's Banking Centre* (London: Aims for Industry, 1964) pp. 5, 13–15; Paish, 'The London New Issue Market', pp. 2, 13; Henderson, *The New Issue Market and the Finance of Industry*, p. 154; P.L. Cottrell,

bolster support for the existence of a City/Industry Divide, the 1970s Labour government established another inquiry into the link between finance and industry. This was chaired by Harold Wilson, the ex-Labour Prime Minister and an Oxford-trained economist. When this inquiry reported in 1980, it concluded, despite opposition from some, that the evidence for a City/Industry Divide was lacking, and that the causes of manufacturing's difficulties lay elsewhere.[77] Nevertheless, there were those who would not give up on the existence of the Divide. Though the US editors of volume on the decline of the British economy cast doubt on the existence of the Divide, the two British academics, Best and Humphries, who contributed the chapter on the City and Industrial Decline, did not, while others continued to find new variations that gave credibility to the thesis.[78] However, the Divide was increasingly regarded as a myth and discounted as a significant explanation for the problems experienced by British manufacturing over the past century.[79] To those

---

Industrial Finance, pp. 34–35; S.J. Prais, *The Evolution of Giant Firms in Britain: A Study of the Growth and Concentration in Manufacturing Industry, 1909–1970* (Cambridge: 1976) pp. 90–91, 105–106, 116–117, 123–124, 129; Hannah, *The Rise of the Corporate Economy*, pp. 3, 58–60, 69, 76, 105, 133, 152–153, 216; Thomas, *The Finance of British Industry*, pp. 145–147, 177–178, 184, 189–190, 335–336. See F. Capie and M. Collins, *Have the Banks Failed British Industry* (London: 1992); N. Dimsdale and M. Prevezer (eds) *Capital Markets and Corporate Governance* (Oxford: 1994), chapters by Marsh, Sykes, McWilliams and Sentence, Hughes, and Schneider-Lenne.

[77] Committee to Review the Functioning of Financial Institutions: Report (London: 1980) pp. 1–2, 19–20, 62, 72, 123, 127, 257, 371; Committee to Review the Functioning of Financial Institutions: The Financing of Small Firms Interim Report (London: 1979) pp. 9, 12: Evidence from Confederation of British Industry, 1977, p. 1: The Stock Exchange, pp. 187–189, 195–196, 217; Accepting Houses, p. 4, 20; Clearing Banks, pp. 177.

[78] B. Elbaum and W. Lazonick, 'An Institutional Perspective on British Decline', in B. Elbaum and W. Lazonick (eds), *The Decline of the British Economy* (Oxford: 1986) pp. 3–5, 10; M.H. Best and J. Humphries, 'The City and Industrial Decline', in Elbaum and Lazonick (eds), *The Decline of the British Economy*, pp. 223, 236; B. Elbaum and W. Lazonick, 'The Decline of the British Economy: An Institutional Perspective', *Journal of Economic History*, xliv, 570–572 (1984); Carnevali, *Europe's Advantage*, pp. 16, 86–87, 93–102.

[79] Confederation of British Industry, *Investing for Britain's Future*, pp. 1–15; Goodhart and Grant, *Making the City Work*, pp. 1, 3, 6, 9, 15–17, 23; R. Floud and D. McCloskey (eds), *The Cambridge Economic History of Britain Since 1700*, 2nd ed. (Cambridge: Cambridge University Press, 1994) (Vol. 2: 1860–1939: M. Edelstein, Foreign Investment and

committed to a belief in the Divide, no lack of evidence, or even evidence to contradict it, would ever suffice to disprove its existence.[80] With the official sanction of a government inquiry, and the implicit backing of the most influential economist of the twentieth century, the Divide became the go-to explanation for Britain's economic decline after the Second World War. It was only as evidence mounted to contradict the existence of the Divide that alternatives had to be sought. Even then, it continued to attract supporters whose mission was to find new evidence to bolster the thesis.

The City/Bank/Treasury Nexus

Faced with the fading credibility of the City/Industry Divide, a new thesis emerged that combined the failure of the City to provide the economy with finance with an ability to direct government economic policies away from those beneficial for manufacturing.[81] This was labelled the City/ Bank/Treasury Nexus. It built on the nineteenth century belief that the City had privileged access to politicians, and could persuade them to do its bidding.[82] This ability to influence those wielding political power became more important in the twentieth century as the government played an increasingly central role in the management of the economy. This was especially the case after the Second World War. As early as 1944, the Labour Party was concerned that the City would be the "stupid master" of productive enterprise.[83] In 1962, Roger Simon produced a report, *Light on the City*, for the Labour Research Department, that warned that

---

Accumulation, 1860–1914, p. 191, F. Capie and G. Wood, Money in the Economy, 1870–1931, p. 246, M. Thomas, The Macro-Economics of the Inter-War Years, pp. 321–322, 333, 345, Vol. 3: 1939–1992: R. Millward, Industrial and Commercial Performance since 1950, p. 134). See O'Sullivan, *From Crisis to Crisis.*

[80] As an example see L. Harris, J. Coakley, M. Croasdale and T. Evans, *New Perspectives on the Financial System* (London: 1988) pp. 120, 134.

[81] Coates, *The Question of UK Decline*, pp. 261–265; Coates and Hillard (eds), *UK Economic Decline*: B. Fine and L. Harris, The Role of the City (1985) pp. 215–220; J. Zysman, Markets and Growth (1983) pp. 223–224; H. Radice, *Britain in the World Economy: National Decline, Capitalist Success?* (London: Routledge, 1989) pp. 243–244.

[82] Harris and Thane, 'British and European Bankers', pp. 215–216, 225; Elbaum and Lazonick, 'An Institutional Perspective on British Decline', pp. 3–5, 10.

[83] The Labour Party, *Financial Policy and Economic Policy* (1944).

"The economic power wielded by the tiny oligarchy that runs the City is increasing all the time."[84] In 1973, Spiegelberg claimed that the City exercised "Power without accountability," because it controlled the finances of the nation but lacked any democratic mandate.[85] It was during the 1970s that the power of the City to dictate government policy was then linked to the decline of manufacturing, becoming established doctrine for many by the 1980s.[86] As expressed by Longstreth in 1979, the thesis was that "The City has ... largely set the parameters of economic policy and its interests have generally predominated since the late nineteenth century."[87] The argument put forward was that those in the City were able to shape the thinking of the Bank of England, which in turn had influence over the Treasury, the most powerful department within government and able to dictate policy. The actions of the City/Bank/Treasury Nexus led to policies being pursued that favoured the City and damaged manufacturing, whether it was the pursuit of Free Trade before the First World War, a return to the Gold Standard between the wars or a strong £ after the Second World War. Underpinning this thesis was that these policies damaged the manufacturing base of the economy to the benefit of financial services largely located in the City. What the thesis ignored was the shift to a service-based economy that was taking place in all developed

---

[84]R. Simon, *Light on the City* (London: Labour Research Department, 1962) pp. 4–8, 31, 50, 55, 70, 78, 90, 94, 97.

[85]Spiegelberg, *Power Without Accountability*, pp. 6, 62, 81, 192, 243, 247.

[86]See W. Keegan and R. Pennant-Rea, *Who Runs the Economy?* (London: 1979); A. Gamble, *Britain in Decline: Economic Policy, Political Strategy and the British State* (London: 1981); M. Moran, 'Finance Capital and Pressure-Group Politics in Britain', *British Journal of Political Science*, 11 (1981); Moran, *The Politics of Banking*; S. Strange, *Casino Capitalism* (London: 1986); P.A. Hall, *Governing the Economy: The Politics of State Intervention in Britain and France* (Cambridge: 1986); Harris, Coakley, Croasdale and Evans, *New Perspectives on the Financial System*; M. Moran, 'City Pressure: The City of London as a Pressure Group since 1945', *Contemporary Record* (Summer 1988); Pollard, *Britain's Prime and Britain's Decline*; R. Stones, 'Government-finance Relations in Britain, 1964–1967: A Tale of Three Cities', *Economy and Society*, 19 (1990); M. Moran, *The Politics of the Financial Services Revolution: The USA, UK and Japan* (London: 1991); G. Burn, *The Re-emergence of Global Finance* (London: Palgrave Macmillan, 2006); L.S. Talani, *Globalization, Hegemony and the Future of the City of London* (London: Palgrave Macmillan, 2012).

[87]F. Longstreth, 'The City, Industry and the State', in C. Crouch (ed.), *State and Economy in Contemporary Capitalism* (London: 1979) p. 161.

economies, including that of the UK, which meant that manufacturing was in relative decline regardless of the policies pursued by successive governments.[88]

Apart from the identification of manufacturing with the entire economy, the other weakness with the City/Bank/Treasury thesis was that it treated the City as a single coherent unit, united with a common purpose regardless of time or circumstance. Considering the size and diversity of the City, it lacked a collective identity when it came to government policy.[89] The one common desire among those in the City was to be free of political intervention.[90] This was evident in the lead up to the First World War.[91] During the war itself, the Liberal politician and later Prime Minister, David Lloyd George, commented on "the difficulty of reconciling the interests of the different sections of the banking community."[92] In 1917, Lord Cunliffe, the Governor of Bank of England, told Bonar Law, Chancellor of the Exchequer, that "I fully realise that I must not attempt to impose my views upon you."[93] That aim of avoiding political engagement was increasingly difficult to achieve after 1931, when Britain left the Gold Standard, as that placed the government in charge of monetary policy.[94] Nevertheless, the lack of an agreed position in the City on almost

---

[88] S. Newton and D. Porter, *Modernization Frustrated: The Politics of Industrial Decline in Britain since 1900* (London: 1988) pp. 8–10, 66, 81, 121, 201–202; J. Paxman, *Friends in High Places: Who Runs Britain?* (London: 1990) pp. 268–273, 278–279, 287.

[89] S.G. Checkland, 'The Mind of the City, 1870–1914', *Oxford Economic Papers*, 9, 263, 276 (1957); M.J. Daunton, 'Gentlemanly Capitalism and British Industry 1820–1914', *Past and Present*, 122, 138–139, 147–150 (1989); P. Williamson, 'Financiers, the Gold Standard and British Politics, 1925–1931', in J. Turner (ed.), *Businessmen and Politics: Studies of Business Activity in British Politics, 1900–1945* (London: Heinemann, 1984) pp. 107–108.

[90] Cassis, *City Bankers*, pp. 272, 290, 296. See Cassis, 'The Banking Community of London', pp. 109–126.

[91] Public Record Office, *Cabinet Papers* 16/18A Report and Proceedings of Imperial Defence Trading with the Enemy Sub-Committee under Lord Desart, Evidence of Huth Jackson, *Merchant Banker*, 26 November 1911 (pp. 90–91) and Lord Revelstoke, Chairman of Baring Brothers, 19 December 1911 (pp. 96–98, 104); Trading with the Enemy: Report and Proceedings [National Archives], 1912, p. 11.

[92] D. Lloyd George, *War Memoirs* (London: Odhams Press, 1933) Vol. 1: pp. 61–67.

[93] Quoted in G.C. Peden, *The Treasury and British Public Policy, 1906–1959* (Oxford: Oxford University Press, 2000) p. 110.

[94] Truptil, *British Banks and the London Money Market*, p. 325; A. Citizen, *The City Today*, pp. 5–7, 15–23, 29, 33–39. See R. Roberts, 'The City of London as a Financial Centre'.

any policy made it difficult to exercise pressure on the government, as the political commentator, Victor Sandelson, observed in the 1950s.[95] This was at a time when the City was, probably, at its most cohesive, having emerged from the Second World War more inward looking and less socially diverse than it had been in the past.[96] That was to change with the growth of international markets from the late 1950s onwards, which drew in foreign banks and their employees.[97] That made the City much more diverse once again, as well as increasingly international in its outlook, complicating any attempt to achieve an agreed position.[98]

Even if the City had been able to agree on a single policy agenda, there is no evidence to suggest that politicians and civil servants would respond, though they were willing to take note of the various views expressed. The editor of the *Financial Times* from 1950 to 1972, Gordon Newton, wrote in his memoirs that the Labour Prime Minister, Harold Wilson, "always liked to know what was happening in the City."[99] However, there is no evidence that what he learnt had any influence on him or his government.[100] One way of testing the ability of the City to dictate policy to government is to examine the attempts by the London Stock Exchange to do so. These were confined to the years after the Second World War but were restricted to matters of taxation. In 1976, they claimed that "Over the years we have been reasonably successful in having our ideas adopted by Chancellors of both political parties." That

---

[95] Sandelson, 'The Confidence Trick', pp. 116–117, 125, 135.

[96] P. Thompson, 'The Pyrrhic Victory of Gentlemanly Capitalism: The Financial Elite of the City of London, 1945–1990', *Journal of Contemporary History*, 32, 431–434 (1997).

[97] J. Coakley and L. Harris, *The City of Capital: London's Role as a Financial Centre* (Oxford: 1983) pp. 122, 192. See IFSL Research, *International Financial Markets in the UK* (London: 2009); H.M. Treasury, *UK International Financial Services: The Future*; S.R. Choi, D. Park and A.E. Tschoegl, *Banks and the World's Major Banking Centres* (October: 2014).

[98] Leyshon and Thrift, *Money/Space*, pp. 133, 136, 145, 155; P. Augar, *The Death of Gentlemanly Capitalism: The Rise and Fall of London's Investment Banks* (London: 2000) p. 329.

[99] Sir G. Newton, *A Peer Without Equal: Memoirs of an Editor* (London: 1997) p. 127.

[100] See Peden, *The Treasury and British Public Policy*; J. Fforde, *The Bank of England and Public Policy, 1941–1958* (Cambridge: 1992); Capie, *The Bank of England, 1950s–1979*; M. Daunton, *Just Taxes: The Politics of Taxation in Britain, 1914–1979* (Cambridge: 2002); A. Cairncross (ed.), *The Robert Hall Diaries* (London: 1989); M. Reid, 'Mrs Thatcher's Impact on the City', *Contemporary Record*, 2 (1989).

success did not apply to wider policy issues, such as exchange controls, and even ones closer to home. In 1979, for example, the Stock Exchange was told that the Government had considered its request for exemption from the restrictive trade practices legislation "but decided that it would not be appropriate to meet it." The outcome was far-reaching change over which the Stock Exchange had no control.[101] What the evidence suggests was that the London Stock Exchange, as with the City as a whole, lacked the power to dictate to the government. Politicians and civil servants acted according to their own agendas, swayed by the media, and were not responsive to demands that ran counter to those.[102] This can be seen from the actions of the Bank of England, as revealed in the latest instalment of its history by Harold James, covering the 1980s and 1990s. Decision-making became increasingly difficult following the breakdown of the post-war certainties in the 1970s, as the Bank of England tried to navigate between cross-currents at home and abroad. There were no simple answers with tension between the Bank and the City on the one hand and the Bank and the Treasury on the other, along with clear policy divisions between those running the Bank of England and the government of the day, such as over European monetary integration. There was no evidence of a City/Bank/Treasury Nexus.[103]

Further testament to the lack of success the City had in making its influence felt was the attitude of the media towards it. In the 1990s, for example, when the City was enjoying a spell as the most successful financial centre in the world, it received a generally hostile press coverage.[104]

---

[101] London Stock Exchange Annual Report 1976–1992. See C. Bellinger and R.C. Michie, 'Big Bang in the City: An Intentional Revolution or an Accident', *Financial History Review*, 21 (2014).

[102] See E.V. Morgan, R.A Brealey, B.S. Yamey and G.P. Bareau, *City Lights: Essays on Financial Institutions and Markets in the City of London* (London: Institute of Economic Affairs, 1979); Big Bang Seminar, 23rd October 1996: Initial Transcript Provided by Sir Nicholas Goodison; A. Hamilton, *The Financial Services Revolution: The Big Bang Worldwide* (London: 1986) p. 133; 'Save the City', *The Economist*, 7th January 2012.

[103] H. James, *The Making of a Modern Central Bank, The Bank of England 1979–2003* (Cambridge: Cambridge University Press, 2020) pp. 204–207, 224, 228, 230–231, 236–237, 254, 263, 268, 271, 318–319, 322, 348, 358–361, 375, 378, 401–402, 409, 411, 414, 419–423, 427, 432, 447–449.

[104] D. Cobham, 'The Equity Market', in D. Cobban (ed.), *Markets and Dealers: The Economics of the London Financial Markets* (London: 1992) p. 53; P. Bancroft, J. Doyle, S. Glaister, D. Kennedy and T. Travers, *London's Size and Diversity — The Advantages in*

It was in 1995 that the influential journalist Will Hutton published his attack on the City, *The State We're In*, which combined elements from the City/Industry Divide and the City/Bank/Treasury Nexus theses to hold the City responsible for the poor state of the British economy. "The central economic argument is that the weakness of the British Economy, particularly the level and character of investment, originates in the financial system. The targets for profit are too high and the horizons are too short. But British finance has not grown up in a vacuum. Behind the financial institutions stand history, class, a set of values and the political system." To him, "The City of London has become a byword for speculation, inefficiency and cheating, Given the power to regulate their own affairs, City financial markets and institutions have conspicuously failed to meet any reasonable standard of honest dealing with the public or their own kind." Added to that, "the financial system has been uniquely bad at supporting investment and innovation." This was no new phenomenon but could be traced back to the nineteenth century. "By the First World War, a pattern was firmly established: a national banking system disengaged from production; a risk-averse London stock market focused on international investment; equity finance made available only on the most onerous terms, heaping large dividend demands on British producers; a Bank of England concerned to preserve price stability and the international value of sterling; and an industrial base losing ground to foreign manufacturers with higher productivity — and having to respond by bidding down wages to maximise retained profits, the only reliable and cheap form of finance."

---

a Competitive World (London: Corporation of London, 1996) p. 52; A. Rajan, L. Rajan and P. van Eupen, *Capital People: Skills Strategies for Survival in the Nineties* (London: 1990) p. 175; R. O'Brien, *Global Financial Integration: The End of Geography* (London: 1992) pp. 19–20, 34, 74, 97; A.D. Smith, *International Financial Markets: The Performance of Britain and its Rivals* (Cambridge: 1992) pp. 130, 148; Corporation of London, *The Competitive Position of London's Financial Services: Final Report* (London: 1995): preface; E. George, Speech, 7th December 1999; J. Arlidge, 'The Golden Gateway', *Sunday Times*, 3rd December 2006; Paxman, *Friends in High Places*, pp. 268–273, 278–279, 287; J. Coakley, *London as an International Financial Centre*, in L. Budd and S. Whimster (eds), *Global Finance and Urban Living: A Study of Metropolitan Change* (London: 1992) pp. 59, 70; H.M. Treasury, *The Location of Financial Activity and the Euro* (London: 2003) pp. 17, 32; M.E. Porter and C.H.M. Ketels, *UK Competitiveness: Moving to the Next Stage*, DTI Economic Paper No. 3, May 2003, pp. 22, 40.

To Hutton, the only solution was state intervention to correct the failings of the financial system.[105]

Lying at the heart of the division of opinion between those who regarded the City of London as a Jewel in the Crown and those who saw it as the Cuckoo in the Nest was a view on what it was for. To its supporters, the City was a highly successful cluster that, according to a report produced by the UK Treasury in 2003, "over a period of more than a century — moved from being a centre grounded in the UK's dominant global economic position, and the role of sterling, to ... that of making international markets in a variety of currencies and providing international financial services across borders."[106] To its critics, the City was a failed financial centre because, in the words of the eminent economist, John Eatwell, it was of "little help to the problems of British industry," adding that it "may be positively harmful."[107] Faced with analysis backed by selected evidence either attacking the City of London or defending it, the public was left to draw its own conclusions about what to believe. There was no uncontested ground in which the facts could be left to speak for themselves. Instead, there was a battlefield over which protagonists fought with the prize being the public perception of the City. This was especially important after the Second World War when governments were much more willing to intervene in the working of the economy in response to public perception. R.A. Clark warned the City in 1975 that "unless we can get across our real merits and values, we shall not only lose business, we shall also be prey to governments which introduce legislation hostile to our interests."[108] There is little evidence that his words had much effect.

Imagining the City

Providing a means of testing the outcome of this battle over how the City was perceived by the public are novels.[109] The City furnished the novelist with fertile material, especially through its role in events such as

---

[105] Hutton, *The State We're In*, pp. xi, 5, 13, 21–23, 112, 122–124, 130–133, 285, 300–301, 315–317.

[106] H.M. Treasury, *The Location of Financial Activity and the Euro*, pp. 32, 46.

[107] Eatwell, *Whatever Happened to Britain*, p. 79, 159–160.

[108] R.A. Clark, 'The Image of the City', *Journal of the Institute of Bankers*, 96, 11 (1975).

[109] Introduction by H.R.F. Keating in Kitchin, *Death of My Aunt*.

speculative booms and busts, banking collapses and financial crises, as well as hosting individuals and businesses that were immensely wealthy or powerful. A few novelists used their actual experience in the City for material, as with P.G. Wodehouse in 1910 and Michael Ridpath and Paul Kilduff in the 1990s.[110] Most drew upon what appeared in the media at the time or the work of later researchers. For his 2005 novel, *Rogues Gallery*, John Malcolm contrasted the pre-First World War Marconi scandal with current events in the City, to suggest that "The thing about working in the City is that even a thickhead can realise that the whole thing was originally based on insider knowledge. All utterly illegal nowadays, of course."[111] Various City financiers were used as models for characters in novels in both the nineteenth and twentieth centuries. One example is Whitaker Wright, who featured as Stormont Thorpe in Frederic's 1899 novel, *The Market Place*; Edward Ponderevo in H.G. Wells's 1909 novel, *Tono Bungay*; and Walter Sinnett in Salema Nazzal's 2015 novel, *The Folly Under the Lake*.[112] A number of authors also mixed factual descriptions with fictional stories, making it difficult to separate one from the other, as in Meason's stories in the 1860s and Erasmus Pinto's *Ye Outside Fools*, published in 1876.[113] Some writers went even further, using works of fiction as factual evidence to support the argument that they were putting forward, as with the barrister, Montagu Williams, in his 1892 book describing life in London. His description of the City financier, Leopold Stiff, was based on Frith's 1880 series of paintings, "The Race for Wealth," as there is no evidence that such a person as Stiff existed or the companies he promoted.[114] In 1959, Victor Sandelson, used the play "Any Other Business" to support his conclusions about the City in post-war Britain.[115] Roger Simon relied on Hilaire Belloc's novels featuring the

---

[110] D.J. Taylor, 'Before There Was Jeeves: A 100 Years of "Psmith in the City"', *Times Literary Supplement*, 17th September 2010; Wodehouse, *Psmith in the City*; C. Harvie, 'Boom, Bust and Scribble', *Times Higher Education Supplement*, 29 January 1988; M. Ridpath, *Free to Trade*; Kilduff, *Square Mile*.

[111] J. Malcolm, *Rogues Gallery* (London: Allison and Busby, 2005) p. 15.

[112] See Mouat, 'Whitaker Wright'; Frederic, *The Market-Place*; Wells, *Tono-Bungay*; Nazzal, *The Folly Under the Lake*.

[113] Meason, *Three Months After Date*; Pinto, *Ye Outside Fools!*

[114] Frith, *My Autobiography and Reminiscences*, pp. 185, 295, 243, 256–259, 364, 461, 469. See *The Times*, 22nd April 1880 (Review of Frith's The Race for Wealth).

[115] Sandelson, 'The Confidence Trick', pp. 116–117, 125, 135.

City financier I.K. Barnett as evidence of the City's political influence in his book, *Light on the City*, which was published by the Labour Research Department in 1962.[116]

Such use of fiction as evidence of fact by Williams, Sandelson and Simon is dangerous. Fact relies on evidence that can be checked, while fiction is the product of a writer's imagination, regardless of whether they believe it to be true or not. Fiction involves the creation of an imaginary world which may or may not reflect reality. One example of that is the 1964 film, "Mary Poppins." This was set before the First World War and featured a run on a City bank. The film was based on the writings of P.L. Travers, which appeared after the First World War and contains no reference to such an event. The bank run was an invention by the studio designed to resonate with an American audience, as such events were a common feature of the US financial system until the 1930s. A bank run featured in the classic US movie of 1946, "It's a Wonderful Life," for example, which remained a perennial Christmas favourite. The only reference to the City by Travers was in one of the 1934 stories. "The City was a place where Mr Banks went every day-except Sundays, of course, and Bank Holidays-and while he was there he sat on a large chair in front of a large desk and made money. All day long he worked, cutting out pennies and shillings and half-crowns and three-penny-bits. And he brought them home with him in his little bag. Sometimes he would give some to Jane and Michael for their money boxes, and when he couldn't spare any he would say, 'The Bank is broken', and they would know he hadn't made much money that day."[117] Another example of invention masquerading as fact appears in Ben Elton's 2009 novel, *Meltdown*, which weaves the events of the financial crisis of 2007/2008 into a story about five Sussex university graduates. One of these is the City banker, Rupert Bennett, who used information gained as a government advisor to buy shares in the ex-building society, Caledonian Granite, as he knew that they would rise when a rescue package was announced. "Granite is about to get shifted from basket-case to gilt-edged. Triple-A status, government-owned safe haven. ... Watched the news of the government bailout send Caledonian

---

[116]R. Simon, *Light on the City*, pp. 4–8, 31, 50, 55, 70, 78, 90, 94, 97. See Belloc, *Emmanuel Burden*; Belloc, *Mr Clutterbuck's Election*; Belloc, *A Change in the Cabinet*; Belloc, *Pongo and the Bull*.

[117]P.L. Travers, *Mary Poppins* (London: Peter Davies, 1934) p. 15; 'It's A Wonderful Life' [film] (1946).

sky high." This incident was modelled on Northern Rock, but in that case the shareholders lost everything as no compensation for its nationalisation was ever paid.[118] In fiction, a story can be invented to suit the agenda of the author but accounts of the real world must have a basis in fact. What fiction can deliver is evidence of perception not fact. In the case of the City, it is important to survey the work of all novelists if the objective is to provide an accurate account of the changing perception, rather than selective impressions based on the most sensational.

The Physical City

Judging from the novels written in the nineteenth century, the public continued to follow many of the factual accounts and see the City as a distinct location, sandwiched between the East and West End of London. This was despite recognising the vast daily migration that supplied the City with its workforce, as in Merriman's 1898 novel, *Roden's Corner*, or the 1907 one, *The Secret of the Square*, by William Le Queux. The City continued to be regarded as a place where people not only worked in a variety of industrial, commercial and financial occupations but also where they lived. Writers could weave stories around communities and describe occupations they could understand, such as manufacturing and trade and the more basic elements of banking. That was unlike the more complex areas of finance which appeared to be much more of a mystery. One novelist, Sala in 1862, admitted his own ignorance when describing the activities of a discount broker, Sir Japer Goldthorpe. "What did all these chiefs of departments, clerks, messengers, and office-boys do from nine in the morning until five at night? None but those employed by the firm could tell." Instead, novelists writing before 1914 still clung to descriptions of those elements of the City involving trade, in particular, but also saw it as a location for lawyers, advertising agents and art dealers. The First World War appears to mark the end to the City being seen by the public as a residential community, though its commercial importance continued to be recognised into the 1930s. City timber merchants featured in J.B. Priestley's *Angel Pavement* and Maynard Smith's *Inspector Frost in the City*. Both novels were published in 1930. However, the commercial aspects of the City received fewer and fewer mentions in novels before the Second World War and

---

[118]Elton, *Meltdown*, pp. 21, 78–79, 227, 236–237, 270, 277, 281, 311, 390, 442–443, 457–461, 472. (I was a shareholder in Northern Rock!).

disappeared almost completely afterwards. George Bellairs's 1963 novel, *Death in the Wasteland*, does include a commodity broker trying to corner the pepper market, but that was an event that took place between the wars. The City bank that features in the John Malcolm series of novels, beginning with *A Back Room in Somers Town* in 1984, was still engaged in the timber trade but it was pointed that this is very exceptional. By then, the perception of the City was purely as a financial centre.

What emerges from the novels is that the public's perception of the City does diverge from the factual accounts. The public continued to recognise the importance of commerce in the City right up to the First World War and even into the 1930s. The activities of merchants feature in quite a number of stories written before 1914, as well as brief mentions of a large number of other occupations that continued to be pursued in the City. What was lost was any sense of a residential community by the late nineteenth century, as that was replaced by the commuter. It was only with the First World War that the public began to ignore the commercial aspects of the City. This continuing awareness of the commercial importance of the City before the First World War meant that the public was much less willing to condemn it as nothing more than a casino or embrace the City/Industry Divide thesis. The contents of the novels suggest that the public recognised that the City was much more than a financial centre and could appreciate the variety of business that took place there. That understanding of the depth and breadth of what the City had to offer appears to have come to an end between the wars, disappearing almost completely after 1945. Geoffrey Sambrook's 2002 novel, *Tarnished Copper* centred on one of the City's last remaining commodity markets, the London Metal Exchange. However, it was a highly technical account of the successful manipulation of the world copper price by a group of insiders drawn from the USA, Japan and the UK, and hardly contributed to an understanding of the depth and breadth of the activities that took place in the City. Prior to the Second World War, and especially before the First, novelists had contributed to the survival of a balanced perception of the City and helped it withstand the attacks it received because of its association with speculation and fraud and its lack of engagement with domestic manufacturing. That disappeared after 1945, leaving the City to be considered much more in the abstract than as a real place.[119]

---

[119] J. Austen, *Pride and Prejudice* (London: 1813) pp. 318, 326; Surr, *The Magic of Wealth*, Vol. 1: p. 3; Scott, *Rob Roy*, pp. 307, 423–424; Dickens, *Nicholas Nickleby*, p. 956; W.H. Ainsworth, *Old St. Paul's: A Tale of the Plague and the Fire* (London: 1841) pp. 15, 195;

The Financial City

Despite the willingness among novelists to acknowledge the City as the leading commercial emporium of the world, it was its association with finance which came to triumph over all others. As early as 1866, Edmund Yates wrote, in *Kissing the Rod*, that "to the world at large it's only a huge counting-house, a busy beehive, a crowd of places where money is to be made, and of men intent on making it." Increasingly, other novelists took this line with their interest propelled by the publicity attached to bank failures, waves of speculation, foreign governments defaulting on their borrowing and the collapse of newly promoted joint-stock companies. From the 1840s to the First World War, financial activities in the City

---

C. Dickens, 'A Christmas Carol' (1843) in C. Dickens (ed.), *Christmas Books* (London: Chapman and Hall, n.d.) p. 16; Dickens, *Martin Chuzzlewit*, pp. 170–171, 477–478; Reynolds, *The Mysteries of London*, pp. 28, 117; Dickens, *Dombey and Son*, pp. 105, 734; Brontë, *Villette*, p. 109; C. Riddell, *City and Suburb: A Novel* (London: 1861), pp. 8, 24–25, 34–35, 129, 143, 148–149, 274, 297; W. Black, *The Monarch of Mincing Lane* (London: 1861) pp. 110–111; Sala, *The Seven Sons of Mammon*, pp. 6–7; Riddell, *George Geith*, pp. 8, 12–13, 17, 21, 55, 106, 183, 194–197, 203, 307, 380, 393–394, 458–459; Riddell, *The Race for Wealth*, Vol. 1: pp. 8–11, 172–173; Dickens and Collins, *No Thoroughfare*, pp. 7–8; Braddon, *Rupert Godwin*, p. 8; Reade and Boucicault, *Foul Play*, pp. 1–3; Hemyng and Graff, *Telegraph Secrets*, p. 79; C. Riddell, *Austin Friars* (London: 1870) pp. 2, 63–64, 73, 150, 167–169, 194, 235–236, Oliphant, *At His Gates*, p. 251; Riddell, *Mortomley's Estate*, Vol. 1: pp. 1–7; Robertson, *A Lombard Street Mystery*, pp. 7–8; Oliphant, *Neighbours on the Green*, p. 319; Swan, *The Strait Gate*, pp. 1–3, 16; Warden, *The Wharf by the Docks*, pp. 7, 57, 95; Merriman, *Roden's Corner*, p. 121; B. Pain, *Eliza* (London: 1900) p. 43; Bennett, *The Grand Babylon Hotel*, pp. 26, 31, 41, 206; Belloc, *Emmanuel Burden*, pp. 54–58; Le Queux, *The Secret of the Square*, p. 56; Belloc, *Mr Clutterbuck's Election*, pp. 1–3, 11–13, 16, 20–22; W. Le Queux, *The Crooked Way* (London: 1908) p. 5; Wells, *Tono-Bungay*, pp. 325–327; Belloc, *A Change in the Cabinet*, p. 121; H.G. Wells, *The History of Mr. Polly* (London: 1910) pp. 43–44; A.S. Swann, *The Bondage of Riches* (London: 1912) pp. 7–8; E. Wallace, *The Fourth Plague* (London: 1913) p. 63; Wallace, *Bones in London*, pp. 11–13, 17, 225–226; J.B. Priestley, *Angel Pavement* (London: 1930) pp. 166–167, 261; H.M. Smith, *Inspector Frost in the City* (London: 1930) pp. 86–87; Fletcher, *The Mystery of the London Banker*, p. 160; G. Bellairs, *Death in the Wasteland* (London: The Thriller Book Club, 1963) pp. 2, 5, 22, 29, 159; Malcolm, *A Back Room in Somers Town*, pp. 11, 16, 21–25; Malcolm, *Gothic Pursuit*, p. 15; Malcolm, *Simpson's Homer*, p. 9, 14; G. Sambrook, *Tarnished Copper* (London: Twenty First Century Publishers, 2002) pp. 98, 107, 120, 178–179, 194–195, 212–213, 222–238.

generated material that piqued the interest of the public and attracted the pen of novelists. In 1892 alone, writers such as Frederick Wicks (*The Veiled Hand*), Thomas Terrell (*The City of the Just*) and Conan Doyle (*Beyond the City*) published City novels. Each year, one or more novels appeared that based their stories on what had recently taken place in the City. The mania for the shares of gold mining companies, which peaked in 1895, produced a cluster of City novels the next year, including Francis Gribble's *The Lower Life*, Headon Hill's *Guilty Gold* and Florence Warden's *The Wharf by the Docks*. All of them focused on the underlying immorality of the financial City with Warden posing the rhetorical question, "Do you suppose the wives and daughters of the men in the City, financiers and the rest, love them the less because they pass their lives trying to get the better of other people? Isn't it just as dishonest to issue a false prospectus to get people to put their money into worthless companies as to steal a watch? It's nonsense to pretend it isn't."

What emerges from the novels is a love/hate relationship between the British public and the City of London when viewed solely as a financial centre. On the one hand, it generated pride because of its global importance. On the other hand, it repelled many through its association with speculation and fraud whether it was the promotion of worthless mining companies or gambling on the price of stocks and shares on the London Stock Exchange. As William Le Queux put it in the 1907 novel, *The Secret of the Square*, "Really and truly I hate the City, but, you see, I can't very well get on without it." Joseph Hocking's 1912 novel, *God and Mammon*, took much the same view. As a somewhat diminished global financial centre, and its commercial activities increasingly ignored, the fraud and speculation associated with the City of London increasingly took centre stage after the First World War, and especially after the Second. This tilted the Love/Hate balance firmly in the direction of the latter.

Nevertheless, the evidence from novels suggests that the public never embraced the City/Industry Divide though it does rate the occasional mention, as in Mottram's 1931 novel, *Castle Island*. Novelists were also aware of the close relationship between the City and industry, both between the wars and after the Second World War. David Williams's series of novels from 1976 to 1993, and those of John Malcolm between 1984 and 2005, both featured City bankers whose work involved British businesses. Malcolm did suggest that the City was not sufficiently supportive in a number of his 1980s novels but appeared to recognise the dangers of an over-close relationship in those of the early 1990s. This ability of writers to express contrary views on the City in different novels, or even in the same one, reflected the problems the public experienced in agreeing on a single perception. The City was both a club for honourable amateurs who lacked professional expertise and a collection of skilled but fraudulent financiers, with the latter increasingly displacing the former.

This nostalgia for an imagined City of the past, populated by gentleman bankers, and a dislike of the new, dominated by American investment bankers, is what comes across in the City novels published from the 1990s onwards. The old City was identified with the era that immediately preceded Big Bang in 1986, not the City before the First or Second World Wars, which was more like the way it operated by the 1990s. There was no appreciation in these novels that the City had experienced considerable change in the 100 years before Big Bang, as in Grant Sutherland's 1997 novel, *Due Diligence*. "More than a century and a half after our arrival, the time has come for the Carlton family to make its unceremonious exit from the City." This suggests that public perception of the City had no long-term memory. Increasingly, those who wrote about the City after Big Bang focused on its global role and the attractions it had for all who wanted to become rich very quickly. In this new City, greed was the only motivation for those who worked there and the banks that employed them. To Michael Ridpath, in his 1996 novel, *Trading Reality*, the City and Wall Street were interchangeable, and both were home to meritocratic high achievers regardless of race, religion and background. It was a brutal world in which only the single-minded could survive and succeed by selling their soul to the devil. Such a perception of the City in the 1990s had much in common with that of the 1890s, but that escaped notice. Interest in the City appeared to die away after 2000 but was suddenly revived in the wake of the financial crisis of 2007/2008. That led to a rush of novels about the City in which the focus was the lead up to the crisis, the events surrounding it and then its aftermath. These were highly critical of the City, which was cast as the main cause of what happened.[120]

---

[120] J. Hatton, *Christopher Kenrick: His Life and Adventures* (London: 1869) p. 11; Riddell, *Austin Friars*, p. 235; Trollope, *The Way We Live Now*, p. 89; The Spectre, *Ye Vampyres*, p. 24; Besant and Rice, *The Golden Butterfly*, pp. 86, 90, 153–154, 264, 498; Anstey, *Vice Versa*, pp. 4–5; Riddell, *Daisies and Buttercups*, pp. 140, 199–201, 246–247; Besant, *All in a Garden Fair*, pp. 29–30, 45, 57–58, 133–139, 147, 150–153, 156–157, 196–197, 209, 220, 238–240; Riddell, *Mitre Court*, Vol. 1: pp. 72, 80–81; Vol. 2: pp. 14–15, 290–292,

What the novels that focus on the financial City reveal is that it was admired for being one of the most important and successful financial

Vol. 3: pp. 42–43; A. Conan Doyle, *Beyond the City: The Idyll of a Suburb* (London: Everett and Co., 1892) pp. 67, 116, 142, 192; Riddell, *The Head of the Firm*, p. 188; Terrell, *The City of the Just*, pp. 30, 86; Wicks, *The Veiled Hand*, pp. 177–178, 250, 413; Gribble, *The Lower Life*, pp. 20, 101; Hill, *Guilty Gold*, pp. 134–136; Warden, *The Wharf by the Docks*, p. 64; Bennett, *Teresa of Watling Street*, p. 7; Le Queux, *Sins of the City*, pp. 8–9; Le Queux, *The Secret of the Square*, p. 92; Haggard, *The Yellow God*, p. 46; Philips Oppenheim, *A Millionaire of Yesterday*, pp. 61, 102, 117; Hocking, *God and Mammon*, pp. 71–72; Buchan, *The Power-House*, p. 31; Birmingham, *Gossamer*, pp. 54, 73, 106, 164–165, 198–199, 220–221; Galsworthy, *In Chancery*, p. 913; Wallace, *Bones in London*, pp. 11–13, 17, 225–226; Bennett, *Lord Raingo*, p. 72; Wallace, *The Twister*, p. 119; Wallace, *Red Aces*, p. 55; Loder, *Whose Hand?*; Loder, *Murder from Three Angles*; F. Wills Crofts, *Mystery in the Channel* (London: Collins, 1931) pp. 64–66; Mottram, *Castle Island*, pp. 260–262; Creasey, *First Came a Murder*, chs. 1, 2, 4, 12, 13, 19, 20, 23, 24; Seligman, *Bank Holiday*, pp. 2, 28–29, 41, 46–47, L. Charteris, *Prelude for War* (London: Hodder and Stoughton, 1938), pp. 35–39; Shute, *Ruined City*, pp. 87–89, 187; Bellairs, *Dead March for Penelope Blow*, pp. 13, 143, 146–147; Smith, *The Deadly Reaper*, pp. 30, 208; Bellairs, *Death in the Wasteland*, pp. 2, 5, 22, 29, 159; Newby, *The Barbary Light*, pp. 132, 140, 281; Williams, *Unholy Writ*, pp. 26–29; Williams, *Murder for Treasure*, pp. 16, 21; Williams, *Divided Treasure*, pp. 18–19, 29–39, 50, 72, 124–125, 222–223; Williams, *Prescription for Murder*, pp. 7–9, 48, 50, 62, 88–89, 92–93, 98–99, 141, 148, 184–185; Francis, *Banker*, p. 98; Malcolm, *A Back Room in Somers Town*, pp. 11, 16, 21–25; Malcolm, *The Godwin Sideboard*, p. 57; Malcolm, *The Gwen John Sculpture*, pp. 12–15, 22–25, 32–33, 80–82, 130–131, 188–190, 195; Malcolm, *Whistler in the Dark*, pp. 11–13; Malcolm, *Gothic Pursuit*, pp. 15, 82; Malcolm, *A Deceptive Appearance*, pp. 19–20, 115; Malcolm, *The Burning Ground*; Malcolm, *Hungover*, p. 115; Malcolm, *Into the Vortex*, pp. 47–48; Davies, *Nest of Vipers*, p. 50; Ridpath, *Free to Trade*, p. 240; Ridpath, *The Market Maker*, pp. 1–3, 8–9, 27, 105, 147–151, 288–289, 306–307, 356–361, 368–378; Sutherland, *Due Diligence*, pp. 411, 470; Cohen, *The Butchers' Ball*, pp. 22, 160–161, 356–357; Kilduff, *Square Mile*; Kilduff, *The Dealer*, pp. 61, 132–133; Kilduff, *The Frontrunner*, pp. 1–2, 17, 198–199, 212–215, 462, 469–471; Kilduff, *The Headhunter*; McLaren, *Black Cabs*, pp. 10–13, 27, 46, 50–53, 91, 123, 171, 388–390; Faulks, *A Week in December*, pp. 8–13, 62, 32–37, 102–104, 125, 190–191, 231–233, 268–269, 309, 371, 375–377, 390; Elton, *Meltdown*, pp. 21, 29, 59, 78–79, 80–81, 88–89, 211, 231, 236–237, 270–272, 277–281, 303–308, 307–311, 320–325, 328–329, 390, 442–443, 457–461, 472, 477–480; Preston, *This Bleeding City*, pp. 7–9, 14, 17, 21, 63–67, 112–117, 121, 132–134, 173–175, 179, 186–187, 192–193, 225–226, 238–239, 250–251, 277–283, 303, 307–311, 320–325, 328–329; Campbell, *On the Floor*; Cartwright, *Other People's Money*, pp. 71, 182, 238–239; Lanchester, *Capital*, pp. 15–25, 192–194, 345–347, 445–449, 466–467, 476–477, 509, 576.

centres in the world and despised because it was where speculation and fraud flourished and the pursuit of money at all costs was all that mattered. The public could hold both views simultaneously, with one balancing the other. It was this contradictory perception that restrained pressure on the government to intervene in the City. Intervention to suppress speculation and fraud could harm the City's ability to operate as a financial centre and compete globally. Judging from the novels produced before the First World War, the public understood the trade-off between the two elements of the City and so calls for reform were both restrained in extent and limited in duration. That changed between the wars when criticism of the City resonated with a collapse in confidence in the working of the entire financial system, which was blamed for the depressed state of the economy. The balance had tilted in favour of intervention which is what was being advocated from many different quarters, including such authoritative ones as government inquiries and influential economists. That intervention was limited before the Second World War but was greatly expanded afterwards. The Bank of England was taken into state ownership and the London Stock Exchange used as the unofficial regulator of the securities market while exchange and capital controls restricted the City's international role.

With the City no longer recognised as a commercial centre, its international role in decline and New York emerging as a serious rival, what remained was the City's reputation as a location for speculation and fraud. Though neither of these was on a scale approaching what had existed in the past, there was enough to fuel public criticism of the City. Added to that was the well-established belief in the City/Industry Divide which had become the go-to explanation for Britain's poor economic performance in the 1950s, 1960s and into the 1970s. The result was that the City had few supporters in the post-war years, leaving it open to criticism from all sides, to which the public remained bystanders, judging from the absence of comment in the novels of those years. The eventual outcome was the abandonment of exchange controls in 1979 and the Big Bang reforms of 1986 which left the City exposed to foreign competition. Unrecognised by the public was the reinvention of the City as a global financial centre based on the use of the US$ and benefitting from the restrictions and controls imposed on rival financial centres, including New York, Tokyo, Frankfurt, Paris and Zurich. What then emerged was a City that was truly international and this was picked up on by the public, judging from the City novels that began appearing in the 1990s. These were completely different from the banker-sleuth variety of the 1970s and 1980s. In many ways, the treatment of the Financial City by novelists from the late twentieth century onwards was remarkably similar to that of a century earlier, though shorn of anti-Semitism. However, that comparison escaped public notice as novelists, like the public, viewed the City of the past as that from the years immediately preceding the present. There was no appreciation of the fact that the City kept reinventing itself, and that involved numerous twists and turns that could bring the story back to a more distant past. What the novels reveal about the City was that there was no collective memory, only a sense that the present was different from the past.

The Controlling City

The final element of the City that resonated with the public was the power that finance gave it. Up to the 1860s, novels suggest that the public believed the City to be all powerful but that perception then faded away as such references almost disappear. It was not until the early twentieth century that novels paint a picture of a City elite able to dictate to government, especially those of Hilaire Belloc's, but picked up by others, suggesting that it resonated widely with the public, and was perceived to have a malign influence over government policy. During the First World War and into the 1920s, that influence became a positive one. It was not until 1932, with the novel, *The Division Bell Mystery*, by the Labour Member of Parliament, Ellen Wilkinson, that there was a return to the pre-First World War perception of City financiers dictating policy to government. Some City financiers could be trusted to act in the national interest while others could not. In the 1938 novel, *Prelude For War*, by Leslie Charteris, the City financier, Kane Luker, "hobnobs with Foreign Secretaries and ambassadors and Prime Ministers, and calls dictators by their first names," while trying to engineer another war because that would be good for his business. Conversely, in the 1938 novel, *Ruined City* by Nevil Shute, another City financier used political influence to help British industry. That perception that the City possessed political power then largely disappeared from novels until the 1990s, suggesting that the thesis of a City/Bank/Treasury Nexus, popular in academic circles, did not resonate with the public. In 1978, a Bank of England insider, Rupert Pennant-Rea, published a novel, *Gold Foil*, that told the tale of the bank operating on its own agenda, in concert with other central banks, and having little contact with the City. In the John Malcolm novels, for example, it is not until 2005, with *Rogues Gallery*, that he brings up the City's connections with government.

Grant Sutherland, in his 1997 novel, *Due Diligence*, does suggest strong City government connections, but it was in the aftermath of the financial crisis of 2008 that novels really bring out the supposed power of the City over government policy, as in the 2009 novels by Sebastian Faulks, *A Week in December*, and Ben Elton's *Meltdown*. To Elton, "The money men had created massive wealth for themselves and given back nothing to society but resentment and fear. They had destroyed faith in the City and respect for honour and rank, utterly compromising the Labour Party in the process." This could almost have been written by Hilaire Belloc in the years before the First World War. The perception of the association between the City and power had come full circle.[121] Without realising it, the novelists who took their material from the financial crisis of 2008 were painting a picture of the City of London that resonated with those writing about it in the years before the First World War. The City they were describing was one populated by rogue traders and hedge funds, dominated by US investment banks and used technology that operated at the speed of light. In contrast, that of 100 years before was populated by merchant banks and company promoters, was dominated by British banks and relied on trading floors and the telegraph. Nevertheless, there were remarkable similarities as the City was a global financial centre at both times, attracting a constant stream of foreign financiers, while the

---

[121] Scott, *Rob Roy*, pp. 307, 423–424; Disraeli, *Tancred*, pp. 112–114; Thackeray, *Vanity Fair*, pp. 54, 89, 253, 539–542, 713, 771; Gore, *The Money Lender*, pp. 136–137; Sala, *The Seven Sons of Mammon*, pp. 6–7; G. Gissing, *Born in Exile* (London: 1892) pp. 3–5; Belloc, *Emmanuel Burden*, pp. 55–58; Belloc, *Mr Clutterbuck's Election*, pp. 193–198, 216–220; Belloc, *A Change in the Cabinet*, pp. 232–233; Belloc, *Pongo and the Bull*, pp. 3, 13–14, 33, 41–43, 71–80, 88, 94, 237; Hocking, *God and Mammon*, pp. 71–72; Rittenberg, *Swirling Waters*; Buchan, *The Power-House*; Birmingham, *Gossamer*, pp. 54, 103, 164–165, 198–201, 220–221; Christie, *The Secret of Chimneys*, p. 81, Bennett, *Lord Raingo;* Wilkinson, *The Division Bell Mystery*, pp. 101, 194; Charteris, *Prelude For War*, pp. 35–39; Shute, *Ruined City*, pp. 87–89; Christie, *One, Two, Buckle My Shoe*, pp. 15–18; R. Pennant-Rea, *Gold Foil: A Novel* (London: Bodley Head, 1978) pp. 24–25, 86–87, 169; Malcolm, *Rogues Gallery*, p. 15; Sutherland, *Due Diligence*, p. 27; Kilduff, *The Frontrunner*, pp. 1–2, 17, 198–199, 212–215; Faulks, *A Week in December*, pp. 36, 390; Elton, *Meltdown*, pp. 21, 78–79, 227, 236–237, 270, 277, 281, 311, 390, 442–443, 457–461, 472.

telephone and the cable were transforming the operation of markets. There were also speculative outbursts and collapses in both eras that had similar causes and consequences with the exception that the British banking system was stable and resilient before 1914, but not in 2008. In between, the City of London passed through two world wars, a world depression in the 1930s and a period of government control between 1945 and 1975, when market activity was suppressed. It was that period of suppression and control that was taken as representative of the old City by those writing about it from the 1980s onwards, as that was the only past they were aware of.

Conclusion

Before the Second World War, anti-City rhetoric was tempered by a recognition that markets needed freedom to operate and that the City performed a valuable role. That changed in the world depression in the 1930s, when capitalism was widely discredited, and then the Second World War, when government control had delivered military victory after six years of war. The result was that in the years that followed the end of the Second World War belief in the City/Industry Divide went unchallenged, being accepted as an article of faith by the public and the economics profession. It was only in the 1970s that belief in the Divide began to fade as it could no longer be made to account for the failings of British manufacturing industry. In its place, government policy became the preferred explanation, being a product of City influence through the City/Bank/Treasury Nexus, and this breathed new life into the anti-City rhetoric. Combined with a lingering attachment to the City/Industry Divide, this sufficed to condemn the City in the eyes of most.

However, there was some restoration of a more balanced view of the City from the 1980s, as its contribution to the economy was increasingly recognised. The result was that though governments were unwilling to follow policies that were supportive of the City, they were also reluctant to introduce ones that were harmful. This was a return to the world that had existed before the Second World War. What this suggests is that perception matters when it lacks a counterbalance. Judging from the output of novelists, the City never endeared itself to the British public for there were always reasons to distrust what went on there, though that changed over time. As long as alternative views existed, this popular antagonism rumbled along as an underlying resentment that waxed and waned but made little impact. That changed after the Second World War and it was not until after the 1970s that equilibrium returned, and then survived the financial crisis of 2008, when there were numerous calls for the government to act and rein in the City. Though some measures were introduced, aimed at markets and banks, these were minor reforms rather than draconian attempts to curb its power.

What the use of fiction provides is a means of assessing which of the factual scenarios resonated with the public, and thus influenced the content and direction of government policy. The facts were never unambiguous but lent themselves to different and even contradictory interpretations. From the facts, the City of London can be considered either as the Jewel in the Crown or Cuckoo in the Nest. As a highly successful and very resilient financial centre that increasingly served the global community, the City was one of the most important business clusters in the UK, generating prosperity for its host economy and tax revenue for the British government. This was understood by contemporaries and recognised by those who studied the changing microstructure of the City. Conversely, another interpretation of the City was also available that was much less favourable. This saw the City as nothing other than an enormous casino in which outsiders gambled and lost, while the winners were those insiders who knew how to play the game. The City was also an alien presence within Britain, serving the interests of global finance and not that of the economy within which it was located. This separation had damaging consequences as it deprived important sectors of the British economy of the finance they required, leading to their eventual collapse, while influencing government to follow policies that were detrimental for national prosperity. Ultimately, the City of London destroyed the economy which had nurtured it. The contrast between the two scenarios could not be greater and each was in circulation over the nineteenth and twentieth centuries. What people chose to believe then resonated with those whose decisions determined the economic, political and social direction that Britain, collectively, took as they manifested themselves in particular policies or specific legislation.[122]

---

[122] Hamilton, *The Financial Services Revolution*, p. 133.

Chapter 9

Conclusion: The Judgement of Conan Doyle

Introduction

What emerges from a study of the British experience with finance since 1800 is how unreliable are the judgements of contemporaries. This was the case whether they were based on the facts available or impressions generated by rumours and lies. In all cases, the result was a distorted and partial picture. Perspective and context came only with the passage of time, and even those hindsight judgements were subject to bias and a selective use of facts. In some cases, there was a deliberate desire to make the facts fit the argument being put forward rather than the reverse. There is always an element of subjectivity in all factual work as interpretations involve selecting what to include and exclude, the connections to be made, the meaning to be put into evidence and the conclusions to be drawn. At each stage, the choices made are influenced by personal preferences and preconceptions. Conversely, there is an element of objectivity in all fiction as the world created by novelists is based on the knowledge and experience of the writer combined with the working of human imagination. Facts never speak for themselves as all require interpretation, which comes from placing them in the context of time, place and circumstance. Contemporary judgements suffer from a lack of hindsight as the future is never known, and even the direction of travel is uncertain because of the impact made by events, whether they are wars, revolutions or pandemics. While hindsight judgements benefit from knowing what took place after the experience they describe, they also suffer from a lack of foresight, as they do not know what is to follow the period in which they are made. There is never perfect foresight as the future defies accurate prediction, and that affects the judgements made about the past. For those reasons, it is important to know what people were thinking at a particular time, as that influenced the decisions they made. Over the course of the nineteenth and twentieth centuries, democratically elected governments played an increasingly central role in the decision-making process, and they were especially sensitive to public opinion as expressed through the media. This meant that what people believed to be true became as important as reality, especially when the evidence was ambiguous as it was in most financial matters.

Contemporaries derived their views based on what they believed to be true, according to their biases, prejudices and level of knowledge. Even among the best informed, the evidence they had available to them, mainly derived from the reporting of the sensational and the episodic, presented a distorted view. The overall effect was to make even the most knowledgeable and expert, among contemporary observers, unreliable witnesses, including politicians and economists, but they had the power to influence others through the speeches they made and the advice they gave, gaining a permanence when committed to print. Novels provide a great store of these beliefs through which the thinking of past generations can be discovered. The world of British finance before the First World War was one occupied by individuals of enormous wealth and possessed of great confidence in their position in the world, located as they were in the country whose Empire covered a quarter of the globe. They were largely untroubled by government restrictions and taxation, enjoyed the stability provided by the Gold Standard and were free to employ their wealth indiscriminately at home and abroad. The result was huge profits as well as severe losses, and an accumulating portfolio of assets distributed throughout the globe. That world came to an end with the First World War, Britain's forced departure from the Gold Standard in 1931, the global economic depression in the 1930s and then the Second World War. What followed was a world of government controls and heavy taxes, the end of the Empire and a greatly diminished position in the world, which brought about an entirely different perspective. It is only by capturing the radically different thinking that underlay decisions in the past that it becomes possible to understand the British experience of finance, and it is novels that have been used for that purpose.

Investment and Investors

Most investment was done in secret, passing unnoticed by the public regardless of the amount involved or its results. It was the product of decisions made by individuals in private in their own homes or offices, whether operating alone or collectively. In this way, incremental additions were made to the housing stock and infrastructure, for example, or the continuous improvements in agriculture, manufacturing, mining and throughout numerous business activities. What the public increasingly identified as investment, and generated the perspective of contemporaries from the early nineteenth century onwards, was the issue of stocks and bonds by governments and companies, even though these were often the product of the need to finance wars or the capitalisation of past expenditure. These stocks and bonds were given a public profile by being traded on the London Stock Exchange, with prices and activity widely reported in the press, especially during speculative outbursts. This identification of investment with the rise and fall of the stock market created the impression that the process was something of a lottery and was confined to what was in the form of stocks and bonds. Hence the belief that so much flowed abroad through subscriptions to foreign government bond sales or purchases of the shares of companies exploring for minerals throughout the world. As most of these mining companies failed, the association between investment and gambling was further enhanced. What went unrecognised was that most foreign investment was directed into the stocks and bonds of railways operating all around the world, especially the USA, and the areas of the Empire that most attracted investors were long-established colonies like Canada rather than newly acquired territories. Also unrecognised was the enormous peace dividend available between 1815 and 1914, because the government stopped borrowing to finance expensive wars, as it had in the past and was to do so again. Rather than foreign investment being a drain on national savings, it represented the search for attractive assets to purchase by a population enjoying the income and wealth generated by a highly successful economy.

Following on from the identification of investment with activity on the stock market, individuals as investors were seen as vulnerable to fraud, easily seduced by the latest fashion and incapable of taking rational long-term decisions. Adding to that was the accusation that investors avoided taking stakes in domestic industry, and were either unwilling or too willing to take risks. Out of that emerged a belief among many that not only had investors to be protected from themselves and crooked financiers but also that the process of investing should be taken out of the hands of individuals and placed with either the banks or the government. Such views were often driven by an anti-capitalism agenda or a reaction to the aftermath of a huge speculative bubble, spectacular default of a government or massive corporate failure. There was little recognition at the time or later that investors had to take decisions based on the opportunities they faced and without the foresight that came with hindsight. Inevitably, the routine elements of investment, and the actions of the cautious investor, largely escaped notice, even though it comprised the great majority. Instead, even when the perception of investment was confined to what took place on the stock market, it was those elements that generated the greatest publicity that dictated what people believed to be true.

This was all taking place at a time when the nature of investment and the investing public was being transformed. In the century before the First World War, the investor was no longer confined to a tiny minority and investment restricted to a choice between holding the National Debt and channelling savings into loans and property through informal networks. The number of investors expanded rapidly in breadth and depth as more of the middle class accumulated savings and began to purchase corporate stocks and bonds. In turn, these investors had available to them a growing variety of securities including the debts of foreign and colonial governments and the stocks and bonds of companies operating all round the world. What emerges from a review of investors before the First World War was their diversity, with some prioritising safety while others gambled on the current novelty. That directed them both to the railways being constructed around the world as well as those companies exploring for minerals. Some of the choices they made were disastrous while others delivered spectacular returns, but, overall, the results were reasonably satisfactory, contributing to the growing wealth of the British population. Though the dominant view considered investors to be naïve and foolish people who lost their money, there was also an alternative story that recognised them as knowledgeable and skilled individuals capable of making a fortune for themselves

That situation was all to end with the First World War, the depressed state of the British economy in the 1920s and 1930s, and then the Second World War. During that 30-year period, foreign assets were sold off, massive debts were accumulated and the competitive ability of the British economy was seriously undermined, whether it was the traditional manufacturing and mining of the North, Scotland, Wales and Northern Ireland or the commercial and financial services located in cities such as Liverpool, Manchester and also London. The losses and damage inflicted in that period were masked by the rapid growth of the world economy in the 1950s but became increasingly evident from 1960s, compounded by the increasingly uncompetitive nature of much of British industry. It was in those years that contemporaries looked for scapegoats with the financial sector being a prime target, building on the criticism it received between the wars. It was not until the 1980s that the fundamental problems of the British economy began to be addressed, by which time the manufacturing base was in terminal decline. As government intervention had failed to reverse this decline, blame shifted to the influence the financial sector had over policy, not the suppression of risk taking through high levels of taxation and high levels of government control. That changed from the 1980s onwards, but did not result in the reappearance of the individual investor on the scale seen before the Second World War. High levels of taxation combined with the complexities of the whole process of finance placed investment in the hands of professionals. It is only through novels that the fundamentally different mind of the pre-1914 investor, or even that of the inter-war years, can be captured and the world that they occupied be recognised. That different mindset, and the environment they lived in, explains the decisions that they made.

Bankers and Financiers

Prior to the crisis of 2007/2008, bankers had been among the most respected individuals in Britain, custodians of the nation's savings, responsible for the functioning of the payments system and relied upon to provide credit and capital for all. They were trusted, admired and envied, though not by all. Many remained suspicious of bankers because of their association with moneylending while others saw them as occupying a too powerful position within economic, social and political life. This perception was based on a subset of banks, mainly comprising a few large retail banks and a small number of merchant banks. The rest of the banking sector was largely ignored by the public. The large retail banks, in particular, had proved able to withstand financial crises before the First World War and then proved resilient in the face of the shocks experienced between 1914 and 1945, including two world wars, an international financial and monetary collapse and a global economic depression. After the Second World War, these same banks operated within a government-controlled environment which ensured stability but only through collusion and an absence of competition. This encouraged a conservative pattern of behaviour which favoured stability but provided customers with a poor service, stimulating the expansion of rivals such as the building societies and a growing shadow banking sector. That environment came to an end in 1979, when exchange controls were lifted, while the liberalisation of the domestic market in the 1980s fostered competition. The result was an increasingly competitive arena in which banks were forced to take greater risks, and this had implications for stability but that only became apparent in the financial crisis of 2007/2008. From that crisis, bankers emerged as individuals motivated solely by greed.

What the traditional view of British bankers failed to recognise was that the large retail banks were only one component of the banking system. Not only were there numerous other types of bankers, such as the merchant banks, as well as financial institutions that replicated banks, like the building societies, but there were also financiers that went unrecognised as bankers in Britain but not in other countries. Among these were the investment bankers as they were labelled company promoters in Britain and omitted from any discussion of the banking system. As a separate group, company promoters flourished between the mid-nineteenth century and the 1930s and then disappeared. When the business previously done by company promoters developed from the 1950s onwards, it was undertaken by the merchant banks, and they acquired the US label of investment banker. As company promoters were regarded as little more than swindlers, with no role to play in the financial system, it was easy to portray bankers as uninterested in domestic company finance. It was company promoters who made business accessible to investors, whether it involved new or established enterprises. These included high-risk ventures in areas like mining or new technology, and it was failures there that had generated the impression that company promoters were crooks. By either vilifying or marginalising company promoters, it was possible to support the City/Industry Divide thesis, indicating that perception mattered when it came to government policy.

Another group of financiers that generated a negative image were those that were Jewish. There had long been an underlying element of anti-Semitism in Britain, and that extended to financiers, regardless of their position within British social, political and economic life. However, the level of anti-Semitism aimed at Jewish financiers reached an extreme level in the 25 years before the First World War. The mass immigration of Jews from Russia in those years coincided with the arrival of a small number of Jewish bankers and financiers in Britain, coming mainly from Germany. They were attracted to London as the world's financial and commercial centre and the greater freedom they enjoyed there compared to Germany, where the government was attempting to restrict certain types of speculative activity. However, much of the antagonism towards Jewish financiers before the First World War was a by-product of what was happening in the USA. In turn, that was linked to a belief that Jewish financiers were prime movers in imperial expansion, leading Britain to become involved in unpopular wars. Though the situation in Britain was different from that in the USA, and evidence linking finance and imperialism was weak, an open season on Jewish financiers developed. They were painted as heartless moneylenders, crooked company promoters, manipulative brokers and unpatriotic bankers. That attack ended with the First World War, and though a latent hostility towards Jewish financiers remained, it largely disappeared in the second half of the twentieth century.

The City of London

As one of the world's leading financial centres, the City of London served not only the United Kingdom but also the international community, and so faced both inwards towards Britain and outwards towards the rest of the world. The scale and scope of its operations, and the constant changes taking place, made it difficult for contemporaries to fully understand the City, leading them to generalise from those aspects with which they were familiar, while ignoring the rest. For many, the City was forever associated with speculation, especially in shares, which was considered no different from gambling, while others saw it as remote from the industrial heartlands, and thus little interested in providing the finance they required. Even when evidence was presented that the City was engaged in providing finance for industry, there remained a strong belief in a City/Industry Divide, especially among economists. Added to that thesis was another belief, the City/Bank/Treasury Nexus, which held that the City was sufficiently powerful to determine the shape and direction of government policy. Whereas the City/Industry Divide was widely believed to exist in the first half of the twentieth century, it was the City/Bank/Treasury Nexus that was considered to operate after the Second World War, when the government played a central role in the management of the economy. Until the First World War, the criticisms of the City related to its operation as a financial centre were tempered by the recognition that it was also a commercial centre, and that role was widely appreciated. As the importance of its position as the hub of international trade faded from the First World War onwards, so the criticisms grew in strength. That was especially the case after the Second World War when the commercial side of the City rapidly disappeared.

Throughout the nineteenth and twentieth century, a love/hate relationship existed between the British public and the City of London. On the one hand, it generated pride because of its global importance. On the other hand, it repelled many through its association with speculation and fraud. Added to that was the belief that there was something alien about the City that separated it from the rest of Britain, and that its interests were not that of the rest of the country. The presence of numerous foreigners, and an orientation towards international finance, provided support for such theses as the City/Industry Divide and the City/Bank/Treasury Nexus, even without the added element of anti-Semitism that was such a presence before the First World War. By the twenty-first century, there was a tendency to merge the City and Wall Street into a single transatlantic financial centre that could be condemned for plunging the world into a global financial crisis in 2008. What the perception of the City reveals was that the public could simultaneously admire it for being one of the most important and successful financial centres in the world and despise it because of the speculation and fraud that flourished there and where the pursuit of money at all costs was all that mattered. To some degree, the City was used as a proxy in a pro/anti-capitalism debate which could be made real because it existed as an identifiable place. What was not appreciated was the way the City kept reinventing itself, and the numerous twists and turns that involved. There was no collective memory of the City, only a sense that the present was different from a past that had not changed for centuries. Though the public's attitude towards the City changed over time, there were always reasons to distrust what went on there. The facts were never unambiguous but lent themselves to different and even contradictory interpretations.

The Judgement of Conan Doyle

One novelist whose works provide a means of matching reality with perception of the City of London, and through that the British financial system, in the critical period between the 1890s and the 1920s, is Arthur Conan Doyle. Using Conan Doyle as guide, and the 1890–1930 period as a pivot, conclusions can be drawn on the changing perception of finance in Britain and the implications that had. Conan Doyle was born in 1857 in Scotland of Irish parents and died in England in 1930. He trained as a physician but became a writer, immortalised as the creator of the fictional detective, Sherlock Holmes.[1] The City features prominently in three of his novels and eleven Sherlock Holmes stories. The novels are *The Firm Of Girdlestone: A Romance of the Unromantic*, published in 1890; *Beyond the City: The Idyll of a Suburb*, 1892; and *A Duet with an Occasional Chorus*, 1899.[2] Among the mysteries solved by Sherlock Holmes, all of which appeared in the Strand Magazine, those that contain references to the City or finance begin with *The Red-Headed League* (August 1891), and are then followed by *A Case of Identity* (September 1891); *The Man with the Twisted Lip* (December 1891); *The Adventure of the Beryl Coronet* (May 1892); *The Adventure of the Stock-Broker's Clerk* (March 1893); *The Adventure of the Resident Patient* (August 1893); *The Adventure of the Norwood Builder* (October 1903); *The Adventure of the Dancing Men* (December 1903); *The Adventure of Black Peter* (February 1904); *The Adventure of the Sussex Vampire* (January 1924); and finished with *The Adventure of the Blanched Soldier* (October 1926).[3] Considering how popular Conan Doyle was as a writer, especially with regard to those stories featuring Sherlock Holmes, these books and stories offer an opportunity to discover how the City and finance were regarded by someone with no knowledge of its inner workings. In many ways, Conan Doyle's views, as expressed through his fiction, can be taken as representative of his time, because he embraced current beliefs, including capitalism, nationalism and imperialism. In contrast, others who have been chosen to

---

[1] For the details of Conan Doyle's life, see the entry for Sir Ignatius Conan Doyle, 1859–1930 in the *Oxford Dictionary of National Biography*.

[2] Conan Doyle, *The Firm of Girdlestone*; Conan Doyle, *Beyond the City*; Conan Doyle, *A Duet with an Occasional Chorus*.

[3] See M. and M. Hardwick, *The Sherlock Holmes Companion* (New York: Bramhall House, 1962).

represent the years between 1890 and 1930, such as H. G. Wells, did not share these beliefs, expressing, instead, those which were to become popular in later years, such as socialism.[4]

The novel, *The Firm of Girdlestone*, was based on Conan Doyle's experience in 1881/1882 as a doctor aboard the steamship Mayumba, which operated out of the port of Liverpool.[5] However, he set his novel around the firm of City merchants and shipowners, run by John Girdlestone and his son, Ezra. They were both ruthless in the pursuit of profits, unwilling to have their ships properly maintained and adequately insured. They were also fond of speculation, leading them to incur large losses on US railroad shares and Cornish tin mines, and an attempt to corner the diamond market, which failed. They were painted as risk takers and rogues who were willing to manipulate markets and resort to kidnap and murder.[6] In his 1892 novel, *Beyond the City: The Idyll of a Suburb*, Conan Doyle wove a story around the residents of a new London suburb and their interactions, both with each other and with the City. This story was based on Conan Doyle's own experience of living in the London suburb of South Norwood.[7] The City that Conan Doyle described was a diverse business community peopled by shipbrokers, solicitors, agents, architects and surveyors as well as brokers of all kinds. Among them was Smith and Hanbury, a firm of moneylenders, referred to as "City sharks." Among the residents in the suburb was a stockbroker, Harold Denver, who "was busy from morning to night on the Stock Exchange.... But the work was never congenial.... You do not know how degrading this City life is, how debasing, and yet how absorbing. Money for ever clinks in your ear. You can think of nothing else. From the bottom of my heart, I hate it, and yet how can I draw back." Whereas Harold hated the City but was honest, his partner, Jeremiah Pearson, was "one of the deepest, slyest foxes in the whole City of London." After robbing the firm, Pearson fled to the USA, leaving Harold to take the blame. Harold survived in business but could only cope with City life through the support of a loving wife and a home

---

[4] Marsh, *Money, Speculation and Finance in Contemporary British Fiction*, pp. vii, 176.

[5] See M. Booth, *The Doctor, the Detective and Arthur Conan Doyle: A Biography* (London: Hodder and Stoughton, 1997) pp. 34, 76, 103; D. Stashower, *Teller of Tales: The Life of Arthur Conan Doyle* (New York: Henry Holt and Co., 1999) p. 45.

[6] C. Doyle, *The Firm of Girdlestone*, pp. 13–14, 42, 76–81, 83, 112, 166–168, 290, 312, 335, 354–355, 358–359.

[7] See Booth, *The Doctor, the Detective and Arthur Conan Doyle*, pp. 168, 218.

in the suburbs. "He has found it possible in spirit also to do one's duties amidst the babel of the City, and yet to live beyond it."[8] Conan Doyle's 1899 novel, *A Duet with an Occasional Chorus*, was also based on his suburban experience.[9] Frank and Maude Crosse were a married couple living in Woking. Frank commuted to the City, where he was an accountant with an insurance company, and Maude's father, who lived St. Albans, was a City banker. Their only brush with the speculative side of the City, as opposed to the daily routine of work, was an investment in a gold mine but they quickly sold out, at a profit, when they realised the risk they were taking.[10]

Though the novels contain much that presents a negative image of the City, they also contain positive elements. In the City, the essential business of managing ships and trading commodities was done, and becoming a City merchant was a route to wealth and respectability "by incessant attention to business and extreme parsimony.... The firm of Dimsdale and Gilray is now among the most successful and popular of all English firms connected with the African trade."[11] Similarly, the stockbroker, Harold Denver, emerges as "a most quiet young gentleman ... he was busy from morning to night on the Stock Exchange....He learned to know where to place his clients' money, which of the jobbers would make a price in New Zealand's, and which would touch nothing but American rails, which might be trusted and which shunned. All this, and much more, he mastered, and to such purpose that he soon began to prosper, to retain the clients who had been recommended to him, and to attract fresh ones."[12] The valuable role played by stockbrokers also emerges in the novel *Duet*. Frank and Maude were in a dilemma of what to invest in as UK government debt paid a very low rate of interest, and so turned to a stockbroker for advice.[13] However, it is in his Sherlock Holmes stories that Conan Doyle reveals a more positive perspective of the City as well as individual bankers and stockbrokers. Criticism is made of a City merchant in *A Case of Identity* and the commercial district bordering the river Thames, in *The Man with the Twisted Lip*, but these are limited. There is no mention in the

---

[8]C. Doyle, *Beyond the City*, pp. 9, 27–28, 67, 118, 123, 142, 192.

[9]Booth, *The Doctor, the Detective and Arthur Conan Doyle*, pp. 168, 218.

[10]C. Doyle, *A Duet with an Occasional Chorus*, pp. 11–12, 249, 254–255.

[11]C. Doyle, *The Firm of Girdlestone*, pp. 1–5, 7, 108, 112–113, 209, 290, 358–359.

[12]C. Doyle, *Beyond the City*, pp. 9, 27–28, 127–129, 172–173, 190.

[13]C. Doyle, *A Duet with an Occasional Chorus*, pp. 250–251, 258–262.

Sherlock Holmes stories of speculative excesses, market manipulation, fraudulent company promoters and absconding financiers. Bankers and stockbrokers come across as honest and respectable people.[14]

Conan Doyle points out in the Sherlock Holmes stories that the City, in general, and banks, in particular, were exposed to the actions of criminals. The man, in *The Adventure of the Resident Patient*, who says, "I would never trust a banker," turned out to be part of a gang of bank robbers. In *The Red-Headed League*, there was a plot to rob the City and Suburban Bank.[15] Another bank robbery was at the centre of *The Adventure of the Beryl Coronet*. Holder and Stevenson of Threadneedle Street was the second largest private bank in the City trusted by royalty and the aristocracy to provide them with credit whenever required. "There are many noble families to whom we have advanced large sums upon the security of their pictures, libraries, or plate." They were relied upon "to be discreet and to refrain from all gossip."[16] In *The Adventure of Black Peter*, it was assumed that the banker, John Hopley Neligan, had stolen securities from his own bank, Dawson and Neligan, and then fled. According to Neligan's son, "It has always been said that my father stole all the securities and fled. It is not true. It was his belief that if he were given time in which to realize them, all would be well and every creditor paid in full. He started in his little yacht for Norway just before the warrant was issued for his arrest. I can remember that last night when he bade farewell to my mother. He left us a list of the securities he was taking, and he swore that he would come back with his honour cleared, and that none who had trusted him would suffer. Well, no word was ever heard from him again. Both the yacht and he vanished utterly. We believed, my mother and I, that he and it, with the securities that he had taken with him, were at the bottom of the sea. We had a faithful friend, however, who is a business man, and it was he who discovered some time ago that some of the securities which my father had with him had reappeared on the London market. You can imagine our amazement. I spent months in trying to trace them, and at last, after many doubtings and difficulties, I discovered that the original seller had been Captain Peter Carey." Sherlock Holmes pieced the events together and showed that the banker had been murdered by Peter Carey,

---

[14] Stashower, *Teller of Tales*, p. 220.

[15] *The Strand Magazine*: 'A Case of Identity', September 1891, 'The Man with the Twisted Lip', December 1891, 'The Adventure of the Resident Patient', August 1893.

[16] 'The Adventure of the Beryl Coronet', *Strand Magazine*, May 1892.

who was the captain of a whaling vessel, after he had been rescued from his sinking yacht.[17] The impression generated is this and other stories was that bankers were decent family men who cared about their reputations and would not steal from those who trusted them.[18]

While it might be expected that bank robberies would feature prominently in stories about a fictional detective, Conan Doyle also included other City businesses as victims of criminal activity. In *The Adventure of the Stock-Broker's Clerk*, it was a stock broking firm that was targeted. In contrast to the robbers, the stockbroker's clerk, Hall Pycroft, whom they duped was "a smart young City man, of the class who have been labelled cockneys, but who give us our crack volunteer regiments, and who turn out more fine athletes and sportsmen than any body of men in these islands." One of the robbers impersonated Pycroft so as to gain access to the vaults of the stockbroking firm, but was caught with a bag containing "Nearly a hundred thousand pounds' worth of American railway bonds, with a large amount of scrip in mines and other companies."[19] This praise of stockbrokers was also evident in one of the last Sherlock Holmes stories, *The Adventure of the Blanched Soldier*. James M. Dodd, a City stockbroker, was described as "a big, fresh, sunburned, upstanding Briton" who had fought as a volunteer in the war the Boer War.[20] In another Sherlock Holmes story, *The Adventure of the Norwood Builder*, there was an attempt to frame a City solicitor for murder.[21] Those in the City were also regularly duped by professional beggars, as in *The Man with the Twisted Lip*.[22]

Conclusion

Conan Doyle was a realist when it came to writing about finance and the City of London. As such, he can act as representative of finance in fact and fiction. He was able to see finance and the City from a number of different angles and used all of them for dramatic effect in his novels of contemporary life and his Sherlock Holmes stories. As an outsider, he was

---

[17] 'The Adventure of Black Peter', *Strand Magazine*, February 1904.

[18] See Oxford D.N.B. Entry.

[19] 'The Adventure of the Stock-Broker's Clerk', *Strand Magazine*, March 1893.

[20] 'The Adventure of the Blanched Soldier', *Strand Magazine*, October 1926.

[21] 'The Adventure of the Norwood Builder', *The Strand Magazine*, October 1903.

[22] 'The Man with the Twisted Lip', *Strand Magazine*, December 1891.

forced to rely on the usual sources available to writers for those of his works with a contemporary setting and for the plots of his Sherlock Holmes stories. These sources included a mixture of personal experience, the daily newspapers and suggestions made by friends, relatives and even complete strangers. As Booth, himself a novelist, commented in his biography of Conan Doyle, "Authors get their ideas from a wide variety of sources, the important thing being that they use them with originality."[23] Interaction with friends and relatives as well as unsolicited advice provided Conan Doyle with inspiration. In the novel, *Girdlestone*, Conan Doyle thanks Mr P.G. Houlgrave for "the accuracy of my African chapters ... and the copious details with which he furnished me."[24] What Conan Doyle chose to ignore, unlike other authors of his age, were most sensational events in finance such as speculative booms and bursts or the failure of financiers. Here, Conan Doyle had available to him his own experience as a successful investor. By 1900, Conan Doyle's success lay as a writer of highly popular novels and short stories. He was generating an income in excess of £2,000 per annum. By then, he had assets valued at between £20,000 and £30,000. Though he spent part of his income in building a small country house for himself and helping his relatives financially, much was also invested. As a result, Conan Doyle became familiar with banks and bankers while his activity as an investor made him acquainted with stockbrokers and this gained him an extensive experience of using the Stock Exchange. An insight into his philosophy as an investor can be found from his letters. As those editing his correspondence have noted, "Conan Doyle often conveyed tedious financial information to his mother in his letters, with scrupulous attention to the status and outlook of their investments." Some of the shares that he held were given to him as presents, notably 500 Newnes Ltd. preference shares, as they were the publishers of the *Strand Magazine* in which the Sherlock Holmes stories appeared. However, most were the product of decisions he made.

Conan Doyle invested widely in companies engaged in a diverse number of activities and operating at home and abroad. His philosophy as an investor can be found in a letter he wrote to his mother in September 1900. There, Conan Doyle reflected that whereas he had lost money investing in a coffee plantation company, having been "advised by experts," he had made money on his mining shares through backing his own judgement.

[23] Booth, *The Doctor, the Detective and Arthur Conan Doyle*, pp. 176–177.
[24] C. Doyle, *The Firm of Girdlestone*, preface.

"I don't call well proved and old fashioned mining or land shares in South Africa speculative. If they have kept up their values during this war they are not likely to lose in the future.... I am very discreet in my purchase of these, and never make a mistake while I often by using my wits make a considerable gain. Last week for example I sold a stock at an advance of £361 clear gain. I could not lose on it as it was a dividend paying stock and I was prepared to keep it as an investment.... Naturally it is better to hold African stock than to sell it while the war keeps down the price, but those stocks bought before the war are steadily creeping up to their old figure. Australia is a failure, I acknowledge. I will never again touch an Australian mine. But I have no considerable investment out there....I call it gambling when you take up stock and don't pay for it. It is legitimate speculation and using of your wits when you choose your stock and buy it right out, prepared either to retain it as an investment or to sell it at a large advance." As the war in South Africa concluded, these mining stocks crept up in value, much to Conan Doyle's pleasure. In September 1902, he wrote to his mother, "The mining market shows signs of righting itself after the convulsion it has undergone. Our financial position is strong now but will be stronger still when that comes about." In addition to these South African mining securities, Conan Doyle also dabbled in a number of high-risk investments in Britain. He was involved in the attempt to mine coal in Kent, which proved to be a financial disaster. More successful was his involvement in a company developing a combination pedal and motorised bicycle. His motivation in making this investment was clear. "The Autowheel is great. I hope it will mean a fortune." He also backed his own literary success by buying shares in the magazine publishers Newnes and Tit-Bits, both of which published his stories.[25]

This experience as an investor does appear to have influenced Conan Doyle when writing his novels and stories. In *The Firm of Girdlestone*, which appeared in 1890, it is the losses made by John Girdlestone, through speculating in US railroad shares and Cornish tin mines, that are the focus.[26] In contrast, later works emphasise the difficulties of finding suitable investments and the money to be made if the search was

---

[25] J. Lettenberg, D. Stashower and C. Foley, *Arthur Conan Doyle: A Life in Letters* (London: Harper Press, 2007) pp. 15, 328, 390, 409, 456, 460, 500, 505, 512, 515, 548–550, 564, 591–592, 550; Booth, *The Doctor, the Detective and Arthur Conan Doyle*, p. 167.

[26] C. Doyle, *The Firm of Girdlestone*, pp. 13–14, 42, 76–81, 166–168, 290, 335.

successful. In *The Adventure of the Beryl Coronet*, published in May 1892, the banker, Alexander Holder, told Sherlock Holmes, "It is, of course, well known to you that in a successful banking business as much depends upon our being able to find remunerative investments for our funds as upon our increasing our connection and the number of our depositors."[27] The solution to this dilemma was found through investing in a wide range of stocks and bonds, as revealed in the February 1904 story, *The Adventure of Black Peter*. When the notebook left by the banker who had disappeared was studied, it revealed the nature of the bank's holdings. "On the second page were the printed letters 'C.P.R.,' and then came several sheets of numbers. Another heading was 'Argentine,' another 'Costa Rica,' and another 'San Paulo,' each with pages of signs and figures after it. 'What do you make of these?' asked Holmes. 'They appear to be lists of Stock Exchange securities. I thought that "J.H.N." were the initials of a broker, and that "C.P.R." may have been his client.' 'Try Canadian Pacific Railway,' said Holmes."[28] Holmes was clearly familiar with the range of securities available to the professional investor at the beginning of the twentieth century.

Faced with such a diversity of investment opportunities, it was no surprise that stockbrokers featured in Sherlock Holmes stories as in *The Adventure of the Stock-Broker's Clerk* of March 1893. It was those in the City that possessed the knowledge and expertise required by investors.[29] In *Beyond the City*, the novel dating from 1892, the stockbroker, Harold Denver, "learned to know where to place his clients' money."[30] The advantage that came to an investor from using a stockbroker was emphasised in the 1899 novel, *A Duet with an Occasional Chorus*. Faced with a windfall of £50, Frank and Maude were in a quandary about what to invest in. Though they invested in the shares of the El Dorado Proprietary Gold Mine, on the advice of a stockbroker, and emerged with a profit, Frank and Maude were so traumatised by the experience that they switched to consols despite the low rate of interest.[31] The attractions of the shares issued by gold mining companies even tempted Dr Watson, as in the December 1903 Sherlock Holmes story, *The Adventure of the Dancing*

---

[27] 'The Adventure of the Beryl Coronet', *Strand Magazine*, May 1892.

[28] 'The Adventure of Black Peter', *Strand Magazine*, February 1904.

[29] 'The Adventure of the Stock-Broker's Clerk', March 1893.

[30] C. Doyle, *Beyond the City*, p. 9.

[31] C. Doyle, *A Duet with an Occasional Chorus*, pp. 250–251, 258–262.

Men. "'So, Watson,' said he, suddenly, 'you do not propose to invest in South African securities?' I gave a start of astonishment. Accustomed as I was to Holmes's curious faculties, this sudden intrusion into my most intimate thoughts was utterly inexplicable. 'How on earth do you know that?' I asked... 'Now, it was not really difficult, by an inspection of the groove between your left forefinger and thumb, to feel sure that you did NOT propose to invest your small capital in the gold fields.' 'I see no connection.' 'Very likely not; but I can quickly show you a close connection. Here are the missing links of the very simple chain: (1) You had chalk between your left finger and thumb when you returned from the club last night. (2) You put chalk there when you play billiards, to steady the cue. (3) You never play billiards except with Thurston. (4) You told me, four weeks ago, that Thurston had an option on some South African property which would expire in a month, and which he desired you to share with him. (5) Your cheque book is locked in my drawer, and you have not asked for the key. (6) You do not propose to invest your money in this manner.' 'How absurdly simple!' I cried."[32]

His success as an investor, and his willingness to accept the risks of losses in the pursuit of gains, marks Conan Doyle out as different from many of his fellow novelists in the late nineteenth and early twentieth century. They were either reluctant to invest in companies, though willing to accept the dividends they received, as with William Morris, or experienced losses which they blamed on those who advised them.[33] As Caroline Dakers has observed, "In their novels excessive wealth, and the desire for it, are mostly linked to excessive and immoral behaviour. Bankers, merchants, industrialists and money-lenders appear as villains (rarely heroes.)."[34] The period when Conan Doyle was writing was a difficult time for investors as the traditional domestic outlets of land, mortgages, property and the National Debt were no longer attractive. The inevitable consequence was a search among investors for higher-yielding securities leading them to the shares issued by British and overseas companies operating in increasingly diverse areas. Those companies mining gold, at a time when most of the world's money was on the gold standard, appeared

---

[32] 'The Adventure of the Dancing Men', *Strand Magazine*, December 1903.

[33] P. Waller, *Writers, Readers and Reputations: Literary Life in Britain, 1870–1918* (Oxford: Oxford University Press, 2006) pp. 344–348, 535, 649.

[34] C. Dakers, *A Genius for Money: Business, Art and the Morrisons* (New Haven/London: Yale University Press, 2011) pp. 5–6.

to be a particularly attractive option. Also favoured were UK industrial and commercial companies manufacturing and selling products that were likely to be always in demand, such as beer, soap and steel.[35] Inevitably, many of these companies disappointed investors either because of unrealistic expectations, high production costs, competitive market conditions as well as outright fraud, and this did produce an inevitable media backlash. However, when it came to the City's role in serving the needs of the investor, Conan Doyle was in the position of an insider who had not only participated in the process but also profited from the result, willing to accept the gains and losses that came with risk taking. This helped him to take a realistic view of the City as he was aware of the problems involved in directing investors into profitable openings at a time of falling yields on once safe domestic investments and the uncertainties that existed overseas.[36]

Conclusion

There is a large and enduring gulf between the role and importance of the financial sector in the British economy and the way those engaged in financial activities are perceived. Whereas governments, and the public to a degree, recognise the contribution made by the financial sector to the functioning of the economy and general prosperity, there also exists a very negative picture of those engaged in such activities. Sarah Gordon picked up on this recently when she noted that "The popular caricature of business, filled with profiteering bankers, simply does not reflect reality."[37] This negative imagery is not confined to those with an anti-capitalism agenda, as might be expected, but has long pervaded society as a whole, if the writings of major novelists are used as evidence. In the nineteenth century, negative images of those in finance are found in the work of Charles Dickens and Anthony Trollope, whereas today it is found in those of Ken Follett and Sebastian Faulks. However, there were others who cast the banker, broker and even accountant in the role of hero, though much

---

[35] Michie, *The London Stock Exchange: A History*, pp. 88–89; Michie, 'Gamblers, Fools, Victims or Wizards?', pp. 156–183. Figures on national debt, railway capital and new issues can be found in B.R. Mitchell, *British Historical Statistics* (Cambridge: 1989) pp. 543–544, 601–602, 678, 685.

[36] I would like to thank Catherine Wynne of the University of Hull for suggesting that I look at Conan Doyle as an investor.

[37] S. Gordon, 'Making Sense of the City', *Financial Times*, 9th March 2019.

more common was either the murdered financier, for whom no one grieved, or the evil financier robbing investors and spreading financial chaos. In the past, merchants and manufacturers were cast in a similar light, but, over time, they have been rehabilitated, judging from novels, reappearing as honourable men contributing to the nation's wealth and Britain's international success. In contrast, collectively, those in finance have not experienced a similar makeover though individual groups were either never subjected to negative characterisation, such as accountants, or moved in and out of favour, as with bankers. As a profession, with a high level of technical competence, accountants always generated a positive image but came across as dull and uninteresting and were largely ignored. In contrast, bankers figured prominently in novels, becoming increasingly respectable over time, but largely in the form of the cold and boring manager of a commercial bank or the aloof and cultivated partner in a merchant bank. That image was then reversed in the wake of Big Bang in the 1980s, when the term "merchant banker" was replaced in the UK with that of "investment banker," commonly used in the USA. The investment banker was a person without ethical standards who was focused on making money regardless of the damage inflicted on others. The image of the respectable and conservative banker was then further reversed with the financial crisis of 2007–2008, as that tarnished the reputation of the entire banking profession. Stockbrokers also went through a similar metamorphosis, becoming respectable in the first half of the twentieth century, when they took on the characteristics of the accountant as sources of expertise and sound advice, but losing it when they were subsumed into investment banking. Throughout, however, financiers remained subjected to a very negative imagery. The company promoter was generally portrayed as the most untrustworthy figure in British finance, as they duped innocent investors of their money by selling them shares in worthless companies and manipulating prices on the London Stock Exchange through insider trading. Whether before or after the First World War, their death was never regretted, being the inevitable outcome of the life they had led. Though the term company promoter faded in usage after the Second World War, it was replaced by the likes of investment banker or hedge fund manager, each of which was used in novels to conjure up a figure in finance that was motivated solely by personal greed. Their collective home was the City of London, which made it such an easy target for those who believed in the City/Industry Divide or the City/Bank/Treasury Nexus.

Bibliography

Fact

Aberdeen Free Press 1853–1896.

Aberdeen Herald 1832–1876.

Ackrill, M. and Hannah, L., *Barclays: The Business of Banking, 1690–1996* (Cambridge: Cambridge University Press, 2001).

Adler, D.B., *British Investment in American Railways, 1834–1898* (Charlottesville, USA: 1970).

Alborn, T.L., *Conceiving Companies: Joint-stock Politics in Victorian England* (London: 1998).

Alderman, G., *Controversy and Crisis: Studies in the History of Jews in Modern Britain* (Boston: 2008).

Ali, Omar UK Financial Services Leader, Ernst and Young, *Financial Times*, 9th May 2017.

Alison, A., *England in 1815 and 1845* (London: 1845).

Anderson, B.L., 'The Social Economy of Late-Victorian Clerks', in G. Crossick (ed.), *The Lower Middle Class in Britain, 1870–1914* (London: 1977).

Anderson, B.L. and Cottrell, P.L., 'Another Victorian Capital Market: A Study of Banking and Bank Investors on Merseyside', *Economic History Review*, 28 (1975).

Anderson, M., Edwards, J.R. and Matthews, D., 'A Study of the Quoted Company Audit Market in 1886', *Accounting, Business and Financial History*, 6 (1996).

Angel, N., *The Great Illusion* (London: 1909).

Anon., *The Bank–The Stock Exchange–The Bankers–The Bankers' Clearing House–The Minister, and the Public: An Expose* (London: 1821).

Anon., 'Scottish Banking Institutions', in W. Chambers, *The Book of Scotland* (Edinburgh: 1830).

Anon., *The Curious and Remarkable History of the Royal British Bank* (London: 1850).

Anon., *Exposure of the Stock Exchange and Bubble Companies* (London: 1854).

Anon., *Commercial Tales and Sketches* (London: 1864).

Anon., 'A Black Year for Investors', *Blackwood's Edinburgh Magazine*, 127, 1875.

Anon., 'Outlying Professions', *Blackwood's Edinburgh Magazine*, 136, 1884.

Anon., 'Scottish Capital Abroad', *Blackwood's Edinburgh Magazine* 136, 1884.

Anon, 'Prospects of Canadian Land Mortgage Companies', *Accountants' Magazine*, 111, 1899.

Anon., 'The Mystery of Room 11', *Union Jack*, January 1910.

Anon., 'Business on the Provincial Stock Exchanges', *Economist*, 31st October 1914.

Anon., 'The Meeting with Marsh', *The Pluck Library*, 22nd May 1915.

Anon., 'The Scotland Yard Scandal', *The Pluck Library*, 29th May 1915.

Anon., 'The Third Shot', *The Pluck Library*, 10th April 1915.

Anon., 'The City in War', *The Banker*, lix, August 1941.

Anon., *Two Centuries of Lewis and Peat*, 1775–1975 (London: 1975).

Anon., *Hambros Bank Ltd, London*, 1839–1939 (London: 1939).

Anon., *Child & Co: A History*, Royal Bank of Scotland Group Publication (2002).

Anon., 'The New City', *Financial Times*, 27–30th March 2006.

Anon., 'The World's Wallet', *Sunday Times Magazine*, 3rd December 2006.

Anon., 'Save the City', The Economist, 7th January 2012.

Anson, M. and Gourvish, T., *Leopold Joseph: A History* (London: 2002).

Aris, S., *The Jews in Business* (London: 1970).

Arlidge, J., 'The Golden Gateway', *Sunday Times*, 3rd December 2006.

Armstrong, J., 'Hooley and the Bovril Company', *Business History*, 28 (1986).

Armstrong, J., 'The Rise and Fall of the Company Promoter and the Financing of British Industry', in J.J. van Helten and Y. Cassis (eds.), *Capitalism in a Mature Economy: Financial Institutions, Capital Exports and British Industry, 1870–1939* (Aldershot: Edward Elgar, 1990).

Arnold, P., *The Bankers of London* (London: 1938).

Artifex and Opifex, *The Causes of Decay in a British Industry* (London: Longmans, Green and Company, 1907).

Attard, B., 'From Free-Trade Imperialism to Structural Power: New Zealand and the Capital Market, 1858–68', *Journal of Imperial and Commonwealth History*, 35 (2007).

Attfield, J.B., 'The Advantages, or Otherwise, of the Establishment of Branches by Bankers, from the Point of View (a) of the Bankers and (b) of the General Interests of the Community', *Journal of the Institute of Bankers*, 13 (1892).

Aubrey, W.H.S., *Stock Exchange Investments: The Theory, Methods, Practice and Results* (London: 1896).

Augar, P., *The Death of Gentlemanly Capitalism: The Rise and Fall of London's Investment Banks* (London: 2000).

Austin, P.E., *Baring Brothers and the Birth of Modern Finance* (London: Pickering and Chatto, 2007).

Ayer, J., *A Century of Finance, 1804 to 1904: The London House of Rothschild* (London: 1905).

Ayres, G.L., *Fluctuations in New Capital Issues on the London Money Market, 1899 to 1913*, University of London M.Sc. (1934).

Baillie Grohman, W.A., 'Cattle Ranches in the Far West', *Fortnightly Review*, xxviii (1880).

Baillie Grohman, W.A., *Camps in the Rockies* (London: Sampson Low, Marston, Searle & Rivington, 1882).

Baines, A., *The Popular Handbook of Finance* (London: 1894).

Baker, W.J., *A History of the Marconi Company* (London: 1970).

Ball, M. and Sunderland, D., *An Economic History of London, 1800–1914* (London: Routledge, 2001).

Bancroft, P., Doyle, J., Glaister, S., Kennedy, D. and Travers, T., *London's Size and Diversity — The Advantages in a Competitive World* (London: Corporation of London, 1996).

Bank for International Settlements, Committee on the Global Financial System, *Long Term Issues in International Banking* (July 2010).

Banner, S., *Anglo-American Securities Regulation: Cultural and Political Roots, 1690–1860* (Cambridge: 1998).

Barker, T.C. and Robbins, M., *A History of London Transport*, Vol. 1 (London: 1963).

Barnett, D., *London, Hub of the Industrial Revolution: A Revisionary History, 1775–1825* (London: I.B. Tauris, 1998).

Barnett, R.W., 'The Effect of the Development of Banking Facilities upon the Circulation of the Country', *Journal of the Institute of Bankers*, 2 (1881).

Barnett, R.W., 'The History of the Progress and Development of Banking in the United Kingdom from the Year 1800 to the Present Time', *Journal of the Institute of Bankers*, 1 (1880).

Barnett, R.W., 'The Reign of Queen Victoria: A Survey of Fifty Years of Progress', *Journal of the Institute of Bankers*, 6 (1887).

Bartlett, W. and Chapman, H., *A Handy-Book for Investors* (London: 1869).

Barty-King, H., *The Baltic Exchange: The History of a Unique Market* (London: 1977).

Bassett, H.H. (ed.), *Business Men at Home and Abroad* (London: 1912).

Bassett, H.H. (ed.), *Men of Note in Finance and Commerce* (London: 1900/1901).

Bassett, H.H., *British Commerce* (London: 1913).

Baster, A.S.J., 'A Note on the Colonial Stock Acts and Dominion Borrowing', *Economic History*, 2 (1930/3).

Baster, A.S.J., *The International Banks* (London: 1935).

Bauer, P.T., *West African Trade: A Study of Competition, Oligopoly and Monopoly in a Changing Economy* (London: 1954).

Beavan, A.H., *Imperial London* (London: 1901).

Bell, B. and Cowan, S., Edinburgh, *Monthly Circular* January 1883, July 1885, May 1893, October 1895, December 1895, January 1896.

Bellinger, C. and Michie, R.C., 'Big Bang in the City: An Intentional Revolution or an Accident', *Financial History Review*, 21 (2014).

Benson, R.H., 'Episodes of Business and Finance', in *Lady Wantage, Lord Wantage: A Memoir* (London: 1907).

Best, M.H. and Humphries, J., 'The City and Industrial Decline', in B. Elbaum and W. Lazonick, *The Decline of the British Economy* (Oxford: 1986).

Billings, M. and Capie, F., 'Financial Crisis, Contagion and the British Banking System between the World Wars', *Business History*, 53 (2011).

Bills, M. and Knight, V. (eds.), *William Powell Frith: Painting the Victorian Age* (New Haven and London: 2006).

Binham, C. and Arnold, M., 'Season of Goodwill to Bankers Began Soon After Tory Victory', *Financial Times*, 23rd December 2015.

Blainey, G., 'Lost Causes of the Jameson Raid', *Economic History Review*, 18 (1965).

Blair, M., *The Paisley Thread Industry* (Paisley: 1907).

Blakey, G.B., *The Post-War History of the London Stock Market, 1945–92* (Didcot: Mercury, 1993).

Bloomfield, A.I., *Short-Term Capital Movements Under the Pre-1914 Gold Standard* (Princeton: 1963).

Blunden, G., 'The Supervision of the UK Banking System', *Journal of the Institute of Bankers*, 96 (1975).

Booth, M., *The Doctor, the Detective and Arthur Conan Doyle: A Biography* (London: Hodder and Stoughton, 1997).

British Warehouseman 1889–1902.

Broadberry, S., *Market Services and the Productivity Race, 1850–2000: British Performance in International Perspective* (Cambridge: 2006).

Broadberry, S. and Harrison, M. (eds), *The Economics of World War 1* (Cambridge: Cambridge University Press, 1998).

Brodrick, G.C., *English Land and English Landlords* (London: 1881).

Brook, S., *The Club: The Jews of Modern Britain* (London: 1989).

Brooks, C., *Something in the City: Men and Markets in London* (London: 1931).

Brown, R., 'The Genesis of Company Law in England and Scotland', *Juridical Review*, 13 (1901).

Burdett's Official Intelligence (London: 1885).

Burke, P., Harrison, B. and Slack, P. (eds.), *Civil Histories* (Oxford: 2000).

Burn, G., *The Re-emergence of Global Finance* (London: Palgrave Macmillan, 2006).

Burn, J., *Stock Exchange Investments in Theory and Practice* (London: 1909).

Burt, R., 'The London Mining Exchange, 1850–1900', *Business History*, xiv (1972).

Busby, J.H., *The London Trust Company Ltd, 1889–1964* (London: 1964).

Butt, J., 'The Scottish Oil Mania of 1864–6', *Scottish Journal of Political Economy*, 12 (1965).

Cain, P., 'J.A. Hobson, Financial Capitalism and Imperialism in Late Victorian and Edwardian England', *Journal of Imperial and Commonwealth History*, 13 (1985).

Cain, P.J. and Hopkins, A.G., *British Imperialism: Crisis and Deconstruction, 1914–1990* (London: 1993).

Cain, P.J. and Hopkins, A.G., *British Imperialism: Innovation and Expansion, 1688–1914* (London: 1993).

Cairncross, A. (ed.), *The Robert Hall Diaries* (London: 1989).

Cairncross, A., *Economics and Economic Policy* (Oxford: 1986).

Cairncross, A.K., *Home and Foreign Investment, 1870–1913* (Cambridge: 1953).

Cairncross, A.K., *The British Economy since 1945: Economic Policy and Performance, 1945–1990* (Oxford: Blackwell, 1992).

Camplin, J., *The Rise of the Plutocrats: Wealth and Power in Edwardian England* (London: 1978).

Canadian Financial Post 1907–1914.

Cannadine, D., 'Aristocratic Indebtedness in the Nineteenth Century: The Case Re-opened', *Economic History Review*, 30 (1977).

Cannadine, D., 'The Landowner as Millionaire: The Finances of the Dukes of Devonshire, c.1800–c.1926', *Agricultural History Review*, 25 and 26 (1977/1978).

Capie, F., *The Bank of England, 1950s–1979* (Cambridge: Cambridge University Press, 2010).

Capie, F. and Collins, M., *Have the Banks Failed British Industry?* (London: 1992).

Capie, F. and Woods, G., *Money over Two Centuries: Selected Topics in British Monetary History* (Oxford: Oxford University Press, 2012).

Capital and Investment 1873.

Cardigan, Earl of, 'Can Money be Profitably Invested in Land?', *Financial Review of Reviews*, 2, August 1906.

Carnevali, F., *Europe's Advantage: Banks and Small Firms in Britain, France, Germany, and Italy since 1918* (Oxford: 2005).

Carosso, V.P., 'The Wall Street Money Trust from Pujo through Medina', *Business History Review*, xlviii (1973).

Carosso, V.P., *Investment Banking in America: A History* (Cambridge, MA: 1970).

Carosso, V.P., *The Morgans: Private International Bankers, 1854–1913* (Cambridge, MA: 1987).

Carr Saunders, A.M. and Jones, D.C., *A Survey of Social Structure of England and Wales* (Oxford: 1927).

Cassis, Y. (ed.), *Finance and Financiers in European History, 1880–1960* (Cambridge: 1992).

Cassis, Y., 'Bankers in English Society in the Late Nineteenth Century', *Economic History Review*, 38 (1985).

Cassis, Y., 'The Banking Community of London, 1890–1914: A Survey', *Journal of Imperial and Commonwealth History*, 13 (1984–85).

Cassis, Y., *Capitals of Capital: A History of International Financial Centres, 1780–2005* (Cambridge: Cambridge University Press, 2006).

Cassis, Y., *City Bankers, 1890–1914* (Cambridge: Cambridge University Press, 1994).

Channon, D.F., *The Service Industries: Strategy, Structure and Financial Performance* (London: 1978).

Chapman, S., 'British-Based Investment Groups before 1914', *Economic History Review*, 38 (1985).

Chapman, S., 'Rhodes and The City of London: Another View of Imperialism', *Historical Journal*, 28 (1985).

Chapman, S., *Merchant Enterprise in Britain: From the Industrial Revolution to World War 1* (Cambridge: 1992).

Chapman, S.D., 'Aristocracy and Meritocracy in Merchant Banking', *British Journal of Sociology*, 37 (1986).

Chapman, S.D., 'The Establishment of the Rothschilds as Bankers', *Transactions of the Jewish Historical Society*, 29 (1988).

Chapman, S.D., *Raphael Bicentenary, 1987* (London: 1987).

Checkland, S.G., 'The Mind of the City, 1870–1914', *Oxford Economic Papers*, 9 (1957).

Checkland, S.G., *The Mines of Tharsis: Roman, French and British Enterprise in Spain* (London: 1967).

Chiozza Money, L.G., *Riches and Poverty*, 11th ed. (London: 1914).

Chiozza Money, L.G., *The Nation's Wealth: Will It Endure?* (London: 1914).

Choi, S.R., Park, D. and Tschoegl, A.E., *Banks and the World's Major Banking Centers* (October: 2014).

Christie, J.R., 'Joint-Stock Enterprise in Scotland before the Companies Acts', *Juridical Review*, 21 (1909).

Christmas, H., *The Money Market: What It is, What It Does, and How It is Managed* (London: Frederick Warne & Co., 1866).

Churchill, R.S., *Men, Mines and Animals in South Africa* (London: 1892).

A. Citizen, *The City Today* (London: New Fabian Research Bureau, 1938).

City of London Council: Report by the Improvements and Town Planning Committee on the Preliminary Draft Proposals for Post-War Reconstruction in the City of London (London: 1944).

City of London, *City of London Day Census, 1911: Report* (London: 1911).

City Research Project, *The Competitive Position of London's Financial Services: Final Report* (London: 1995).

Clapham, J., *The Bank of England: A History* (Cambridge: Cambridge University Press, 1944).

Clark, R.A., 'The Image of the City', *Journal of the Institute of Bankers*, 96 (1975).

Clarke, M., *Citizens' Financial Futures: The Regulation of Retail Investment Financial Services in Britain* (Aldershot: 1999).

Clarke, W.C., *The City's Invisible Earnings* (London: 1958).

Clarke, W.M., *The City in the World Economy* (London: 1965).

Clayton, G. and Osborn, W.T., *Insurance Company Investment: Principles and Policy* (London: 1965).

Cleary, E.J., *The Building Society Movement* (London: 1965).

Clemenson, H.A., *English Country Houses and Landed Estates* (London: 1982).

Coakley, J., *London as an International Financial Centre*, in L. Budd and S. Whimster (eds.), *Global Finance and Urban Living: A Study of Metropolitan Change* (London: 1992).

Coakley, J. and Harris, L., *The City of Capital: London's Role as a Financial Centre* (Oxford: 1983).

Coates, A., *The Commerce in Rubber: The First 250 Years* (Singapore: 1987).

Coates, D. and Hillard, J. (eds.), *UK Economic Decline: Key Texts* (London: 1995).

Coates, D., *The Question of UK Decline: State, Society and Economy* (London: 1994).

Cobham, D., 'The Equity Market', in D. Cobban (ed.), *Markets and Dealers: The Economics of the London Financial Markets* (London: 1992).

Cochran, T.C., *Business in American Life: A History* (New York: McGraw-Hill, 1972).

Cockburn, H., *Journal, 1831–1854* (Edinburgh: 1874).

Cockburn, H., *Memorials of His Time* (Edinburgh: 1856).

Cockerell, H.A.L. and Green, E., *The British Insurance Business, 1547–1970* (London: 1976).

Collins, B. and Robbins, K. (eds), *British Culture and Economic Decline* (London: 1990).

Colquhoun, P., *A Treatise on the Wealth, Power, and Resources of the British Empire* (London: 1815).

Committee on Finance and Industry: Report, Cmd 3282 (1931).

Committee on Industry and Trade: Final Report, Cmd 3282 (1929).

Committee on the Working of the Monetary System: Report (London: 1959).

Committee to Review the Functioning of Financial Institutions: Report (London: 1980).

Comparative Account of the Population of Great Britain in the Years 1801, 1811, 1821 and 1831, British Parliamentary Paper 348 (1831).

Confederation of British Industry, *Investing for Britain's Future: Report of the CBI City/Industry Task Force* (London: 1987).

Cordero, H.G. and Tarring, L.H., *Babylon to Birmingham* (London: 1960).

Corporation of London, *The Competitive Position of London's Financial Services: Final Report* (London: 1995).

Cottier, F.E., 'London Representatives of Foreign Banks', *The Banker*, xvi (1930).

Cottrell, P.L., 'The Business Man and Financier', in S. and V.D. Lipman (eds.), *The Century of Moses Montefiore* (Oxford: 1985).

Cottrell, P.L., *Industrial Finance, 1830–1914: The Finance and Organization of English Manufacturing Industry* (London: 1980).

Cottrell, P.L., *Investment Banking in England, 1856–1882: Case Study of the International Financial Society*, University of Hull Ph.D. (1974).

Cottrell, P.L., 'London's First "Big Bang"? Institutional Change in the City, 1855', in Y. Cassis and P.L. Cottrell (eds.), *The World of Private Banking* (Farnham: Ashgate, 2009).

Cottrell, P.L., 'The Steamship on the Mersey, 1815–1880: Investment and Ownership', in P.L. Cottrell and D.H. Aldcroft (ed.), *Shipping, Trade and Commerce: Essays in Memory of Ralph Davis* (Leicester: 1981).

Cowen, H.C., 'The London Stock Exchange and Investment', in *Current Financial Problems and the City of London* (London: Institute of Bankers, 1949).

Crafts, N., *British Relative Economic Decline Revisited*, CEPR Discussion Paper (2011).

Craig, R., 'William Gray and Company: A West Hartlepool Shipbuilding Enterprise, 1864–1913', in P.L. Cottrell and D.H. Aldcroft (ed.), *Shipping, Trade and Commerce: Essays in Memory of Ralph Davis* (Leicester: 1981).

Craik, J., Eadie, J. and Galbraith, J. *Memoirs and Portraits of One Hundred Glasgow Men* (Glasgow: 1886).

Crammond, E., 'The Economic Relations of the British and German Empires', *Journal of the Royal Statistical Society*, lxxvii (1914).

Crathorne, N., *Tennants' Stalk: The Story of the Tennants of the Glen* (London: 1973).

Crick, W.E. and Wadsworth, J.E., *A Hundred Years of Joint-Stock Banking* (London: Hodder and Stoughton, 1936).

Critchell, T. and Raymond, J., *A History of the Frozen Meat Trade* (London: 1912).

Currie, A.W., 'British Attitudes toward Investment in North American Railroads', *Business History Review*, xxxiv (1960).

Dakers, C., *A Genius for Money: Business, Art and the Morrisons* (New Haven and London: Yale University Press, 2011).

Dallas Brett, R., *Usury in Britain* (London: 1945).

Darbyshire, M., 'NS&I Rate Cut Drives Savers into Investments', *Financial Times*, 9th January 2021.

Darling, P.S., *City Cinderella: The Life and Times of Mercury Asset Management* (London: 1999).

Daunton, M.J., *Just Taxes: The Politics of Taxation in Britain, 1914–1979* (Cambridge: 2002).

Daunton, M.J., 'Gentlemanly Capitalism and British Industry 1820–1914', *Past and Present*, 122 (1989).

Davenport-Hines, R.P.T. and van Helten, J.J., 'Edgar Vincent, Viscount D'Abernon, and the Eastern Investment Company in London, Constantinople and Johannesburg', *Business History*, 28 (1986).

Davies, E., *What to Look for in a Prospectus* (London: 1926).

Davis, H.P., *The Davis Handbook of the Cobalt Silver District* (Toronto: Canadian Mining Journal, 1910).

Day, J.E., *Stockbroker's Office Organisation, Management and Accounts* (London: 1911).

Dennett, L., *The Charterhouse Group, 1925–1979: A History* (London: Gentry Books, 1979).

Deuchar, C., 'Investments', *Journal of the Federation of Insurance Institutes of Great Britain and Ireland*, 1 (1898).

Diaper, S., 'Merchant Banking in the Inter-War Period: The Case of Kleinwort, Sons and Company', *Business History*, 28 (1986).

Dick, J., 'Banks and Banking in the United Kingdom in 1891, Compared with Former Years', *Journal of the Institute of Bankers*, 14 (1892).

Dimsdale, N. and Horsewood, N., 'The Financial Crisis of 1931 and the Impact of the Great Depression on the British Economy', in Dimsdale, N. and Hotson, A.C. (eds.), *British Financial Crises since 1825* (Oxford: Oxford University Press 2014).

Dimsdale, N. and Prevezer, M. (eds.), *Capital Markets and Corporate Governance* (Oxford: 1994).

Dot, *The Stock Exchange and Its Victims* (London: 1851).

Drury, A.C., *Finance Houses: Their Development and Role in the Modern Financial Sector* (London: 1982).

Duffy, I.P.H., *Bankruptcy and Insolvency in London during the Industrial Revolution*, Oxford D.Phil (1973).

Duffy, F. and Henney, A., *The Changing City* (London: 1989).

Dumett, R.E., 'Edwin Cade and Frederick Gordon: British Imperialism and the Foundations of the Ashanti Goldfields Corporation, West Africa', in *Mining Tycoons in the Age of Empire, 1870–1945: Entrepreneurship, High Finance, Politics and Territorial Expansion* (Farnham: 2009).

Dumett, R.E., 'Exploring the Cain/Hopkins Paradigm: Issues for Debate; Critique and Topics for New Research', in *Gentlemanly Capitalism and British Imperialism: The New Debate on Empire* (London: Longman, 1999).

Dumett, R.E. (ed.), *Gentlemanly Capitalism and British Imperialism: The New Debate on Empire* (London: Longman, 1999).

Dumett, R.E. (ed.), *Mining Tycoons in the Age of Empire: Entrepreneurship, High Finance and Territorial Expansion* (Farnham: Ashgate, 2009).

Dundee, Perth and Cupar Advertiser 1823–79.

Dunn, J.F., 'Banking in 1837 and in 1897 in the United Kingdom, India and the Colonies: A Comparison and a Contrast', *Journal of the Institute of Bankers*, 19 (1898).

Dunnett, A.M., *The Donaldson Line: A Century of Shipping, 1854–1954* (Glasgow: 1960).

Dunning, J.H. and Morgan, E.V., *An Economic Study of the City of London* (London: 1971).

Durran, W., 'How the Public Forms an Opinion on Stocks', *Financial Review of Reviews*, 9, September 1913.

Hopkins, L.E. (ed.), *The Universal Railway Manual* (London: 1911).

Eatwell, J., *Whatever Happened to Britain: The Economics of Decline* (London: 1982).

Economist

Economist Intelligence Unit, *The London Metal Exchange* (London: 1958).

Edelstein, M., *Overseas Investment in the Age of High Imperialism: The United Kingdom, 1850–1914* (London: 1982).

Edinburgh Weekly Journal 1824–45.

Edwards, D., Edwards, M. and Matthews, D., 'Accountability in a Free-Market Economy: The British Company Audit, 1886', *Abacus*, 33 (1997).

Einzig, P., 'Foreign Bank Branches during the War', *The Banker'*, lix (August 1941).

Einzig, P., 'Internal and International Banking', *The Banker*, xxviii (1933).

Einzig, P., 'The Jews in International Banking', *The Banker*, xxviii (October 1933).

Einzig, P., *The Fight for Financial Supremacy* (London: Macmillan & Co., 1931).

Einzig, P., *Why London Must Remain the World's Banking Centre* (London: Aims for Industry, 1964).

Elbaum, B. and Lazonick, W., 'An Institutional Perspective on British Decline', in Elbaum, B. and Lazonick, W. (eds.), *The Decline of the British Economy* (Oxford: 1986).

Elbaum, B. and Lazonick, W., 'The Decline of the British Economy: An Institutional Perspective', *Journal of Economic History*, xliv (1984).

Elliot, G., *The Mystery of Overend Gurney: A Financial Scandal in Victorian London* (London: 2006).

Ellis, A., *Heir to Adventure: The Story of Brown, Shipley and Company, Merchant Bankers, 1810–1960* (London: 1960).

Endelman, T.M., *The Jews in Britain, 1656 to 2000* (Berkeley/Los Angeles: University of California Press, 2002).

Escher, F., *Elements of Foreign Exchange* (New York: 1911).

Escott, T.H.S., *England: Its People, Policy, and Pursuits* (London: 1879).

Essex-Crosby, A., *Joint-Stock Companies in Great Britain, 1890–1930*, University of London M.Com. (1938).

Evitt, H.E., 'Exchange Dealings Under Current Conditions', *Journal of the Institute of Bankers*, 52 (1931).

Feldman, D., 'The Importance of Being English: Jewish Immigration and the Decay of Liberal England', in D. Feldman and G. Stedman Jones (eds.), *Metropolis London: Histories and Representations since 1800* (London: Routledge, 1989).

Fenn, C., *A Compendium of the English and Foreign Funds and Principal Joint-stock Companies* (London: 1838).

Ferguson, N., *High Financier: The Lives and Time of Siegmund Warburg* (London: Penguin, 2010).

Ferguson, N., *The Cash Nexus: Money and Power in the Modern World, 1700–2000* (London: 2001).

Ferguson, N., *World's Banker. The History of the House of Rothschild* (London: 1998).

Fforde, J., *The Bank of England and Public Policy, 1941–1958* (Cambridge: 1992).

Field, F.W., 'How Canadian Stocks are Held', *Monetary Times Annual*, 53, January 1915.

Field, F.W., *Capital Investments in Canada* (Toronto: 1911).

Financial Facilities for Trade: Report 1st July 1916, Cd 8346.

Financial News, The City, 1884–1934 (London: 1934).

Financial Review of Reviews 1905–1914.

Financial Times 1971–2022.

Financial Times, Investor's Guide (London: 1913).

Findlay, J.A., *The Baltic Exchange* (London: 1927).

Fishman, J.J., *The Transformation of Threadneedle Street: The Deregulation and Re-regulation of Britain's Financial Services* (Durham, NC: 1993).

Fithian, E.W., 'The Beneficial Effect of International Investment on British Trade', *The Financial Review of Reviews*, 5, February 1909.

Floud, R. and McCloskey, D. (eds), *The Cambridge Economic History of Britain since 1700: Vol. 2: 1860–1939*, 2nd ed. (Cambridge: Cambridge University Press, 1994).

Floud, R., Humphries, J. and Johnson, P. (eds.), *The Cambridge Economic History of Modern Britain: Vol. 2, Growth and Decline, 1870 to the Present* (Cambridge: Cambridge University Press, 2014).

Ford, A.G., *The Gold Standard, 1880–1914: Britain and Argentina* (Oxford: 1962).

Foster, A.R., 'Cotton Spinning Companies as Investments', *The Financial Review of Reviews*, 3, February 1907.

Frankel, S.H., *Investment and the Return to Equity Capital in the South African Mining Industry, 1887–1965* (Oxford: Blackwell, 1967).

Franklin, J., *The Gentleman's Country House and Its Plan, 1835–1914* (London: 1981).

Fraser, S., *Everyman a Speculator: A History of Wall Street in American Life* (New York: Harper Collins Publishers, 2005).

Fraser, T.W.L., 'Issuing Houses and the Raising of Long-term Capital in London', in *The Pattern and Finance of Foreign Trade, with Special Reference to the City of London* (London: Institute of Bankers, 1949).

Fraser, W.L., *All to the Good* (London: 1963).

Freeman, M., Pearson, R. and Taylor, J., 'A Doe in the City: Women Shareholders and Early Nineteenth Century Britain', *Accounting, Business and Financial History*, 16 (2006).

French, D., *British Economic and Strategic Planning, 1905–1915* (London: 1992).

French, W., *Port of London: Handbook of Rates, Charges and General Information* (London: 1937).

Freshfields Bruckhaus Deringer, 'The Legal Impact of Brexit on the UK-based Financial Services Sector', report for The City UK (London: Financial Times, 9th May 2017).

Frith, W.P., *My Autobiography and Reminiscences* (London: 1888).

Fuchs, C.J., *The Trade Policy of Great Britain and Her Colonies since 1860* (London: 1905).

Fun

Gairdner, C., *The Constitution and Course of the Money Market* (Glasgow: 1888).

Gamble, A., *Britain in Decline: Economic Policy, Political Strategy and the British State* (London: 1981).

Garrard, J.A., *The English and Immigration, 1880–1910* (Oxford: 1971).

Gartner, L.P., 'Notes on the Statistics of Jewish Immigration to England 1870–1914', *Jewish Social Studies*, 22 (1960).

Gayer, A.D., Rostow, W.W. and Schwartz, A.J., *The Growth and Fluctuations of the British Economy, 1790–1850* (Oxford: Clarendon Press, 1953).

Geisst, C.R., *Wall Street: A History*, updated ed. (Oxford: Oxford University Press, 2012).

Gibbon, J.M., *The Scot in Canada: A Run through the Dominion* (Aberdeen: 1907).

Gibson, A.H., *The Fall in Consols and Other Investments since 1897* (London: 1908).

Giffen, R., *Stock Exchange Securities* (London: 1877).

Giffen, R., *The Growth of Capital* (London: 1889).

Gilbert, J.C., *A History of Investment Trusts in Dundee, 1873–1938* (London: 1939).

Gleeson, A., *People and Their Money: 50 Years of Private Investment* (London: 1981).

Godley, A., *Jewish Immigrant Entrepreneurship in New York and London, 1880–1914: Enterprise and Culture* (Basingstoke: Palgrave, 2001).

Goldman, C.S., *South African Mines: Their Position, Results, and Development, Together with an Account of Diamond, Land, Finance, and Kindred Concerns* (London: 1895–1896).

Goldsmith, R.W., *Comparative National Balance Sheets: A Study of Twenty Countries, 1688–1978* (Chicago: 1978).

Good, T., 'Some Shareholding Hazards', *Financial Review of Reviews*, 9, October 1913.

Goodhart, D. and Grant, C., *Making the City Work* (London: Fabian Trust, 1988).

Gordon, S., 'Making Sense of the City', *Financial Times*, 9th March 2019.

Gourvish, T.R. and Reed, M.C., 'The Financing of Scottish Railways before 1860: A Comment', *Scottish Journal of Political Economy*, 28 (1971).

Graham, W., *The One Pound Note in the History of Banking in Great Britain* (Edinburgh: 1911).

Grant, A.T.K., *A Study of the Capital Market in Post-War Britain* (London: 1937).

Green, D.R., *From Artisans to Paupers: Economic Change and Poverty in London, 1790–1870* (Aldershot: 1995).

Green, D.R. and Owens, A., 'Gentlewomanly Capitalism? Spinsters, Widows, and Wealth Holding in England and Wales, c. 1800–1860', *Economic History Review*, lvi (2003).

Green, D.R., Owens, A., Maltby, J. and Rutterford, J., 'Lives in the Balance: Gender, Age and Assets in Late Nineteenth Century England and Wales', *Continuity and Change*, 24 (2009).

Green, E., 'Export Bankers: The Migration of British Bank Personnel to the Pacific Region, 1850–1914', in O. Checkland, S. Nishimura and N. Tamaki (eds), *Pacific Banking, 1859–1959: East Meets West* (London: 1994).

Greenhill, R., 'Merchants and the Latin American Trades: An Introduction', in D.C.M. Platt (ed.), *Business Imperialism, 1840–1930* (Oxford: 1977).

Grossman, R.S., *Unsettled Account: The Evolution of Banking in the Industrialized World Since 1800* (Princeton: Princeton University Press, 2010).

H.M. Treasury, *The Location of Financial Activity and the Euro* (London: 2003).

H.M. Treasury, *UK International Financial Services: The Future* (London: 2009).

H.M., *On the Analogy between the Stock Exchange and the Turf* (London: 1885).

Habakkuk, H.J., 'Fluctuations and Growth in the 19th Century', in M. Kooy (ed.), *Studies in Economics and Economic History* (London: 1972).

Hadden, T., *Company Law and Capitalism* (London: 1972).

Hall, A.R., 'A Note on the English Capital Market as a Source of Funds for Home Investment Before 1914', *Economica* n.s. xxiv (1957).

Hall, A.R., 'The English Capital Market Before 1914: A Reply', *Economica* n.s. xxv (1958).

Hall, A.R., *The London Capital Market and Australia, 1870–1914* (Canberra: 1963).

Hall, P., *Cities in Civilization: Culture, Innovation, and Urban Order* (London: Weidenfeld and Nicholson, 1998).

Hall, P.A., *Governing the Economy: The Politics of State Intervention in Britain and France* (Cambridge: 1986).

Hamilton, A., *The Financial Services Revolution: The Big Bang Worldwide* (London: 1986).

Hammond, R.J., 'British Food Supplies, 1914–1939', *Economic History Review*, 16 (1946).

Hannah, L., 'Mergers in British Manufacturing Industry, 1880–1918', *Oxford Economic Papers*, 26 (1974).

Hannah, L., 'The Moral Economy of Business: A Historical Perspective on Ethics and Efficiency', in P. Burke, B. Harrison and P. Slack (eds.), *Civil Histories* (Oxford: 2000).

Harley, C.K., 'Goschen's Conversion of the National Debt and the Yield on Consols', *Economic History Review*, 29 (1976).

Harley, P., *My Life in Shipping, 1881–1938* (London: 1938).

Harris, J. and Thane, P., 'British and European Bankers, 1880–1914: An Aristocratic Bourgeoisie?' in P. Thane, G. Crossick and R. Floud (eds.), *The Power of the Past* (Cambridge: 1984).

Harris, L., Coakley, J., Croasdale, M. and Evans, T., *New Perspectives on the Financial System* (London: 1988).

Harrison, A.E., *Growth, Entrepreneurship and Capital Formation in the United Kingdom's Cycle and Related Industries, 1870–1914*, University of York Ph.D. (1977).

Harvie, C., 'Boom, Bust and Scribble', *Times Higher Education Supplement*, 29 January 1988.

Hatch, F.H. and Chalmers, J.A., *The Gold Mines of the Rand: A Description of the Mining Industry of Witwatersrand, South African Republic* (London: 1895).

Hawke, G.R. and Reed, M.C., 'Railway Capital in the United Kingdom in the Nineteenth Century', *Economic History Review*, 22 (1969).

Haxey, S., *Tory MP* (London: Victor Gollancz (Left Book Club), 1939).

Hayes Fisher, W., *Investing at Its Best and Safeguarding Invested Capital* (London: 1912).

Hein, L.W. *The British Companies Acts and the Practice of Accountancy, 1844–1962* (New York: 1978).

Heinemann, K., 'Investment, Speculation and Popular Stock Market Engagement in 20th-Century Britain', *Archiv für Sozialgeschichte*, 56 (2016).

Heinemann, K., *Popular Investment and Speculation in Britain, 1918–1987*, University of Cambridge Ph.D. (2017).

Henderson, R.F., *The New Issue Market and the Finance of Industry* (Cambridge: 1951).

Hickman, W. and Aubrey, S., *Stock Exchange Investments: Their History, Practice, and Results* (London: 1897).

Hidy, R.W., *House of Baring in American Trade and Finance, 1763–1861* (New York: Russell and Company, 1949).

Hirst, F.W., *British Capital at Home and Abroad: An Examination of Recent Statements as to Exports of Capital Abroad* (London: 1910).

Hirst, F.W., *The Six Panics and Other Essays* (London: 1913).

Hirst, F.W., *Wall Street and Lombard Street: The Stock Exchange Slump of 1929 and the Trade Depression of 1930* (New York: 1931).

Hobson, C.K., *The Export of Capital* (London: 1914).

Hobson, J.A., 'Do Foreign Investments Benefit the Working Classes?' *The Financial Review of Reviews* 5 (March 1909).

Hobson, J.A., 'Foreign Investments and Home Employment', *Financial Review of Reviews* 6 (October 1910).

Hobson, J.A., *Imperialism: A Study* (London: 1902).

Hobson, J.A., *The Economic Interpretation of Investment* (London: 1911).

Hobson, J.A., *The Evolution of Modern Capitalism* (1926 ed.).

Hobson, J.A., *The War in South Africa: Its Causes and Effects* (London: 1900).

Hobson, O.R., 'The Stock Exchange and the Public', *The Banker* xlii (July 1947).

Hobson, O.R., *How the City Works* (London: 1940).

Hoffman, R.J.S., *Great Britain and the German Trade Rivalry, 1875–1914* (Philadelphia: 1937).

Holden, C.H. and Holford, W.G., *The City of London: A Record of Destruction and Survival* (London: 1951).

Holden, W.C., *The Espuela Land and Cattle Company* (Austin, Texas: 1970).

Hollow, M., Akinbami. F. and Michie, R.C. (eds.), *Critical Perspectives on the Evolution of American and British Banking* (Cheltenham: Edward Elgar, 2015).

Hollow, M., *Rogue Banking: A History of Financial Fraud in Inter-War Britain* (Basingstoke: Palgrave Macmillan, 2015).

Holmes, C., *Anti-Semitism in British Society, 1876–1939* (New York: 1979).

Homer, S., *A History of Interest Rates* (New Brunswick: Rutgers University Press, 1963).

Hooker, A., *The International Grain Trade* (London: 1936).

Hooper, W.E., *The Motor Car in the First Decade of the Twentieth Century* (London: 1908).

Hughes, J., *The Vital Few: American Economic Progress and Its Protagonists* (New York: Houghton Mifflin, 1966).

Hunt, B.C., *The Development of the Business Corporation in England, 1800–1867* (Cambridge, MA: 1936).

Hunt, W., *Heirs of Great Adventure: A History of Balfour, Williamson and Company Limited* (London: 1951, revised 1960).

Hutton, W., *The State We're In* (London: 1995).

Hyamson, A.M. and Silberman, A.M. (eds.), *Valentine's Jewish Encyclopaedia* (London: 1938).

Hyndman, H.M., *Commercial Crises of the Nineteenth Century* (London: 1892).

IFSL Research, *International Financial Markets in the UK* (London: 2009).

Illustrated London News 1843–1914.

Ingham, G., *Capitalism Divided? The City and Industry in British Social Development* (London: 1984).

Innes, J., 'Managing the Metropolis: London's Social Problems and Their Control, c. 1660–1830', in P. Clarke and R. Gillespie (eds.), *Two Capitals: London and Dublin 1500–1840* (Oxford: Oxford University Press, 2001).

Inouye, J., *Problems of the Japanese Exchange, 1914–1926* (London: 1931).

Inter-Bank Research Organisation, *The Future of London as an International Financial Centre* (London: 1973).

Inverness Journal and Northern Advertiser 1822–5.

Investor's Monthly Manual 1880–1914.

Irving, R.J., *The North Eastern Railway Company, 1870–1914: An Economic History* (Leicester: 1976).

Jackson, F.H. (ed.), *Lectures on British Commerce, Including Finance, Insurance, Business and Industry* (London: 1912).

Jackson, W.T., *The Enterprising Scot: Investors in the American West After 1873* (Edinburgh: 1968).

Jacobs, J., 'The Stock Exchange', in *Jewish Encyclopaedia* (New York: Funk & Wagnalls, 1901–6).

Jacobs, J., *Jewish Contributions to Civilization: An Estimate* (Philadelphia: 1919).

Jacobs, J., *Jewish Ideals and Other Essays* (London: 1896).

Jacobs, J., *Studies in Jewish Statistics: Social, Vital and Anthropometric* (London: 1891).

James, H., *The Making of a Modern Central Bank, The Bank of England 1979–2003* (Cambridge: Cambridge University Press, 2020).

Jamieson, G., 'Chinese Investments and Finance', *Financial Review of Reviews*, 2 (December 1906).

Jamieson, G.A., 'On Some of the Causes and Effects of the Fall in the Rate of Interest', *Accountants' Magazine*, 1 (1897).

Japhet, S., *Recollections from My Business Life* (London: Privately printed, 1931).

Jarvie, J.G., 'Finance for Small Industries', *The Banker*, xxxii (November 1934).

Jarvie, J.R., *The Old Lady Unveiled: A Criticism and an Explanation of the Bank of England* (London: 1933).

Jefferys, J.B., 'The Denomination and Character of Shares, 1855–1885', *Economic History Review*, xvi (1946).

Jefferys, J.B., *Retail Trading in Britain, 1850–1950* (Cambridge: 1954).

Jefferys, J.B., *Trends in Business Organisation in Great Britain since 1856, with Special Reference to the Financial Structure of Companies, the Mechanism of Investment and the Relations between the Shareholder and the Company*, University of London Ph.D. (1938).

Jenkins, A., *The Stock Exchange Story* (London: 1973).

Jenkins, P., 'Brexit Can Mean London Loses Even if the EU Doesn't Gain', *Financial Times*, 11th January 2021.

Jenks, L.H., The Migration of British Capital to 1875 (New York: 1927).

Johnson, P., 'Civilizing Mammon: Laws, Morals and the City in Nineteenth Century England', in P. Burke, B. Harrison and P. Slack (eds.), *Civil Histories* (Oxford: 2000).

Johnson, P., *Making the Market: Victorian Origins of Corporate Capitalism* (Cambridge: 2010).

Johnson, T., *The Financiers and the Nation* (London: 1934).

Johnston, J. and Murphy, G.W., 'The Growth of Life Assurance in UK since 1880', *Economic and Social Studies*, 25 (1957).

Jones, C.A., *British Financial Institutions in Argentina, 1860–1914*, University of Cambridge Ph.D. (1973).

Jones, C.A., *International Business in the Nineteenth Century: The Rise and Fall of a Cosmopolitan Bourgeoisie* (Brighton: 1987).

Jones, H. and Sayers, H.J., *The Story of Czarnikow* (London: 1963).

Jones, I.F., *The Rise of a Merchant Bank: A Short History of Guinness Mahon* (Dublin: 1974).

Jones, S. (ed.), *Banking and Business in South Africa* (New York: 1988).

Jonker, J. and van Zanden, J.L., *A History of Royal Dutch Shell: From Challenger to Joint Industry Leader, 1890–1939* (Oxford: 2007).

Joseph, L., 'Industrial Finance: A Comparison between Home and Foreign Developments', a Paper Delivered to the National Electric Manufacturers' Association, Institution of Electrical Engineers, London, 25th April 1911.

Josephson, M., *The Robber Barons: The Great American Capitalists, 1861–1901* (New York: Harcourt Brace, 1934).

Julius, A., *Trials of the Diaspora: A History of Anti-semitism in England* (Oxford: Oxford University Press, 2010).

Karo, M., *City Milestones and Memories* (London: 1962).

Keegan, W. and Pennant-Rea, R., *Who Runs the Economy?* (London: 1979).

Keene, D., 'The Setting of the Royal Exchange: Continuity and Change in the Financial District of the City of London, 1300–1871', in A. Saunders (ed.), *The Royal Exchange* (London: 1997).

Kennedy, P., *Strategy and Diplomacy* (London: 1983).

Kennedy, W.P., 'Foreign Investment, Trade and Growth in the United Kingdom, 1870–1913', *Explorations in Economic History*, 11 (1974).

Kennedy, W.P., *Industrial Structure, Capital Markets and the Origins of British Economic Decline* (Cambridge: Cambridge University Press, 1987).

Kerr, W.G., 'Scottish Investment and Enterprise in Texas', in P.L. Payne (ed.), *Studies in Scottish Business History* (London: 1967).

Kerr, W.G., *Scottish Capital on the American Credit Frontier* (Austin, Texas: Texas State Historical Association, 1976).

Kessler, D., *The Rothschilds and Disraeli in Buckinghamshire* (Waddesdon: Rothschild Waddesdon, 1996).

Kettle, R., *Deloitte and Company, 1845–1956* (Oxford: 1958).

Keynes, J.M., 'The Prospects of Money', *Economic Journal*, 24 (1914).

Keynes, J.M., *The General Theory of Employment, Interest and Money* (London: Macmillan, 1935).

Keyworth, J., 'The Old Lady of Threadneedle Street', *Bank of England Quarterly Review*, 53 (2013).

Kindleberger, C.P. and Aliber, R.Z., *Manias, Panics, and Crashes: A History of Financial Crises* (London: Palgrave, 2011).

Kinross, J., *Fifty Years in the City: Financing Small Business* (London: 1982).

Kirkaldy, A.W., *British Finance During and After the War, 1914–21* (London: 1921).

Knowles, F.C., *Monetary Crisis Considered* (London: 1837).

Kubicek, R.V., 'The Randlords of 1895: A Reassessment', *Journal of British Studies*, 11 (1972).

Kubicek, R.V., *Economic Imperialism in Theory and Practice* (Durham, NC: Duke University Press, 1979).

Kushner, A.J., *British Anti-Semitism in the Second World War*, Sheffield University Ph.D. (1986).

Kynaston, D., *The City of London*, 4 Vols. (London: 1994–2001).

Labour Party, *The City: A Socialist Approach: Report of the Labour Party Financial Institutions Study Group* (London: 1982).

Laing, S., *The Great City Frauds of Cole, Davidson and Gordon* (London: 1856).

Lambert, R., 'Charlatans: Financial Scandals of the 20th Century', *Financial Times*, 1st January 2000.

Lambourne, L., *Victorian Painting* (London: 1999).

Landells, W., 'The London Stock Exchange', *Quarterly Review* (1912).

Larkworthy, F., *Ninety-One Years* (London: Mills and Boon, 1924).

Lavington, F., *The English Capital Market* (London: 1921).

Lawson, W.R., 'The Rubber Madness in the City: The Gamble in Shares', *The Financial Review of Reviews*, 6 (June 1910).

Lawson, W.R., *The Scottish Investors' Manual* (Edinburgh: 1884).

Lee, C.H., *British Regional Employment Statistics, 1841–1971* (Cambridge: 1979).

Lee, T.A., 'Bankrupt Accountants and Lawyers: Transition in the Rise of Professionalism in Victorian Scotland', *Accounting, Auditing and Accountability Journal*, 24 (2011).

Leighton-Boyce, J.A.S., *Smiths the Bankers, 1658–1958* (London: 1958).

Lenfant, J.H., *British Capital Export, 1900–1913*, University of London Ph.D. (1949).

Lenman, B. and Donaldson, K., 'Partners' Incomes, Investment and Diversification in the Scottish Linen Area, 1880–1921', *Business History*, 13 (1971).

Lentin, A., *Banker, Traitor, Scapegoat, Spy? The Troublesome Case of Sir Edgar Speyer* (London: Hans Publishing Ltd, 2013).

Lepler, J., '"There Is No Need for Anyone to Go to America": Commercial Correspondence and Nineteenth-Century Globalisation', *The Rothschild Archive: Review of the Year 2007/8*.

Leslie, A., *Mr Frewen of England: A Victorian Adventurer* (London: 1966).

Lettenberg, J., Stashower, D. and Foley, C., *Arthur Conan Doyle: A Life in Letters* (London: Harper Press, 2007).

Levi, L., 'Joint-stock Companies', *Journal of the Royal Statistical Society*, xxxiii (1870).

Lewis, C., 'British Railway Companies and the Argentine Government', in D.C.M. Platt (ed.), *Business Imperialism, 1840–1930* (Oxford: 1977).

Leyshon, A. and Thrift, N., *Money/Space: Geographies of Monetary Transformation* (London: 1997).

Lipman, V.D., 'The Victorian Jewish Background', in A. and R. Cowen (eds.), *Victorian Jews through British Eyes* (Oxford: 1986).

Lisle-Williams, M., '"Beyond the Market", The Survival of Family Capitalism in the English Merchant Banks', *British Journal of Sociology*, 35 (1984).

Lisle-Williams, M., 'Merchant Banking Dynasties in the English Class Structure: Ownership, Solidarity and Kinship in the City of London, 1850–1960', *British Journal of Sociology*, 35 (1984).

Lloyd George, D., *War Memoirs* (London: Odhams Press, 1933).

Lloyd, J., *Rolls-Royce: The Growth of a Firm* (London: 1978).

Lobban, M., '*Erlanger v. The New Sombrero Phosphate Company* (1878)', in C. Mitchell and P. Mitchell (eds.), *Landmark Cases in the Law of Restitution* (London: Hart Publishing, 2006).

Lobban, M., 'Nineteenth Century Frauds in Company Formation: *Derry v. Peek* in Context', *Law Quarterly Review*, 111 (1996).

Loftie, W.J., *London City: Its History, Streets, Traffic, Buildings, People* (London: 1891).

London Stock Exchange: Annual Report 1976–1992.

London Stock Exchange Commission: *Report of the Commissioners and Minutes of Evidence* (London: HMSO, 1878).

London Stock Exchange: Committee of Trustees and Mangers, Minutes 1914–1939.

London Stock Exchange: Sub-Committee on the Limitation of Members: Report 6th May 1904.

Longstreth, F., 'The City, Industry and the State', in C. Crouch (ed.), *State and Economy in Contemporary Capitalism* (London: 1979).

Lorimer, J.C., 'Accountants in Their Relation to Public Companies', *Accountants' Magazine*, 3 (1899).

Low, R., *The History of the British Film, 1906–1914* (London: 1949).

Lowenfeld, H., 'How to Select Investments', *The Financial Review of Reviews*, 3 (March 1907).

Lowenfeld, H., 'Investment Crazes', *The Financial Review of Reviews*, 2 (March 1906).

Lowenfeld, H., 'The Investor's Mind', *The Financial Review of Reviews*, 3 (November 1907).

Lowenfeld, H., 'The Money Market Article and the Private Investor', *The Financial Review of Reviews*, 3 (February 1907).

Lowenfeld, H., 'Shares as Investments', *The Financial Review of Reviews*, 7 (February 1911).

Lowenfeld, H., *All About Investment* (London: 1909).

Macauley, T.B. (Lord Macauley), *The History of England* (London: 1848).

MacGregor, D.H., 'Joint-Stock Companies and the Risk Factor', *Economic Journal*, xxxix (1929).

Mackenzie, J., 'Ship Owning by Shares and by Single Ship Limited Companies', *Accountants' Magazine*, 2 (1898).

Mackinnon, L., *Recollections of an Old Lawyer* (Aberdeen: 1935).

Macrae, N., *The London Capital Market: Its Structure, Strains and Management* (London: 1955).

Maddison, E.C., *On the Stock Exchange* (London: 1877).

Magee, G.B. and Thompson, A.S., *Empire and Globalisation: Networks of People, Goods and Capital in the British World, c. 1850–1914* (Cambridge: Cambridge University Press, 2010).

Malenbaum, W., *The World Wheat Economy, 1885–1939* (Cambridge, MA: 1953).

Mallock, W.H., *The Nation as a Business Firm: An Attempt to Cut a Path through Jungle* (London: 1910).

Maltby, J., 'A Sort of Guide, Philosopher and Friend: The Rise of the Professional Auditor in Britain', *Accounting, Business and Financial History*, 9 (1999).

Maltby, J. and Rutterford, J., 'She Possessed Her Own Fortune: Women Investors from the Late 19th Century to the Early 20th Century', *Business History*, 48 (2006).

Manley, P.S., 'Clarence Hatry', *Abacus: A Journal of Accounting and Business Studies*, 12 (1976).

Manley, P.S., 'Gerard Lee Bevan and the City Equitable Companies', *Abacus: A Journal of Accounting and Business Studies*, 9 (1973).

Marchildon, G.P., *Promotion, Finance and Mergers in Canadian Manufacturing Industry, 1885–1918*, London School of Economics Ph.D. (1990).

Marsh, N., *Money, Speculation and Finance in Contemporary British Fiction* (London: 2007).

Marshall, A., *Industry and Trade* (London: 1919).

Marshall, C.H., 'Dundee as a Centre of Investment', in British Association, Handbook of the Dundee Meeting (1912).

Martin, P.F., 'How Latin Americans Invest Their Money', *Financial Review of Reviews*, 7 (August 1911).

Martin, P.F., 'Local Investments in British India', *Financial Review of Reviews*, 4 (July 1908).

Martin, P.F., 'Mexico as a Field for Investment', *Financial Review of Reviews*, 5 (August 1909).

Martins, S.W., *A Great Estate at Work: The Holkham Estate and Its Inhabitants in the 19th Century* (Cambridge: 1980).

Marwick, W.H., 'Scottish Overseas Investment in the 19th Century', *The Scottish Bankers Magazine*, XXVII (1935/6).

Mason, M.M., 'Dangers of Colliery Shares', *Financial Review of Reviews*, 9 (November 1913).

Matthews, D., *A History of Auditing: The Changing Audit Process in Britain from the 19th Century to the Present Day* (London: 2006).

Matthews, R.C.O., Feinstein, C. and Odling-Smee, J., *British Economic Growth 1856–1973: The Post-War Period in Historical Perspective* (Oxford: Oxford University Press, 1982).

Matthias, P., *Retailing Revolution* (London: 1967).

Maude, W., *Anthony Gibbs & Sons, Merchants and Bankers, 1808–1958* (London: 1958).

Maughan, C., *Markets of London* (London: 1931).

May, H., 'The London Stock Exchange', *Fortnightly Review*, 37 (1885).

McCullough, T.R., *Dictionary of Commerce* (London: 1832).

McKie, D., 'The Fall of a Midas', *The Guardian*, 2nd February 2004.

McKie, D., *Jabez: The Rise and Fall of a Victorian Rogue* (London: 2004).

McLaren, C., 'Prospects for Iron and Steel Investments', *Financial Review of Reviews*, 2 (October 1906).

Meredith, H., *The Drama of Money-Making: Tragedy and Comedy on the London Stock Exchange* (London: 1931).

Mewburn, F., *The Larchfield Diary: Extracts from the Diary of the Late Mr Mewburn, First Railway Solicitor* (London: 1876).

Mikkelsen, A.L., *The Market Practice and Techniques of London Issuing Houses in Connection with Sovereign Bond Issues and Their Role in Facilitating Access to Sovereign Borrowers to the London Capital Market, 1870–1914*, Kings College, London Ph.D. (2014).

Mitchell, B.R., *British Historical Statistics* (Cambridge: 1989).

Mitchell, J., *Reminiscences of My Life in the Highlands* (London: 1883).

Mitchell, W., *Our Scotch Banks* (Edinburgh: 1879).

Moffat, A., *Scottish Railways: Their Present and Future Value Considered as an Investment for Capital* (Edinburgh: 1849).

Money Trust Investigation: Investigation of financial and monetary conditions in the United States under House Resolutions numbers 429 and 405 before the subcommittee of the Committee on Banking and Currency, Washington (1912).

Monteon, M., 'John T. North, The Nitrate King, and Chile's Lost Future', in R.E. Dumett (ed.), *Mining Tycoons in the Age of Empire, 1870–1945: Entrepreneurship, High Finance, Politics and Territorial Expansion* (Farnham: 2009).

Moran, M., 'City Pressure: The City of London as a Pressure Group since 1945', *Contemporary Record*, 2 (Summer 1988).

Moran, M., 'Finance Capital and Pressure-Group Politics in Britain', *British Journal of Political Science*, 11 (1981).

Moran, M., *The Politics of Banking: The Strange Case of Competition and Credit Control* (London: 1984).

Moran, M., *The Politics of the Financial Services Revolution: The USA, UK and Japan* (London: 1991).

Morgan, E.V. and Thomas, W.A., *The Stock Exchange: Its History and Functions* (London: 1962).

Morgan, E.V., Yamey, B.S., Brealey, R.A. and Bareau, G.P., *City Lights: Essays on Financial Institutions and Markets in the City of London* (London: Institute of Economic Affairs, 1979).

Morier Evans, D., *City Men and City Manners: The City or the Physiology of London Business* (London: Groombridge and Sons, 1852).

Morier Evans, D., *Facts, Failures and Frauds* (London: 1859).

Morier Evans, D., *Speculative Notes, and Notes on Speculations, Ideal and Real* (London: 1864).

Morier Evans, D., *The Commercial Crisis of 1847* (London: 1848).

Morier Evans, D., *The History of the Commercial Crisis, 1857–8* (London: 1859).

Morris, C.K., *Canada: For British Gold and British Enterprise* (London: 1910).

Morris, R.J., 'The Middle Class and the Property Cycle during the Industrial Revolution', in T.C. Smout (ed.), *The Search for Wealth and Stability* (London: 1979).

Morrison, T., *The Economic Transition in India* (London: 1911).

Mortimer, T., *Every Man His Own Broker* (London: 1761).

Mothershead, H.R., *The Swan Land and Cattle Company Limited* (Norman, Oklahoma: 1971).

Mouat, J., 'Whitaker Wright, Speculative Finance, and the London Mining Boom of the 1890s', in R.E. Dumett (ed.), *Mining Tycoons in the Age of Empire, 1870–1945: Entrepreneurship, High Finance, Politics and Territorial Expansion* (Farnham: 2009).

Moyle, J., *The Pattern of Ordinary Share Ownership, 1957–1970* (Cambridge: 1971).

Mulhall, M.G., *Industries and Wealth of Nations* (London: 1896).

Mulhall, M.G., *The English in South America* (Buenos Ayres: 1878).

Murray, A.J., *Home from the Hill: A Biography of Frederick Huth, Napoleon of the City* (London: 1970).

Myers, G., *History of the Great American Fortunes* (New York: The Modern Library, 1909, 1936).

Napier, T.B., 'The History of Joint-Stock and Limited Liability Companies', in *A Century of Law Reform* (London: 1901).

Nash, R.L., *A Short Inquiry into the Profitable Nature of Our Investments*, 3rd ed. (London: 1881).

Nash, R.L., *Money Market Events* (London: Effingham Wilson, 1869).

Nash, R.L., *The Australasian Joint-Stock Companies Year Book* (Sydney: 1900).

Newbury, C., 'Cecil Rhodes, de Beers and Mining Finance in South Africa: The Business of Entrepreneurship and Imperialism', in R.E. Dumett (ed.), *Mining Tycoons in the Age of Empire, 1870–1945: Entrepreneurship, High Finance, Politics and Territorial Expansion* (Farnham: 2009).

Newbury, C., *The Diamond Ring: Business, Politics and Precious Stones in South Africa, 1867–1947* (Oxford: Oxford University Press, 1989).

Newton, G., *A Peer Without Equal: Memoirs of an Editor* (London: 1997).

Newton, S. and Porter, D., *Modernization Frustrated: The Politics of Industrial Decline in Britain since 1900* (London: 1988).

Newton, L. and Cottrell, P., 'Female Investors in the First English and Welsh Commercial Joint-Stock Banks', *Accounting, Business and Financial History*, 16 (2006).

Nicholas, T., 'Enterprise and Management', in R. Floud, J. Humphries and P. Johnson (eds.), *The Cambridge Economic History of Modern Britain: Vol. 2, Growth and Decline, 1870 to the Present* (Cambridge: Cambridge University Press, 2014).

Nicholls, E., *Crime Within the Square Mile: The History of Crime in the City of London* (London: 1935).

Nicholson, S., *A Victorian Household* (London: 1988).

Nicholson, S., *An Edwardian Bachelor: Roy Sambourne, 1878–1946* (London: 1999).

Noakes, A., *William Frith: Extraordinary Victorian Painter* (London: 1978).

Norton, G., *Commentaries on the History, Constitution and Chartered Franchises of the City of London* (London: 1828).

Norton, Trist and Gilbert, 'A Century of Land Values: England and Wales', *The Times*, 20th April 1889.

Nye, J.G.D., *The Company Promoter in London, 1877–1914*, Kings College London Ph.D. (2011).

O'Brien, D.P. (ed.), *The Correspondence of Lord Overstone* (Cambridge: 1971).

O'Brien, R., *Global Financial Integration: The End of Geography* (London: 1992).

O'Hagan, H.O., *Leaves from My Life* (London: John Lane, The Bodley Head, 1929).

O'Sullivan, B., *From Crisis to Crisis: The Transformation of Merchant Banking, 1914–1939* (London: Palgrave Macmillan, 2018).

Offer, A., *Property and Politics 1870–1914: Landownership, Law, Ideology and Urban Development in England* (Oxford: Oxford University Press, 1981).

Olsson, U., *Furthering a Fortune: Marcus Wallenberg, Swedish Banker and Industrialist, 1899–1982* (Stockholm: Ekerlids Forlag, 2001).

Omnium, G., *A Handy Guide to Safe Investments* (London: 1858).

Orbell, J., *Baring Brothers & Co: A History to 1939* (London: 1985).

Paish, F.W., 'The London New Issue Market', *Economica* n.s. xviii (1951).

Paish, F.W., *Business Finance* (London: 1961).

Paish, F.W., *Long-Term and Short-Term Interest Rates in the United Kingdom* (Manchester: 1966).

Paish, G., 'Great Britain's Capital Investments in Individual Colonial and Foreign Countries', *Journal of the Royal Statistical Society*, lxxiv (1911).

Paish, G., 'Great Britain's Capital Investments in Other Lands', *Journal of the Royal Statistical Society*, lxxii (1909).

Paish, G., 'The Export of Capital and the Cost of Living', *The Statist*, 14th February 1914.

Paish, W., *Business Finance* (London: 1961).

Pak, S., *Gentleman Bankers: The World of J.P. Morgan* (Cambridge, MA: Harvard University Press, 2013).

Parker, R.H., 'Regulating British Corporate Financial Reporting in the Late Nineteenth Century', *Accounting, Business and Financial History*, 1 (1990).

Parkes, J., 'The History of the Anglo-Jewish Community', in M. Freedman (ed.), *A Minority in Britain: Social Studies of the Anglo-Jewish Community* (London: 1955).

Parliamentary History and Review — Reports of the proceedings of the two houses of Parliament during the session of 1825 (London: 1826).

Paulet, H.W., *Statesmen, Financiers and Felons* (n.p.: 1934).

Paxman, J., *Friends in High Places: Who Runs Britain?* (London: 1990).

Payne, P.L., 'The Early Scottish Limited Companies, 1856–1895: An Historical and Analytical Survey', *California Institute of Technology Working Paper*, 222 (1977).

Pearce, W.M., *The Matador Land and Cattle Company* (Norman, OK: 1964).

Peden, G.C., *The Treasury and British Public Policy, 1906–1959* (Oxford: Oxford University Press, 2000).

Perren, R., *The Meat Trade in Britain, 1840–1914* (London: 1978).

Perry, S.E., 'The History of Companies' Legislation in England in Its Practical Aspect, and Its Effect upon Our Industrial and Banking Development', *Journal of the Institute of Bankers*, 29 (1908).

Peters, H.E., *The Foreign Debt of the Argentine Republic* (Baltimore, MD: 1934).

Phillips, H., *Phillips' Investors Manual* (London: 1887).

Phimister, I., 'Corners and Company-Mongering: Nigerian Tin and the City of London, 1909–12', *Journal of Imperial and Commonwealth History*, 28 (2000).

Pickford, J., "London" in 'Big Hubs Keep the Wheels of Industry Turning', *Financial Times*, 9th May 2009.

Pike, J.R., *Britain's Metal Mines: A Complete Guide to the Laws, Usages, Localities and Statistics* (London: 1864).

Platt, D.C.M., *Latin America and British Trade, 1806–1914* (London: 1972).

Playford, F., *Practical Hints for Investing Money: With an Explanation of the Mode of Transacting Business on the Stock Exchange* (London: 1856 and 1865).

Pohl, M. and Burk, K., *Deutsche Bank in London, 1873–1998* (Munich: 1998).

Poley, A.P. and Gould, F.H., *The History, Law, and Practice of the Stock Exchange* (London: 1911).

Political and Economic Planning, *Report on the Location of Industry* (London: 1939).

Pollard, A. (ed.), *The Representation of Business in English Literature* (London: 2000).

Pollard, S., *Britain's Prime and Britain's Decline: British Economy, 1870–1914* (London: Edward Arnold, 1989).

Pollard, S., *The Development of the British Economy, 1914–1990*, 4th ed. (London: Edward Arnold, 1992).

Pollard, S., *The Wasting of the British Economy; British Economic Policy 1945 to the Present* (London: 1982).

Pollins, H., 'The Marketing of Railway Shares in the First Half of the 19th Century', *Economic History Review*, 8 (1954–5).

Pollins, H., *Economic History of the Jews in England* (London: 1982).

Porter, M.E. and Ketels, C.H.M., *UK Competitiveness: Moving to the Next Stage*, DTI Economic Paper No. 3 (May 2003).

Powell, E.T., *The Mechanism of the City* (London: 1910).

Prais, S.J., *The Evolution of Giant Firms in Britain: A Study of the Growth and Concentration in Manufacturing Industry, 1909–1970* (Cambridge: 1976).

Preda, A., 'The Rise of the Popular Investor: Financial Knowledge and Investing in England and France, 1840–1880', *The Sociological Quarterly*, 42 (2001).

Prosser, J., 'The Incorporation of Trading Companies', *Accountants' Magazine*, 2 (1898).

Public Record Office, *Cabinet Papers* 16/18A Report and Proceedings of Imperial Defence Trading with the Enemy Sub-Committee under Lord Desart, Evidence of Huth Jackson, merchant banker, 26 November 1911.

Radice, H., *Britain in the World Economy: National Decline, Capitalist Success?* (London: Routledge, 1989).

Raffalovich, M.A., 'Russia as a Field for Investment', *Financial Review of Reviews*, 8 (August 1912).

Railway Record 1844–5.

Rajan, A., Rajan, L. and van Eupen, P., *Capital People: Skills Strategies for Survival in the Nineties* (London: 1990).

Ramsay MacDonald, J., 'The Export of Capital', *The Financial Review of Reviews*, 5 (April 1909).

Raymond, H., *B.I. Barnato: A Memoir* (London: 1897).

Reader, W.J., *A House in the City: A Study of the City and of the Stock Exchange Based on the Records of Foster and Braithwaite, 1825–1975* (London: 1979).

Reader, W.J., *Imperial Chemical Industries: A History, Vol.1: The Forerunners, 1870–1926* (London: 1970).

Rees, G.L., *Britain's Commodity Markets* (London: 1972).

Rees, G.L., *The History of the London Commodity Markets* (London: 1978).

Reeves, J., *The Rothschilds: The Financial Rulers of Nations* (London: 1887).

Reid, M., 'Mrs Thatcher's Impact on the City', *Contemporary Record*, 2 (1989).

Reid, T.H., 'The Rubber Madness in the City: The Risks and Dangers of Rubber Cultivation', *The Financial Review of Reviews*, 6 (June 1910).

Report of an Enquiry by the Board of Trade into Working Class Rents, Housing and Retail Prices: London and Certain Outer Districts (London: 1908).

Report of Governor Hughes's Committee on Speculation in Securities and Commodities (New York: 7th June 1909).

Report of the Committee Appointed to investigate the Concentration of Control of Money and Credit, US Congressional House Committee, 28th February 1913.

Report of the Company Law Amendment Committee (London: 1918).

Reunert, T., *Diamonds and Gold in South Africa* (London: 1893).

Richards, A., 'Transmission Revamp Will Reshape the Financial World', *Financial Times*, 18th August 2021.

Richards, A.B., *Touche Ross and Company, 1899–1981: The Origins and Growth of the United Kingdom Firm* (London: 1981).

Richardson, P. and van Helten, J.J., 'The Development of the South African Gold-Mining Industry, 1885–1918', *Economic History Review*, 37 (1984).

Rippy, J.F., *British Investments in Latin America, 1822–1949* (Minneapolis: 1959).

Ritchie, A.E., *The Kent Coalfield—Evolution and Development* (London: Iron & Coal Trades Review, 1919).

Robb, G., *White-Collar Crime in Modern England: Financial Fraud and Business Morality, 1845–1929* (Cambridge: 1992).

Roberts, R. (ed.), *Global Financial Centres: London, New York, Tokyo* (Aldershot: Edward Elgar, 1994).

Roberts, R. (ed.), *International Financial Centres: Concepts, Development and Dynamics* (Aldershot: Edward Elgar, 1994).

Roberts, R. (ed.), *Offshore Financial Centres* (Aldershot: Edward Elgar, 1994).

Roberts, R., 'The City of London as a Financial Centre in the Era of Depression, the Second World War and Post-War Official Controls" in A. Gorst, L. Johnman and W.S. Lucas (eds.), *Contemporary British History, 1931–61* (London: 1991).

Roberts, R., *Saving the City: The Great Financial Crisis of 1914* (Oxford: Oxford University Press, 2013).

Roberts, R., *Schroders: Merchants and Bankers* (London: 1992).

Robinson, K., *The Mining Market* (London: 1907).

Rolleston, J.F.L., 'Commercial and Financial Aspects of "Back to the Land"', *Financial Review of Reviews*, 3 (September 1907).

Rolleston, J.F.L., 'The Taxation of Land Values', *Financial Review of Reviews*, 4 (April 1909).

Romney, A., *Three Letters on the Speculative Schemes of the Present Times and the Projected Banks* (Edinburgh: 1825).

Rose, M.B., 'Diversification of Investment by the Greg Family, 1800–1914', *Business History*, xxi (1979).

Rosenberg, E., *From Shylock to Svengali: Jewish Stereotypes in English Fiction* (London: 1961).

Ross, D.M., 'Industrial and Commercial Finance in the Interwar Years', in R. Floud, J. Humphries, and P. Johnson (eds.), *The Cambridge Economic History of Modern Britain: Vol. 2, Growth and Decline, 1870 to the Present* (Cambridge: Cambridge University Press, 2014).

Rossi, P., 'A Non-Political Explanation of the Fall in Consols', *The Financial Review of Reviews*, 9 (May 1913).

Roth, C., *The Jewish Contribution to Civilization* (London: 1938).

Roubini, N., 'Future of Finance', *Financial Times*, 2nd November 2009.

Rowe, J.W.F., *Primary Commodities in International Trade* (Cambridge: 1965).

Roy, H., *The Stock Exchange* (London: 1860).

Royal Commission on the Geographical Distribution of the Industrial Population: Minutes of Evidence (1938).

Rubinstein, W.D., 'The Victorian Middle Classes: Wealth, Occupation and Geography', *Economic History Review*, 30 (1977).

Rubinstein, W.D., 'The Wealth Structure of Britain in 1809, 1860–61, and 1906', in D.R. Green, A.J. Owens, J. Maltby and F. Rutterford (eds.), *Men, Women and Money: Perspectives on Gender, Wealth, and Investment, 1850–1930* (Oxford: 2011).

Rubinstein, W.D., *A History of the Jews in the English-Speaking World: Great Britain* (London: 1996).

Rubinstein, W.D., *Capitalism, Culture and Decline in Britain, 1750–1990* (London: 1993).

Rubinstein, W.D., Jolles, M.A. and Rubinstein, H.L., *The Palgrave Dictionary of Anglo-Jewish History* (London: Palgrave Macmillan, 2011).

Rubinstein, W.D., *Men of Property: The Very Wealthy in Britain since the Industrial Revolution*, 2nd ed. (London: 2006).

Rubinstein, W.D., *Wealth and Inequality in Britain* (London: 1986).

Russell, C. and Lewis, H.S., *The Jew in London: A Study of Racial Character and Present-day Conditions* (London: 1900).

Russell, N., *The Novelist and Mammon: Literary Responses to the World of Commerce in the Nineteenth Century* (Oxford: 1986).

Rustin, S., 'New Style Crime Wave in the City', *Financial Times*, 1st January 2000.

Rutterford, J. and Hannah, L., 'The Rise of Institutional Investors', in D. Chambers and E. Dimson (eds.), *Financial Market History: Reflections of the Past for Investors Today* (CFA Institute Research Foundation, 2016).

Rutterford, J., 'The Merchant Banker, the Broker and the Company Chairman: A New Issue Case Study', *Accounting, Business and Financial History*, 16 (2006).

Samuel, H.B., *Shareholder's Money: An Analysis of Certain Defects in Company Legislation with Proposals for Their Reform* (London: 1933).

Sandelson, V., 'The Confidence Trick: Sir Norman Tullis and Partners', in H. Thomas (ed.), *The Establishment* (London: 1959).

Saul, S.B., *Studies in British Overseas Trade, 1870–1914* (Liverpool: 1960).

Sayers, R.S., *Lloyds Bank in the History of English Banking* (Oxford: Oxford University Press, 1957).

Sayers, R.S., *The Bank of England, 1891–1944* (Cambridge: 1976).

Schneer, J., *London 1900: The Imperial Metropolis* (New Haven, CT: Yale University Press, 1999).

Scott, B., *A Statistical Vindication of the City of London* (London: 1867).

Scott, J. and Hughes, M., *The Anatomy of Scottish Capital* (London: 1980).

Scott, L.G., 'The Rich Man Can Speculate: The Poor Man Dare Not', *Financial Review of Reviews*, 2 (June 1906).

Scott, P., *The Triumph of the South: A Regional Economic History of Early Twentieth Century Britain* (London: 2007).

Scottish Land: The report of the Scottish Land Enquiry Committee (London: 1914).

Scottish Railway Gazette 1845–51.

Scrathley, A., *On Average Investment Trusts* (London: 1875).

Sebag-Montefiore, D., *The Story of Joseph Sebag and Co. and Its Founding Families* (London: 1996).

Select Committee on Loans to Foreign States, Report (London: 1875).

Shannon, H.A., 'The Coming of General Limited Liability', *Economic History Review*, 2 (1931).

Shannon, H.A., 'The Limited Companies of 1866–1883', *Economic History Review*, 4 (1933).

Share Pushing: Report of the Departmental Committee appointed by the Board of Trade, 1936/7, cmd 5537(London: 1937).

Shaw, E.R., *The London Money Market* (London: 1975).

Shiller, R.J., *Irrational Exuberance* (New York: 2000).

Siegel, J., *For Peace and Money: French and British Finance in the Service of Tsars and Commissars* (Oxford: Oxford University Press, 2014).

Simmons, A., 'The Early Twentieth Century: Uniformity, Drudgery and Economics', in A. Pollard (ed.), *The Representation of Business in English Literature* (London: IEA, 2000).

Simon, R., *Light on the City* (London: Labour Research Department, 1962).

Smalley, G.W., *Society in London, by a Foreign Resident* (London: Chatto and Windus, 1885).

Smart, P.E., 'Bankers in Fiction', *Journal of the Institute of Bankers*, 82 (1961).

Smith, A.D., *International Financial Markets: The Performance of Britain and Its Rivals* (Cambridge: 1992).

Smith, A.E., *George Smith's Money: A Scottish Investor in America* (Maddison, Wisconsin: 1966).

Smith, R., 'An Oldham Limited Liability Company, 1875–1896', *Business History*, 4 (1961/2).

Smith, W.N., *Robert Fleming, 1845–1933* (Haddington: Whittinghome House, 2000).

Sowels, N., James, D. and Hunter, I., *Britain's Invisible Earnings* (Aldershot: 1989).

Speare, C.F., 'Europe's Interest in American Securities', in T. Gibson (ed.), *Special Market Letters for 1898* (New York: 1909).

Speare, C.F., 'Selling American Bonds in Europe', in W.H. Hull (ed.), 'Bonds as Investment Securities', *Annals of the American Academy of Political and Social Science*, Volume 18 (Philadelphia, PA: September 1907).

Spence, C.C., *British Investments and the American Mining Frontier, 1860–1901* (Ithaca, NY: 1958).

Spiegelberg, R., *Power Without Accountability* (London: 1973).

Stahl, K.M., *The Metropolitan Organization of British Colonial Trade: Four Regional Studies* (London: 1951).

Stashower, D., *Teller of Tales: The Life of Arthur Conan Doyle* (New York: Henry Holt and Co., 1999).

Steele, F.E., 'Bank Amalgamations', *Journal of the Institute of Bankers*, 18 (1897).

Steffenburg, C.E., 'Merchant Banking in London', in *Current Financial Problems and the City of London* (London: Institute of Bankers, 1949).

Stock and Share Review 1883.

Stock Exchange Official Intelligence (London: 1914).

Stone, I., *The Global Export of Capital from Great Britain, 1865–1914: A Statistical Survey* (London: 1999).

Stones, R., 'Government-finance Relations in Britain, 1964–7: A Tale of Three Cities', *Economy and Society*, 19 (1990).

Strange, S., *Casino Capitalism* (London: 1986).

Sturmey, S.G., *The Economic Development of Radio* (London: 1958).

Sturrock, J.B., *Peter Brough: A Paisley Philanthropist* (Paisley: 1890).

Sunderland, D., *Financing the Raj: The City of London and Colonial India, 1858–1940* (Woodbridge: Boydell Press, 2013).

Supple, B., *The Royal Exchange Assurance: A History of British Insurance, 1720–1970* (Cambridge: 1970).

Supple, B.E., 'A Business Elite: German-Jewish Financiers in Nineteenth Century New York', *Business History Review*, 31 (1957).

Sutherland, D., *The Landowners* (London: 1968).

Swinson, C., *Regulation of the London Stock Exchange: Share Trading, Fraud and Reform, 1914–1945* (London: Routledge, 2018).

Swinson, C., *Share Trading, Fraud and the Crash of 1929: A Biography of Clarence Hatry* (London: Routledge, 2019).

Sykes, J., *The Amalgamation Movement in English Banking, 1825–1924* (London: 1926).

Tait, J.S., *The Cattle Field of the Far West* (Edinburgh: 1884).

Talani, L.S., *Globalization, Hegemony and the Future of the City of London* (London: Palgrave Macmillan, 2012).

Talbot, F.A., *The Railway Conquest of the World* (London: 1911).

Taylor, A.J., 'The Economy', in S. Nowell-Smith (ed.), *Edwardian England* (London: 1964).

Taylor, C.W., 'The Case Against the Nationalisation of the Banks', *Journal of the Institute of Bankers*, 56 (1935).

Taylor, D.J., 'Before There Was Jeeves: A hundred years of "Psmith in the City"', *Times Literary Supplement*, 17th September 2010.

Taylor, G.R., *Thomas Dunlop and Sons: Ship-owners, 1851–1951* (Glasgow: 1951).

Taylor, J., *Boardroom Scandal: The Criminalization of Company Fraud in Nineteenth-Century Britain* (Oxford: Oxford University Press, 2013).

Taylor, J., *Creating Capitalism: Joint-stock Enterprise in British Politics and Culture, 1800–1870* (Woodbridge: Boydell and Brewer, 2006).

Thane, P., 'Financiers and the British State: The Case of Sir Ernest Cassel', *Business History*, 28 (1986).

The Bailie 1872–1914.

The Bankers' Circular 1828–58.

The Bankers' Magazine and Journal of the Money Market 1844–5.

The Corporation of London, The Competitive Position of London's Financial Services: Final Report (London: 1995).

The Economist 1843–1914.

The Edinburgh Property Review.

The Editors of Institutional Investment, *The Way It Was: An Oral History of Finance, 1967–1987* (New York: William Morrow & Co., 1988).

The Estates Gazette, 1880–1914.

The Financial Register and Stock Exchange Manual, 1877.

The Financial Review of Reviews, 1904–1914.

The Financier: A Daily Record of the Money Market, Investments and Trade 1870.

The Investment Journal, Money, Land and Share Market Chronicle, 1863.

The Investor's Monthly Manual 1880–1914.

The Investors' and Stock Exchange Magazine, 1863.

The Investors' Guardian, 1863.

The Investors' Review, 1890–3.

The Labour Party, Financial Policy and Economic Policy (London 1944).

The Land: The Report of the Land Enquiry Committee (London: 1914).

The Money-Maker Manuals for Investors No. 1: How to Commence Investing (London: 1901).

The Money-Maker Manuals for Investors No. 4: Scientific Speculation (London: 1901).

The Scottish Banking and Insurance Magazine, 1879–86.

The Scottish Financier, 1883.

The Scottish Railway Shareholder's Manual (Edinburgh: 1849).

The Stock Exchange Gazette: A Weekly Journal for Investors and Their Advisers, 1880, 1895–6, 1901.

The Stock Exchange Observer, 1875.

The Stock Exchange Official Yearbook, 1875–1914.

The Stock Exchange Review, 1870.

The Times, 1840–1914.

Thomas, D., 'UK Banks Push for Ambitious Financial Services Strategy', *Financial Times*, 22nd February 2021.

Thomas, S.E., *British Banks and the Finance of Industry* (London: 1931).

Thomas, W.A., *The Big Bang* (Oxford: 1986).

Thomas, W.A., *The Finance of British Industry, 1918–1976* (London: 1978).

Thomas, W.A., *The Provincial Stock Exchanges* (London: 1973).

Thomas, W.A., *The Stock Exchanges of Ireland* (Liverpool: 1986).

Thompson, F.M.L., 'Britain', in D.S. Spring (ed.), *European Landed Elites in the 19th Century* (Baltimore: 1977).

Thompson, F.M.L., *English Landed Society in the Nineteenth Century* (London: 1963).

Thompson, F.M.L., *Gentrification and the Enterprise Culture: Britain 1780–1980* (Oxford: 2001).

Thompson, P., 'The Pyrrhic Victory of Gentlemanly Capitalism: The Financial Elite of the City of London, 1945–90', *Journal of Contemporary History*, 32 (1997).

Thompson, P., *The Edwardians: The Remaking of British Society* (London: 1975).

Thomson, T., 'The Effect on Commerce of the Law of Limited Liability', *Journal of the Institute of Bankers*, lvii (1886).

Tomlinson, B.R., 'Economics and Empire: The Periphery and the Imperial Economy', in J.M. Brown and W.R. Louis (eds.), *Oxford History of the British Empire* (Oxford: Oxford University Press, 1997).

Tomlinson, B.R., 'Imperialism and After: The Economy of the Empire on the Periphery', in J.M. Brown and W.R. Louis (eds.), *Oxford History of the British Empire* (Oxford: Oxford University Press, 1997).

Toms, S., 'Financial Scandals: A Historical Review', *Accounting and Business Research*, 49 (2019).

Tooke, T., *A History of Prices*. 6 Vols. (London: 1838–1857).

Toronto Daily Star 1900–1914.

Trading with the Enemy: Report and Proceedings [National Archives] (1912).

Truptil, R.J., *British Banks and the London Money Market* (London: Jonathan Cape, 1936).

Turner, J., 'Holding Shareholders to Account: British Banking Stability and Contingent Capital', in N. Dimsdale and A. Hotson (eds.), *British Financial Crises since 1825* (Oxford: Oxford University Press, 2014).

Turner, J.D., *Banking in Crisis: The Rise and Fall of British Banking Stability, 1800 to the Present* (Cambridge: Cambridge University Press, 2014).

Turrell, R.V. and van Helten, J.J., 'The Rothschilds, The Exploration Company and Mining Finance', *Business History*, 28 (1986).

UK International Financial Services, *The Future: A Report from the UK Based Financial Services Leaders to the Government* (H.M. Treasury, May 2009).

Utton, M.A., 'Some Features of the Early Merger Movements in British Manufacturing Industry', *Business History*, xiv (1972).

Vallance, A. *The Centre of the World* (London: 1935).

Vamplew, W., 'Banks and Railway Finance: A Note on the Scottish Experience', *Transport History*, 4 (1971).

Vamplew, W., 'Sources of Scottish Railway Share Capital before 1860', *Scottish Journal of Political Economy*, 17 (1970).

Van Cleef, E., *Trade Centers and Trade Routes* (New York: 1937).

Van Helten, J.J., 'Empire and High Finance: South Africa and the International Gold Standard, 1890–1914', *Journal of African History*, 23 (1982).

Van Oss, S.F., *American Railroads and British Investors* (London: 1893).

Van Oss, S.F. and Mathieson, F.C., *Stock Exchange Values: A Decade of Finance, 1885–1895* (London: 1895).

Von Peter, G., 'International Banking Centres: A Network Perspective', *BIS Quarterly Review* (10th December 2007).

Wagner, T.S., *Financial Speculation in Victorian Fiction: Plotting Money and the Novel Genre, 1815–1901* (Columbus, OH: Ohio State University Press, 2010).

Wagstaff Blundell, J., *Telegraph Companies Considered as Investments* (London: Effingham Wilson, 1869).

Wainwright, D., *Government Broker: The Story of an Office and of Mullens & Co.* (East Molesey: 1990).

Wainwright, D., *Henderson: A History of the Life of Alexander Henderson, First Lord Faringdon, and of Henderson Administration* (London: 1985).

Walker, D. and Watson, *Investor's and Shareholder's Guide* (Edinburgh: 1894).

Wall, W.W., *How to Invest in Railways* (London: 1903).

Waller, P., *Writers, Readers and Reputations: Literary Life in Britain, 1870–1918* (Oxford: Oxford University Press, 2006).

Ward, R.A., *A Treatise on Investments* (London: 1852).

Ward-Perkins, C.N., 'Banking Developments', in G.D.M. Worwick and P.H. Ady (eds.), *The British Economy, 1945–1950* (Oxford: Oxford University Press, 1952).

Watson, K., *Industrial Finance in the UK: The Brewing Experience, 1880–1913*, Oxford D.Phil. (1990).

Webb, A.D., *The New Dictionary of Statistics* (London: 1911).

Weiner, M.J., *English Culture and the Decline of the Industrial Spirit, 1850–1980* (Cambridge: 1981).

Weir, R.B., *A History of the Scottish American Investment Company Limited, 1873–1973* (Edinburgh: 1873).

Welsh, F., *Uneasy City: An Insider's View of the City of London* (London: 1986).

Welsman, M.S., *A Guide to the Unprotected in Every-Day Matters Relating to Property and Income, by a Banker's Daughter* (London: 1891).

Wernette, J.P., 'The English Banking System', *Harvard Business Review*, 13 (1935).

Wheeler, J.F., *The Stock Exchange* (London: 1913).

Whyte, A.G., *The Electrical Industry: Lighting, Traction and Power* (London: 1904).

Wilgress, L.D., 'The London Money Market', *Journal of the Canadian Bankers Association*, 20 (1912–13).

Williams, E.E., 'British Capital and Legal Protection in Foreign Countries', *Financial Review of Reviews*, 5 (July 1909).

Williams, M.S., *Round London, Down East and Up West* (London: 1892).

Williamson, P., 'Financiers, the Gold Standard and British Politics, 1925–1931', in J. Turner (ed.), *Businessmen and Politics: Studies of Business Activity in British Politics, 1900–1945* (London: Heinemann, 1984).

Wilson, A.J., 'Can Home Railway Common Stocks Solidly Rally?', *Financial Review of Reviews*, 2 (June 1906).

Wilson, S., *The Origins of Modern Financial Crime: Historical Foundations and Current Problems in Britain* (London: Routledge, 2014).

Withers, G., 'Collective and Individual Stability', *The Financial Review of Reviews*, 3 (January 1907).

Withers, G., 'English Investors and American Securities', *The Financial Review of Reviews*, 3 (March 1907).

Withers, G., 'Patent Rights and Latent Dangers', *The Financial Review of Reviews*, 2 (April 1906).

Withers, H., *International Finance* (London: 1916).

Withers, H., *Money-Changing: An Introduction to Foreign Exchange* (London: 1913).

Withers, H., *Stocks and Shares* (London: 1914).

Withers, H., 'The Work of the New Issue Market', in Financial News, *The City, 1884–1934* (London: 1934).

Wolff, H.D., *Rambling Recollections* (London: 1908).

Wood, C., *Victorian Panorama: Paintings of Victorian Life* (London: 1976).

Wood, C., *William Powell Frith: A Painter and His World* (Stroud: 2006).

Wood, J.H., *A History of Central Banking in Great Britain and the United States* (Cambridge: Cambridge University Press, 2005).

Woolf, F.A.H., *The Stock Exchange: Past and Present* (London: 1913).

Wright, R.E., *One Nation under Debt: Hamilton, Jefferson, and the History of What We Owe* (New York: 2008).

Wynne-Bennett, H.D., *Investment and Speculation* (London: 1924).

Ziegler, P., *The Sixth Great Power: Barings 1762–1929* (London: 1988).

Zysman, J., Markets and Growth (1983).

Fiction

Ainsworth, W.H., *John Law: The Projector* (London: 1864).

Ainsworth, W.H., *Old St. Paul's: A Tale of the Plague and the Fire* (London: 1841).

Alexander, Mrs, *A Crooked Path* (London: Hurst and Blackett, 1890).

Alexander, Mrs, *Mammon* (Leipzig & London: Heinemann and Balestier, 1892).

Alexander, Mrs, *What Gold Cannot Buy: A Novel* (London: F.V. White, 1895).

Allen, G., 'The Great Ruby Robbery' (1892), in M. Cox (ed.), *Victorian Tales of Mystery and Detection* (Oxford: 1992).

Allen, G., *An African Millionaire: Episodes in the Life of the Illustrious Colonel Clay* (London: 1897).

Anderson, J.R.L., *Death in the City* (London: Victor Gollancz, 1977).

Anon., *Commercial Tales and Sketches* (London: 1864).

Anon., *The Financial House that Jack Built* (London: 1819).

Anstey, F., *Vice Versa* (London: 1882).

Archer, J., *Not a Penny More, Not a Penny Less* (London: Jonathan Cape, 1976).

Austen, J., *Pride and Prejudice* (London: 1813).

Aytoun, W.E., *How We Got Up the Glenmutchkin Railway and How We Got Out of It* (1845) reprinted in W.L. Renwick (ed.), *W.E. Aytoun: Stories and Verse* (Edinburgh: 1964).

Barker, G., *The Voysey Inheritance* (London: 1903) [play].

Barr, R., *The Face and the Mask* (London: 1894).

Bell, R., *The Ladder of Gold: An English Story* (London: 1850).

Barr, R., *Lord Stranleigh Abroad* (London: Ward, Lock & Co., 1913).

Barr, R., *Lord Stranleigh Philanthropist* (London: Ward, Lock & Co., 1911).

Barr, R., *Stranleigh's Millions* (London: Eveleigh Nash, 1909).

Barr, R., *Young Lord Stranleigh* (London: Ward, Lock & Co., 1908).

Bellairs, G., *Calamity at Harwood* (London: 1945).

Bellairs, G., *The Case of the Headless Jesuit* (London: John Gifford, 1950).

Bellairs, G., *Dead March for Penelope Blow* (London: The Thriller Book Club, 1951).

Bellairs, G., *Death in the Wasteland* (London: The Thriller Book Club, 1963).

Belloc, H., *A Change in the Cabinet* (London: 1909).

Belloc, H., *Emmanuel Burden, Merchant, of Thames St, in the City of London, Exporter of Hardware: A Record of His Lineage, Speculations, Last Days and Death* (London: 1904).

Belloc, H., *Mr Clutterbuck's Election* (London: 1908).

Belloc, H., *Mr Petre: A Novel* (London: Arrowsmith, 1925).

Belloc, H., *New Cautionary Tales* (London: Duckworth, 1930).

Belloc, H., *Pongo and the Bull* (London: 1910).

Bennett, A., *Anna of the Five Towns* (London: 1902).

Bennett, A., *Buried Alive* (London: 1908).

Bennett, A., *The Card* (London: 1911).

Bennett, A., *Clayhanger* (London: 1910).

Bennett, A., *The Grand Babylon Hotel* (London: Chatto and Windus, 1902).

Bennett, A., *Hilda Lessways* (London: 1911).

Bennett, A., *The Loot of Cities: Being the Adventures of a Millionaire in Search of Joy (a Fantasia) and Other Stories* (London: 1905).

Bennett, A., *Lord Raingo* (London: 1926).

Bennett, A., *A Man from the North* (London: 1898).

Bennett, A., *The Regent: A Five Towns Story of Adventure in London* (London: 1913).

Bennett, A., *Teresa of Watling Street: A Fantasia on Modern Times* (London: 1904).

Bennett, A., *These Twain* (London: 1916).

Benson, E.F., *Mammon and Co.* (London: 1899).

Benson, E.F., *The Money Market* (London: 1898).

Benson, E.F., *The Osbornes* (London: 1910).

Bentley, E.C., *Trent's Last Case* (London: 1913).

Berkeley, A., *The Silk Stocking Murders* (London: Penguin, 1941).

Besant, W., *The Alabaster Box* (London: 1900).

Besant, W., *All in a Garden Fair: The Simple Story of Three Boys and a Girl* (London: 1883).

Besant, W., *All Sorts and Condition of Men* (London: 1882).

Besant, W., *Beyond the Dreams of Avarice* (London: 1895).

Besant, W., *The Fourth Generation* (London: Chatto and Windus, 1900).

Besant, W. and Rice, J., *The Golden Butterfly* (London: 1877).

Besant, W. and Rice, J., *Ready-Money Mortiboy: A Matter-of-Fact Story* (London: 1872).

Birmingham, G.A., *Gossamer* (London: 1915).

Black, R., *Love or Lucre: A Novel* (London: George Routledge and Sons, 1878).

Black, W., *The Monarch of Mincing Lane* (London: 1861).

Blackwood, A., *A Prisoner in Fairyland* (London: Macmillan & Co., 1913).

Blyth, H., 'The Accusing Shadow', in M. Cox (ed.), *Victorian Tales of Mystery and Detection* (Oxford: 1992).

Boland, J., *The Golden Fleece: A Slightly Criminous Novel* (Crowborough: Forrest House Books, 1961).

Boothby, G., 'The Duchess of Wiltshire's Diamonds' (1897), in H. Greene (ed.), *The Complete Rivals of Sherlock Holmes* (Harmondsworth: 1983).

Boothroyd, B., 'The Adventures of Mr. Pitkin, Bank Manager', *The Dark Horse* [Lloyds Bank Staff Magazine] (London: 1937).

Braddon, M.E., *Aurora Floyd* (London: Downey and Company, 1863).

Braddon, M.E., *Birds of Prey: A Novel* (London: Ward, Lock and Tyler, 1867).

Braddon, M.E., *Charlotte's Inheritance* (London: Ward, Lock and Tyler, 1868).

Braddon, M.E., *John Marchmont's Legacy* (London: Downey and Company, 1863).

Braddon, M.E., *Lady Audley's Secret* (London: 1862).

Braddon, M.E., 'Levison's Victim' (1870), in M. Cox (ed.), *Victorian Tales of Mystery and Detection* (Oxford: 1992).

Braddon, M.E., *Only a Clod* (London: Downey and Co., 1865).

Braddon, M.E., *Rupert Godwin* (London: John and Robert Maxwell, 1867).

Bramah, E., *The Bravo of London* (London: Cassell & Co., 1934).

Bretherton, R.H., *An Honest Man* (London: 1909).

Brontë, C., *Villette* (London: 1853).

Brophy, J., *The Day They Robbed the Bank of England* (London: Chatto and Windus, 1959).

Buchan, J., *Mr Standfast* (London: 1919).

Buchan, J., *The Gap in the Curtain* (London: 1932).

Buchan, J., *The Power-House* (London: 1913, reprinted 2007).

Budden, D., *No Accounting for Murder* (London: 1986).

Bulwer-Lytton, E., *The Disowned* (London: 1828).

Burnett, F.H., *A Little Princess* (London: 1905).

Butler, S., *The Way of All Flesh* (London: 1903).

Byron, L., *Don Juan* (1818/23).

Campbell, A., *On the Floor* (London: Serpent's Tail, 2012).

Capra, F. [Director & Producer], 'It's A Wonderful Life' [film] (1946).

Cartwright, J., *Other People's Money* (London: Bloomsbury, 2011).

Charteris, L., *Boodle: Stories of the Saint* (London: Hodder and Stoughton, 1934).

Charteris, L., Prelude For War (London: Hodder and Stoughton, 1938).

Chesterton, G.K., *The Innocence of Father Brown* (1910/11), in *The Complete Father Brown* (London: 1981).

Christie, A., *One, Two, Buckle My Shoe* (London: 1940).

Christie, A., *Parker Pyne Investigates* (London: 1932).

Christie, A., *Poirot Investigates* (London: Bodley Head, 1924).

Christie, A., *The Secret of Chimneys* (London: John Lane, The Bodley Head, 1925, reprinted by Pan Books).

Churchill, C., *Serious Money: A City Comedy* (London: 1987).

Cohen, M.B., *The Butchers' Ball* (London: Hodder and Stoughton, 1999).

Cole, G.D.H. and Cole, M., *Big Business Murder* (London: Collins, 1935).

Collins, W., *A Rogue's Life* (London: 1856).

Collins, W., 'The Biter Bit' (1859), in R.C. Bull (ed.), *Great Tales of Mystery* (London: Weidenfeld and Nicholson, 1960).

Collins, W., *The Dead Secret* (London: 1857).

Collins, W., *The Evil Genius* (London: 1886).

Collins, W., *The Haunted Hotel* (London: 1878).

Collins, W., *The Moonstone* (London: 1868).

Collins, W., *Who Killed Zebedee?* (London: 1881).

Collins, W. and Besant, W. *Blind Love* (London: 1890).

Conan Doyle, A., 'The Adventure of the Beryl Coronet', *Strand Magazine*, October 1892.

Conan Doyle, A., 'The Adventure of the Blanched Soldier', *Strand Magazine*, October 1926.

Conan Doyle, A., 'The Adventure of the Dancing Men', *Strand Magazine*, December 1903.

Conan Doyle, A., 'The Adventure of the Norwood Builder', *Strand Magazine*, October 1903.

Conan Doyle, A., 'The Adventure of the Stock-Broker's Clerk', *Strand Magazine*, March 1893.

Conan Doyle, A., *Beyond the City: The Idyll of a Suburb* (London: Everett and Co., 1892).

Conan Doyle, A., *A Duet with an Occasional Chorus* (London: 1899).

Conan Doyle, A., *The Firm of Girdlestone: A Romance of the Unromantic* (London: Collins, 1890).

Conan Doyle, A., 'The Man with the Twisted Lip', *Strand Magazine*, December 1891.

Connington, J.J., *Nordenholt's Million* (London: 1923).

Conrad, J., *Chance* (London: 1914).

Conrad, J., *Heart of Darkness* (London: 1902).

Corelli, M., *The Sorrows of Satan* (London: 1895).

Courlander, A., *Mightier than the Sword* (London: T. Fisher Unwin, 1912).

Creasey, J., *Death Round the Corner* (London: 1935).

Creasey, J., *The Case of the Murdered Financier* (London: 1937).

Creasey, J., *First Came a Murder* (London: 1935).

Cutcliffe Hyne, C.J., *Thompson's Progress* (London: 1903).

Danby, F. (Mrs Julia Frankau), *Pigs in Clover* (London: William Heinemann, 1903).

Davies, L., *Nest of Vipers* (London: Vigliano, 1995, reprinted 2014).

Davis, H.C., *Trouble in the Bank* (London: Ward, Lock and Co., 1960).

De Vere Stacpoole, M., *London 1913: A Novel* (London: 1914).

Delderfield, R.F., *Come Home Charlie and Face Them* (London: Hodder and Stoughton, 1969).

Dickens, C., 'A Christmas Carol' (1843), in *Christmas Books* (London: Chapman and Hall, n.d.).

Dickens, C., *Dealings with the Firm of Dombey and Son, Wholesale, Retail, and for Exportation* (London: 1848).

Dickens, C., 'Hunted Down' (1859), in M. Cox (ed.), *Victorian Tales of Mystery and Detection* (Oxford: 1992).

Dickens, C., *The Life and Adventures of Martin Chuzzlewit, 1843–4* (London: Chapman and Hall, 1842).

Dickens, C., *The Life and Adventures of Nicholas Nickleby* (London: Chapman and Hall, 1838).

Dickens, C., *Little Dorrit* (London: 1857).

Dickens, C., *Our Mutual Friend* (London: 1864/5).

Dickens, C., *A Tale of Two Cities* (London: Chapman and Hall, 1859).

Dickens, C. and Collins, W., *No Thoroughfare* (London: 1867).

Disraeli, B., *Coningsby* (London: 1844).

Disraeli, B., *Lothair* (London: 1870).

Disraeli, B., *Tancred or the New Crusade* (London: 1847).

Du Cross, A., *Wheels of Fortune: A Salute to Pioneers* (London: 1938).

Du Maurier, G., *The Martian: A Novel* (London: 1898).

Edwards, A.B., *Half a Million of Money* (London: George Routledge and Sons, 1865).

Elliot, G., *Middlemarch* (London: 1871/2).

Ellis, G.U., *Every Man's Desire* (London: Duckworth, 1925).

Elton, B., *Meltdown* (London: Bantam Press, 2009).

Faulks, S., *A Week in December* (London: Hutchinson, 2009).

Fletcher, J.S., *The Bartenstein Case* (London: John Long, 1913).

Fletcher, J.S., 'Blind Gap Moor' (1918), in *The Secret of the Barbican and Other Stories* (London: Hodder and Stoughton, 1925).

Fletcher, J.S., *The Charing Cross Mystery* (London: 1923).

Fletcher, J.S., *The Chestermarke Instinct* (London: 1921).

Fletcher, J.S., 'The Contents of the Coffin' (1909), in H. Greene (ed.), *The Complete Rivals of Sherlock Holmes* (Harmondsworth: 1983).

Fletcher, J.S., *The Herapath Property* (London: 1920).

Fletcher, J.S., 'The Magician of Cannon Street', in *Paul Campenhage, Specialist in Criminology* (London: Ward, Lock & Co., 1918).

Fletcher, J.S., *The Middle Temple Murder* (London: Ward, Lock and Co., 1920).

Fletcher, J.S., 'The Murder in the Mayor's Parlour' (1922), in *The Secret of the Barbican and Other Stories* (Hodder & Stoughton, 1925).

Fletcher, J.S., *The Mystery of the London Banker: Being Entry Number Seven in the Case-Book of Ronald Camberwell* (London: George G. Harrap and Co., 1933).

Fletcher, J.S., 'The Tobacco Box', in *Paul Campenhage, Specialist in Criminology* (London: Ward, Lock & Co., 1918).

Follett, K., *A Dangerous Fortune* (London: Macmillan, 1993).

Follett, K., *Paper Money* (London: 1977).

Forester, C.S., *Payment Deferred* (London: The Bodley Head, 1926).

Forester, C.S., *Plain Murder* (London: The Bodley Head, 1930).

Forester, C.S., *The Pursued* (1935) (London: Penguin Books, 2011) [not published until 2011].

Forster, E.M., *Howards End* (London: 1910).

Fox-Davies, A.C., *The Finances of Sir John Kynnersley* (London: The Bodley Head, 1908).

Francis, D., *Banker* (London: Michael Joseph, 1982).

Francis, D. and Francis, F., *Crossfire* (London: Michael Joseph, 2010).

Francis, D., *Risk* (London: Michael Joseph, 1977).

Fraser, R., *Financial Times* (London: Jonathan Cape, 1942).

Frederic, H., *The Market-Place* (London: 1899).

Galsworthy, J., *The Country House* (London: 1907).

Galsworthy, J., *On Forsyte 'Change* (London: Heinemann, 1930).

Galsworthy, J., *The Man of Property* (London: Heinemann, 1906. [Vol. 1 of the Forsyte Saga].

Galsworthy, J., *In Chancery* (London: 1920) [Vol. 2 of the Forsyte Saga].

Galsworthy, J., *To Let* (London: 1921) [Vol. 3 of the Forsyte Saga].

Galsworthy, J., *The White Monkey* (London: 1924) [Vol. 4 of the Forsyte Saga].

Galsworthy, J., *The Silver Spoon* (London: 1928) [Vol. 5 of the Forsyte Saga].

Galsworthy, J., *Maid in Waiting* (London: 1931) [Vol. 7 of the Forsyte Saga].

Galsworthy, J., *Swan Song* (London: 1928) [Vol. 6 of the Forsyte Saga].

Galsworthy, J., *Flowering Wilderness* (London: 1932) [Vol. 8 of the Forsyte Saga].

Galsworthy, J., *Over the River* (London: 1933) [Vol. 9 of the Forsyte Saga].

Galt, J., *A Rich Man; or, He has Great Merit, being the Autobiography of Archibald Pack, esq. Late Lord Mayor of London* (1836), reprinted in W. Roughead, *A Rich Man and Other Stories by John Galt* (London & Edinburgh: T.N. Foulis, 1925).

Gaskell, E., *Cranford* (London: 1853).

Gaskell, E., *North and South* (London: 1855).

Gaspey, T., *Calthorpe, or Fallen Fortunes: A Novel* (London: Longman, Hurst, Rees, Orme and Brown, 1821).

Gilbert, W.S. and Sullivan, A.S., 'Utopia, Limited, or, the Flowers of Progress' (London: 1893), in *The Complete Plays of Gilbert and Sullivan* (New York and London: 1976).

Gissing, G., *Born in Exile* (London: 1892).

Gissing, G., *The Crown of Life* (London: 1899).

Gissing, G., *Eve's Ransom* (London: 1895).

Gissing, G., *The Nether World* (London: 1889).

Gissing, G., *The Whirlpool* (London: 1897).

Gissing, G., *Will Warburton: A Romance of Real Life* (London: 1905).

Glyn, E., *The Reason Why* (London: 1911).

Gore, Mrs, *The Banker's Wife or Court and City* (London: Henry Colburn, 1843).

Gore, Mrs, *The Man of Business, or Stokeshill Place* (London: J. and C. Brown, 1837).

Gore, Mrs, *Men of Capital* (London: James Blackwood, 1857).

Gore, Mrs, *The Money Lender* (London: 1854).

Gowing, Mrs A., *Gods of Gold* (London: 1896).

Gribble, F., *The Lower Life* (London: 1896).

Griffiths, A., *Ford's Folly, Ltd.* (London: George Bell and Sons, 1900).

Grossmith, G. and Grossmith, W., *The Diary of a Nobody* (London: 1892).

Gunter, A.C., *Miss Dividends: A Novel* (London: 1892).

Haggard, W., *The Money Men, a Novel* (London: Hodder and Stoughton, 1981).

Hamilton, M.A., *Dead Yesterday* (London: 1916).

Hardwick, M., Hardwick, M. and Paget, S. *The Sherlock Holmes Companion* (New York: Bramhall House, 1962).

Hare, C., *Tenant for Death* (London: Faber and Faber, 1937).

Hartley, L.P., *A Perfect Woman* (London: 1955).

Harvey, W.N., *A Tale of Two Nations* (Chicago: Coin Publishing Company, 1894).

Hatton, J., *By Order of the Czar: The Tragic Story of Anna Klosstock, Queen of the Ghetto* (London: 1890).

Hatton, J., *Christopher Kenrick: His Life and Adventures* (London: 1869).

Hatton, J., *Clytie: A Novel of Modern Life* (London: 1874).

Hatton, J., *Cruel London: A Novel* (London: Frederick Warne & Co., 1878).

Hatton, J., *In the Lap of Fortune; A Story Stranger than Fiction* (London: Frederick Warne and Co., 1873).

Hatton, J., *John Needham's Double* (London: 1885).

Hatton, J., *The Banishment of Jessop Blythe: A Novel* (London: 1895).

Hatton, J., *The Gay World* (London: S. Blackett, 1877).

Hatton, J., *The Tallants of Barton* (London: Frederick Warne & Co. 1867).

Heddle, E.F., *The Pride of the Family* (London: James Bowden, 1899).

Hemyng, B. and Graff, J.H., *Too Sharp by Half, or, the Man Who made Millions* (London: 1871).

Hemyng, B. and Graff, J.H., *Telegraph Secrets* (London: Chapman and Hall, 1868).

Hemyng, B., *The Stockbroker's Wife and Other Sensational Tales of the Stock Exchange* (London: John and Robert Maxwell, 1885).

Heseltine, W., 'A Family Scene during the Panic at the Stock Exchange in May 1835', *The Lady's Magazine* (London), 9 July 1836.

Hill, H., 'The Sapient Monkey' (1893), in M. Cox (ed.), *Victorian Tales of Mystery and Detection: An Oxford Anthology* (Oxford: Oxford University Press, 1992).

Hill, H., *Guilty Gold: A Romance of Financial Fraud and City Crime* (London: 1896).

Hill, H., *Millions of Mischief: The Story of a Great Secret* (London: 1905).

Hill, H., *The One Who Saw* (London: 1905).

Hilton, J., *Ill Wind: Contango* (London: 1932).

Hocking, J., *God and Mammon* (London: 1912).

Hocking, J., *The Man Who Rose Again* (London: 1906).

Hodder, M., *Sexton Blake Internet Archive* [online].

Hope, A., *Tristram of Blent: An Episode in the Story of an Ancient House* (London: 1901).

Hornung, E.W., 'The Black Mask' (1901), in *The Collected Raffles Stories* (Oxford: Oxford University Press, 1996).

Hornung, E.W., *Raffles: The Amateur Cracksman* (London: 1899).

Hume, F., 'The Greenstone God and the Stockbroker' (1893), in M. Cox (ed.), *Victorian Tales of Mystery and Detection* (Oxford: 1992).

Hume, F., *Lady Jim of Curzon Street* (London: 1905).

James, H., *The Awkward Age* (London: 1899).

Jerome, J.K., *Three Men in a Boat* (London: 1889).

Jerrold, D., *A Man Made of Money* (London: 1849).

Keen, H., 'The Tin Box' (1896), in M. Cox (ed.), *Victorian Tales of Mystery and Detection: An Oxford Anthology* (Oxford: Oxford University Press, 1992).

Kilduff, P., *The Dealer* (London: 2000).

Kilduff, P., *The Frontrunner* (London: 2001).

Kilduff, P., *The Headhunter* (London: 2003).

Kilduff, P., *Square Mile* (London: Coronet Books, 1999).

Kingsley, C., *Yeast: A Problem* (London: 1851).

Kitchin, C.H.B., *Crime at Christmas* (London: Faber and Faber, 1934).

Kitchin, C.H.B., *Death of His Uncle* (London: Constable & Co., 1939).

Kitchin, C.H.B., *Death of My Aunt* (London: Hogarth Press, 1929).

Kuppord, S., *A Fortune from the Sky* (London: 1903).

Lanchester, J., *Capital* (London: Faber and Faber, 2012).

Le Queux, W., *The Bond of Black* (London: 1899).

Le Queux, W., *The Crooked Way* (London: 1908).

Le Queux, W., *The Great War in England* in 1897 (London: 1894).

Le Queux, W., *Guilty Bonds* (London: 1891).

Le Queux, W., *The Invasion of 1910* (London: 1906).

Le Queux, W., *The Secret of the Square* (London: The London Book Company, Le Queux, W., *Sins of the City: A Story of Craft, Crime and Capital* (London: 1905), 1907).

Le Queux, W., *The Stretton Street Affair* (London: 1922).

Le Ros, C., *Christmas Day; and How It Was Spent by Four Persons in the House of Fograss, Fograss, Mowton and Snorton, Bankers* (London: George Routledge & Co., 1854).

Lever, C., *Davenport Dunn or the Man and the Day* (Leipzig: 1859).

Lever, C., *That Boy of Norcott's* (London: 1869).

Linnaeus Banks, Mrs G., *The Manchester Man* (London: 1876).

Loder, V., *Murder from Three Angles* (London: 1934).

Loder, V., *Red Stain* (London: 1931).

Loder, V., *Two Dead* (London: 1934).

Loder, V., *Whose Hand* (London: 1929).

Macdonell, A.G., *Lords and Masters* (London: 1936).

Malcolm, J., *A Back Room in Somers Town* (Glasgow: William Collins, Sons and Co., 1984).

Malcolm, J., *The Burning Ground* (London: 1993).

Malcolm, J., *Circles and Squares* (London: 2003).

Malcolm, J., *A Deceptive Appearance* (London: Macmillan, 1992).

Malcolm, J., *The Godwin Sideboard* (Glasgow: William Collins and Sons, 1984).

Malcolm, J., *Gothic Pursuit* (London: Harper Collins, 1987).

Malcolm, J., *The Gwen John Sculpture* (London: Collins, 1985).

Malcolm, J., *Hung Over* (London: 1994).

Malcolm, J., *Into the Vortex* (London: 1996).

Malcolm, J., *Mortal Ruin* (London: Harper Collins, 1988).

Malcolm, J., *Rogues Gallery* (London: Allison and Busby, 2005).

Malcolm, J., *Sheep, Goats and Soap* (London: Harper Collins, 1991).

Malcolm, J., *Simpson's Homer* (London: 2001).

Malcolm, J., *Whistler in the Dark* (London: Collins, 1986).

Malcolm, J., *The Wrong Impression* (London: Collins, 1990).

Marsh, N., *Death at the Bar* (London: 1940).

Marshall, B., *The Bank Audit* (London: 1958), published in the USA as *The Accounting* (Boston: Houghton Mifflin, 1958).

Martineau, H., *Berkeley the Banker* (London: 1832–4).

Mason, A.E.W., *The House in Lordship Lane* (London: Hodder and Stoughton, 1946).

Mason, A.E.W., *The Turnstile* (London: 1912).

McCutcheon, G.B., *Brewster's Millions* (London: 1909).

McIlroy, A., *A Banker's Love Story* (London: T. Fisher Unwin, 1901).

McLaren, J., *Black Cabs* (London: Simon and Schuster, 1999).

Meason, M.L., *Three Months After Date and Other Tales* (London: Ward, Lock and Tyler, 1874).

Mel, F.H., *The Accountant* (London: Remington & Co., 1894).

Merrick, L., *Violet Moses* (London: Richard Bentley & Son, 1891).

Merriman, H.S., *Roden's Corner* (London: 1898).

Merriman, H.S., *The Last Hope* (London: 1904).

Milwain, P., *The Honest Accountant* (Lochmaben: Solway Publishing Company, 2006).

Morrison, A., 'The Affair of the "Avalanche Bicycle and Tyre Co. Limited"' (1897) reprinted in H. Greene, *The Complete Rivals of Sherlock Holmes* (Harmondsworth: 1983).

Morrison, A., *A Child of the Jago* (London: 1896).

Morrison, A., *The Case of Laker, Absconded* (1895), in H. Greene, *The Complete Rivals of Sherlock Holmes* (Harmondsworth: 1983).

Mottram, R.H., *The Boroughmonger* (London: Chatto and Windus, 1929).

Mottram, R.H., *Castle Island* (London: Chatto and Windus, 1931).

Mottram, R.H., *Our Mr Dormer* (London: Chatto and Windus, 1927).

Mullock, D.M. (Mrs Craik), *John Halifax, Gentleman* (London: 1856).

Murray, D.C., *In His Grip* (London: John Long Limited, 1907).

Nazzal, S., *The Folly Under the Lake* (Dartford: Pneuma Springs Publishing UK, 2015).

Newby, P.H., *The Barbary Light* (London: Faber and Faber, 1962).

Nicholson, B.D., *Business Is Business* (London: 1933).

Oliphant, L., *Piccadilly* (London: 1870).

Oliphant, Mrs M., *At His Gates* [serialized in *Good Words*] (London: Strahan and Co., 1872).

Oliphant, Mrs M., 'An Elderly Romance' (1879), in *Neighbours on the Green* (London: Macmillan and Company, 1889).

Oliphant, Mrs M., *The Fugitives* (London: 1879).

Oliphant, Mrs M., *Hester: A Study in Contemporary Life* (London: Macmillan and Co., 1883).

Oliphant, Mrs M., 'The Lady's Walk' (1883), in M. Cox (ed.), *Victorian Ghost Stories* (Oxford: Oxford University Press, 1997).

Oliphant, Mrs M., 'Mademoiselle' (1889), in *A Widow's Tale and Other Stories* (London: 1898).

Oliphant, Mrs M., *Mrs Merridew's Fortune* (1869), in *Neighbours on the Green* (London: Macmillan and Company, 1889).

Oliphant, Mrs M., 'My Faithful Johnny' (1880), in *Neighbours on the Green* (London: Macmillan and Company, 1889).

Oliphant, Mrs M., 'Queen Eleanor and Fair Rosamund' (1886), in *A Widow's Tale and Other Stories* (London: 1898).

Oliphant, Mrs M., 'The Stockbroker at Dinglewood' (1868), in *Neighbours on the Green* (London: Macmillan and Company, 1889).

Oliphant, Mrs M., 'The Strange Adventures of John Percival' (1896), in Mrs Oliphant, *A Widow's Tale and Other Stories* (London: 1898).

Oliphant, Mrs M., 'The Wonderful History of Mr Robert Dalyell' (1892), in *The Ways of Life and Other Stories* (London: Smith, Elder & Co., 1897).

Orczy, B., 'The Mysterious Death on the Underground Railway' (1901), in H. Greene (ed.), *The Complete Rivals of Sherlock Holmes* (London: 1983).

Orczy, B., 'The Theft at the English Provident Bank' (1901), in *The Old Man in the Corner* (London: 1909).

Ouida, *The Massarenes: A Novel* (London: 1897).

Oxenham, J., *Profit and Loss* (London: 1906).

Oxenham, J., *Rising Fortunes: The Story of a Man's Beginnings* (London: 1899).

Pain, B., *Deals* (London: Hodder and Stoughton, 1904).

Pain, B., *Eliza* (London: 1900).

Pain, B., *Eliza Getting On* (London: 1911).

Pain, B., *Eliza's Husband* (London: 1903).

Pain, B., *Eliza's Son* (London: 1913).

Pain, B., *Exit Eliza* (London: 1912).

Parker, G., *The Judgement House* (London: 1913).

Payn, J., *The Burnt Million* (London: Chatto and Windus, 1890).

Payn, J., *Fallen Fortunes* (London: Chatto and Windus, 1876).

Peacock, T.L., *Crotchet Castle* (London: 1831).

Peacock, T.L., *Levi Moses* (1806).

Peacock, T.L., *Paper Money Lyrics* (1825–6).

Pemberton, M., *The Impregnable City* (London: 1895).

Pennant-Rea, R., *Gold Foil: A Novel* (London: Bodley Head, 1978).

Penny, R., *The Talkative Policeman* (London: 1937).

Pettman, G., *A Study in Gold* (London: 1912).

Phillips Oppenheim, E., *Anna, the Adventuress* (London: 1904).

Phillips Oppenheim, E., *The Bank Manager* (London: Hodder and Stoughton, 1934).

Phillips Oppenheim, E., *Havoc* (London: 1912).

Phillips Oppenheim, E., *Jeanne of the Marshes* (London: 1909).

Philips Oppenheim, E., *A Millionaire of Yesterday* (London: 1912).

Phillips Oppenheim, E., *Mr Wingrave, Millionaire* (London: 1906).

Phillips Oppenheim, E., *The Mysterious Mr Sabin* (London: 1905).

Phillips Oppenheim, E., *A Prince of Sinners* (London: 1903).

Phillpotts, E. and Bennett, A., *The Sinews of War: A Romance of London and the Sea* (London: T. Werner Laurie, 1908).

Pickersgill, W., *Washington Grange: An Autobiography* (London: 1859).

Pinto, E., *Ye Outside Fools! Glimpses Inside the Stock Exchange* (London: 1876).

Preston, A., *This Bleeding City* (London: 2010).

Priestley, J.B., *Angel Pavement* (London: 1930).

Reade, C. and Boucicault, D., *Foul Play* (London: 1868).

Reade, C., *Hard Cash; A Matter-of-fact Romance* (London: 1863).

Reade, C., *Love Me Little, Love Me Long* (London: Chatto and Windus, 1859).

Reynolds, G.M., *The Mysteries of London* (London: 1844–56) (edited by T. Thomas, Keele University Press, 1996).

Riddell, C., *Austin Friars* (London: 1870).

Riddell, C., *City and Suburb: A Novel* (London: 1861).

Riddell, C., *Daisies and Buttercups: A Novel of the Upper Thames* (London: Sampson Low, Marston, Searle and Rivington, 1882).

Riddell, C., *Far Above Rubies* (London: 1867).

Riddell, C., *George Geith of Fen Court* (London: 1864).

Riddell, C., *The Head of the Firm* (London: William Heinemann, 1892).

Riddell, C., *Joy after Sorrow* (London: 1873).

Riddell, C., *Mitre Court: A Tale of the Great City* (London: Richard Bentley and Son, 1885) Vol. 2.

Riddell, C., *Mortomley's Estate: A Novel* (London: 1874).

Riddell, C., *The Race for Wealth* (Leipzig: 1866).

Rider Haggard, H., *Colonel Quaritch V.C.* (London: 1888).

Rider Haggard, H., *Love Eternal* (London: Cassell and Company, 1918).

Rider Haggard, H., *People of the Mist* (London: Longmans, Green and Co., 1894).

Rider Haggard, H., *Queen Sheba's Ring* (London: The Thames Publishing Company, 1910),

Rider Haggard, H., *The Yellow God: An Idol of Africa* (London: 1909).

Ridpath, M., *Fatal Error* (London: Michael Joseph, 2003).

Ridpath, M., *Final Venture* (London: Michael Joseph, 2000).

Ridpath, M., *Free to Trade* (London: Heinemann, 1995).

Ridpath, M., *The Market Maker* (London: Michael Joseph, 1999).

Ridpath, M., *On the Edge* (London: Michael Joseph, 2005).

Ridpath, M., *The Predator* (London: Michael Joseph, 2001).

Ridpath, M., *See No Evil* (London: Michael Joseph, 2006).

Ridpath, M., *Trading Reality* (London: Heinemann, 1996).

Rittenberg, M., *Swirling Waters* (London: 1913).

Robertson, M., *A Lombard Street Mystery: A Novel* (London: W. Bartholomew, 1888).

Robinson, E., *The City Banker or Love and Money* (London: 1856).

Robinson, E., *The Gold-Worshippers; or, the Days We Live in* (London: G. Routledge and Co., 1851).

Robinson, F.W., *True to Herself* (London: 1870).

Robinson, P., *Dry Bones that Dream* (London: Constable and Co., 1995).

Saki (H.H. Munro), 'When William Came', in *The Penguin Complete Saki* (London: 1982).

Sala, G.A., *The Seven Sons of Mammon* (London: Tinsley Brothers, 1862).

Sambrook, G., *Tarnished Copper* (London: Twenty First Century Publishers, 2002).

Sayers, D.L., *Whose Body?* (London: T. Fisher Unwin, 1923).

Scarborough Jackson, W., *Nine Points of the Law* (London: 1903).

Schreiner, O., *Trooper Peter Halket of Mashonaland* (London: 1899).

Scott, W., *Rob Roy* (London: 1818).

Seligman, V., *Bank Holiday* (London: 1934).

Shand, A.I., *Against Time* (London: 1870).

Shand, A.I., *Fortune's Wheel: A Novel* (Edinburgh & London: William Blackwood and Sons, 1886).

Shaw, G.B., *An Unsocial Socialist* (London: Constable and Company 1887, reprinted 1914).

Sheridan Le Fanu, J., *Checkmate* (London: 1871).

Shute, N., *Ruined City* (London: Heinemann, 1938).

Sims, G.R., *In London's Heart* (London: Chatto and Windus, 1900).

Sims, G.R., *Living London* (London: Cassell, 1901–3).

Sims, G.R., *Rogues and Vagabonds* (London: Chatto and Windus, 1885).

Sinclair, C., *The Mysterious Marriage or Sir Edward Graham* (London: Clarke Beeton and Company, 1854).

Smart, H., *The Great Tontine* (London: 1881).

Smedley, F.E., *Frank Fairleigh, or Scenes from the Life of a Private Pupil* (London: 1850).

Smith, C., *The Case of Torches* (London: Hammond and Hammond, 1957).

Smith, C., *The Deadly Reaper* (London: Hammond and Hammond, 1956).

Smith, C., *The Speaking Eye* (London: Hammond and Hammond, 1955).

Smith, H., *The Moneyed Man or the Lesson of a Life* (London: Darton and Company, 1841).

Smith, H.M., *Inspector Frost in the City* (London: 1930).

Spectre, The, *Ye Vampyres, A Legend or The National Betting-Ring, Showing What Became of it* (London: 1875).

St. John Sprigg, C., *Death of an Airman* (London: 1934).

Stafford Northcote, W., Earl of Iddesleigh, *Luck o' Lassendale* (London: John Lane, The Bodley Head, 1882).

Stanton, C. and Hosken, H., *The Sinners' Syndicate* (London: Hurst and Blackett, 1907).

Stead, W.T., '"Two and Two Make Four," A Christmas Story for the Times', in *The Review of Reviews*, viii July–December (London: 1893).

Stevenson, R.L., *The Dynamiter* (London: 1885).

Stoker, B., *The Lady and the Shroud* (London: 1909).

Stuart, D., *The Man Outside* (London: 1934).

Surr, T.S., *The Magic of Wealth: A Novel* (London: 1815).

Sutherland, G., *Due Diligence* (London: Hodder Headline, 1997).

Sutherland, G., *East of the City* (London: 1998).

Swan, A.S., *The Bondage of Riches* (London: 1912).

Swan, A.S., *The Strait Gate* (London: 1894).

Sykes, W.S., *The Missing Moneylender* (London: 1931) (reprinted by Penguin).

Terrell, T., *The City of the Just* (London: Trischler and Company, 1892).

Tey, J., *The Man in the Queue* (London: Peter Davies, 1953).

Thackeray, W.M., *The Book of Snobs: Sketches of Life and Character* (London: 1846).

Thackeray, W.M., *The Diary of C. Jeames De La Pluche, Esq.* (London: 1854), in *The Works of William Makepeace Thackeray* (London: 1872).

Thackeray, W.M., *The History of Samuel Titmarsh and the Great Hoggarty Diamond* (London: 1841).

Thackeray, W.M., *The Newcomes: Memories of a Most Respectable Family* (London: 1854).

Thackeray, W.M., *Vanity Fair* (London: 1847/8).

Thorne, G. and Custance, L., *Sharks: A Fantastic Novel for Business Men and Their Families* (London: 1904).

Travers, P.L., *Mary Poppins* (London: Peter Davies, 1934).

Travers, P.L., *Mary Poppins and the House Next Door* (Glasgow: William Collins and Sons, 1988).

Travers, P.L., *Mary Poppins Comes Back* (London: Peter Davies, 1935).

Travers, P.L., *Mary Poppins in Cherry Tree Lane* (Glasgow: William Collins and Sons, 1982).

Travers, P.L., *Mary Poppins in the Park* (London: Peter Davies, 1962).

Travers, P.L., *Mary Poppins Opens the Door* (London: Peter Davies, 1944).

Trollope, A., *Can You Forgive Her?* (London: Chapman & Hall, 1864/6).

Trollope, A., *The Last Chronicle of Barset* (London: 1867).

Trollope, A., *The Prime Minister* (London: 1876).

Trollope, A., *The Three Clerks: A Novel* (London: 1857).

Trollope, A., *The Way We Live Now* (London: 1875).

Wade, H., *The Duke of York's Steps* (London: 1929).

Wade, H., *Gold Was Our Grave* (London: Constable and Co., 1954).

Wade, H., *The Verdict of You All* (London: 1926).

Wallace, E., *The Admirable Carfew* (London: Ward Lock and Co., 1914).

Wallace, E., *Bones in London* (London: Ward, Lock & Co., 1921).

Wallace, E., *A Debt Discharged* (London: 1916).

Wallace, E., *The Four Just Men* (London: 1905).

Wallace, E., *The Fourth Plague* (London: 1913).

Wallace, E., *The Guv'nor* (London: Hodder and Stoughton, 1932).

Wallace, E., *The Joker* (London: Hodder and Stoughton, 1926).

Wallace, E., *The Melody of Death* (London: Allied Newspapers Ltd, 1915).

Wallace, E., *Mr J.G. Reeder Returns* (London: 1932).

Wallace, E., *The Nine Bears* (London: Ward Lock, 1910).

Wallace, E., *Red Aces* (London: 1929).

Wallace, E., *The Twister* (London: 1928).

Warden, F., *City and Suburban: A Novel* (London: F.V. White and Company, 1890).

Warden, F., *The Financier's Wife* (London: T. Werner Laurie, 1906).

Warden, F., *Something in the City* (London: John Long, 1890).

Warden, F., *The Wharf by the Docks: A Novel* (London: 1896).

Weldon, F., *The Life and Loves of a She-Devil* (London: Hodder and Stoughton, 1983).

Wells, H.G., *Ann Veronica* (London: 1909).

Wells, H.G., *Kipps: The Story of a Simple Soul* (London: 1905).

Wells, H.G., *Mr. Britling Sees It Through* (London: Cassell and Company, 1916).

Wells, H.G., *The History of Mr. Polly* (London: 1910).

Wells, H.G., *Tono-Bungay* (London: 1909).

Weyman, S.J., *Ovington's Bank* (London: John Murray, 1922).

White, F.M., 'A Bubble Burst', in F.M. White, *The Doom of London* (London: 1903) (originally published in *Pearson's Magazine*, May 1903).

White, F.M., *The House of Mammon* (London: Ward Lock and Co., 1914).

Wicks, F., *The Veiled Hand: A Novel of the Sixties, the Seventies, and the Eighties* (London: 1892).

Wilde, O., *An Ideal Husband*, in Oscar Wilde, *The Major Works* (Oxford: 1989).

Wilde, O., *The Importance of Being Earnest*, in Oscar Wilde, *The Major Works* (Oxford: 1989).

Wilde, O., *The Model Millionaire* (1891), in *The Complete Works of Oscar Wilde* (London: 1948/66).

Wilkinson, E., *The Division Bell Mystery* (London: George G. Harrap & Co., 1932).

Williams, D., *Advertise for Treasure* (London: 1984).

Williams, D., *Banking on Murder* (London: Harper Collins, 1993).

Williams, D., *Copper, Gold and Treasure* (London: Collins, 1980).

Williams, D., *Divided Treasure* (London: 1988).

Williams, D., *Holy Treasure* (London: 1989).

Williams, D., *Murder for Treasure* (London: Collins, 1980).

Williams, D., *Murder in Advent* (London: Macmillan, 1986).

Williams, D., *Planning on Murder* (London: 1992).

Williams, D., *Prescription for Murder* (London: 1991).

Williams, D., *Treasure by Degrees* (London: Collins, 1977).

Williams, D., *Treasure by Post* (London: 1992).

Williams, D., *Treasure in Oxford* (London: 1989).

Williams, D., *Treasure in Roubles* (London: 1987).

Williams, D., *Treasure Preserved* (London: Collins, 1983).

Williams, D., *Treasure up in Smoke* (London: Collins, 1978).

Williams, D., *Unholy Writ* (London: Collins, 1976).

Williams, D., *Wedding Treasure* (London: Macmillan, 1985).

Wills Crofts, F., *Inspector French's Greatest Case* (London: Wm. Collins Sons & Co., 1924).

Wills Crofts, F., *Mystery in the Channel* (London: Collins, 1931).

Witting, C., *Measure for Murder* (London: Hodder and Stoughton, 1941).

Wodehouse, P.G., *Psmith in the City* (London: 1910).

Wood, Mrs H., *A Life's Secret: A Story* (London: Richard Bentley and Son, 1862).

Wood, Mrs H., *Adam Granger and Other Stories* (London: Richard Bentley and Son, 1876).

Wood, Mrs H., *The Channings: A Story* (London: Macmillan and Company, 1862).

Wood, Mrs H., *East Lynne* (London: 1861).

Wood, Mrs H., *Oswald Cray: A Novel* (London: 1864).

Wood, Mrs H., *Roland Yorke* (London: Richard Bentley and Son, 1869).

Wood, Mrs H., *The Shadow of Ashlydyat* (London: Richard Bentley and Son, 1863).

Woolf, V., *The Voyage Out* (London: 1915).

Wynne, A., Death of a Banker (London: 1934).

Yates, E.H., *Kissing the Rod: A Novel* (London: Tinsley Brothers, 1866).

Yonge, C.M., *The Pillars of the House* (London: Macmillan & Co., 1873).

Yorke, C., *A Romance of Modern London: A Novel* (London: 1892).

Zangwill, I., 'Cheating the Gallows' (1893), in M. Cox (ed.), *Victorian Tales of Mystery and Detection: An Oxford Anthology* (Oxford: Oxford University Press, 1992).

Index

Printed in the United States
by Baker & Taylor Publisher Services